China: Lost Mission?

Nicholas Maestrini, PIME

PIME WORLD PRESS
17330 Quincy Avenue
Detroit, Michigan 48221

First published under the title *MY TWENTY YEARS
WITH THE CHINESE, LAUGHTER AND TEARS,
1931-1951* by Magnificat Press, February 1991.

Second edition under the title: *CHINA: LOST
MISSION?* by PIME WORLD PRESS, October 1992.

Copies of this book can be ordered from the publisher

PIME WORLD PRESS
17330 Quincy Avenue
Detroit, Mi. 48221

If you wish to have an autographed copy by the author
write to:

Fr. Nicholas Maestrini
1550 Beach Road
Tequesta, Fl. 33469

Suggested donation to the missions: $11.95 per copy
(Please add $2.00 for postage)

Cover photo courtesy of Maryknoll Missioners

Dedication

To Mary, Mother of Confidence
and Queen of the Apostles,
on the sixtieth anniversary of my ordination
to the priesthood,
with my love and gratitude

—Nicholas Maestrini, PIME

Contents

Acknowledgments

I wish to acknowledge my debt of gratitude to all my friends who in various ways have made the writing and publication of this book possible. Without their encouragement and collaboration, I could not have brought this project to a successful conclusion. It would take far too many pages to list them all here, but since this is impossible I want at least to assure them that they all are in my heart and prayers. I have to limit myself here to mention only those who had a major role in the long and laborious preparation of the manuscript.

First of all I have to mention three of my dear friends in Detroit, Allen Abramson, Grace Garland Janisz, and Mary Lou Zieve. Without their loving insistence, this book would probably never have been written. For the last thirty years they have insistently asked, begged and cajoled me into writing my autobiography. They thought that the events of my life, which has spanned three continents (Europe, Asia and America), would be of interest to American readers. As a result of their insistence, I did start writing my autobiography early in 1985 but, after drafting ten chapters, I decided against continuing it for a multitude of reasons. However, I did resolve to keep writing about my experiences with Chinese people in Hong Kong and China. This book is the result of that decision. To Allen, Grace and Mary Lou I owe undying gratitude.

Another person without whom this book would never have been written is my devoted and faithful secretary, Mrs. Nancy Reilley MacKenzie, who for the last sixteen years has worked for me here in Florida with unlimited patience and devotion beyond the call of duty.

The writing of this book has been a long and complicated process over a period of three years. I first wrote the draft of each chapter in longhand, dictated it on a dictaphone for Mrs. MacKenzie and then had it keyed into the computer. When we had the computer printout, Mrs. MacKenzie and I started the time-consuming work of revising and correcting the rough copy for grammar, style and content. In view of the many changes I made in the manuscript, she had to read, reread and correct the entire 700-page manuscript, checking for corrections, additions and typos due to my two-finger typing ability and lack of experience in computer work. By now, she probably knows the whole manuscript by heart.

I also owe a posthumous tribute of gratitude to the memory of the late Brother Pius Cremasco, PIME, my friend for the last forty years and faithful companion for the last twelve years. He spent endless hours making numerous photocopies of the thirty chapters as I was writing and correcting them. He even copied for me several entire books that are now out of print but which I needed for reference.

I owe a debt of gratitude to the librarian and staff of the Maryknoll Fathers Mission Library in Ossining, NY. They always fulfilled my request for help with promptness and courtesy and helped me immensely by providing books and information that were otherwise unavailable.

Other persons who helped me immensely in preparing this manuscript are: Mariellen Howell of Gratiot, OH, who patiently revised all the chapters and gave me invaluable suggestions: Anne Saldich of Palo Alto, CA; Mary Louise Tully of Menlo Park, CA; Mabel Chen of Hong Kong; Mary Fong of the University of California at Davis; Man Wah Bentley of England; Mr. Peter Treves of New York, NY; Eileen Burns, Carol Anne Moens, Mrs. Mary Ann Lindberg and Kathy Rooney, all of whom at various stages of writing read part of the manuscript and gave me invaluable advice.

In the technical preparation of the book I owe a great deal of gratitude to Mrs. Marcia Rommack, founder and owner of Presentations, Inc., and to her husband Tom. Marcia scanned all my manuscript into the computer as a work of love. Moreover, both she and her husband Tom gave me invaluable assistance in solving many of the problems that every novice faces in learning the use of a modern computer.

I also have to thank Mr. Duke Peters; Mr. Frank Riddle of Computer Support; Mary Ellen Keemer, a computer teacher who edited the entire manuscript on the computer; and Mr. Stanton Bloom, a computer programmer and consultant, who calls me "his favorite student" because of my young age of eighty-two.

I have also to mention Mr. Joe Mullally, a sea captain, who in his vacation time between trips copied the photos I could obtain from the Diocesan Archives of Hong Kong and from other sources.

Special thanks are due to Mr. Stephen Dunham, my editor and publisher, who had the intelligence to read my manuscript instead of rejecting it without reading it, as sixty-four other publishers in the USA, England and Hong Kong have done.

In spite of all the preparatory work done by so many people, this book would probably have never seen the light of day without the generous donations of so many friends who helped me finance its publication. I have to mention first of all the late Dr. Samuel W. Lindsay, Pastor of the Royal Poinciana Chapel in Palm Beach and a dear friend of mine, who as far back as 1978, on his own initiative, gave me $100 to pay for secretarial work to write my memoirs.

In more recent days, the following friends have generously contributed to make this publication possible: Mr. Allen Abramson; Dr. and Mrs. Vincent Adams; Mr. and Mrs. Thomas V. Angott; Mr. and Mrs. M. H. Antonini; Mr. Frank Bader; Mrs. J. Merriam Barnes; Mr. and Mrs. Ermo Bartoletti; Mrs. Claire A. Baum; Mr. and Mrs. J. M. Belanger; Mr. and Mrs. Henry Bellaimey; Mr. and Mrs. Carl Benson; Mr. T. W. Berube; Mr. and Mrs. Phillip J. Bifulk; Mr. Donald Bosco; Mr. Louis C. Bosco, Sr.; Mr. and Mrs. Louis Bosco, Jr.; Mr. and Mrs. Thomas G. Bosco; Mr. and Mrs. L. Bridenstine; Mr. John J. Brogan; Mr. and Mrs. Arthur A. Burck; Mr. and Mrs. Ronald Burton; Mr. and Mrs. D. S. Caputo; Mrs. George L. Cassidy; Mr. I. B. and Dr. Ava Coleman; Mr. and Mrs. Perry Como; Mrs. C. D. Connelly; Mr. and Mrs. W. J. Cunningham; Mr. and Mrs. John D. Daniels; Mrs. Gertrude Davis; Mr. and Mrs. Albert De Mascio; Hon. and Mrs. R. DeMascio; Mr. and Mrs. Gino DiClemente; Mr. and Mrs. G. G. Diehl; Dr. and Mrs. D. Doll; Mrs. Ralph Doria; Mr. and Mrs. Joseph Doria; Mr. and Mrs. D. Dossin; Mr. and Mrs. Spencer Drayton; Mrs. Adele Dunn; Mr. King Dunn; Dr. and Mrs. H. B. Fenech; Mr. and Mrs. G. A. Ferris; Mr. and Mrs. Richard T. Finn; Mr. and Mrs. Louis Fisher; Mr. and Mrs. Ben Fretti; Mr. and Mrs. John L. Gardella; Mr. and Mrs. Thomas A. Gardella; Mr. and Mrs. Steve Garrisi; Mr. and Mrs. John H. Giba; Mrs. Glenn S. Glass; Mrs. Erma G. Grogan; Mrs. John C. Hadges; Mr. and Mrs. Sam C. Hakemian; Mr. and Mrs. Frank J. Heinrich; Mrs. Andrew L. Hellmuth; Mr. and Mrs. Dan. S. Holefca; Mr. and Mrs. C. Holloway; Mrs. Margaret L. Hope; Mr. and Mrs. William M. Husak; Mrs. T. Janisz; Mrs. Leona W. Jertson; Mr. and Mrs. John Kehrig; Dr. Alexandria M. Klein; Mr. and Mrs. Bernard J. Kolar; Mr. and Mrs. Joseph A. Kolar; Mrs. Constance E. Langner; Dr. and Mrs. Albert J. Latorra; Mr. and Mrs. and Arnold L. Lindberg; Dr. and Mrs. Michael A. Longo; Mr. and Mrs. Ray W. MacDonald; Mr. and Mrs. George Manderioli; Mr. and Mrs. Christopher C. Mannino; Mr. and Mrs. Joseph Mariani; Mr. and Mrs. A. R. Marzelli; Mrs. Jo Anne McCarthy; Mr. and Mrs. H. Richard McCord; Mr. and Mrs. Paul McGlone; Mr. and Mrs. Paul Mirabito; Mr. and Mrs. Armand L. Moens, Jr.; Mr. and Mrs. R. John Moore; Mr. and Mrs. Thomas A. Murphy; Mr. and Mrs. James Nemec; Mr. and Mrs. T. O'Brien; Mr. and Mrs. R. M. O'Connor; Mrs. Lee Visconsi Olsen; Mr. and Mrs. Hubert

Opici; Michael and Rayleen Page; Mr. and Mrs. R. R. Palombit; Mr. and Mrs. Paul E. Parsons; Mr. and Mrs. D. Pollack; Mr. and Mrs. Robert Probst; Mrs. Dominic Pucci; Mrs. Constanzo Pucillo; Mr. and Mrs. D. Raso; Mr. and Mrs. John J. Raymond; Mr. and Mrs. Edward M. Ricci; Mr. and Mrs. V. Riportella; Mr. and Mrs. John Roland; Mr. and Mrs. John F. Rooney; Mr. and Mrs. Edward Rusin; Dr. and Mrs. Richard M. Ryan, Jr.; Mrs. Ann Saldich; Mr. and Mrs. A. Salerno; Mrs. Don Schaaf; Mr. and Mrs. J. G. Schafer; Mr. and Mrs. William Shannon; Mr. and Mrs. G. E. Shena; Mrs. Irene Stanley; Mr. and Mrs. F. D. Stella; Mrs. John Stetson; Mrs. M. Ternes; Mrs. Robert E. Thibodeau; Mr. and Mrs. James Toohey, Jr.; Mr. and Mrs. Lynn Townsend; Mr. and Mrs. E. E. Tracy; Mr. and Mrs. Leo Vecellio, Sr.; Mr. and Mrs. Pat Valenti; Raymond and Kathleen Van Winkle; Mr. William E. Walle; Mr. and Mrs. M. M. Welshons; Mrs. Hugh Wichert; Mr. and Mrs. Jay Young; Mr. and Mrs. V. J. Zerbo, Jr.; Mr. and Mrs. Mort Zieve; and several others who wish to remain anonymous.

Last, but not least, I have to thank the publishers and authors who kindly granted me permission to quote from their publications:

Burns & Oates of London, England, for permission to quote from *The Jesuit Under Fire* by Fr. Thomas F. Ryan.

The Century Hutchinson Publishing Group Limited of London, England, for permission to quote from *Twilight in Hong Kong* by Ellen Field.

The National Catholic Reporter of Kansas City, MO, representative for Sheed & Ward, for allowing me to quote several pages from Dr. John C. H. Wu's autobiography, *Beyond East and West.*

The Oxford University Press of Hong Kong for permission to quote from *Hong Kong Eclipse* by G. B. Endacott.

Pan Books of London, England, for permission to quote from *The Fall of Hong Kong* by Tim Carew.

To all the persons I have mentioned above, and to the many more whose names I could not include here, I extend my undying gratitude and I promise grateful prayers.

Preface

This is a book about love. Not exactly the type of love described by
Professor Leo Buscaglia in his books, but the kind of love made up
of service, self-sacrifice and dedication; the kind of love of God and
neighbor the Bible describes, which Christ exemplified throughout His
life from the cradle in Bethlehem to the cross on Calvary, and which
God alone can help us to practice in times of joy and sorrow. This is a
book about the practice of love, not its theories. It presents practical
examples of how people found serenity and a solution to their problems
in the development of the spiritual dimension in their lives. It speaks of
people in Hong Kong and China, school girls, young men, university
students, homeless street sleepers, professors, businessmen, rich and
poor, widows, victims of war, politicians, even suicidal persons.

This book deals with man's work for God; not the labor of servants
in fear of a tyrannical Master, but the serene, unselfish work for others
inspired by true love for the Man who died for love of us. From personal
experiences, I write here about the work for others done by people such
as a British VIP, Irish and Chinese ladies enduring wartime circumstances, the zeal of a poor widow in bringing Christ to non-Christians,
the eagerness of a converted and sick prostitute in teaching religion to
prospective converts, the twenty-seven-year ordeal of a young woman in

Communist labor camps, the zeal and activities of lay missionaries who came from America and Australia to work in Hong Kong to witness for Christ.

This book covers my work during twenty years of my life, a life buffeted by war, hunger, military occupation, communist persecution, success, disappointment and failure. It is the book of my personal experiences throughout the most critical twenty years in the history of China. It covers the period from China's unification in 1933 under Chiang Kai-shek, through the Japanese invasion, the following eight years of war, the devastation and incredible sufferings caused by the Japanese military victory, and China's rise to the status of a world power in 1945 and its final sinking behind the Bamboo Curtain under the tyranny of communism.

In the following chapters I give the reader a glimpse of the agony and despair that prevailed in Hong Kong during the Japanese occupation, of a pastor's work in time of war under a foreign power, of the starvation of three million people, of missionaries reduced to selling the wood of a church belfry and the gold sacred vessels of the cathedral to survive four years of famine and starvation. I give here a personal account of the seventeen-day war and of the four years of Japanese occupation from the Church's point of view.

This book is also the story of the growth and development of the diocese of Hong Kong, with its millions of non-Christian Chinese, from the thirties to the fifties, through the dark hours of the Japanese war in China, the destruction of many of our missionary institutions, the bombing and destruction of our Catholic Chinese Hospital, the rape of Hong Kong and the ravaging Japanese occupation, to its resurgence and reconstruction in the postwar period.

Why did I write this book? Because I wish to inform, to inspire and to motivate people. This has been the program of action through my sixty years as a priest and missionary, and I want to be faithful to it to the end.

My long life, which began in 1908, has spanned three generations: the prewar generation (1920-45), the postwar generation (1945-60), and the post-Vatican II generation (1960 to today)—three very different generations. During the last thirty years, technology has made more progress than in the last three centuries. As a result, the world's way of life, its thinking, philosophy, views of religion and of morality, have changed a great deal and people have lost the sense of history. Most people of the present generation know hardly anything about what happened in the world barely fifty years ago.

They forget that history is the greatest teacher of men.

Rev. Nicholas Maestrini, PIME
1550 Beach Rd.
Tequesta, FL 33469

FOREWORD TO THE SECOND PRINTING
THE NEW TITLE "CHINA: LOST MISSION?"

It was only eighteen months ago-February 1991-that this book was first released to the public, but as our stock is fast being depleted, we have to rush into the second printing. The fast sale of this book is remarkable in view of the fact that the former publisher, the Magnificat Press, went out of business shortly after the book was put on sale and consequently there was no advertising campaign on a national scale, no book reviews in major papers and no help from the media to promote the book. The quick sale of the book was due only to the fact that readers loved the book and promoted its circulation.

Why a new title? Because several experts in the field of book publishing found the old title too long and unappealing. The present title was suggested by my friend Bill Deneen of New York and it was chosen by the publishers of the Italian translation of the book. Then it became obvious that it was better to use the same title for both editions

This title does represent the true story of my life: my mission to bring Christ to China seemed to end in defeat because of the victory of Communism, but in reality, today, Christianity in China is stronger than ever.

This is the paradox of Christianity: through defeat to victory.

Tequesta, Florida. August 15, 1992.

Fr. Nicholas Maestrini, PIME

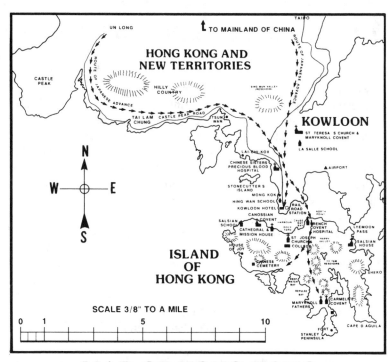

MAP OF HONG KONG
AND NEW TERRITORIES

Introduction

My Birth And Background

It was in a medium-sized city of Central Italy called Cagli that I was born on a cold night on January 9, 1908, the first of six children.

After the birth of the fourth child, in 1912, my father moved his law practice to Nocera Umbra, a little medieval city perched at the top of a hill not far from Assisi, in central Italy. This is the place where I grew up and where I learned from the words and example of my parents the basic Christian values and priorities that have guided me through life. My seminary training confirmed and strengthened those values and gave me the logical rationale and theological basis for their validity, but their roots were planted in my heart by my parents and by the training I received in my early years.

My Family

My father, Anthony, was of medium height (5'5" tall), clean-shaven except for a black mustache, brown eyes, a high forehead and broad shoulders. An able lawyer graduated from the School of Law of the University of Rome, he was soft-spoken and kind, very precise in everything he did, and always logical in his reasoning. He spoke perfect Italian and insisted that we all should do the same. A profoundly convinced Catholic, well educated in Church doctrine, he always acted coherently with his high moral principles. For me he was not only my physical parent but also the best educator I ever had.

My mother, Elizabeth, a few years younger than my father, was slender and petite with rich brown hair and a beautifully delicate oval face. Her graceful figure, which she maintained into her old age, enhanced her distinguished and refined appearance. She was kindness personified, had excellent taste in clothing and even to her dying day, at age eighty-nine, was meticulously dressed. Endowed with a great deal of intuition, she, too, was deeply religious, living out her faith with all her heart and soul, without being in the least pietistic.

There were four of us children each born one year apart. My sister, Anna, was the first to follow me and she was soon followed by Frank, John, and Bepi. Being so close in age we grew up as a closely knit group of which I, the first born, was the natural leader. We had a lot of fun together and lustily indulged in all the usual quarrels and tantrums of normal children. It was altogether a happy childhood and I soon learned how to share and to give, to take an interest in others and to find companionship in a healthy environment.

The Dawn Of A Vocation

Like any normal child thinking about his future work in life, I shifted in my desires from one career to another. Somehow the law career of my father never appealed to me. I thought about being an engineer, a professor of history, a doctor, even an explorer. I remember an almost prophetic incident. I was about twelve years old when one day I began leafing through an illustrated world atlas with my cousin and classmate, Attilio. We came across a full-page map of China. I was fascinated by that immense area and, placing the palm of my hand on the map, said, "Here is where I want to live one day!"

"Not me," said Attilio quickly and emphatically, "not me! How could you live with those foreigners? I like Italy better."

"Well, we will see," I concluded philosophically, but I never forgot the incident.

The first childish whim I had about going to the foreign missions occurred when I was only nine years old. A seminarian at the local Carmelite seminary lent me some issues of a mission magazine published by PIME entitled *Italia Missionaria (Missionary Italy)*. As I was going through the phase of reading novels about exotic countries—the American Wild West and the mysterious countries of Southeast Asia were my favorites—I avidly read every issue I could lay my hands on. Its stories combined adventures in exotic countries with religious ideals and heroism. This combination fascinated me. I still remember one beautiful summer evening just before sunset: I was on the balcony of our house reading a story in *Italia Missionaria* about the difficult life and tragic death of a young and heroic French missionary, Teophane Venard. After a life of great hardships he had been martyred for the faith in Tonkin (Vietnam) during the previous century. Deeply moved, I closed the magazine and said to myself, "One day I, too, will be a missionary!" Of course, that mood passed, but the impression of that evening still lingers in my mind.

Courses in Latin were not offered in the schools of Nocera and so, in October 1919, at age eleven, I entered a private academy at Spello (a little city only twenty miles from Nocera) conducted by a religious society called Somaschi. [2]

Every year in February the students made a short spiritual retreat. It was during the retreat of February 1921 that I began to feel a vague desire to become a priest. Two things attracted me to the priesthood then: helping others and working at something that had everlasting value. I talked about my desire to the confessor and, after a few questions, he concluded, chafing his hands, "Very good, Nicola, you can enter the minor seminary of our society in October. We will make a cute little student for our order out of you!"

I wrote home that next fall I wanted to enter the seminary of that Order in North Italy. My father's answer was: "Only over my dead body will I let you join that religious order now! When you come home for summer vacation we will talk this over." I had the highest regard for my father's opinion and I felt sure that he had good reasons for objecting to my plans, so I lost interest in joining that order.

A Decisive Summer

When I returned home for my summer vacation, my dad called me aside one day and said, "Listen, son, if you really want to become a priest, this is O.K. with your mother and me. However, what we want most of all for you now is to help you make the right decision. If the Lord calls you to become a priest, we will be honored and happy, but never forget that we will also be very happy if you decide to follow any other career in life. But certainly I do not want you to join the Somaschi now. You are too young to understand the difference between secular and order priests. When you are in college, then you will decide. However, if you want to enter a seminary now to better find out if the Lord calls you, then I would recommend the Vatican Seminary in Rome which, I believe, is the best diocesan seminary in Italy.

"If, before you make up your mind, you would like to see some experienced priest, I would recommend you talk to Monsignor F. Roberti, who is the rector of that seminary. I can easily arrange that. Monsignor Roberti is a friend of the family, and he is vacationing not far from here. I will be glad to take you to see him if you want to go. Perhaps a conversation with him might help you to make up your mind. Think it over, son, and let me know what you decide."

It was not very difficult for me to make up my mind. I still wished to become a priest and the idea of studying in Rome appealed to me. I told my father that I would be happy to see Msgr. Roberti.

A few days later we were at his summer residence near my native city of Cagli. He received us with great warmth and kindness and, after talking with my father about our family, he took me into a private room.

Standing by the window, and in a very casual way, he questioned me at length about my values in life and my reasons for wanting to become a priest. After about half an hour of conversation he concluded: "Well, Nicola, I think that you have the right disposition to enter a seminary because the purpose of a seminary is to help a boy to find out whether he has a real vocation or not. I think it would do you good to enter a seminary now. By entering a seminary, you have nothing to lose and you are always free to return home any time you want to do so. If you would like to enter my seminary, I am ready to accept you. I will send you an application by mail and if you decide to come, return it to me by the beginning of October." I returned home elated at the prospect of entering the Vatican Seminary.

However, as weeks went by and July dragged into August and August into September, my feelings of elation subsided. That was the summer when I began to discover girls and to experience the normal attraction to the opposite sex. With her gift of intuition my mother soon noticed my change of mood and correctly guessed that I was having second thoughts. As the summer was coming to an end, I hated more and more the idea of going to the seminary because it meant giving up my freedom and the company of girls. The application for Rome lay on my desk quietly waiting to be filled in, but I could not make up my mind to sign it.

My First Visit To The Seminary

Early in October, my dad brought up the subject of the seminary. Speaking with real affection and understanding he said, "Son, it seems that you have changed your mind and are no longer very enthused about going to Rome. Remember that if you do not want to go, your mother and I are very happy and we will never talk about it again. But, before you make up your mind, would you like to go to Rome first to see the seminary and maybe have another chat with Monsignor Roberti?"

I grasped that opportunity as I was really torn by indecision and off we went to Rome, a mere 150 miles away. Msgr. Roberti was kindness itself. He personally gave us a tour of the building, the dorm and the study room to which I would be assigned, the dining room and the chapel. I loved it all. After visiting the building, he took me aside, and after asking a few questions concluded, "Listen, son, I don't see much change since I saw you last June. You are only going through natural growing pains. You are absolutely free to come or not to come. However, my advice to you is that you enter the seminary this month. What better place than a seminary to find out whether you have a vocation or not? Any time you decide not to become a priest, you are free to leave immediately and go home, but at least you will know for certain whether God is calling you."

His reasoning cleared up all my doubts and I immediately decided to enter the seminary to find out if I had a vocation or not.

October 23, the day of my scheduled departure for Rome, soon arrived. It was still very dark at about 6:00 in the morning when I went to my parents' bedroom to bid farewell to my mother, who was not well and could not accompany me to Rome. Her eyes were red, as she had been crying all night long. When she saw me she again burst into tears and kept repeating, "Nicola, please, assure me that you will come back if you are not happy, if you feel that it is not your way." I really had to tear myself away from her. That was indeed the most painful farewell I have ever had in my life.

My father was eager to show me the sights of Rome and we spent three days visiting the city. The afternoon of Thursday, October 26, 1921, was the day assigned for me to report to the seminary. At 4:00 P.M. my dad and I were at the door of the Vatican Seminary. The farewell to my father was not as emotional as that to my mother, but hardly less painful.

"Son, the time has come for me to say goodbye," he said, restraining his tears with difficulty. "Now is the time for you to remember all that your mother and I have taught you. Remember: duty before pleasure. Study, obey and, if you think the Lord is calling you to be a priest, then be a good seminarian. But if you have any doubt, please come home immediately. Keep in mind that there is nothing wrong about leaving a seminary if you find that you have no vocation. You will always be more than welcome at home. You know that. God bless you."

I hugged him while choking back tears and he left. The door closed behind him and I, lonely and disconsolate, started to slowly climb the four flights of broad marble stairs to my dorm. There were fifteen of us in the fourth-year Latin class, all fine boys with lofty ideals, and I soon loved them all. It was my new family. I was assigned a desk in the study room, a bed in the common dormitory, and a small locker without a lock. Goodbye, privacy! Late in the evening I retreated to the bathroom and, feeling really homesick, I looked at length at the snapshots I was secretly and jealously carrying in my hip pocket, photos of my parents, my family, my girl friends. That evening I went to bed with a very heavy heart.

Two days later we started a three-day spiritual retreat. During that retreat I made the most important decision of my life. The conviction formed deep in my soul that the Lord was calling me to dedicate my life to follow in His footsteps and to serve Him as a priest in the foreign missions.

By the evening of the third and last day of the retreat, my mind was made up: I wanted to be a foreign missionary. I tore up the pictures of my girl friends in a symbolic gesture of farewell to marriage and the secular life. During Mass, on All Saints Day, I promised the Lord that, if He was really calling me, I would serve Him as a missionary priest forever.

Life At The Vatican Seminary

For the sake of those who do not know what seminary life was like in pre-Vatican II days I will describe it briefly here.

Discipline at the Vatican Seminary for high-school students seemed at times petty and vexatious. Even though we were all teenagers, we were not allowed to go home on vacation except for a couple of weeks every two or three years. Summer was spent at a seminary villa on the hills not far from Rome. We were allowed to see our parents only once a month on a certain appointed Sunday, and then just for a couple of hours. We were not allowed to display any form of affection for one another. If two boys were seen together frequently, they were suspected of homosexual tendencies and expelled promptly after a warning.

The subject of girls was taboo; sex was considered an improper subject of conversation and was never mentioned. Most of the sermons and meditations dealt with angelic purity, consecrated chastity, sublimation of one's energies, eternal punishment for sins of the flesh. Theoretical teachings were accompanied by the strictest measures to protect chastity. Not only did we not have the remotest possibility of meeting or simply talking to any person of the opposite sex, but we were not even allowed to read the daily paper nor even hum any of the popular airs about love and life. Two or three times a year we were shown a movie, but only selected ones with love scenes censored.

The day's schedule reflected the type of Spartan education imparted to us. A typical school day started with rising at 5:30. One hour in the chapel, 6:00 to 7:00, for meditation and Mass; study period from 7:00 to 8:00; breakfast of milk, coffee and bread; then three class periods of fifty minutes each. Lunch at 12:30; one hour of recreation playing soccer; two more classes from 2:00 to 4:00, and a one-hour passeggiata (walk) to visit and pray in some nearby church. Study period followed from 5:00 to 7:00, then rosary and benediction; supper at 8:00, half an hour of recreation sitting in our study room, and at 9:00 off to bed and lights out.

Going into the city alone was unheard of. The vice rector would do our shopping, and if we had to go to a doctor or a dentist we would be accompanied by a priest. The meals were good, nutritious, with plenty of fresh fruits, but no dessert except at Christmas and Easter. We were never allowed to eat or nibble between meals.

Our fun time: long walks in groups within the city of Rome visiting some old church or Roman ruins, attending special lectures in some other seminary, and occasionally participating in religious celebrations in St. Peter's when the pope officiated.

The whole purpose of the strict discipline was to test the students. In fact, those who resented it left in a hurry or were sent home. We who remained enjoyed our simple way of life and accepted the stern discipline as a necessary condition to reach our goal: the priesthood. We were in love with that ideal and we accepted our disciplined life as a training in line with the spiritual values that we had chosen as our priorities.

Of course, this did not mean that all was rosy and that there were no storms. But, all things considered, we were a happy bunch of youths preparing for the priesthood, willing to fight hard and sacrifice a lot to reach our coveted goal.

A Change Of Seminary

After three years of uninterrupted seminary life, the time came for me to return home for a short vacation. Home now was Perugia, the capital of Umbria Province, to which my father had transferred his law practice. I had left home at thirteen and was now returning at sixteen with the added prestige of coming from the nation's capital and wearing the clerical cassock.

I had three glorious weeks at home. It was one of the happiest periods of my life. However, for the first time I realized that a priest can never be an integral part of the lay world. I began experiencing the full import of the words of St. Paul about priests: "a man set aside." I did not belong to the lay world any longer.

I greatly enjoyed the company of my sister and brothers, but they had their own lives to live, their friends, their parties, their youthful escapades. I could no longer be the gang leader. Wearing the black clerical cassock and sporting a short, military-type haircut set me aside from them. I did not belong to their world because we no longer had much in common, except the affection that came from our blood ties. I was naturally shy of girls and the few I met looked at me with that mixture of pity and contempt that, as A. J. Cronin said, the mere sight of a clerical soutane seems to evoke in Latin countries. Some boys in the streets laughed at me openly; some even shouted after me, "Black crow! Sack of charcoal!" It annoyed me. The friends of my family were very kind and considerate, full of admiration or compassion according to their religious views. Those prone to adore anyone with a Roman collar were full of respect and veneration; those of a worldly type commiserated my choice of the priesthood.

The three weeks were soon over and upon my return to Rome I entered the Lateran Seminary, the seminary of the Diocese of Rome for College and Theology. I enjoyed my new status as college student, but it did not last long. My desire and determination to be a missionary had constantly grown through the years of high school. My spiritual director, Msgr. Alfredo Ottaviani (who later became famous Cardinal Ottaviani of the Vatican Council) encouraged me to pursue the vocation to the foreign missions but suggested that I wait until the end of college.

However, at the new seminary I felt uneasy because my ideals and plans for the future were totally different from those of my classmates. They were talking about and planning their future ministries in Italy or careers in the diplomatic service of the Vatican. On the contrary, I was dreaming of nothing except being a missionary. Gradually I realized that a specific missionary formation in a mission seminary would be a better preparation for my future work. PIME[3] was the society of my choice and I decided to join it at the end of the school year.

On January 9, my seventeenth birthday, I wrote to my parents telling them about my decision and asking for their permission and blessing. On February 2, I received their reply. My dad wrote: "Dear son, your mother and I have thought hard and prayed a lot about your request to join PIME. Our friend Bishop Curi of Cagli was favorably impressed with his visit to you and thinks we should give you our permission. Nicola dear, we both are heartbroken at the prospect of your leaving for the missions. However, we repeat to you what we told you when you entered the Vatican Seminary: If this is God's will for you, His will be done. We want you to be happy and you can be happy only if you do what God wants you to do. You have our permission to become a missionary and to join PIME. But please remember, should you change your mind and want to return home, do not hesitate one moment to do so. You will always be most welcome back at home."

The following day I wrote to PIME's headquarters in Milan and much to my surprise a few weeks later Fr. Paul Manna, PIME,[4] came to interview me at the Lateran. A few weeks later I was formally accepted by PIME and told to report to the College Seminary in Monza, near Milan, at the beginning of October. I left the Lateran Seminary at the end of the school year and for the first time I enjoyed a three-month vacation with my family in Perugia.[5]

A Disappointing Impression

It was raining in Milan on the morning of October 1, 1925. As the train from Perugia was slowly winding its way through the suburbs of the city, I felt very low in spirit. When I finally arrived by taxi at the door of PIME's headquarters at Via Monterosa 81 in Milan, the PIME brother at the door was not overly impressed at the sight of a genteel-looking seminarian from the South. (To the good people of Milan, any person coming from Central or South Italy is a hillbilly.) A couple of hours later I was on a screeching and groaning streetcar headed for PIME's College Seminary in Monza.

When I finally reached my destination, saw the seminary building, and met my future classmates, I was totally devastated. Here everything was so different and inferior compared with Rome. The seminary building was small, economically built, poorly furnished. The seminarians were wearing ill-fitting, faded greenish cassocks, spoke Milanese dialect, had none of the refinement of the seminarians at the Roman seminary, and the vice rector, a young priest, tucked his cassock under his belt while playing soccer, thus uncovering his ankles and legs.[6] I was shocked!

That evening in bed, when lights were out, I could not help crying. I was desolate. I felt I could not take that kind of life, but at the same time I did not know what to do. During the following few days, my worst impressions were confirmed and I practically decided to return to the Lateran Seminary, so disappointed was I with the PIME seminary. I was told, however, that on October 5 there would be the departure ceremony of the new missionaries at the PIME headquarters in Milan, and all the college students were invited to attend. I decided to go and see what it was all about and then make my decision.

A Change Of Mind

The sun finally showed its face again on the morning of October 5, and forty of us students climbed aboard an old, screeching streetcar on the way to Milan, all in a happy mood. Nothing could dampen the spirit of forty teenagers on a trip to the big city.

When the religious service began, we seminarians from Monza led the procession into the spacious and crowded church of St. Francis Xavier, attached to our headquarters in Milan. The theology students, the sixteen bearded departing missionaries, and His Eminence the cardinal archbishop of Milan, accompanied by all the missionaries residing in the motherhouse, followed and took their places around the altar. I could not take my eyes off all those elderly missionaries. White beards, sallow faces, and bent backs were evident signs of many years of hard work and sacrifices endured in the mission fields.

There was no doubt about what the crowd assembled that morning in St. Francis Xavier Church thought of the departing missionaries; priests, seminarians, relatives, friends and benefactors were there to bid their last farewell to the sixteen bright-eyed, strong, energetic young men whom they definitely regarded as true heroes.

The most pertinent and emotionally charged moment came when, after a stirring homily, the cardinal blessed the "mission crosses" and presented one to each missionary, saying, "Behold, my son, the inseparable companion of your missionary life, your comfort in sufferings and dangers, your strength in life and death."

Then Fr. Andrew Granelli, the senior of the departing missionaries, gave the farewell address. Among other things he said: "A few days ago someone told me: 'You missionaries have no heart. If you had one, you'd not leave your families and your country.' I consider this the worst insult one could offer to a missionary and to truth itself. It is because of love that a missionary sacrifices himself to save others, that he understands the good shepherd's lament: 'I still have other sheep who do not belong to this fold'; and that he offers his life to extend to the whole world Christ's promises to man." There was not a dry eye in the whole audience when he left the lectern.

Soon after the ceremony, with emotions at a high pitch, we crowded around the sixteen young heroes, hugging them, kissing their crosses, asking their blessing. We followed them for the traditional last visit to a famous shrine of Our Lady and then on to the railroad station. This last farewell was heartrending. Mothers, sisters, brothers were crying desperately; we seminarians were crying, too, and finally even the missionaries themselves broke down and many could not restrain hot, honest tears.

When at last the train slowly left the station and disappeared down the tracks into a bright October sun, it left behind many bleeding hearts, but also many enthused souls.

It was then that I realized how wrong I was in pining for the niceties of Rome and in looking down on the patched, faded cassocks of my classmates, the old, weather-stained building, and the "scandalous" vice rector who tucked his cassock under his belt while playing soccer! My eyes were finally open. The Roman system was the proper system to produce such men as popes, cardinals and Church diplomats, but the PIME system was also the right and proper system to produce men of the caliber of the sixteen missionaries to whom we had just bade farewell.[7] That night I returned to Monza a changed and happy man. I never again regretted that I had left Rome to join PIME.

Acquiring The Missionary Mind

The seminary discipline in Monza was as strict and severe as that at the Lateran seminary. Every minute of the waking day was regulated by the sound of the community bell. We obeyed it promptly under pain of being reprimanded. Our mail, both incoming and outgoing, was always read by the vice rector; we couldn't read books other than our textbooks without permission, and permission was often denied. There was no school library. Eating between meals was considered lack of mortification and of self-discipline. At recreation time, willy-nilly we had to play soccer. In winter the cold was intense and the building unheated, and chilblains caused us a lot of misery. There was really nothing to alleviate the routine and the drudgery of the school days. Why, then, were we there? We were all normal, red-blooded Italian youths, ranging in age between seventeen and twenty-two. We were free to quit and leave for greener pastures any moment we wanted. No effort whatever was made to lure us to remain there. There were no locks or bolts on the doors. There wasn't even the slightest attempt at coaxing or cajoling us into staying. On the contrary, mission life was portrayed to us in all its stark reality as it was lived in those days; total lack of human comforts, lots of hard work and difficult travels, loneliness, dangers, ingratitude, betrayal, scant visible results, a long trip to a faraway destination and little probability of ever returning home.

Why, then, did we remain there? And remain we did, because actually over ninety percent of us went through to the priesthood and to mission life. There is only one answer: the power of love. We were in love with Christ, with our ideal of "saving" souls, with the ideal of total dedication. For that ideal we were ready to sacrifice anything, anytime, no matter the cost.

What did we feel about women and sex? The normal throbbing of passion at that age, the insatiable curiosity of human nature, the irresistible urge to experiment with new, forbidden adventures, so normal in youth, were all kept under control by the vigorous type of life and a conscious effort to keep away from any unnecessary external stimulus.

However, what helped us most to win the battle was the clear identity we had of ourselves: we clearly knew who we were, what we wanted above everything else, and we knew that human love and the hugging of bodies in sexual embrace did not mix with our ideal of a dedicated life.[8] Therefore, even though fully conscious of the greatness and nobility of the married state, we felt that we were called to something different, to a spiritual, wider fatherhood. We did not hesitate to sacrifice one for the other.

The Theology Years

After one year of theology at Monza, my classmates went to our Milan seminary to continue their studies while I was sent to the Gregorian

University in Rome. I found the intellectual atmosphere of this great institution of learning very stimulating, but I felt no attraction to higher studies. A doctorate in theology would have landed me in some seminary teaching theology, and that was not what I wanted. I told Fr. Manna about my feelings and he allowed me to go to our PIME seminary in Milan to finish my theological studies.

I enjoyed the company of my classmates. There were about fifty of us. The seminary building was brand new and each seminarian had his own bedroom. The faculty was excellent, theology classes were stimulating and there was a good library, too. Among us students there was not only an intense family spirit but also a strong missionary spirit that was constantly nurtured by frequent visits from returning missionaries. We came from different parts of Italy, from different family backgrounds, we had different views about many subjects, but we were all united in one common ideal: to go to the foreign missions.[9]

A Priest Forever

The date of our ordination was set for Saturday, September 20, 1930, at the beginning of our fourth year of theology. That day my classmates were ordained to the priesthood in the Milan Duomo by the cardinal archbishop. However, I was ordained in the cathedral of Perugia because Archbishop Rosa, being a friend of the family, had requested this privilege.

The dawn of that Saturday came after a restless night due to the excitement that the most important day of my life, the day of my ordination to the priesthood, was arriving at last. I think it is very difficult to adequately describe the thoughts and emotions of a young man on the day of his ordination. This very special event really has no counterpart in ordinary lay life. It is quite different, for instance, from the day of graduating to pursue a professional career or even of one's wedding day. Ordination to the priesthood is the complete, lifelong surrender of oneself, body and soul, to divine, eternal, demanding love. As it was written: it is the surrender of one's will to obedience, of one's body to chastity, of one's desire for possessions, to follow Christ in poverty.

My first Mass in my parish in Perugia was attended by all my relatives and family friends. During the following days I revisited and celebrated Mass in the places where I had lived for some length of time: the church where I had been baptized in Cagli, the church of the Carmelite Fathers in Nocera, which had been my spiritual cradle, the chapel of a cloistered convent where one of my aunts lived. One of my first Masses was also celebrated in the great Franciscan Shrine of St. Mary of the Angels in Assisi, where St. Francis had lived and died. The "honeymoon" lasted eight glorious days, eight days that could never be duplicated in my life, eight days that left a tremendous imprint on my soul.

Then I took a train back to Milan for one more, and last, year of studies and hard discipline, but also the first year of a new life as a priest.

Mission Assignment: China

After the day of ordination to the priesthood, the most important day in the life of a PIME missionary is the day when he receives his first mission assignment. We saw it as a real manifestation of God's will and therefore we were ready to go anywhere we were sent. This also meant accepting the new country to which we were assigned as our new, adopted fatherland regardless of our personal feelings. We were taught that to obey God's will was the paramount duty of the missionary.

Late in the afternoon of June 29, 1931, the Feast Day of Sts. Peter and Paul, the whole student body and the faculty of the PIME Theological Seminary in Milan assembled in the chapel for the solemn event of mission assignments. When, after the ritual songs and prayers, Fr. Paul Manna, our superior general, read from the altar the list of assignments, one could have heard a pin drop in that tense atmosphere. He started reading the names in alphabetical order. Finally he arrived at the letter M and read in a routine fashion, "Maestrini and Orlando are assigned to the diocese of Hong Kong." So China was to be my new country. I had always cherished the idea of going to Burma, and for a moment I was disappointed. Realizing, however, that this was God's will for me, I told the Lord: "Thy will be done! China it will be." From that moment, China became my second fatherland.

In the meantime, Fr. Orlando, who sat next to me, was all excited and, tugging at my elbow, kept repeating, "Nicola, rejoice, rejoice, we are going!"[10]

Farewell To My Family

The day after this ceremony I left for a final visit to my family. That last month at home was a real strain on the emotions of all of us. Of course, I found strength in my youthful idealism and the satisfaction of reaching my goals, but nonetheless I felt the pain of separation. My poor mother and dad, already in their fifties, felt that my departure was like a death knell. They expected never to see me again here on earth. Very often I would catch my mother crying or would notice her red eyes. My father did not cry openly, but I could read his pain in every line of his face. He wanted to spend every minute of the day with me.

The conversations with relatives and friends always revolved around the same subject: "Why do you have to leave and go to work among those barbarians? There is so much good to be done here!" Some people were very outspoken and openly blamed my parents for letting me go. "If he were my son," they would say, "I would never let him go." It was not easy to answer such human reasoning, but my dad always came to his own defense, and he developed an answer all his own.

"Remember," he told his friends, even priests, "the parable of Lazarus and the rich man. When the rich man asked Abraham to send Lazarus back into the world to warn his brothers to change their way of living, lest they, too, fall into that place of torments, Abraham answered, 'They have Moses and the prophets. Let them hear them; if they do not listen to Moses and the prophets, they will not be convinced even if one should rise from the dead!' We have Moses and our prophets here. If we do not listen to them it is our fault. But those poor souls in China, India and Africa have never even heard about Christ, and if my son is called by God to do that kind of work, well, God's will be done." It was a good theological argument and no Catholic worthy of the name could argue with it.

I wanted to spend the last day of my vacation with all my relatives, in Cagli, where I had been born, and leave for the missions from there. Therefore I asked all of those who could come to gather there at my uncle's house, on August 1, the last day of my leave. They all decided to see me off at the railroad station. When at about 10:00 P.M. the train pulled into the station a flood of tears was let loose. Trying to smile, pretending to be cheerful, encouraging, hugging, kissing everybody, I finally sighed with relief when the conductor shouted, "All aboard!" Slowly the train moved away from the dim light of the station and started speeding into the night. In a semi-deserted compartment of the train, and finally alone, I cried, too.

The Departure Ceremony

As I mentioned before, it was the departure ceremony I had attended in

October 1925 that had strengthened my vocation to the missions. During the following years I had never failed to attend this yearly event and each time I had again been deeply moved, anticipating the day of my own departure.

Finally that day came, on August 21, 1931. There were twenty-two of us, eighteen priests and four lay brothers, assigned to the different missions of PIME in India, Burma and China. The night before, at a solemn ceremony in our PIME church, Fr. Manna had given each of us the Official Document from the Sacred Congregation for the Evangelization of the Peoples signed by the cardinal prefect, conferring upon us the official title of "Apostolic Missionary." That certificate gave us an official status in the Church, but to us it was more than the Church's official recognition of our missionary vocation. It meant that the Church was officially "sending" us ("missionary" means "one who is sent") to the non-Christian nations, as Christ sent His apostles to bring the Good News to the whole world. I believe that no doctor or lawyer has ever cherished his university diploma more than we cherished that document, which made us official envoys of Christ.

The church ceremony was followed by the traditional farewell banquet at which superiors, students, close friends and benefactors joined together to honor the departing missionaries. It was one of the distinguishing characteristics of the family type of life in PIME.

August 21 was to be our last day in Italy and the most emotionally trying day of our lives.

At 9:00 A.M. a convoy of luxury cars, supplied by a group of businessmen friends of PIME, took us to the very old Church of St. Simpliciano in Milan. The pastor had invited us to hold the departure ceremony there in order to stimulate his parishioners to a greater love for the missions. The church was filled to capacity by relatives and friends. This solemn departure ceremony was a civic event for the city and there had been extensive publicity in the local press. Cardinal Ildefonso Schuster (an Italian with a German name), Archbishop of Milan, came personally to perform the ceremony. His vibrant, emotional farewell speech impressed all of us. The theme of his talk, which I remember to this day, was: "For you departing missionaries, this day is the beginning of a lifelong Mass. Mass is essentially a sacrifice and your very life must be a continuous Mass. As Christ was priest and victim in His own sacrifice on Calvary, so, imitating Him, you, too, will make your lives a perennial sacrifice for the salvation of souls."

One from our group gave the traditional farewell speech and touched everybody's heart. When the ceremony was over and we came out sporting our brand-new, shiny crucifixes, thunderous applause greeted us. People crowded around us to kiss our crucifixes, to shake hands with us, to give us a personal farewell. Soon we were on the way to the Shrine of Our Lady of St. Celso for the traditional farewell to Our Blessed Mother and to ask for her protection during the long journey ahead. This last visit to that shrine was an old tradition; it had originated with the very first departure ceremony of Blessed John Mazzucconi in 1853.

From the shrine we proceeded immediately to the railroad station. More heartrending farewells, more tears, more hugging on the part of the agonizing parents and relatives, and finally we left on the 12:00 express for Venice.

For me the worst part was still to come. My parents wanted to give me a last farewell in Venice and were waiting for me at the station there. They gave me their parting gifts: my mother put around my neck a gold chain with a medal of Our Blessed Mother. My father gave me a silver locket with a picture of mother and himself. Then we exchanged our last promises. Mother promised to write to me every day and mail the letters on the first and fifteenth of every month. In return I promised to write every week as far as I possibly could.[11]

When the time came for them to board the train they gave me a last, teary farewell and climbed aboard. More frantic waving of hands, some· fluttering of handkerchiefs, some throwing of kisses, and they were gone. This time it was I who remained glued to the platform until the little red light of the last car of the train disappeared down the track in the fading light of the sunset. Finally I turned around and hurried down to the harbor to rejoin my companions and catch the ship for China.

Farewell To Italy

It was early evening. The sun was slowly setting on the horizon in a blaze of colors. The beautiful city of Venice with its red-tiled roofs, its white marble balconies and Doric columns, its fabulous palaces and its silent waterways was gradually assuming that air of peace, of silence, of mystic and ethereal beauty that is characteristic of this unique city. Only down at the harbor was there life, feverish life. Dozens of huge liners with their black hulls, white decks, and multicolored stacks stood out in the growing darkness of the evening. They were tied up at different piers, loading and unloading their human cargo and commercial goods. Among them the liner *Cracovia*, the flagship of the Italian line Lloyd

Triestino, was getting ready to sail on a long journey to India and China. The last gangway had been lifted, the last line was being untied, and only the paper streamers billowing in the air between the people on board and those on land seemed a last fragile line keeping the huge ship tied to the pier. Frantic shouts of farewell were being exchanged between the passengers on board and the people on the jetty below.

Three ear-piercing blasts of the whistle made the ship quiver; then the huge liner began slowly, ever so slowly, to move away from the shore. High on the ship in a corner of the deck was our group of sixteen bright-eyed young men in the prime of youth. Each one of us was sporting a black, untrimmed beard, was dressed in a black clerical cassock, was wearing a black sash and a shiny, new bronze crucifix, and each was bound for missionary life in China. The conversation was subdued but all at once, as the ship glided slowly from the pier, we all burst forth in a mighty, vibrant song, the classical Gregorian melody of the "Magnificat." Every voice vibrated with emotion and every eye had a tear, but there was joy in that song, the joy that crowned ten or more long years of willing self-denial and deprivation. It was the joy of reaching the goal for which we had sacrificed our youthful years: to go to the missions.

Thirty-one days later we landed in Hong Kong.

The Hong Kong Of The Thirties

Certain aspects of Hong Kong today are very different from the Hong Kong of the thirties. The life style of the people, the size of the population, the number, size and height of buildings, the volume of business transacted, the religious activities of the different regions and Christian denominations, etc., are now much different from then. However, the basic structure of the government, the makeup of the population, and, of course, the topography of the place, were basically the same as today. These short notes are necessary to familiarize the reader with the Hong Kong of my days.

Geography. The British crown colony of Hong Kong, founded in 1841 by agreement between the governments of Great Britain and China, is adjacent to the Guandong Province in southeast China, south of the Tropic of Cancer, at approximately the same latitude as Mexico City. It is forty miles east of Macao, which was colonized by the Portuguese in the sixteenth century.

The British colony consists of the main island, Hong Kong, with its capital city, Victoria, the Kowloon peninsula (ceded to England in 1860) across the harbor from Victoria, and adjoining New Territories (leased 1898), along with several small islands. It has an area of 398 square miles (approximately the size of New York City). It had a population of about three million when I arrived in 1931. Today it has over 6,500,000. Then, as now, ninety-eight percent are Chinese.

Government. The colony governor was appointed by the British Foreign Office in London. He had supreme power and ruled in consultation with an appointed Advisory Council comprising prominent British and Chinese, all of whom were nominees approved by the governor. It was the typical colonial government on which the British Empire was built. In the case of Hong Kong its benevolent rule was of great benefit to the Chinese, British and people of other nationalities who flocked there "to make a bundle." To us missionaries, Hong Kong was not only a field of missionary work, but also a springboard for our religious work in China.

Religion. From the beginning of the colony the British government adopted a very broad policy of collaboration with both Protestants and Catholics and with the major non-Christian religions. It followed the general principle of separation of church and state: it regarded all organized religions as equals and collaborated with them in social and educational matters. In my days relations among the various religions and Christian denominations were good. In fact, long before Vatican II started the ecumenical movement, we Catholics in Hong Kong were already practicing it by heartily collaborating with Protestants and non-Christian religions.

The Catholic Church in Hong Kong is as old as the colony itself. It was there in 1841 when the colony started and in 1842 it was established as a prefecture apostolic (a territory on the way to becoming a diocese)[12] under the jurisdiction of the Congregation for the Evangelization of Peoples. In 1858 the very first members of PIME started to work there and the whole prefecture was officially entrusted to PIME in 1869. It was later raised to the status of diocese.

The area of work assigned by the Congregation to the new prefecture included then—as it still does—the British-administered territory of the crown colony and three Chinese prefectures on the mainland (Haifeng, Huiyang and Paoan) for a total of six thousand square miles.

When I arrived in 1931 the total population of the diocese, including Catholics and non-Catholics in Hong Kong and on the mainland, was about seven million. In Hong Kong itself the Catholic Church consisted of about three thousand Portuguese Catholics, scarcely one thousand

Chinese, eight parishes, half a dozen Chinese priests, about sixty missionary priests and about one hundred fifty missionary sisters of different nationalities. All worked under Italian-born Bishop Henry Valtorta of PIME. They conducted a vast array of Catholic activities, such as several hospitals, schools, both in English and Chinese, with several tens of thousands of students (mostly non-Christian), orphanages for boys and girls, houses for the elderly, etc.

The Chinese and the PIME priests constituted the diocesan clergy and were in charge of all the parishes, except one entrusted to the Salesians. The religious (non-diocesan) clergy comprised the Salesians and the Irish Jesuits, who specialized in educational work. Others, such as Maryknoll missionaries, the Dominicans and the French missionaries, had only administrative offices.

The sisters, too, were running an imposing array of charitable works. The Sisters of St. Paul de Chartres from France, popularly known in Hong Kong as the French Sisters, were the first to arrive in the colony, in 1850, for religious work among the European and Chinese girls. The Canossian Sisters, founded by St. Magdalen of Canossa in Italy in 1808, were known in Hong Kong as the Italian Sisters. As the result of the great work of these two societies among Chinese women, a flourishing society of Chinese Sisters was later established in the diocese. Many other societies of women came later and they, too, did great work.

By the time I arrived in Hong Kong, the French, Italian and Chinese sisters were running dozens of girls' schools, orphanages and hospitals, educating several tens of thousands of girls in both English and Chinese schools. The La Salle Brothers were running the best-known Catholic school for boys, St. Joseph College, not far from the cathedral.

The cathedral, the oldest church in the colony (1888) and the attached mission house (which also included the bishop's residence) on Caine Road in the heart of Victoria, midway up the hill from the harbor, were the headquarters of the diocese and the nerve center of all its charitable and religious activities.

The mission house, also called the bishop's residence, was then an imposing four-story building with a beautiful view of the harbor and of the Kowloon peninsula on the other side. The building housed the bishop's quarters—one room, which he used as his office and bedroom the chancery, which also consisted of one room, the pastor's office and residence, fifteen bedrooms for resident and visiting missionaries from the mainland, a private chapel, a library, one large dining room and a couple of conference rooms. Besides the bishop and the pastor, other resident priests included the chancellor of the diocese, the administrator in charge of finances, the bishop's secretary, occasional priest students or retired priests, and the PIME priests from the mainland when they came to town to see the bishop and to buy supplies.

The bishop, who was then a PIME member, the Chinese and we Italian priests of PIME lived a community life and shared the same dining room. It was a small but closely knit family of dedicated missionary priests bound together by the common ideal of evangelizing China. We then had no secretaries and no lay employees, with the exception of a couple of Chinese men who took care of the kitchen and house cleaning.

A unique place. The brief information I have given here about Hong Kong is, of course, totally inadequate to describe the place, the people, the ambience that prevailed there in 1931. Then, as now, Hong Kong was a unique city.

Han Suyin in her article in *Life* magazine in 1959 aptly called Hong Kong a borrowed place on borrowed time. I like to add: with a mystique all its own.

Even in 1931 Hong Kong could be described in the words of Richard Hughes: "an anachronistic mixture of British colonialism and the Chinese way of life, a jumble of millionaires' mansions and horrible slums, a teeming mass of hard-working humans, a well ordered autocracy."[13] Hong Kong has always been unashamedly materialistic. Its simple formula for success as given by Hughes is: "low taxes, no controls, quick profits, hard work and laissez-faire."[14] But behind this facade, Hong Kong has, and always had, a heart: the compassionate heart of the teeming masses of China combined with the philanthropic heart of the Anglo-Saxon race.

Hong Kong was and still is Chinese to the core. With a population that is constantly ninety-eight percent Chinese it cannot be anything else but Chinese, yet it is different from China: it is a unique combination of the best and worst in both East and West.

I was fascinated by Hong Kong when I first saw it from the deck of the SS *Cracovia* in the early dawn of September 21, 1931, and I am still fascinated fifty-nine years later as I write this in 1990.

Notes

1. Another sister, Mary, was born while were were at Nocera, but died after a few months. My last brother, Joseph ("Bepi"), was born in 1921 shortly after I had entered the seminary in Rome.

2. It was founded by St. Jerome Emiliani (1486-1537) in northern Italy for the education of youth.

3. PIME stands for the Italian words that mean "Pontifical Institute for Foreign Missions" and it is popularly called the PIME Missionary Society. Its members are known as PIME missionaries. For further information read the appendix about PIME.

4. Fr. Paul Manna, PIME, was one of the greatest pioneers in the development of modern foreign missions. It all began on a rainy day in April 1907, in Toungoo, Burma, when old Bishop Rocco Tornatore, PIME, called young Fr. Paul Manna to his room. In a voice quivering with emotion the bishop said, "Father Paul, I hate to tell you this but you are under a death sentence. You are in an advanced stage of tuberculosis and the English doctor in Rangoon gives you no more than a couple of months to live. However, he says that if you leave soon for Italy and your native climate of Naples, your chance of living a few more years will improve."

Fr. Manna was then only thirty-five. He had spent twelve years doing pioneer work among the primitive population of northeast Burma, where no foreign missionary had even penetrated before. He was looking forward to new conquests for Christ, and now he was under a sentence of death.

"If you order me to go, I will go. God's will be done." With this humble reply Fr. Manna accepted God's plan for his life. Back in Italy he went on to become one of the greatest mission promoters of the twentieth century until his death in 1952 at age eighty.

Fr. Manna was only 5′5″, of stocky build. He sported a full beard, wore thick lenses in gold-rimmed eyeglasses, and had deep, dark, intelligent eyes. He was a man of vision, he had a soul on fire, and he worked endlessly, sixteen hours a day, to make the Christian world realize the urgent necessity of bringing Christ's message of love to the non-Christian nations.

What impressed me most about him was his total dedication to the mission ideal; to him nothing else mattered but the foreign missions. He did not think, speak, or dream of anything else. Nothing else mattered. I owe him not only my missionary vocation through the magazine he founded in 1917, *Italia Missionaria*, but also my whole missionary formation and spirituality. During my two years in Milan he spent quite some time with the students, and the profound influence of his personality was felt in every detail of our seminary life.

His influence was also felt here in the United States. His book *The Workers Are Few* was one of the first books on foreign missions ever published in the United States and it deeply influenced the foundation of the Maryknoll Foreign Missions Society in 1911.

The cause for his beatification has already been successfully concluded and before too long he may be raised to the Honor of the Altars.

5. Many of the people I met at the Roman seminary were later elevated to the highest positions of authority in the Church. I will mention only a few: Msgr. Angelo Roncalli became Pope John XXIII; my spiritual director, Msgr. Alfredo Ottaviani, became Cardinal Ottaviani; my first rector, Msgr. Roberti, became His Eminence Francesco Cardinal Roberti, one of the greatest contemporary authorities on Canon Law; my two prefects, Ferretto and Cenci, became diplomats and cardinals. Among my classmates: Egidio Vagnozzi became the Apostolic Delegate to the USA and, later, a cardinal; Francis T. Furey and Joseph McShea, both from Philadelphia, became respectively the bishops of San Diego in California and Allentown in Pennsylvania.

6. That young priest later became His Excellency Bishop Fernando Guercilena of Kengtung, Burma, and a great friend of mine.

7. I want to briefly mention here some of the great events that later occurred in the lives of the missionaries who so inspired me that day. Only seven years later, tall and handsome Fr. Granelli became the first pastor of the new St. Teresa's parish in Kowloon, Hong Kong, and I his assistant. He died in Hong Kong in 1976 at age 84.

Fr. Diego D'Ayala Valva came from a noble family of Spanish descent. After losing his faith for a time in his youth and being active in the Communist Party, he abandoned politics, returned to his faith, joined PIME for life, and was assigned to Hong Kong. He was my mission companion for all the years I was in Hong Kong. Since leaving Italy on October 5, 1925, he has never returned.

For the well-girthed Fr. Antonio Barosi, who read the prayer of dedication at the departure ceremony, the words "even more blessed that day when I may be found worthy to shed my blood in Your witness" became a glorious reality. After a very active and fruitful mission life in Henan Province in central China, he was a candidate to become bishop.

In the afternoon of November 19, 1941, he and three other PIME missionaries were attacked in their own mission house by a roving band of Chinese guerrillas, cruelly tortured and killed.

The same glorious martyrdom was reserved for two other missionaries of the group that left for the missions in 1925. On two separate days in February of 1953, Frs. Alfredo Cremanesi and Pietro Manghisi died violently at the hands of Burmese bandits.

8. Today, judging the seminary training of those days in the light of the reforms of Vatican II, I admit that the old system had some deficiencies. It stunted our emotional growth, it warped our views about sex and love, it failed to teach us how to assume responsibilities and make decisions, etc. But these drawbacks were only temporary and we made up for them later as we grew in years and maturity.

After living sixty full years as a priest in a tremendous variety of circumstances and different environments from Italy to China to the USA, I am still grateful for the type of training I received and I owe to it the deep spirituality it taught me.

9. An important step in preparation for our ordination was to start growing a beard. In those days, the Catholic clergy in Europe (with the exception of the Capuchin Friars) were not allowed to grow a beard, but foreign missionaries were encouraged to do so. The official thinking was that since we had to live abroad, it was better to grow a beard because in many countries, such as China, a full-grown beard made a person look older and, therefore, more respectable. The unofficial, but no less important, thinking was that the beard would make the young missionary look less physically attractive to women.

It was only early in June that our class received official permission to let our beards grow. Therefore, a few weeks later, when I arrived home for my summer vacation, I looked more like a man who had simply not shaved for a couple of weeks than like a young man with a beard. When I stepped down from the train in Perugia and rushed to hug my mother, she really had a feeling of revulsion, hesitated before hugging me, and could not help blurting out, "Son, you really look ugly!" but she soon got over it. I wore a beard all through my years in Hong Kong, and only shaved it in 1951 when I came to the States, at the suggestion of the then apostolic delegate to the USA, Archbishop Cicognani.

10. Today, the beautiful concept of a mission assignment as the manifestation of God's will, to be accepted as an act of total obedience, has been utterly destroyed. This is true not only of PIME but of all the missionary societies in general. As a result of the effort to "naturalize" Christian life in the aftermath of Vatican II, the mission assignment today comes about through a three-party dialogue: the General Directorate, which is assigning the missionary; the missionary himself, who is free to discuss his assignment and, if he insists, select a country of his choice; and the receiving mission, which is free to accept or refuse the missionary. Thus the will of God and the act of obedience have ended in a merely human dialogue!

11. My dear mother faithfully kept her promise until she died thirty-eight years later at eighty-nine years of age. From the day I left she started writing a kind of diary of daily family events. The last thing she did at night before retiring was to write at least a few lines to her missionary son far away. Even through the four years of World War II she wrote a few lines every day and tucked her letters away in a drawer until the Italian Post Office would again accept mail for Hong Kong. When the war was over she mailed to me all she had written through the four years, and for days on end I read of what my family had gone through in those hard times. In the last year of her life her eyesight failed badly, but still every day she scribbled a few lines.

12. According to the old Canon Law of the Church, the Congregation of "Propaganda Fide" (the Foreign Affairs Ministry of the Vatican), which was in charge of the evangelization work of the Church in non-Christian nations, assigned and defined the area of work in mission territories within which each religious order was responsible for the promotion of Christianity and the planting of the Church.

For administrative purposes these areas were called by different names according to their respective stages of development. At the initial stage a mission territory was called a prefecture apostolic and was ruled by a prefect apostolic, who had the title of "monsignor" but was not a bishop. In the second stage, when the prefecture had developed considerably and had a good number of local and foreign clergy, of converts, churches, etc., it was raised to the status of a vicariate apostolic, and was governed by a bishop called the vicar apostolic. Finally, when the Church had made considerable progress in the whole nation, the "hierarchy" was established and the vicariates were raised to the status of dioceses governed by bishops. Hong Kong was made a prefecture apostolic in 1842, a vicariate apostolic in 1869 and finally a diocese in 1947. In this book, for the sake of clarity, I always refer to Hong Kong as a diocese, regardless of the proper title it had in the year I am writing about.

13. *Hong Kong,* p. 9.

14. Ibid, page 17.

The author when he left Italy for China on August 21, 1931.

1

Beginning A New Life In The Orient

Hong Kong The Beautiful

It was 4:30 in the morning, September 22, 1931. After a thirty-one-day
sea voyage, the SS *Cracovia*, flagship of the Italian Lloyd Triestino line,
was sailing the calm waters of the China Sea, approaching the China
mainland. Sixteen newly ordained priests pressed against the ship's rail
for a first glimpse of land. My classmate Fr. C. Orlando and I were
among them.

The five hundred passengers on board slept peacefully while the eager,
bearded Italians strained to see the coastline through the darkness of the
moonless night. Nature has her own rhythms; despite our concerted
willpower, she would not unveil the moon or raise the sun. In due course,
patience was rewarded. Intermittent beams of light began to appear in the
darkness. They came from the lighthouses located on the deserted islands
along the south China coast. As dawn broke, a line of jagged hillcrests
emerged from the haze on the far horizon. It was China at last.

China! My lifelong dream of being a foreign missionary was finally
being realized! In a few hours I would land in Hong Kong, the mission
Divine Providence had assigned to me, where I would begin my life of
service to the Chinese, following Christ's invitation "Come, follow Me."
I was only twenty-three, and after ten years of seminary training, it
seemed I had been waiting a lifetime. Now I had arrived.

At 7:30 A.M. the massive liner slowly maneuvered through the
Lyemoon pass into Hong Kong Harbor and sailed majestically toward
the Kowloon dockside, opposite the mountainous, tropical island of
Hong Kong. I was stunned by the beauty of the scenery. It impressed

me as one of the world's most spectacular ports. As we crossed the harbor, it seemed we were sailing through a vast water basin completely surrounded by hills and bustling with hundreds of ships and boats of all sizes and shapes, from majestic liners to ancient Chinese junks, down to diminutive "walla-walla" motor boats. On one side, imposing Victoria Peak rose steeply 1,800 feet above the water, its verdant slopes dotted with white villas and trim gardens surrounded by luscious, tropical vegetation. The city of Victoria, with its typical, somber-looking colonial buildings, its congested tenement houses crawling halfway up the hills, sprawled at its feet along the seashore. On the opposite side of the harbor was the teeming Kowloon Peninsula, flat and spread out to the slopes of the Lionhead and the jagged hills at the horizon.

While the liner slowly docked to the cheers of thousands of friends and sightseers, we, from high on the ship could clearly see a little group of men dressed in clerical cassocks in the midst of a large mass of Chinese people. We soon recognized them as our fellow priests from PIME who had come to welcome us. I soon recognized Fr. Ambrose Poletti, my close friend from our year of theology in Rome, Frs. A. Granelli and D. D'Ayala, whose departure ceremony in 1925 had changed my mind about leaving PIME, and many other former fellow students who had preceded us there. They were thinner, dusty, sun-tanned, but now veteran missionaries still bubbling with enthusiasm. They were my new family. When we finally landed, they received us with typical Italian enthusiasm, hugs, and kisses. After this festive, exuberant welcome, still on our sea legs, all sixteen of us were rushed across the harbor on the ferryboat and up the hill to the cathedral to meet our bishop. Stocky, bespectacled, sporting a full, untrimmed beard with a tinge of gray, in his late forties, debonair Bishop Henry Valtorta received us with the typical enthusiasm of his Milanese fatherland, slapping our shoulders, shaking our hands till we cringed with pain. He was happy to add two young missionaries to his overburdened diocesan personnel.

After a brief visit to the large, Gothic-style cathedral, we were escorted around town for a quick tour by bus and streetcar of the sights of the city. Late in the afternoon we went back to the Cracovia and bade farewell to our fourteen confreres who were continuing on to Shanghai to reach their final destinations in various parts of China. Fr. Orlando and I went back to the bishop's house for dinner and a good night's sleep. We were dead tired but could not have been happier!

A Missionary At Last!

What left me stunned on that first day in Hong Kong was the number of people milling in the streets. Everywhere I saw overcrowded shops, over-crowded buses and streetcars, overcrowded tenement houses, men, women, children, shopkeepers, street vendors and beggars all squeezing and pressing each other and everyone else . . . people everywhere. They were similar to, yet so different from the people with whom I was accustomed to living. Their appearance, their dress, the way they shuffled along in the streets, their language and their customs seemed so strange to me that day. The cultural shock was tremendous, yet I felt love and admiration for them.

I kept on repeating to myself: these are my people, these are the souls I have come to save. What can I do or will I be able to do for them? Of course, I realized that they could not care less about me, but that did not disturb me. I was there among the Chinese people because Someone higher than all of us had invited me there. As long as He wanted me there, I would be happy to remain there with my new, adopted family, whether they would accept me or not.

At no other time in my life have I experienced such a keen sense of futility as I did that evening. In the peace and silence of my room, sitting on the only chair, looking at the poor, drab furniture around me, I reviewed the main events of that day: from the human point of view I certainly was the greatest fool on earth. What was I doing in that room, alone, on foreign soil, thousands of miles away from everything I loved and appreciated, without even being able to speak the language? To convert the Chinese? But they, steeped in their centuries-old culture and religious tradition, with their profound dislike for everything foreign, could not care less about me and my religion. Wasn't I a fool? Why had I left my country, my family, even the Roman seminary, which might have opened a path to a diplomatic career in the church? Why? Why?

From the human point of view, nothing made sense, yet I was happy. I thought of Peter, John, Andrew and the other apostles, the days after they had left their families, their businesses, their ways of life to follow an unknown, itinerant teacher who did not even possess a house and did not enjoy a good reputation among the church leaders. The people of their times must have called them fools, but they knew what they were doing and time proved that they were right and the people wrong. I, too, was there to follow in the footsteps of Christ, and I knew I was right and could have not asked for a more important role in life.

As I prepared for bed I could not help thinking of my family, of my mother especially. It was more than a month since I had left them. Were they thinking of me? Were they worrying about me?

After thirty-one days on the ship, that night was the first night I slept in a real bed on land. What a relief! But at the same time what a torture. Orlando and I had been assigned rooms on the fourth floor at the mission house with a beautiful view of the harbor and the Chinese mainland, but the bed, like all Chinese beds, consisted of three narrow wooden boards resting on a low trestle and a flimsy bamboo mat. It was the first time I had ever slept on a hard bed and, in spite of my youthful years, my bones were aching all over. Finally I fell asleep and when I awakened the next morning I felt like a new man.

The First Mass On Mission Soil

It was still early morning when Orlando and I entered the cathedral to celebrate our first Mass on mission soil. The words Cardinal Ildefonso Schuster of Milan had addressed to us only a month before at the departure ceremony were still ringing in my ears: "For you departing missionaries, this day is the beginning of a lifelong Mass. Mass is essentially a sacrifice and your very life must be a continuous Mass, a perennial sacrifice to bring souls to Christ."

In the life of every missionary, the first Mass on mission soil is always an event of great spiritual importance, and it was such for Orlando and me. What made it even more interesting for us was the fact that the cathedral was dedicated to Our Blessed Mother; we both shared a tender devotion to her. We believed strongly in Mary's power of intercession with God as beautifully expressed by Dante in the thirty-third canto of his *Paradise*:

"Lady, thou art so great and so dear to God
that who seeks help and does not seek it through thee
would have his wish to fly without wings."

We celebrated Mass separately at a side altar, as was the custom of those days, and a Chinese gentleman served it pronouncing the Latin words with a strong Chinese accent.

I did not know that morning that a few years later I would be the pastor of that very church and that I would spend the most tragic years of my life there under Japanese occupation. But that morning the future was hidden from my eyes and, as any other young man would have felt, I was eager to get acquainted with our new world.

For Fr. Orlando and me breakfast with Bishop Valtorta proved a thrilling experience: continental breakfast—coffee, milk, and bread served by A-Wong, the diminutive head man of the small household staff who was waiter, cook, receptionist, "Mister Do-it-all," and who, we soon learned, was worth his weight in gold.

The bishop was eager to get to know us and we to know him. In mission lands, where priests are few, the bishop is very much a father, a companion, a guide. We admired good bishop Valtorta, who, through his long experience as a missionary on the China mainland and in the city of Hong Kong, had acquired a great knowledge of the Chinese, loved them deeply, and was totally committed to them. That morning he was in the best of moods, seemed to like us, and told us story after story about his mission life.

After breakfast, Fr. Poletti took us under his wings and led us on a visit to the parishes and Catholic institutions in the colony. Our first visit was to venerable Fr. John Spada, the dean of our PIME missionaries in Hong Kong, who had been working there since 1892. He was then the pastor of Rosary Church, the first and oldest church on the Kowloon side, which he had built in the year 1900. He received us warmly and urged us to get down to studying English and Chinese promptly. Only four months later he became my first pastor.

At Rosary we also met Fr. Lam, one of the oldest Chinese priests of the diocese, and we spoke Latin with him. I could not help marveling at the way he had mastered this difficult language. We were not so lucky at the Chinese sisters' convent, where we admired the work of the nuns in the orphanage and the school but could not communicate with them as we spoke neither English nor Chinese.

Communications were easier at the French convent at Causeway Bay, where, with our high-school French, we managed to get through to the sisters as they led us through the imposing array of their work, which included the best-run Catholic hospital in the colony at that time, the English and Chinese schools with thousands of students, the orphanage for girls, and the novitiate for the training of Chinese sisters.

The visit to the Canossian sisters at the Italian convent, only a few hundred yards from the cathedral, was most rewarding because, at last, we could communicate without the need of an interpreter. The good sisters were delighted to see us as they too felt the need of more priests in their work.

This concluded our first day's tour of the main Catholic institutions in the colony. We were impressed by the terrific work done by the Church in less than a century, but we were only slightly interested in all that we saw. We believed then that only the missionaries working in the country-side of the China mainland under primitive conditions were the real mis-sionaries. Those working in the cities were, in our eyes, kind of second-class missionaries and we wanted none of that. We were eager to be assigned to work in the interior of China, and all that city work did not interest us very much.

My First Encounter With China

Two days after we arrived, Bishop Valtorta invited Fr. Orlando and me to accompany him on a trip to the Chinese mainland, where he was to officiate at the solemn baptism of a whole village. We both were ecstatic at the opportunity to see the "real" China and accepted with enthusiasm.

At 6:00 the next morning Bishop Valtorta and the two of us boarded a train at the Kowloon station of the British railroad linking Hong Kong and Guangzhou. The car was unbelievably overcrowded with cages of pigs, chickens, birds, and bales of cargo, and people were everywhere, standing, sitting, lying down, leaning against mountains of cargo. I must confess that at the beginning I felt rather uneasy among that crowd of foreigners, as I regarded them, but I soon realized that I was the for-eigner, that those people pressing against me on every side, smelling of sweat, chatting, coughing, chewing, were my people. I had to adapt to them, not they to me, and I slowly began to enjoy them and to feel at home.

About one hour later we left the train at the railroad station of Tai-po in the New Territories. That little village in those days was like thou-sands of similar villages all over the China mainland, except for the presence of the British police station. The houses were typical of the one-floor structures seen in all the Chinese villages, the shops were small and crowded, the streets narrow and unpaved.

We walked through the village down to the little harbor trailed by a line of half-naked coolies carrying our luggage on bamboo poles across their shoulders. A large Chinese junk, bobbing up and down, was tied up at the pier and, judging from the crowd of people milling around it, was being readied for a trip. We followed the bishop and, walking on a rickety gangplank, finally boarded the old boat. On board, the bishop told us that the junk was the regular "liner" plying between the British New Territories and the Chinese mainland and was used mostly by Chinese shopkeepers, traders and businessmen.

I was in a completely new world. Everything looked so different from my usual environment, so strange, so new to me. Even though it was only 7:00 A.M., the tropical sun was scorching and the heat intense. Chinese peasants were everywhere. The women wore long, black pants and jackets and large, round bamboo hats with black fringe. They were doing all the menial work, washing, scrubbing, handling the light cargo, cooking on little portable earthen stoves. They all seemed middle-aged and I could not tell the difference between young and old. Hard work and poor nutrition made them all look alike. The men wore wide pants made of black cloth, and white cotton vests. The coolies and deckhands wore only dirty shorts. Their tanned skin gleamed in the sun while rivulets of perspiration ran down their bodies as they handled the cargo.

In the midst of this shabbily dressed crowd, we walked along in our strictly European attire of long, white cassocks, new sun helmets, black leather shoes and white stockings. Our black beards and protruding noses stuck out among the beardless and flatnosed Chinese. In their eyes we surely were an odd-looking group. I understood then why the Chinese call us "foreign devils." My mind wandered back to the days when the apostles traveled through the roads of the Roman empire. Did they wear Jewish clothes? Did they, too, look like oddities to the sophisticated citizens of Athens and Rome?

The typical Chinese junk, flat-bottomed and with battered sails, offered no shelter from the scorching sun. We could only squat on the wooden deck or sit on our luggage with sweating people and animal cages pressing us on every side. What a difference from the seminary world in which I had grown up!

Finally the sails were hoisted and the junk moved away from land in a faint breeze. For five hours the bobbing junk moved along, skimming the waves of a calm, copper-colored sea ever so slowly, bound northward first along the coast, then across a large, beautiful bay. There was no room to move even a few steps, and there were no rest rooms. The only food available was bananas and hot Chinese tea served in small china cups that did not look too clean to me. They were used by everybody.

Finally at 1:00 P.M. we sighted Nam-tau, a tiny village on the China coast, north of Hong Kong. Even though our final destination was the village of Shui-ten-sa, about one mile away, we were scheduled to leave the junk in Nam-tau for "public relations" purposes. As there were no Christians yet in Nam-tau, the missionary in charge of that district, Fr. Andrew Maglio, PIME, had planned to have the bishop land there and to give him a big reception in order to impress the non-Christian villagers.

As the old junk with its yellow sails billowing approached land, firecrackers burst out with a deafening sound all along the shore. We saw hundreds of people gathered at the pier waiting for the boat to dock. The local Chinese band with handmade bamboo flutes, string instruments, and drums struck up a thunderous sound. When the gangplank was securely tied, the bishop was the first to debark. He shook hands with stocky, sunburned Fr. Maglio, who introduced him to the elders of Shui-ten-sa. They in turn greeted him effusively, bowing in Chinese style with joined hands. There were hundreds of bystanders attracted by the noise who wondered who that long-nosed, bearded foreign devil might be as he was being received with such pomp.

All the people from Shui-ten-sa who were to be baptized the next day were lined up along the shore and the bishop inspected them all as they knelt before him asking for his blessing. Orlando and I tagged along like two simpletons, shaking hands, smiling, understanding nothing of what was being said but enjoying the scene like two young children on a family outing.

It was a beautiful sight. Under a scorching sun, two long rows of people—men, women and children in their Sunday best—paid homage to the bishop, smiling, bowing and crossing themselves while hundreds of non-Christian onlookers in work clothes were milling around. They seemed surprised, confused, and unable to understand why so much homage was being paid to a foreign dignitary.

I was impressed by the fact that all these people were fishermen; like many fishermen in the rest of the world they were poor and uneducated. The bishop had told us that there was no other trade in that desolate coastal area and that fishing was still done by the same primitive methods that had prevailed for centuries. The whole scene reminded me of Galilee as we read about it in the Gospel. Here, on the Chinese seashore, twenty centuries after Christ trod this earth and ten thousand miles away from Israel, a bishop, successor of the original Fishermen of Galilee, was also raising his hand in blessing as Christ himself had with the crowds along the shores of His beautiful lake. History repeats itself.

Finally the parade of new converts began to march toward Shui-ten-sa, led by a man carrying a white cross. This cross bearer was obviously a leper: his hands were all gnarled and several fingers were missing. Children, men and women followed the cross while the band played. The bishop, Orlando and I brought up the rear while Fr. Maglio ran up and down the line talking to people, giving final instructions for the complicated ceremony planned for the following day, keeping people in line.

The Great Ceremony

The baptismal ceremony took place the next morning during a Mass celebrated along the seashore under the open sky. The little chapel was far too small to accommodate all the guests and visitors who came from nearby Christian villages to share in the joy of the new Catholics of Shuiten-sa. Their strong sense of community was remarkable.

In order to speed up the long ceremony, the catechumens were divided into several groups and different priests were assigned to baptize each group. Orlando and I had our own group of about twenty each. As Latin was the language then used for the baptismal ceremony, we had no trouble with that!

The big celebration would not have been complete without a festive meal. The communal banquet was prepared by the whole village for themselves and their guests. For Orlando and me that banquet was an unforgettable experience. The food was cooked in the open air among swarms of flies; the old, much-used and abused pots and pans seemed crusted with dirt, as were the once white rice bowls. The menu, in true Chinese style, consisted of at least twenty different varieties of food, and, except for the pure white steaming rice, looked discouraging enough for our European taste. We had been told by Fr. Maglio that somewhere in the midst of all those dishes there was dog meat and even snake meat. We did not believe him but since we could not speak Chinese, we could not ask anyone for the facts.

When the time to eat finally arrived, Orlando and I looked at each other questioningly and I, yielding to my finicky taste, asked him in Italian: "Do we really have to eat this dirty stuff in such dirty bowls?"

The bishop overheard me. Turning to us with a broad smile and a tinge of friendly irony in his voice he said, "Listen, you two. Either you eat what these poor people offer you or you starve. Make your choice! Remember, this is China, not Italy."

We were racked by hunger and parched with thirst, as it was almost noon and we had not had any breakfast because of the late Mass and Eucharistic fast. In a joyous mood all the people squatted on the grass to eat their meal, and we two sat next to the bishop at a ramshackle, grimy old table in the shade of an ancient tree, trying desperately but unsuccessfully to keep the flies away. In keeping with the old Chinese traditions of kindness, the good people around us were very solicitous and tried to show us how to use chopsticks. I was still hesitating whether to eat or not, but finally sheer hunger proved more powerful than my squeamish fear of germs and my lack of skill in handling the chopsticks. We tasted the food, found it flavorful, and ate ravenously, no longer caring about what we were eating. The bishop watched us with obvious satisfaction and congratulated us on our valiant efforts. Shortly afterward we were served a meat dish that was especially tasty and we told the bishop so. He laughingly commented, "Gentlemen, what you have finished eating just now was dog meat! Did you enjoy it?"

"No!" we exclaimed, totally horrified. "It can't be! It's so good!"

"Exactly," he continued, "and this is why in China dog meat is considered a delicacy and is eaten only on festive occasions."

It was my first Chinese meal and I truly enjoyed it in spite of the dirty bowls and swarms of flies. After that experience we enjoyed everything served, including shark's fin and soup of birds' nests, old eggs, chicken, pork, and different types of fish.

That evening, after the community night prayers were over in the chapel, the women rushed home to attend to their chores but the men came out on the beach, just in front of the church, to talk with the bishop. Fr. Maglio told us later that the talk rambled from petty matters to questions about religion. It was a beautiful scene. A full moon shone in a cloudless sky and its silvery light was reflected by the shimmering blue ocean on the wrinkled faces of the hard-working fishermen. They were now all followers of Christ.

I could not help but think of similar scenes in Jesus' days on the beaches of Galilee. There, too, Christ had tarried late into the night to talk to fishermen—His apostles. They and their fellow fishermen crowded around Him hungry for words of life, just as these Chinese fishermen asked their bishop for light and guidance. Again history was repeating itself.

On the following day the return trip to Hong Kong by junk was harder than the first trip. We had to squat in a corner of the crowded deck, near a bamboo cage of chickens squawking their heads off, for hours on end. There was hardly any breeze and the old junk moved very slowly. As a result of the long hours in the sun and in spite of my new sun helmet I had a mild sun-stroke and a bad headache which lasted for days afterwards—the first of several to come.

Back To School: Learning Two Languages

Back in Hong Kong we had to face the problem of learning two languages at the same time. We had hardly any knowledge of English and we needed to learn it first in order to study Cantonese (the Chinese dialect spoken in Hong Kong) because all the available textbooks for learning it were in English.

The bishop sent us first to St. Joseph High School and College, conducted by the La Salle Brothers, to learn English. We were placed in a sixth-grade class with twelve-year-old Chinese and Portuguese boys. They were already proficient in English while we were still at zero level and did not have much opportunity to practice conversational English. Realizing this, the bishop asked a retired English-speaking Chinese businessman, Mr. Yeung, to spend some time with us to practice talking English. Needless to say, Mr. Yeung spoke English with a marked Chinese accent, and I got my English pronunciation from him. This is why I call my accent "Sino-British," as I learned to speak English from a Chinese gentleman in the British Colony of Hong Kong.

While learning English, we also started to study Chinese. The mission's professional Chinese teacher was Mr. Lo Pak-to, a seventy-year-old man and former Protestant catechist who neither spoke nor understood a word of English. Needless to say, his teaching methods were very, very primitive.

We accepted all these arrangements without questioning them. That was the way our confreres had learned English and Chinese before us and, if those methods had been good enough for them, they would also be good enough for us.

Thanks to God things have changed now. Today in many foreign countries there are scientifically run language schools for foreigners. Foreign missionaries go there to learn not only the language but also the history, the culture, and the ethnic characteristics of the nation where they have to work. But back in 1931 we had none of these facilities. We were then just at the beginning of the modern growth of the church's missions. Lacking modern facilities for the study of languages, we worked hard at them because our life's work depended on learning them.

A Simple Case Of Misunderstanding

One morning as I entered the community dining room at the mission house, I decided to have an apple for breakfast and in faltering, childish Chinese, I asked the man in charge of the kitchen, "A-Wong, can you please bring me a . . . a . . . an ap?"

"Father wants ap?" he answered, also in Chinese, with surprise in his tone of voice.

"Yes, A-Wong, give me an ap, please," I replied in Chinese. Proud of my progress in the new language, I went to sit at the dining table to wait for the apple. A few minutes later the diminutive, old A-Wong appeared in the dining room carrying a dish full of meat.

"A-Wong, what's that? I don't want meat, I asked you for an apple!" I exclaimed in English while all the priests at the table burst out laughing.

"Father asked for roast duck, I bring roast duck," answered A-Wong, unperturbed.

I was very embarrassed. What had happened was this. I did want an apple but could not remember the English word for apple and vaguely remembered that it started with "ap." I had also learned a Chinese word pronounced "ap," so I thought that probably "ap" meant apple in both English and Chinese. I totally forgot that in Chinese "ap" meant duck. By sheer coincidence the community had had roast duck for dinner the day before so, when I asked for "ap," good A-Wong, who knew very little English, thought that I wanted duck meat for breakfast. Though it was a very unusual request even in China, obligingly he had brought me duck meat!

This is just one of the countless mixups that happen to all missionaries while learning foreign languages.

Progress In English

In spite of attending classes at St. Joseph's College I found that my progress in learning English was too slow for my taste, so I decided to take matters into my own hands. I asked the teacher for a good English novel to read. He recommended *A Tale of Two Cities* by Charles Dickens. He added, "It is not easy reading, but if you can understand that book then you can understand any book in English." I immediately bought the book, along with a small English-Italian dictionary.

To tell the truth, when I started reading the book I could not make any sense out of it. Undaunted, I started methodically to look up each word in the English-Italian dictionary, to make a list of the new words and to note their position and grammatical function within the structure of each sentence. It was slow work, but after a week or so I began to understand the plot of the novel.

After another week I understood almost fifty percent of every page. Impatient as usual, I gave up making lists of new words, and kept on reading, as I was fascinated by the plot of the novel and could not put the book down. In three weeks I finished the entire book and then reread it without opening the dictionary once. I understood about ninety-five percent of it. From then on, I read a great number of books and this reading gave me my basic dictionary for conversation. After three months I was able to carry on a conversation, to write the draft of my sermons and even to hear confessions. The painful apprenticeship was over. However, to this day I regret the fact that I learned English in such a haphazard way and that I never had the opportunity for formal study of this beautiful language.

Back To Childhood

The process of learning a foreign language and adapting to a new culture is one of the sacrifices of missionary life. A university graduate can normally begin exercising his profession immediately after graduation, but for a foreign missionary the situation is totally different. Despite his scholastic achievements, a missionary in a foreign country has to begin all over again by going back to elementary school. All the years of studying, all the learning he has accumulated and all the techniques he has mastered are of no help until he can talk and communicate. His main work is to be a communicator, namely to communicate the Word to those who do not know it, and without a sufficient knowledge of the language he cannot even begin his ministry.

Orlando and I had to plod through those early months in real agony, learning not only how to speak two languages but also how to handle every aspect of life. We had to get accustomed to Chinese meals and how to eat Chinese food, how to dress in Chinese fashion, how to survive in tropical weather, how to handle Chinese people, and how to conduct church services according to the local customs. All the knowledge so painfully acquired through ten or twelve years of seminary life seemed almost irrelevant since we could not communicate.

I remember the many times I would stop in the street to watch Chinese children playing and I envied them because they could talk and communicate while I could not. Of course, I remembered that the truly universal language is love and that that language does not need words. I remembered, too, that great missionaries performed great deeds even with a very inadequate knowledge of the language, but I was young, I saw the immense work to be done, and I wanted to work. While waiting for the day when we could leave the nest and plunge into work, Orlando and I plodded along cheerfully and patiently, comforting each other and dreaming of all the great work we wanted to do.

A Matter Of Blankets

Besides studying, there were other practical problems to be solved. Cold weather in the tropics was another thing we had to learn to cope with. After the balmy, bright October days, November arrived with occasional frigid air pouring in from the north, and temperatures at night dropped to the lower forties and even dipped into the thirties. Blankets had not been necessary until then and the only bed sheet I had was no longer sufficient to keep me warm. I asked the houseboy for one blanket, then a second one, then a third one and I still could not sleep because of the cold.

One day at breakfast, after an especially cold night, as I was sitting at the table opposite the bishop, and he asked me, "Did you sleep well, Maestrini?"

"No, bishop, not at all," I replied grouchily, "and I cannot understand why. I had three blankets on top and yet I could not get warm."

"You had three blankets on top! That's too much. But how many did you have underneath you?"

"None, of course. Just the wooden boards and the bamboo mat."

"Of course you can't warm up! You need to put something between the boards and the mat to keep your body heat from dissipating. Can't you understand that, young man? Tonight put one blanket underneath you and one on top and you will sleep like a log!"

That evening I did just that and I never again had trouble sleeping in chilly weather.

2

China Through Western Eyes

Before I write about my twenty years of work with the Chinese I want to
record my impressions of these great people and give a brief description
of their habits, mentality, religion, and philosophy of life. I trust this will
help the reader to better understand this book. However, I wish to
emphasize that I have no intention of doing an academic study of China
in depth. I simply want to summarize my general impressions, which are
the result of the many years I worked with the Chinese.

A Complex Nation

China is so vast, so complex, so old, so varied from area to area and,
above all, so secretive, that it is absolutely impossible to know the nation
as a whole or to write accurately when making general statements.
Things are now even more complicated by the fact that there is a very
substantial difference between pre-communist and communist China. In
fact, no other country in the world has undergone such tremendous
cultural upheaval and change as China has in recent years. However,
many cultural characteristics remain the same and are as valid today as
they were in my days. The China I write about is the traditional China of
the days before communism's rise to power in 1949. Today, after over
forty years of communist rule, the life style of the people, the
communications systems, and the political and religious situations are
profoundly changed, but the typical characteristics of the Chinese
mentality remain substantially the same.

Differences Between East And West

The most serious error Westerners commit in dealing with the people of
the East is to assume that they are just like us, that they feel like us, think
like us, react like us. The truth is that, even though we are all humans,
there are profound differences in our national characteristics.

After a first hurried visit to China, one might conclude that the
differences seem rather superficial: the Chinese eat with chopsticks while
we use knives and forks; on formal occasions men wear long tunics while
we always wear pants; Chinese women wear long tunics split to well
above the knee while Western women prefer skirts; the Chinese carry
fans not only when it is hot but even in cold weather; they drink hot tea
even on the hottest days; on certain occasions, such as New Year's Day,
they offer guests great varieties of food that are only to be looked at and
not eaten; they use white as the color of mourning instead of black, and
consider the left as the place of honor instead of the right.

Such differences, however, are only the external manifestation of far
deeper differences. Henry Van Stralen put it like this: "We differ from
the Orientals not only in language, traditions, point of view, but in the
very type of mind and process of thinking."[1]

The difference between East and West is so deep that it affects the
way of thinking and the whole gamut of emotional reactions. This is why
it has been said: "East is East and West is West and never the twain shall
meet." The differences between Eastern and Western minds, outlooks,
and philosophies of life are far deeper than the differences between
peoples of the same race, such as between English and Germans or
between Italians and French. Therefore, it is very important to know at
least the basic differences between Eastern and Western mentalities in
order to understand each other. The common saying "East meets West"
means only an understanding of each other, not a fusion of the two
streams.

Perhaps the ultimate union is possible only, as Dr. John C. H. Wu put
it in his biography, "in a meeting beyond East and West."[2]

A Different Process Of Thinking

We Westerners believe that the shortest way to one determined point is a
straight line to that point, but the Chinese are convinced that the shortest
way is the longest way "all around the bush." For them a frank, direct
approach to anything means a lack of good manners. For instance, if you

need an important favor from a friend, you never go directly to him, but use an intermediary, a mutual friend or a relative. For the Chinese this process is very logical: if your friend says no directly to you, you suffer a loss of face and your friendship is in jeopardy, but if he says no to an intermediary, you pretend that nothing ever happened, so your face is saved and your friendship preserved.

If you have a business proposition to make, you do not lay it on the table as Western businessmen do, give your potential partner a pat on the shoulder and ask: "A deal? Here, shake hands." Oh, no! This is certainly not the way the Chinese do business. In China you first drink endless cups of tea, talk about everything under the sun, praise your partner to the sky, and then slowly, ever so slowly, you begin to unfold your plan, emphasizing all along that he will have all the advantages.

According to many writers the Chinese way of thinking and reasoning is different from ours. Generally speaking, we of the West like an analytical approach to problems. Our minds are of the discursive type and we are prone to making endless distinctions, to establishing logical principles, to philosophizing and arriving at logical conclusions by reasoning from established premises. These qualities have produced a scientific approach that has given the West its vast technological heritage. The Chinese mind, on the contrary, is of the intuitive type, more artistic and contemplative than discursive. This is why in the past China has excelled in poetry and the arts rather than in the sciences, even though Chinese history is also full of examples of great subtlety of thought, of humor and of scientific discovery. The recent book *China, Land of Discovery and Invention*, by Robert K. G. Temple,[3] is a popular and impressive account of the scientific genius of the Chinese.

Lin Yutang, the well-known Chinese writer of the twenties and thirties, in his book *Importance of Living*, described his personal theory about the characteristics of the Eastern mind. He wrote: "We know some of the virtues and deficiencies of the Chinese mind, at least as revealed to us in the historical past. It has a glorious art and a contemptible science, a magnificent common sense, a fine womanish chatter about life and no scholastic philosophy. What does one find as he goes through the field of Chinese literature? One finds there are no sciences, no extreme theories, no dogmas, and really no diversified schools of thought. China is a land where there is no system of philosophy broadly speaking, no formal logic, no metaphysics, no academic jargon; where there is much less academic dogmatism and fewer abstract terms and long words. It is a land where there are no lawyers in business life as there are no logicians in philosophy. In place of well thought-out systems of philosophy, the Chinese have only an intimate feeling of life, and instead of a Kant or Hegel, they have only essayists, epigram writers, and propounders of Buddhist conundrums and Taoist parables."

Generally speaking, I tend to agree with Lin Yutang's view. I recognize, however, that there are other points of view. For instance, Mrs. Man Wah Bentley considered Lin's view simplistic and superficial. She maintained that China has other scholars of philosophy besides Confucius. Some of them are reminiscent of twentieth-century Western philosophical theories. What is certain is that there are deep-seated differences between the Eastern and Western mentalities.

Three Basic Characteristics

Throughout my twenty years of work with the Chinese and through my close association with them, I have come to the conclusion that some of their characteristics are an integral part of their culture and life style. I will mention only a few that impressed me most.

Center of the world. The Chinese masses are profoundly convinced that China is the greatest nation on earth and the center of the world. The very name "China" means, literally, "middle kingdom" or "center of the universe." This idea of national superiority is deeply rooted in the Chinese mind. For example, one of the main reasons for China's isolationism during past millennia was the conviction that she was superior to her "barbarian" neighbors and had nothing to learn from them. She did not need to expand her borders and consequently she did not need to conquer more territories. There were, of course, notable exceptions as, for instance, when the Chinese Imperial Court of the thirteenth century welcomed foreigners such as Marco Polo, and when the Han Chu Court of the seventeenth century welcomed Matteo Ricci and the other Jesuits. However, because of their superiority complex, the Chinese generally regard foreigners with suspicion and contempt. In their presence they disguise their feelings because they do not want to appear ill-mannered, or simply for the sake of friendship and self-interest, but this external behavior does not change their feelings. Anyone who is not Chinese is a "foreign devil." This is the term they use in their private conversations when referring to non-Chinese, and it reflects their innate sense of superiority.

When dealing with the Chinese we foreigners should never forget that feeling superior is part of their cultural heritage and background. They must be approached with a sense of esteem and respect if we do not want to offend and antagonize them. What the Chinese hate most in people of the white race is our own sense of superiority as we often look down on them and consider ourselves superior to them. Ironic, isn't it? The starting point of both the Chinese and the foreign devils is that each feels superior to the other. This is the source of many misunderstandings, incomprehensions, and futile irritations.

It would be a mistake to believe that today this basic attitude of theirs is changed because they come knocking at the door of Western powers seeking technological help. This change is not due to a different attitude but simply to their present needs. At this time they want Western technology because they can no longer afford to be isolated.

It would be wrong to conclude from what I have written above that all the Chinese feel nothing but contempt for the West. Far from it. The cultured classes, especially the scientists, the writers, the artists who are familiar with the achievements of the West, admire our culture and are eager to learn about our achievements as well as to enjoy the advantages of our life style. My personal experience has been that when Chinese meet Western people who love and appreciate them, they are eager to establish solid friendships and often become very loyal and devoted friends for life.

Face. For non-Chinese people it is very difficult to fully understand what the word "face" really means to the Chinese. To them, it is much more than dignity, self respect, prestige. Yes, not only is "face" all of this, but it is infinitely more. It is a feeling deeply rooted in their hearts and minds. It is so profound and pervasive that it overrides any other relationship or tie, such as love, blood, financial security, social position, etc. Obviously, the sense of prestige is also very keenly felt by us of the West. "Loss of face" is well known in Western diplomacy, as well as in high financial and business circles. However, the concept of face and its influence on daily living is far deeper with the Chinese than with Westerners.

To a Chinese, "face" is the most important thing in life. Even a street beggar would rather die than lose face in a serious matter. In China, once a serious loss of face occurs, everything is lost, life is not worth living. Loss of face is the main reason for lingering, invincible hatreds.

In pre-World War II China, one of the main reasons Chinese disliked foreigners so intensely was that during the last 150 years the Western powers had inflicted a series of humiliations on their country. Britain forced the opium trade on China and compelled it to cede Hong Kong

(1839-42). Following the Boxer Rebellion in 1900, England, France, and Italy forced China to grant them "concessions," that is, areas of Chinese territory that were placed under foreign jurisdiction. Russian expansion in the Far East robbed China of vast territories (1859), from the Amur and Ussari Rivers to the Pacific and the naval base of Vladivostok.

In addition to loss of face through wars, China was deeply humiliated by unfair trade practices forced upon her by arrogant colonial powers of the West and their unscrupulous businessmen. Up until 1941 large signs in French and Chinese at the entrance of a public park in the French Concession in Shanghai loudly proclaimed: "Dogs and Chinese not allowed!"

It is because of the humiliations inflicted on China by foreign powers that the main theme of the Chinese Revolution that started in 1911 was "to free China from the oppression of foreigners," as Sun Yat Sen put it.

In China, face controls all interpersonal relationships. Even in the most intimate ones, such as between husband and wife, and even between parents and children, teachers and pupils, employers and employees, the supreme rule is saving face. Once face is lost, hatred replaces it, no matter how long and intimate the relationship might have been.

Patient suffering and resilience. Another Chinese characteristic that impressed me most was their power to withstand hardships and their ability to suffer patiently without becoming discouraged or yielding to despair. Many writers attribute this attitude to the so-called "Oriental fatalism," namely to the belief that all events are predetermined by blind fate and cannot be changed by human beings or by their actions.

Chinese people have a phrase that is probably the expression most widely used every day all over the country. In Cantonese it sounds like this: "Mo fat tsz!" Its literal translation is: "There is no remedy," but its real meaning is much more than a simple statement affirming that things cannot be changed. It implies patience, resignation, endurance, tolerance and acceptance of suffering, and it excludes rebellion, resentment, wrath, cursing and despair. "Mo fat tsz" is a great philosophy of life that has certainly permitted China to survive and flourish through constant sufferings, misfortunes and reverses, which crowd every page of its long history.

From the day I set foot in China to the day I left, day after day, I watched the people suffering. It was suffering in all forms: spiritual, mental, physical, moral, private, public, in times of great tragedies and in common everyday events, in the form of sickness, starvation, poverty, ignorance, of lack of basic human comforts, affecting men and women, young and old, rich and poor, healthy and sick, learned and ignorant, in cities, in villages, in desolate shacks and in rich mansions, in the turmoil of big cities and in the deadly silence of lonely dwellings, in peace and in war. Everywhere I saw people suffering intensely, inconsolably, but always resignedly. "Mo fat tsz" were the words I heard most often from Christians and non-Christians, the almost magic words that have given Chinese people resilience, endurance, patience, an unshakable will to carry on through and despite hardships of all kinds and of all intensity

Believe me, I am not romanticizing this Chinese characteristic. I simply describe what I saw. Through the rest of this book I prove my assertions.

It may be remarked that widespread suffering and high tolerance of physical pain are common throughout the Orient. True, but I believe that the Chinese have this quality in a somewhat higher degree than the rest of the people of Asia. I have visited and read a great deal about Japan, the Philippines, Thailand, Singapore, and India. There, too, I have seen lots of people enduring many sufferings, but nowhere have I seen the quiet acceptance of sufferings accompanied by a spirit of resilience and determination to overcome obstacles such as I saw every day in China. In my mind, the Chinese ability to endure resignation to suffering, accompanied by a determination to overcome all obstacles, is one of the greatest virtues of Chinese people.

During the eight painful years of the Sino-Japanese War I saw, time after time, Chinese cities and villages ravaged by the war, bombed out of existence, destroyed by fire, with hundreds and thousands of victims. In every case, the very first day following the attack, when fires were still smoldering and the ashes still hot, the humble, patient Chinese would appear again. Rummaging through the ruins they would salvage whatever trinkets could be used, then, stretching a piece of canvas or a bamboo mat across two dilapidated walls, they offered for sale a few salvaged articles and started in business again!

Notes

1. *Through Eastern Eyes* (Loveland, OH: Grailville, 1951). Fr. Van Stralen was a missionary to China.

2. John C. H. Wu, *Beyond East and West* (Sheed and Ward).

3. Mr. Temple's book describes one hundred Chinese discoveries in agriculture, astronomy, engineering, domestic and industrial technology, medicine, mathematics, the physical sciences, music and warfare. His book is published by Patrick Stephens Ltd., Wellingborough. Robert K. G. Temple is a graduate in Oriental studies from the University of China and renowned for his writings on unusual scientific subjects. His book *China: Land of Discovery and Invention* has an introduction by Dr. Joseph Needham, Director of the Needham Research Institute at Cambridge, who is considered the world's foremost authority on China.

3

Self-Restraint, Medicine, Snake Bites

A Children's Christmas Party

Preparations for the children's Christmas party in the parish hall of the Hong Kong Cathedral had just been completed. The long tables were crammed with goodies in a colorful array: bright golden oranges, candies, cookies, sweets, fresh fruits, souvenirs—all that a child might dream about on an occasion such as this. There was a place and a portion for each child.

Finally the doors were opened, and over one hundred children—age three to ten—from poor families marched in escorted by parents, all very orderly, very solemn. They quietly lined up behind the tables and remained standing. I had expected a lot of gleeful noise, a mad rush, a grabbing of food. But no, the children remained standing, eating the goodies in front of them only with their eyes, but no one touched even a candy, no one spoke, no one pushed or shoved. Dressed in their Sunday best, with their soft, round faces gleaming, they looked adorable, but they were not eating. Suddenly I was alarmed: had I done something wrong?

"Why don't they eat?" I asked one of the young Chinese ladies who had worked hard to prepare the party.

"Because, Father, they expect you to invite them to eat. In China, it is very improper and ill-mannered to start eating without being asked to do so."

Those lovable children taught me an important lesson. Restraint of emotions is an integral, essential part of Chinese culture and all are taught this from childhood.

If we Westerners believe that the Chinese are cold and unemotional, we are wrong. At all ages, in all walks of life, they have the same intense emotions and feelings as we have, but through education and training they are much more restrained in displaying them.

Here is one example, a true story Fr. Poletti told me. One day in the countryside a young soldier, carrying a heavy bag, was returning home after a long period of absence. Just outside the house he noticed his elderly father tilling the family vegetable garden.

"Father, good morning," the young man said, without a trace of emotion in his voice, turning to the older one without stopping. "Did you eat?" (The usual Chinese greeting, which means: Are you well?)

"Yes, son! Are you well?" the man replied, hardly raising his head and continuing to work.

When the young man reached the house, he entered without knocking and, laying down his heavy bag on the floor, just as if he were returning from a shopping trip, simply said, "Mother, I'm home."

"Good," was the simple reply of the elderly lady. "Are you well, son? Would you like some tea?" And she got busy serving him.

Generally speaking, this scene is typical of the way the Chinese restrain their emotions. In our country very likely the father and mother would have traveled hundreds of miles to welcome back a son returning home after years of absence. When finally they met, they would embrace, kiss, scream, eat a big meal, invite neighbors and relatives, and have a big celebration. In China, nothing like this. A simple "Father, are you well?" "Mother, are you well?" However, we would be wrong if we concluded from this that the Chinese love their children less than we Westerners do. It is strictly a matter of culture. The Chinese simply refrain from showing emotions in public.

This is an unwritten rule that applies to every one, at every time of life, in every social situation. Kissing, for instance, even as a simple manifestation of affection between parents and children or brothers and sisters, is never done in public. The only exception perhaps is that of mothers kissing their babies. Vigorous hand-shaking, embracing, patting on the shoulders, are not Chinese habits.

Physical Pain

In China even physical pain is generally borne with stoic endurance. One day, I saw a poor coolie who had been badly mauled by a runaway handcart on a steep street in Hong Kong. The flesh of his naked thighs

was shredded and it hung in large chunks. The man was bleeding pro-
fusely. The poor fellow just sat on the curb of the sidewalk, supporting
his head with his hands, and did not scream or even shed a tear. Passers-
by ignored him. I ran to offer him help, but he flatly refused. I knew that
he did not want to have anything to do with a foreigner. I remained
watching from a distance to see how it would end. After over one hour,
finally, a man arrived, roughly threw the coolie on his shoulders, and
took him away.

I was dumbfounded at the man's endurance of pain. When I mentioned this episode to one of my fellow missionaries, he assured me that
there was nothing unusual in what I had seen because Chinese, in
general, have a very high threshold of pain. Is it perhaps, as some people
say, because of their diet? Is it because they are inured to physical
suffering from childhood? The fact is that their endurance is much
greater than that of sophisticated Westerners.

There are, however, a few occasions in life when they barely exercise
restraint.

One of them is funerals. Here they display their feelings with no
inhibition. They cry, they lament, they mourn like people do all over the
world. But the Chinese go even a bit further. In order to placate the spirit
of the deceased, they hire professional criers who for hours, even days in
the case of rich families, continue their monotonous lamentations and
high-pitched crying.

Another occasion is anger. When the Chinese are mad, they show
scarcely any restraint in venting their wrath upon each other. Village
women are particularly famous in this regard. One day, as I was in the
countryside visiting a Haka-speaking village (Haka is a Chinese dialect
different from Cantonese) with my friend Poletti, I heard two women
quarreling and shouting at each other at the top of their voices. I thought
it was only a short outburst of wrath, but they kept on and on. The noise
was so disturbing that I could not concentrate on anything. Moreover, as
they were talking in the Haka dialect, I could not understand a word.
After about half an hour I turned in disgust to Poletti and said, "When
will those two women stop screaming?"

"Oh, don't worry, Nicholas. They have just started."

"But it is already over a half hour," I replied in surprise.

"That's nothing," answered Poletti. "They might keep it up for hours.
You see, when they get mad, they curse each other's family. The Chinese
have a very rich vocabulary describing every possible degree of relationship, whether they are relatives on the wife's side or the husband's side,

whether on the mother's or father's side, whether on the younger or older brother's or sister's side, and so on and on. When they are mad, they curse every degree of relationship, and then they conclude: 'Ham ka tchan!' which means: 'May all your relatives and your family be destroyed.' Then, when you think they are finished, they start all over again."

That day, the litany of curses lasted about three hours. But it started again later in the evening, and the next morning when we left the village the two women were still at it.

An Exercise In Futility

Generally speaking, if foreigners in China get mad at their domestics or at business people in commercial transactions and speak in anger, all they accomplish is an exercise in futility. The reason is that by raising our voices in a fit of temper, we fail to pronounce the words according to the proper "tones" and thus our speech is absolutely unintelligible to them. It happened a few times to me, too. Once, as I raised my voice in anger against my domestic, the poor guy stood there staring at me with a stolid face and an ironic smile that seemed to say: "Shan-fou, shout all you want, to your heart's content. I don't understand a word of what you are saying and I couldn't care less!" That was certainly not the best way to calm the temper of a hot-blooded missionary—from Italy or from any other country.

Suicides

Protesting and expressing wrath take different forms in different countries. In the China of my days, the expression of wrath often took the form of suicide.

One of the most frequent cases was that of young brides who committed suicide as a retaliation against tyrannical mothers-in-law. In the patriarchal life style of the Chinese families, it was impossible for a young wife to escape the clutches of a wicked and dominating mother-in-law. What made the situation worse was that the unfortunate wife could not even expect much help from her husband. Due to the ingrained sense of filial piety, very rarely would a young man take the side of his wife against his mother. If the poor wife ran away, she would be caught and returned to her husband's family and her fate would be even worse than before because she would have made her husband's family lose face.

As a result, the young wife was defenseless, and suicide was her only escape. According to Chinese customs, when a young bride committed suicide, her own family would descend on the husband's family and take a terrific revenge in order to placate her spirit. The revenge consisted of demanding enormous sums of money in reparation, as an alternative to the vengeful destruction of their houses and businesses.

Chinese Medicine

One of my first impressions of China was the sight of large numbers of sickly people roaming the streets. Everywhere you could see them, grown-ups and children, with hideous sores on arms, legs and heads. Children's heads especially were often a mass of sores covered with dirty, smeared bandages, from which strangely colored concoctions oozed out. When I inquired about the health situation in China, I was told that there were two types of medicines–Chinese and Western.

Chinese medicine is as ancient as China itself. There are medical books dating back to the fourth century B.C. One of the largest medical works is a collection of fifty-two volumes by Li Shi-zhen, published in 1596. It catalogs and describes the medical properties of over two thousand remedies and it gives ten thousand medical prescriptions.

The Chinese approach to medicine is empirical rather than scientific like that of the West.

Acupuncture is certainly the most famous branch of Chinese medicine. It seems that its earliest origins go back to the Stone Age, when sharp-edged stone instruments were used to alleviate pain and cure diseases. When bronze was discovered, metal needles were introduced and acupuncture was more fully developed. Later on, silver and gold needles were used largely to cure specific diseases. Today both the physiological and pathological aspects of acupuncture have been developed, and it is used in Western hospitals. I never had the need to use acupuncture during my twenty years in China, but I knew a number of friends, both Chinese and Westerners, who derived great benefit from it.

Chinese pharmacology is completely based on the use of natural elements. Both preventive and therapeutic medicines use mostly herbs prepared through infusions and concoctions. There are detailed norms about the age of the plants, the parts to be used, the localities where they have to be grown, the way they have to be prepared, and even the times when they are to be taken according to the conjunction of planets and stars.

Even though some prescriptions are obviously useless, and some even harmful—especially those applied to open wounds—Chinese medicine has kept the nation healthy and vigorous to the point of being overpopulated. The Orientals have contributed a great deal to the Western world's knowledge of the medicinal properties of many herbs.

The old China of the Emperors did not believe in hospitals, at least not in the Western sense of this word. Sick people remained at home and, as long as they could walk, moved around freely in the streets. When, after the 1911 revolution, China officially opened its doors to Western culture and methods, Western medicine was well received. Hospitals and medical universities were immediately introduced, but they remained mostly confined to the large cities. A person living in the countryside would often have to travel hundreds of miles before finding a Western-type hospital or doctor.

Medicine And Christianity In China

Both Catholic and Protestant missionaries took advantage of the health situation in China to open medical facilities, which ranged all the way from "mission dispensaries" (a kind of outpatient clinic) to first-class medical institutions of the Western type, staffed by qualified Chinese and foreign doctors.

Mission dispensaries, often lacking qualified personnel, limited themselves to distributing simple medicines supplied by benefactors at home and to treating such common diseases as boils, abscesses, blood poisoning, ringworm, and sore eyes. People flocked to these dispensaries because, especially in the countryside, there were no government medical facilities available. The dispensary was meant not only to heal diseases but also to make friends and to prepare the way for Christianity. That, of course, was the ultimate goal of our presence as missionaries. As Christ had used the healing of bodies as an instrument to reach the souls of the people of His time, so we used the same method (minus the miracles) to introduce Christ to China.

We did not use the dispensaries to "preach" to the Chinese, and we never connected the needed medical treatment to religious affiliation. We treated their bodies and relied on their natural sense of gratitude to prompt them to ask, "Why are you, foreign devils, doing this for us?"

A variety of methods were devised to answer this all-important question. I will quote only one example. Fr. Bernard Meyer of Maryknoll prepared a Chinese leaflet and used an old Confucian proverb as a title:

"When you drink water, think of the source." The leaflet explained in simple language the ultimate goal of the Christian missionary presence in China: to bring to the Chinese the Good News of Christ and to offer them the opportunity to know Christianity. In collaboration with Fr. Meyer I had the Catholic Truth Society of Hong Kong print tens of thousands of copies of this leaflet, which we used widely in South China.

According to official statistics from the Vatican, when the communists took over China in 1949, the Catholic Church was running 847 dispensaries (with over fifteen million consultations a year) and 216 Western-type hospitals with a total of 7500 beds. The communists closed, took over, or destroyed all these facilities.

Snake Bites And Acupuncture

My friend Fr. A. Poletti personally witnessed the following episode and told me the details of what happened. Late in the afternoon of a summer day in the village of Tam-tong in south China, a strong, healthy young man was seriously bitten on the hand by a poisonous snake. Soon the village was in motion to find the local man who knew the well-kept secret of curing snake bites.

While people went to fetch him, the poor boy lay in the street in great pain, moaning and asking for help. After about fifteen minutes the "snake doctor" arrived: just a plain farmer, as illiterate as most of his peers in that village. He had a superficial look at the boy's wound, asked him a couple of questions and, turning to the parents, very nonchalantly asked, "How much?" He meant, "Yes, I can cure the boy, but how much are you going to pay me?" Yielding to the innate Chinese habit of haggling about prices, they spent five more minutes discussing the fee.

When finally they agreed on the moderate sum to be paid, the "doctor," instead of getting busy about his work, sat down on the steps of a house, leisurely extracted from his pocket a small sheet of cigarette paper and a pinch of tobacco and wrapped for himself a bulging cigarette. He lit it and began smoking leisurely, totally unconcerned about the suffering boy.

The swelling on the boy's arm was growing rapidly. Parents and bystanders became restless and urged the doctor to take care of the boy. "What's the hurry! Take it easy. I know what I have to do," the man replied, with a tinge of resentment in his voice.

After what seemed to Fr. Poletti and to the bystanders an eternity, the "doctor" finished his smoke, then slowly got up, and walked aimlessly around the edges of a nearby field, picking up different kinds of wild herbs. Everyone knew that he picked up some good and some useless herbs so as to confuse the people watching him. Then he put a handful of herbs in his mouth and chewed them. He went to the boy, who was now in a coma, spat a little of the chewed herbs into his hands, and pressed that green paste on the wound in the boy's hand.

He waited a few more minutes, then, squatting on the ground, took the dying boy's head in his hands, opened his clenched teeth with a knife, and forced another large portion of the chewed herbs into the boy's mouth. This work done, he stood up. Smiling complacently and wrapping another cigarette, he told the parents, "Don't worry. In about half an hour he will be all right."

Fr. Poletti, who had witnessed the whole incident from a little distance, was now certain that the doctor was a charlatan and that the boy was going to die. He moved closer to the scene to better see the end of the tragedy. Contrary to what he had expected, he actually saw the swelling slowly beginning to decrease from the shoulder down to the hand. Within half an hour it was gone. The boy opened his eyes, looked around to his parents and friends and said, "I feel fine now!" In a few more minutes he stood up and quietly walked away.

The secret of curing snake bites is a very old science in China and it has been handed down as a family secret from generation to generation.

4

The Religions of China

A Devout Lady

On one of my first days in Hong Kong a fellow missionary and I passed one of the more than three hundred small neighborhood temples in the city. My eyes spotted a thin, elderly lady walking gingerly on her small, bound feet, carrying a black cane, dressed in the customary black coat and trousers of Chinese peasant women, approaching the temple door. Her concentration and obvious devotion impressed me deeply. I wanted to see a Chinese temple and decided to follow her into the building. My fellow priest agreed and we went in.

Without looking right or left the old lady went straight to a small makeshift counter and bought several incense sticks. Then, totally oblivious to the presence of tourists and other devotees around her, she went to the front of an altar that was covered with statues, name tablets and other religious symbols, lit her incense sticks and, after placing them in a container with others already burning, bowed down with joined hands several times. Finally, in a kneeling position, she rested on her haunches and began to pray silently, moving her lips and bowing repeatedly with her head touching the ground each time.

"Is this a Confucian temple?" I asked my companion and mentor.

"No," he said, "it's just a neighborhood temple that serves Confucianists, Buddhists and Taoists." Then he went on to explain the religious situation in China.

Three Religions

Contrary to the popular belief that Chinese people are all Confucianists, the truth is that in China there are three major religions: Confucianism, Taoism and Buddhism.[1] The three religions have neither a well-defined dogmatic body of doctrines nor hordes of priests and ministers proselytizing for their denominations or fighting for followers. A popular Chinese proverb says: "The three religions are but one religion" (San jiao shi yi jiao). This saying expresses very well the Chinese religious syncretism, namely the trend to combine and reconcile different beliefs regardless of their being historical truth or plain legend.

The fact is that, despite our Western penchant for analytical thinking and carefully worded definitions, there is probably no other country in the world where natural religion has influenced the culture and lifestyle of the people as it has in China.[2]

Chinese Religiosity

Fr. Thomas F. Ryan, SJ, in his book *China Through Catholic Eyes* remarked that, even though according to general belief the Chinese in pre-communist China were considered too pragmatic, too engrossed in material things, to be interested in religious abstract speculation, it is wrong to assume that they were not a religious people. Certainly they pursued human pleasure and material well-being like any other people on earth, but not to the point of completely ignoring religious values. He wrote: "Matter of fact they certainly are, but not in a crude, materialistic sense, and it would be difficult to find any literature which is inspired by such a constantly idealistic spirit as theirs."

My personal experience with Dr. John C. H. Wu, Francis Yeh, and hundreds of other Chinese has convinced me that the Chinese are indeed a religious people. Allow me to review briefly some of the popular religious practices.

Worship Of Ancestors

Ancestor worship is not a religious act in itself, but it helped people to keep alive belief in the afterlife, in some kind of reward or punishment after death, and in the power of the living to help the dead. These beliefs are also an integral part of Catholic doctrine.

Propitiation Of The Spirits

The belief in spiritual beings who are superior to man and the belief in the survival of man's soul after death are an integral part of the Chinese religious heritage. Even though there never was a priestly caste in China, still the popular cult of the spirit flourished as the most common expression of popular devotion. This religiosity gave birth to countless places of worship, which ranged from the great national temples to small neighborhood pagodas, to small shrines built in honor of the spirits along the roads, in small wooded areas, along river banks and other odd places, but especially in the homes. In pre-Communist China there was hardly a home without some kind of religious symbol. The burning of incense sticks, the offering of food to their ancestors, the bowing and kowtowing before statues and name tablets were the natural outlet of the soul's need of believing in someone beyond the human realm of things, in something spiritual and permanent.

Divination

The worship of the spirits led the Chinese to their form of divination, called "fung shui" ("wind and water"), which consists basically of consulting the spirits to ensure their blessings on any new undertaking. This form of divination is practiced in such occurrences as determining the right orientation of a new building, selecting the place of a grave, choosing the right day for the beginning of a trip or of a business venture, and the like. We may call this "superstition," but superstition has its roots in religion.

The 1985 official Hong Kong guide states: "If you want to see Chinese culture in Hong Kong, the best living museum is all around you. The Chinese "culture" is a way of life, a set of creeds and customs. Skyscrapers soar where dragons used to roam, but the dragons aren't ignored—nor are the ancestral and evil spirits and all the forces of Nature.

"Why are there so many little eight-sided mirrors hanging outside windows? To deflect evil spirits. Why does the Regent Hotel have a see-through lobby with a massive harbour-gazing wall of glass? So that the neighborhood dragon can go and bathe in the harbor without any hindrance! Why did a pair of bronze lions guard The Hong Kong and Shanghai Bank Group HQ for so many years? To protect occupants from water-borne dangers. Many of Hong Kong's buildings have been specially designed to take account of ancient fung shui (wind-water) beliefs. The scientific alignment of walls, doors, desks, even beds, is crucial if humans are to balance correctly the eight elements of Nature and the spirit of the yin (female-passive) and yang (male-active) forces that control our world. Note the large number of fish tanks in offices; if you can't look out over water (good fung shui) then you bring the water inside.

"Every Hong Kong resident accepts 'fung shui' principles. Look at all the Hang Seng Bank branches and note their odd diagonally positioned main doors. Notice how many buildings have front doors where you'd expect to find back doors. Try to find a desk whose occupant will have his back exposed to the room's entrance."[3]

Filial Piety

Filial piety is a virtue rather than a cult, but it was so deeply welded into the Chinese soul that it certainly was part of Chinese religiosity. It was developed by a group of neo-Confucianists under the Sung Dynasty (A.D. 960-1279) who "broadened the idea of filial piety by transporting it to our relations with the Earth, which is the Chinese expression for the Cosmos. Their philosophy is pantheistic rather than theistic. When Confucius used the word 'Heaven' he meant God; but when the neo-Confucianists used 'Heaven and Earth' they meant the Cosmos."

Filial piety became deeply rooted in the Chinese mind and was an essential part of one's behavior in society.

Chinese Religions From The Christian Point Of View

Chinese religions have many of the basic elements of Christianity. This is natural because all men came from one source, and all had a monotheistic form of religion in the beginning.

From the theological point of view, Christianity and the Chinese religions have in common the basic idea of a supreme being. According to many writers, the "Tao" or "Supreme Being" of Lao-tsu (600 B.C.) has definite characteristics that are very similar to the Christian concept of God. Dr. John C. H. Wu saw in the "Tao" the equivalent of the Greek concept of "Logos" who was called "The Word" in the prologue of St. John's Gospel.

From the point of view of morality we fully share at least five of the Ten Commandments with the Chinese, namely: Respect for parents (Honor your father and your mother); respect for life (You shall not kill);

respect for other people's property (You shall not steal; you shall not covet your neighbor's house); honesty and sincerity (You shall not bear false witness).

Unfortunately, in Chinese religions, except for the general principle of adhering to the Tao, there is nothing similar to our commandments that teach a filial love of God. There is not even the remotest hint of the basic Christian principle that God has created man out of love and that the goal of human life is to pursue a constant growth in the love of God and the service of his fellow creatures. The Chinese idea of the relationship between men and the spirits is based entirely on fear. Its only purpose is to propitiate them. The idea of an interpersonal relationship with the spirits does not in any way include the idea of self-sacrificing love, which is central to Christianity. Even the Chinese Buddhists who have developed the idea of self-sacrifice, purification, and expiation ignore the concept of love as proclaimed by Christ.

Chinese religions are essentially self-centered instead of God-centered. According to them one's well-being is the beginning and end of happiness. There is absolutely no idea of loving God as a Father, of seeking the glory of God, of seeing God in our fellow humans, of being a member of the people of God and, much less, of being a child of God. They are baffled by the mystery of life and death but cannot find any solution in the worshiping of their spirits.

The greatest joy in my work as a missionary in China was always that of opening the eyes of a prospective convert to the unsurpassable beauty of God's love. It was a joy to see such souls opening up like flowers in the radiant warmth of a newly discovered life of love, to liberate them from the fear of spirits and launch them into the arms of the all-powerful love of God.

I want to quote the following passage from Dr. John C. H. Wu's *The Science of Love*. Writing about St. Teresa's words, he commented: "The TAO is such an impersonal entity that it appears to me to be of the ice, icy; whereas Jesus is such a living flame of love that He enkindles every fiber of my heart. To me as a Chinese, the great thing about Christianity is that it combines the profound mysticism of Lao Tzu with the intense humanism of Confucius. It differs from Taoism in that the Tao or the Word has taken on flesh and a warm pulsating heart. It differs from Confucianism in that it is the Word, and nothing short of the Word, that has done so. Confucius said: 'One who has given offense to God prays in vain.' Lao Tzu said: 'Why did the ancients prize the Tao? Is it not because, through It, whoever seeks finds, and whoever is guilty is relieved of punishment?' The Confucian idea of God is personal but narrow, while the Taoist idea is broad but impersonal . . . Only Christianity can satisfy my mind completely, because its idea of God is at once broad and personal. And it is Therese (of Lisieux) who has confirmed my faith in my religion, for her mind is as subtle and detached as that of Lao Tzu, while her heart is as affectionate and cordial as that of Confucius."

Can Chinese Religions Lead To Christ?

This question has vexed missionaries to China for centuries. Some missionaries and even some religious authorities viewed Chinese religions through their foreign mentality and condemned them wholesale as the work of the devil. On the contrary, more enlightened missionaries believed that they contained all the basic elements of natural law, which are a prerequisite to accepting Christianity.

For me the question was solved when I met Dr. John C. H. Wu in 1938 and he confided to me the story of his journey to the Faith. In 1951, when he wrote his biography, he repeated what he had told me in Hong Kong eleven years earlier. Rather than trusting my memory, I am reporting here his thinking as he wrote it in his biography. For him the three religions of China were definitely the instrument God used to bring him to Christianity.

In his biography, writing about "The Religions of China," John Wu declared: "The three religions of China served as my tutors, bringing me to, Christ, so that I might find justification in faith (Gal. 3.24). Of course, every conversion is due to the grace of God; but there is no denying that in my case God used parts of the teachings of Confucius, Lao Tzu and Buddha as instruments to open my eyes to the Light of the world."

Notes

1. Here is a short description of the three major religions in China.

Confucianism: The philosophy of Confucius (551-549 B.C.) was developed by subsequent generations of scholars to provide a moral basis for the social and political structure of China and to embrace the traditional forms of ancestor worship. Confucianism is more an ethical code than a religion or a school of philosophy.

Taoism: It derives from Lao-Tsu, who in the sixth century B.C. taught a form of religion emphasizing simplicity and conformity to the Tao, the way (tao) of nature. Superstitious practices, mixed with magic, were added later to Taoism in its popular form.

Buddhism: Founded by Buddha in India, about six centuries before Christ, teaches how to avoid suffering by suppressing human desires. A sect of Buddhism called 'Mahayana Buddhism' (Great Vehicle) was brought to China in the first century A.D. and soon mingled with Confucianism and Taoism. Before 1940 there were about five million Buddhist monks and nuns in China. The communists confiscated the monasteries, dispersed the monks, and forced the nuns to marry.

2. To these religions we must add Islam, which was introduced into Western China by Arab merchants under the Sung Dynasty (960-1280) and was later embraced by non-Chinese tribes. However, it always remained confined to some provinces in the far west and it never had a significant influence on the bulk of the Chinese population.

3. This is how the same Hong Kong guide describes the practice of popular Chinese religion in that city today: "Spiritual beliefs and superstitions still abound in modern Hong Kong. Visit some of its 350-plus temples. Look at their gaily colored roof decorations. The curving roofs deter the evil spirits, while the carved animals protect the temple-goers.

"The Chinese may be great gamblers, but not in spiritual matters. They cover their bets by worshiping both Buddhist and Taoist deities and their families' ancestral spirits. Look for the small shrines that are tended in almost every home or shop and in many offices; the lighting of joss sticks does bring luck. So does the burning of paper tributes; every full moon, and during major festivals, you'll see housewives setting fire to paper "clothes," "motorcars," "houses" or Bank of Hell "bank notes" on sidewalks or stairwells.

"Many temples offer fortune-telling services for small fees. You shake a bamboo container of sticks, discover your lucky number and then have its particular cryptic messages interpreted for you."

Are the Chinese very different from us in this respect? Fr. Ryan wrote: "Our scientific age has not abandoned its mascots, and if the Chinese were loathe to undertake anything without picking a lucky day, so, to judge by the weekly horoscopes in the press, are the people of the West in our own day."

Rosary Church in Kowloon, Hong Kong.

5

Mission Life In China

My First Assignment

After the general remarks about China in previous chapters, I feel it is time to begin narrating the events of my life there. It is impossible to relate these events in a strict chronological order because many of them overlap each other; therefore I will follow a logical order.

As I mentioned in chapter 1, soon after Fr. Orlando and I arrived in Hong Kong, we were assigned to reside at the mission house while studying English and Chinese. Barely three months later, at the beginning of January 1932, Bishop Valtorta called us to his room one morning and gave us our first mission assignment. Orlando was appointed to work in a Cantonese-speaking area on the China mainland in the Paoan Prefecture in order to become more proficient in Chinese while caring for the few Christian villages in that area. I was to go to Rosary Church, on the Kowloon side, as assistant to the old pastor, Fr. John Spada.

To tell the truth, I was disappointed with my assignment because I wanted to work on the China mainland. I asked the bishop if he would consider changing my appointment.

"Remember, young man," the bishop answered with a smile and a tone of voice that took away the harshness of his reply, "that you have been assigned to China to work under your bishop. The needs of our diocese require that you work at Rosary Church now. Of course, whenever you have time, feel free to take a trip to our inland missions in order to get acquainted with the priests and the work there, but your China for the time being is Rosary Church."

So, a few days later Orlando and I parted after having been classmates and close friends for over six years. He left Hong Kong by boat for his missionary work in the Paoan district and I envied him his good luck. On the contrary, I took the ferry to Rosary Church, just across the harbor from the bishop's house, to continue my study of English and Chinese and at the same time to work with the parishioners, who were practically all Portuguese Catholics.

Before I narrate my apprenticeship at Rosary and the errors and bloopers I committed, I want to write about some of my experiences and the trips I made to visit my confreres on the China mainland according to the bishop's suggestion.

A Trip To The Chinese Countryside

It was raining steadily that Monday afternoon in July 1932 when the rickety little Chinese boat docked at an equally rickety old pier in the primitive harbor of Tai-sun along the south China coast of Paoan County, less than one hundred miles south of Hong Kong.

I was on my way to the China mainland in order to spend some time practicing how to speak Cantonese. The one-day trip from Hong Kong on the small Chinese steamboat had been a nightmare. I had been the only foreigner in the overcrowded boat that carried nearly three hundred Chinese passengers in a space designed for a hundred. As I was too shy to engage in any conversation either in English or Chinese, I had felt lonely and very, very uneasy in that new, strange surrounding. Bales of cargo, rattan baskets filled to the brim with all kinds of goods, bamboo cages of all shapes and sizes filled with squawking chickens and squealing pigs had been stacked all over the boat, leaving hardly any room to walk even a few steps. There had been barely room to sit. I had been nervous and restless, not only because of the noise and the loneliness in spite of the overcrowded conditions: I knew that pirates worked the sea on which we sailed and that foreigners were occasionally kidnapped for ransom. The possibility of falling into pirates' hands did not ease my peace of mind.

As the boat docked I scanned the crowd on the pier through sheets of falling rain, looking for someone who might be there to greet me. At last I saw a black Western umbrella and a man dressed in a white cassock. Both stood out from the mass of shabbily dressed peasants wearing their conical bamboo hats. My heart was flooded with joy and relief. That could only be my classmate and host, Fr. Orlando, who had invited me to pay him a visit. I had not seen him for six months and now I was going to spend a few weeks in one of his mission villages where people spoke good Cantonese.

As soon as I landed, he rushed over to me and I felt as though I were home again. I told him that he looked thinner and sun-burned, and he told me that I looked fatter and sassier, a real city boy.

After kidding each other under the rain, he informed me that there were no Catholics in Tai-sun and therefore no church where we could spend the night. We had to go to Sun-chun, a Christian village a few miles away.

So, off we went on foot in the humid, stifling, monsoon heat, picking our way carefully along muddy, slippery, narrow paths that crisscrossed the rice paddy fields. That area, south of the mighty Pearl River, is the "rice bowl" of the Guangdong Province in south China, and paddy fields are everywhere.

A-yun, Fr. Orlando's "houseboy" (a married man servant), lean but brawny, carried our luggage in two large bamboo baskets on a pole slung across his shoulders. He was dressed in the characteristic cotton shirt and black trousers of the Chinese peasant, and his large bamboo hat was his only umbrella in the pouring rain.

We followed, limping along, careful not to slip into the mud of the rice fields. Dressed in long, white Chinese tunics, tropical sun-helmets and each carrying a black umbrella, we were the perfect picture of the traveling missionary of those days. I had seen that kind of picture hundreds of times in mission magazines: a Chinese landscape, endless rice fields, little pagodas scattered everywhere, and the missionary walking behind his Chinese guide carrying two rattan baskets, one at each end of a bamboo pole. In my seminary days that picture seemed very romantic, but now the reality was something else! The heat, the mosquito bites and fatigue made it much less exciting than the dream.

I will not recount here the details of my arrival at that desolate little village except to say that our meal of boiled rice and salted fish left me still hungry, that my bed of wooden boards made my bones ache, and that mosquitoes and fleas feasted on my blood. The stifling heat in the windowless, low-ceilinged room made me gasp for breath, and sleep was very fitful.

I celebrated Mass the next morning in the local "church," which was nothing but a hovel with cracked mud walls and peeling white paint. Our makeshift altar was adorned with an old Italian-made crucifix, a faded picture of Our Lady cut from some religious magazine, and some dusty, discolored artificial flowers in a bottle. The few Catholics who came to

Mass were a sorry sight: shabbily dressed old farm hands, a couple of wrinkled old ladies, and a young woman who nursed her baby while squatting on the earthen floor.

Fr. Orlando introduced me to the local catechist, who was to be my Chinese teacher; after promising to come back to see me soon, he left to visit other Christian villages. I was to be alone in order to learn Chinese faster.

Loneliness

The days went by very slowly. Except for several hurried visits from Orlando, I was there all alone, absolutely unable to communicate with my teacher or with anybody else, for that matter. At night I was scared. During the day I was lost and lonely, miles away from any communication center. My entire body itched from mosquito and flea bites. I was famished for lack of decent food. At age twenty-four most people are hardy and optimistic. I was misery itself.

In addition to physical suffering, I experienced an inner agony because it seemed that my life was being spent in vain. Living in a non-Christian culture and feeling lost in the midst of masses of pagans weighed heavily on me. And yet, those people who, humanly speaking, seemed to me so unfortunate, so poor and dirty were my people, the people I had adopted to follow Christ's invitation in my new fatherland; the people I wanted to serve and save.

But the situation seemed hopeless. I could not even talk with them. I could do no good for them and they certainly cared nothing for me. In the eyes of those very non-Christians I wanted to bring to Christ, I was simply a fool, a "foreign devil," living all alone in a shack that differed from the others only because it had a meaningless (to them) little cross on the front wall. They thought I must have done something very bad in my country, otherwise why would I have run away to hide in such a forsaken place? It was beyond their belief that I could live without a woman. In fact, no woman, not even a Catholic, ever came near the house unless in the company of others. My sole visitor was the old, faithful catechist. He came twice a day to bring me the unchanging fare of boiled rice, salted fish and watery vegetables. He did make some effort to talk to me, but the good man was no teacher. We could not communicate and I made no progress in learning Cantonese.

My Faith was telling me that those anguished days were not in vain, that, as I had learned in the seminary, souls are saved through sacrifice.

However, all that did very little to diminish the pain of my loneliness.

Lepers In The Night

One morning, about 2:00, I was suddenly awakened out of my fitful sleep by people screaming, the noise of running steps in the street, and what sounded like real bedlam. I thought that bandits were attacking the village and that my last hour had come. I expected them to break down the flimsy house door at any moment and kill me right on the spot, or take me away as a hostage to hold for ransom.

Kneeling by the bedside I commended my soul to the Lord, and did not fail to add that, if it were His Will, I wouldn't mind living a little longer . . . and I waited and waited. As I heard no sound of firearms I thought that perhaps it wasn't, after all, a bandits' attack. After a while, as nobody knocked on my door, I quietly got to my feet and, without lighting the kerosene lamp, tiptoed in darkness toward the small window high on the wall and, climbing on a stool, peered outside.

All I could see were men, women, and children scurrying in all directions, carrying flaming torches, shouting at the top of their lungs, and looking everywhere as if hunting some hidden enemy. After about half an hour of noise and tumult, things seemed to quiet down. People went back to their homes, the streets were plunged into darkness again and silence returned. I, too, went back to bed, but my heart was still beating hard.

The next morning I tried in vain to learn from my teacher the reason of that night's commotion, because my Chinese was not yet good enough for me to understand him. I had to wait until Orlando returned to know what had happened. After telling him about the noise and the tumult, I asked if he knew what had happened.

"Of course, I know about it," he answered. "The day before, some of the lepers living in the countryside came to the village to beg for food. As the villagers are terribly frightened of lepers, they chased them out quickly and even threw stones at them. The poor lepers ran away threatening revenge. One of their favorite forms of vengeance is to get into the village pool, which also serves as water tank. As this is the only source of water for the village, if it is contaminated by lepers, the village women have to walk miles and spend hours to get water from some other village for cooking, drinking and washing. This would be a disaster for the whole village and would prevent women from working in the fields.

"Well, what happened that night is that someone returning home late thought that he saw some people near the pool and assumed they were the vengeful lepers. He gave the alarm and the whole village was in an uproar trying to frighten the lepers away. Were you frightened, Nicola?" "Of course I was frightened. At least you, rascal, could have warned me!"

"I am sorry, old man. I forgot to do it. After all, these things don't happen too often, but they do happen."

"Are there a lot of lepers around here?" I asked out of curiosity, and also out of interest in these poor people.

"Even though leprosy here in south China is not as widely spread as in India and Burma, there still are quite a number of cases. Here in my district there certainly are a few hundred. No one cares for them, and they are not allowed to live in any village. They live in huts in deserted places, but occasionally they come to a village to beg for food or clothing. How they live nobody knows because they have no jobs and no source of income. But whenever they come near a village, they are chased away . . . like lepers."

"And what are you doing for them, my friend?"

"Honestly, there is not much I can do for them now. With having to care for twenty villages, I have my hands full. Moreover, they are afraid of foreigners, so it is not easy to approach them. Whenever I succeed in contacting them, I try to persuade them to go to the leper colony of Sheklung conducted by the French missionaries, and if they agree, I give them a letter of introduction to the missionary who is in charge there."

Having finally solved the mystery of the commotion of that frightening night, we both had a good laugh at my expense.

Not long after that incident, I returned to my work at Rosary Church.

A Missionary's Daily Routine

Whenever we speak of a "parish" in the United States, we usually think of a fairly large church with Catholics living within relatively short distances. On the contrary, when we missionaries speak of a "mission parish" or "district," we mean a rather large area—sometimes even much larger than a county—with many small Christian communities scattered in villages separated by various distances. The village where there are the most Catholics becomes the main residence of the missionary.

As the people of the different communities could not easily go to the main residence of the district because of distance and lack of transportation, the missionary went to visit them several times a year.

Some districts, such as that of my friend Fr. A. Poletti, comprised as many as forty-eight villages. Even visiting one village per day, it took about two months to visit the entire parish. This is why every Sunday morning, under the guidance of the local catechist or community head, the Catholics gathered in the chapel, if there was one, or in one of the largest houses, to recite their community prayers. However, the real Sunday for them was the day the missionary visited them.

The daily routine of a missionary's life in the Chinese countryside (where most of the Catholic population lived then) was something like this . . .

We rose before dawn to say our prayers. Then, as daylight came, we opened the door of the little church, rang a small bell and waited for the women to come for Confession. The men arrived later and we celebrated Mass while the congregation recited their community prayers in the beautiful sing-song melody typical of the Chinese language. The sermon was brief but to the point because it was an important tool for the education of our parishioners. We tailored it to the needs of each particular community.

After Mass everyone rushed away for the morning meal and then to work in the fields. We, on the contrary, would sit down with our faithful houseboy to a small breakfast of rice gruel and vegetables. Then we packed our suitcases, closed the church, and started traveling to the next village, almost always on foot, with our houseboy carrying our luggage and the other implements for Mass on the customary pole slung across his shoulders.

Usually we arrived at our destination around three or four in the afternoon. The houseboy soon opened up the little church or chapel while we went around the village to inform parishioners of our arrival and remind them to come to church in the evening. In some cases the head catechist would sound a horn or a bell to let people know we were there. When there was no chapel, we would lodge at the house of one of our Catholics.

In our tour of the village we visited the sick, distributed some simple home remedies, arranged Baptism for the newborn, checked on the progress of adults who were preparing for Baptism, and tried to settle the inevitable quarrels.

About 6:00 P.M. we finally sat down to a meal of rice, vegetables, salted fish and, occasionally, a piece of boiled chicken if some family had given us one. Toward 7:00 people would start coming in for night prayers and religious instruction. As darkness approached, the women rushed home and we started hearing the Confessions of the men.

Finally the social hour began, a friendly gathering of the priest and flock. In winter it took place in one of the stables; in summer it was in the open air. Always it was in an atmosphere filled with the smoke of hand-wrapped, cheap cigarettes, the smell of dozens of sweating men, the drone of mosquitoes, and the bites of various insects sucking one's blood.

Those nightly gatherings offered a great opportunity to a missionary to communicate with his people, to listen to their stories, to advise and to guide them. Religion was not the only subject: we talked about almost everything under the sun, but mostly about what the people felt close to their hearts: families, animals, fields, crops, local politics and their very routine lives. Two or three months might pass before their priest came again. It was through these long talks that a missionary could inspire the dull existence of earthy men and raise their sights beyond the strictly material cares that absorbed them.

It would often be midnight or later when the men went home. While they were finding their way through the silent black alleys with the light of the flaming torches they were carrying, the visiting missionary would kneel by his bed for a final prayer and then stretch out on a board-bed, hoping there were no mosquitoes inside the mosquito net.

Traveling In China

Traveling was the source of many adventures and some rough times. It was done mostly on foot and in the company of a.houseboy who knew the roads. Horses were costly and scarce. In most cases bicycles could not be used because the roads were mere narrow strips laid out among rice fields and unsuitable for biking.

Back in the twenties Fr. Bernard Meyer of Maryknoll wrote a letter to his headquarters in New York describing the missionary travel of those days: "One must travel in all sorts of circumstances and weather, exposed to thorough soaking, perhaps more than once a day, with no chance to change clothes; he must sleep in noisy and unsanitary surroundings; he must often eat what is not the best of food. The summer is extremely hot and enervating, so humid at times that one cannot sleep for nights on end."[1]

Fr. John E. Donovan, his biographer, commented: "There was nothing in these mission journeys that approached luxury: 'I walked all day in the rain.' They were often wearisome: 'Walked two days in the blazing sun for 40 miles.' And getting back to his central mission, after being on the road for a week or two was a welcome relief for 'a day or two, a good bed and a taste of home cooking, before going off in another direction.' "

Germs And Viruses

Even though I never worked long enough on the China mainland to have a parish of my own, I often visited many of my fellow missionaries and accompanied them on their travels to Christian villages.

On August 14, 1933, I was visiting Fr. Ottavio M. Liberatore in his Huichou County mission district, and he asked me to go along with him to a village, about a four-hour walk away, to celebrate the solemn Feast of the Assumption there on the following day.

Because Liberatore thought he knew the road well, he sent the houseboy ahead, by himself. The two of us started on our journey a little later, about 8:00 A.M. For four hours we walked continuously among paddy fields, hills and ravines in the hundred-degree air. By noon not a village was in sight. We then realized that we were hopelessly lost in the middle of nowhere, without water, food, or shade to shelter us from the scorching August sun. We did not dare to stop for a rest because we were afraid that we would not reach some village before night. On and on we trudged under the tropical sun, walking aimlessly, getting more and more dehydrated. We kept praying, one rosary after another, but it seemed that our prayers could not reach heaven through the bronze-colored sky of that torrid afternoon.

After nine hours, when I was on the verge of collapsing, we saw on the far horizon what appeared to be a major road. People and oxcarts were traveling in both directions.

"Nicola, we are saved!" Liberatore exclaimed. "I do not know yet where we are but that surely is a road. Cheer up, young man, you are not going to die today!"

Half an hour later we reached the road and, to our delight, we saw a man selling hot tea at a roadside stand. We rushed toward him and Liberatore said, "Drink, Nicola, drink! This tea is our salvation!"

We rushed forward, but my heart sank when I had a close look at the tea- stand. The small teacups were awash in a dirty dishpan and were black with filth. Probably the water had not been changed since morning. Everyone who drank tea "washed" the cup in that same water. I was flabbergasted. My imagination saw millions of infectious germs of all kinds floating in that fetid water or on the grimy cups. With despair in my voice, I looked up at Liberatore, who was taller than I and said dejectedly, "Do you really expect me to drink from those dirty cups?"

With a patronizing smile, he looked down at me and said, "Listen, Nicola, I know now where we are. It will take at least two more hours of walking to reach our house. You are too tired and dehydrated to make it unless you drink. Do you want to spend the night here in the open air? Come on! Drinking from those dirty cups will not kill you. I have done it hundreds of times!"

Faint with fatigue and disgust, but pushed by the instinct of survival, I gingerly extracted a cup that looked less dirty than the others from the filthy water and poured in some tea. With an effort, I conquered a rising swell of nausea, brought the cup to my lips and took a sip. The tea was hot and delicious! I drank with relish and felt renewed strength flooding throughout my body. I had a second cup, then a third, until I'd drunk twelve cups. Liberatore had sixteen!

When we resumed our walk, I said, "Listen, my friend, if I die of tuberculosis or typhoid fever it is all your fault."

"Don't worry, Nick. I guarantee you will not die, not this time."

For weeks afterwards I expected some foul disease, but none came, and as I write this, I am at the ripe age of eighty-two. That August 14 fifty-three years ago, is the day I lost faith in germs and infectious disease! With the help of Divine Providence I never got an infectious disease during my twenty years in China.

Food And Famine

"Did you ever starve when you were in China?" I have been asked this question hundreds of times, especially by people who in recent years have visited communist China. Probably this question was prompted by the widely spread belief that the Chinese were all starving before Mao brought them his own version of earthly paradise.

My answer has always been an unequivocal: "No. Even though I lived in China over fifty years ago, I can assure you that neither I nor the four hundred million Chinese were on a starvation diet."

To say that in pre-communist China most of the Chinese were starving is a lie spread abroad by communist propaganda. The truth is that as far back as the early thirties there were already four hundred million Chinese! How could China at that time be the most populous nation on earth if the Chinese were dying of starvation? True, there was indeed a lot of poverty and there were local famines due to occasional floods or droughts, but to state that the whole of China was suffering from chronic starvation is a downright falsehood.

In the China of the thirties there was, of course, a lot of poverty, but poverty is very different from famine. Moreover, the concept of poverty is relative to the situation of each case and therefore must be evaluated accordingly. In affluent countries such as ours it is easy to confuse poverty with famine. Poverty means different things in different countries. Here in the States we classify a family of four as poor because it has an annual joint income of less than $10,000. But in most of the nations of the Third World the same family with an income of only $1000 per year would be classified as middle class and well above the poverty level.

Consider, for instance, the case of meat consumption. Here in the States our meat consumption is over seventy pounds per person per year. In China at that time, it was from three to five pounds per person. This difference was due not to poverty but simply to different life styles. Millions of Chinese were as satisfied with their small consumption of meat as we Americans are with ours. Life styles are determined by historical conditions, habitat and climate and not necessarily by lack of money.

China has always been an agricultural country. In my days eighty percent of the people lived in small villages in the countryside doing agricultural work. As in all agricultural societies the world over, the greatest majority were cash-poor, but far from starving.

What did we eat in China? There was, of course, a great difference between the type of food consumed in villages and that eaten in large cities. In the villages we PIME missionaries lived and ate just as the Chinese did. Allow me to describe one of my early meals in China, namely the meal I had the first evening when I went to visit Fr. Orlando as I reported in the previous chapter.

"Carmelo, what are we going to eat tonight?" I asked him with some apprehension in my voice as I saw no preparations being made for the evening meal and I was really hungry—not very unusual for a twenty-five-year-old.

"Listen, Nicola, tonight we are going to have a celebration in your honor. We will have boiled chicken, steamed rice, salted fish, to-fu, and boiled vegetables with plenty of soybean sauce."

With a grimace on my face and a tinge of discontent in my voice I remarked, "Well, chicken and rice don't seem to me much of a celebration!"

"Of course it is! On ordinary days I eat only rice and salted fish with some occasional vegetable just as most of the Chinese do around here."

"Why salted fish?"

"Because rice is cooked without salt. A small piece or two of salted fish add flavor and stimulate the appetite in this hot weather. For the same reason we occasionally add a little curry powder to the vegetables."

"Is this the way all the Chinese eat around here?"

"Yes, and not only around here but practically all over south China, well over one hundred million of them do. Only in central and north China people eat steamed bread in the place of rice because wheat grows there and rice doesn't."

"Isn't this a starvation diet?"

"Silly city boy, of course not!" he answered with just a little friendly irony.

Ignoring the quip, I replied, "It must be a very boring diet! Look, Orlando, you and I are only twenty-five-years-old and we need food. How can you live on salted fish and rice alone? Don't you ever eat beef, pork or some other kind of meat besides boiled chicken?"

"Very seldom, and only on the occasions of weddings, funerals, holidays, or when a cow or a pig or a dog is slaughtered. Here in the countryside the situation is different from the cities. Here we have no shops selling meat because there is no electricity, and ice-boxes are unknown. Most families keep a few chickens and kill one only when there are visitors or there is a sick person in the family. Tonight we eat chicken because a good family gave me one in your honor."

I must confess that that evening as we "celebrated" my arrival with a festive meal I was human enough to feel homesick at the thought of good Italian food and especially of my mother's cooking. The whole atmosphere was depressing and the meal became an exercise in penance.

There was no home-like atmosphere in that residence and the house looked more like a hovel than a rectory. The whole house consisted of one room, fourteen feet by twelve, which had been added as an afterthought to the back of the small church. It served as a sacristy, bedroom for two, living room, study room and dining room all in one. The walls were made of mud bricks, and cracks of various dimensions ran in all directions. The plaster was gone and the grayish earth of the mud bricks was visible all over. The tiny layer of cement over the earthen floor was cracked, dusty and uneven.

The furniture consisted of a Chinese bed (three wooden boards supported by a low trestle) covered by an old mosquito net of undetermined age and undefined color; an antique closet of wormed pine wood containing the church utensils and a beaten-up, tottering old table of the type used for playing mahjong, grimy with food stains. Two rickety old chairs and a three-legged wooden stool completed the furnishings. Two frames with religious images cut out of a religious magazine were hanging on the walls to cover up some of the worst cracks. A small, square opening in the wall, sealed with a dirty glass, was the only source of light and air in the room.

There was no kitchen, just a cupboard containing a few dirty-looking pans. There was a small earthen pot for burning wood shavings or dried grass, the type of fuel used by the peasants in the countryside for cooking meals. There was no running water. The only water available came from the village pool and was used for cooking and in a cracked enameled wash basin when we washed our faces. There were, of course, no toilets. An old-fashioned and smelly latrine was in the yard, just outside the back door.

When dinner time came, we sat at the grimy old table. Of course, there was neither table cloth nor napkins, no silverware, no water glasses, only three chipped rice bowls, three pairs of chopsticks and tea cups for Orlando, his cook and houseboy, A-yun, and me. An old chicken had been killed and immediately placed in a pot to boil hardly one hour before the meal. It was as tasteless and chewy as shoe leather, the salt fish had more bones than meat, and the boiled cabbage was watery and flavorless. Only the bright red to-fu (a kind of Chinese cheese) added flavor and color to the food.

As we sat down to eat at the rickety table with A-yun perched on the three-legged stool, I could not help remarking to my friend Orlando with just a touch of sarcasm in my voice, "Is this the scrumptious Cantonese food everybody is raving about?"

"Nicola, you shock me!" he replied, pretending to be scandalized by my earthly remarks. "Have we come to China all the way from Italy to eat well and to enjoy ourselves or rather to follow Christ in poverty and live as the Chinese do? What you experienced at this meal is China, the real China."

Notes

1. A Priest Named Horse by John F. Donovan. (Our Sunday Visitor.)

6

My First Assignment: Errors And Bloopers

Tangling With Women

I began my assignment as assistant to Fr. John Spada at Rosary Church in January 1932, barely three months after my arrival in Hong Kong. Obviously I could not be of much help to him because of my scant knowledge of English and Chinese. I spent much time locked in my room studying by myself because dear Fr. Spada did not believe in spending money to provide a teacher. Thanks to Divine Providence I met Mr. Lawrence Barton, a gentle Englishman, who soon volunteered to help me with corrections of my sermons. However, during the first few months, except for Sunday Mass, I did not have any ministry to do.

This situation was further complicated by the fact that I did not think much of my pastor as a missionary. I admired his priestly virtues because he was a holy and totally dedicated priest. But he was catering only to Portuguese Catholics and therefore, in my opinion, he was no missionary at all! Since his arrival in Hong Kong in 1892 he had always worked among the Portuguese and spoke very little Chinese.

To make matters worse, like most youths I had a large measure of self-assurance. I was far from being a young, humble assistant eager to be trained. As a result, our relationship was merely cordial. To make matters worse, dear Fr. Spada, in spite of his experience and saintliness, definitely did not know how to train a young assistant and could not understand the generation gap. He was accustomed to doing most of the work by himself so there was not much left for me to do.

The first few months I kept a low profile and concentrated mostly on learning English. Still I could not help noting that there were a lot of things that in my opinion were definitely wrong. I regarded Fr. Spada as far too tolerant and permissive in running the parish. However, I felt that there was no use discussing these matters with him and I decided to act on my own initiative.

At the beginning of the hot season I began to notice that the Portuguese women were coming to church wearing sleeveless dresses, low-cut blouses, and makeup. According to my Italian mentality that way of dressing was positively scandalous and could not be tolerated. As Fr. Spada did not seem to notice it, I decided to get things moving and started a series of sermons on women's modesty in dress, the importance of setting a good example, and God's punishment for scandalmongers. Sunday after Sunday I preached "hell and brimstone" sermons. But, much to my chagrin, nobody listened to my words and the ladies kept coming dressed as usual. I was furious and decided to take action.

One Sunday in July, when the temperature was in the upper nineties, I gave the ladies an ultimatum from the pulpit: "Beginning next Sunday, I will refuse Holy Communion to any lady who comes to the altar rail wearing a sleeveless dress, a low-cut blouse, or too much makeup. This church is no place for modern Jezebels!"

In spite of my ultimatum nobody took me seriously and the following Sunday the ladies came to church again dressed as usual. At Communion time I loudly told each lady who was not dressed according to my rules, "You are not properly dressed. If you want to receive Holy Communion, go home, dress modestly and come back." And I skipped giving Communion to her.

The following Sunday there were fewer offending ladies, but I still loudly scolded each of them. I failed to notice that the attendance was down but rejoiced seeing that several ladies were wearing sweaters in spite of the sweltering July heat! The third Sunday the church was almost empty; there were only a few men and some very old ladies attending my Mass.

I was heartbroken and confused. I wanted to bring souls to God and all I was accomplishing was keeping them away from church. At last it dawned on me that perhaps I was doing something wrong but I was too proud to discuss this matter with Fr. Spada. So I went to consult my spiritual director, Fr. George Byrne, an old and holy Irish Jesuit who had already spent many years in Hong Kong.

After I gave him a brief report of what I was doing, he told me, "My dear Father Nick, haven't you realized yet that Hong Kong is not Italy and that the way of life in the tropics is different from that of European countries? I agree with you that if Italian women went to church dressed as the good Portuguese ladies do at Rosary Church, they would create a scandal there. But here the situation is different. We are in the tropics. The ladies in your parish go to church dressed as they dress at home every day. The use of makeup in the Anglo-Saxon culture is quite normal. It is part of the acceptable way of dressing up. These ladies would feel very disrespectful of the Lord if they came to church without makeup. Yes, you are making a big mistake. So, be sensible. Apologize to your congregation and stop this nonsense."

I did exactly that. The good Portuguese ladies forgave my youthful inexperience and we became great friends after that.

This episode came back to my mind last summer while I was visiting Oxford, England. I was reading Newman by Owen Chadwick. On page 22 Chadwick wrote: "Pastors of sixty rummage among their old sermons preached thirty years before, and are disturbed at their presumption, or sad that the years lowered their standards instead of fostering their growth. They conclude that now they should not dare to say what once they said with sincerity. The reason for this is not only sin. It is a livelier sense of the possible.

"Not so Newman. In the strength of his earlier years he did not shrink from the strongest words; and his disciples saw that his endeavor was consistent with those words. Decades afterwards, in his late sixties, he did not hesitate to republish. Experience taught him what as a young vicar he never quite realized, that not all dedicated men and women ought to aspire to heroism. Nevertheless the aged cardinal saw nothing too fierce in the words of the young Newman."

Certainly it is not so with me. I honestly would not preach again the sermons of my earlier years.

A Victim Of Girlish Pranks

In my early years at Rosary Church I strictly followed the rules I had learned in the seminary about relations with the opposite sex. To put it in a few words, the rule was that we should not speak to a woman (except in the case of one's family) unless there was real necessity, that we had to stick to the subject we had to discuss and keep the conversation as brief as possible. However, what seemed easy and clear in the all-male atmosphere of the seminary did not prove so easy in real life. During my early months at Rosary Church this rule was put to a severe test.

There was a high school for girls right next to Rosary Church. It was not a parish school but was conducted by the Canossian Sisters and we at the rectory had very little to do with it.

Of course, the senior girls soon noticed the presence of the new young missionary in the rectory. Even my unkempt beard did not curtail their girlish curiosity. Occasionally, at recess time, some of the more adventurous girls sneaked over to the church, ostensibly to pray but in reality to see what was going on at the rectory. Old and experienced Fr. Spada knew what they were up to and did not pay much attention to them. I was innocent and trusting and soon fell prey to their pranks.

Two of them, both Chinese, began to come over almost every day and, if I happened to be around, started asking me questions about religion. Knowing that they were "pagans," I was interested in their conversion. In spite of my broken English we managed to understand each other and occasionally talked for a few minutes in front of the church. Before too long our conversations drifted from religion to school matters and complaints against the sisters. They told me all kinds of horror stories about the "nasty" sisters and how badly they treated the students. I took them seriously and started worrying about a possible scandal if those complaints were to become public. I did not feel enough confidence in dear Fr. Spada to tell him about this matter and kept the worries to myself.

The horror stories got worse and worse. One day, with an air of mystery, the girls told me that one of the sisters had warned them to keep away from me and not to speak to me anymore as I was too young, too inexperienced and knew nothing about China.

I could stand it no longer and braced myself to face the lion in her den. The following day I cornered the headmistress in her office and with undisguised resentment in my voice, while trying to hide the identity of the two girls, I told her what they had reported to me about the bad behavior of the nuns and the prohibition of seeing me. I bluntly asked for an explanation.

While telling the story, I noticed that the sister, instead of being upset by my revelations, was fighting hard to suppress her amusement. I was fuming. She let me finish my story and then with a kind smile and a very appeasing tone of voice said, "Father Maestrini, please do not be offended. But you are very young, you have just arrived and obviously you do not know Chinese girls. I bet the two who came to see you are Bella Ma and Ruby Moy."

She was right. I was dismayed that she had identified the culprits, but nodded assent. "Father, it is just a prank!" she continued with a smile on her lips. "You should hear what they have told us about what you and Father Spada say about us! They are playing a game, Father, that's all. Both are intelligent and excellent students, and actually are taking instructions to become Catholics, but they are young and like to play games!"

That day I went back to the rectory like a whipped dog. I had learned a painful lesson at the cost of my pride. I did not scold the girls, but when they realized that I was aware of their tricks the games stopped and we became the best of friends. Eventually both were baptized, married, and became great Christian mothers. Ruby Moy became Mrs. Y. Y. Tang, the sister-in-law of Archbishop Tang of Canton, and Bella Ma married Dr. Sun. When I visited Hong Kong in 1979 we had a very joyful reunion and talked at length about their girlish escapades.

A Chinese Wedding

One day Fr. Spada asked me to perform the wedding ceremony of a Chinese couple. The ceremony was to take place at 11:00 A.M. on a weekday. As it was the first time I was going to perform a wedding, I prepared the ceremony with great care. Fifteen minutes before the wedding was due to take place, I was already in church, lit the candles, and donned the sacred vestments. Much to my surprise, at 11:00 I was still the only person in church. Nobody had showed up. At 11:15 no one had yet, arrived, and I started to pace up and down the aisle, fuming. At 11:30 Fr. Spada happened to come into the church and he immediately realized the situation. Being a very parsimonious man, the first thing he did was to snuff out the candles. Then he came over to me and said, "Father Maestrini, you must learn that the Chinese do not have the same sense of time as we do. If they say that they are coming for a ceremony at eleven, they really mean that they are coming about twelve or later. You may go back and wait in the house. When they arrive, they will surely let you know."

So I did, and they arrived long after 12:00.

I started the ceremony using Latin, as was done in those days, and then changed to Chinese when I asked for the consent. Addressing the groom first I asked, "Do you want to marry so and so?"

"Yes," he answered promptly.

But when I asked the same question of the bride, she did not answer. At first I blamed myself for speaking poor Chinese and patiently repeated the question. Still no answer. Finally, the third time, with obvious impatience in my tone of voice, I asked, "Do you or don't you?"

She noticed my impatience and whispered, "Yes," so faintly that I could barely hear her.

Losing my temper completely, I said loudly, "Come on, please say 'Yes' or 'No' so that the witnesses can hear."

The poor girl was astonished by my ignorance of Chinese customs and, almost crying, answered, "Hai, Shan foo, hai"—"Yes, Father, yes."

When I reported the happening to Fr. Spada he said, "Oh, I forgot to tell you that this is what you might have expected. According to Chinese customs, no girl at the altar will ever answer yes the first time you ask her. This would be considered unmaidenly and highly improper. You're lucky you got away with asking her only three times. Sometimes it takes even longer. But, please, in such cases do not lose your patience because this is very offensive to the Chinese."

Now things are different. Today Westernized Chinese brides in Hong Kong do not hesitate to answer yes like their counterparts in the rest of the world.

A Lesson In Humility

As I am in the mood to confide the story of my bloopers and errors to my readers, I will include in this chapter a couple of episodes even though they took place some time later.

In the early days of my work as assistant to Fr. Andrew Granelli at the new parish of St. Teresa I was very active helping him in the organization of the Chinese Catholic Young Men's Association. The purpose of this organization was to further the religious formation óf the young men of the parish. Most of them came to the Faith through the good work of the La Salle Brothers, who were running the La Salle College, only half a mile away from St. Teresa's. As this kind of work appealed to me, I delved into the project with all my youthful energies, spending a great deal of time with the prospective members and taking an active part in the drafting of the bylaws.

The inaugural meeting was set for a Saturday evening but, unfortunately, that very morning Fr. Granelli became seriously ill and had to be rushed to the French Convent Hospital on the Hong Kong side. Undaunted by this setback and with unlimited confidence in myself, I decided that the show had to go on and that I could very well substitute for him. The meeting was held as scheduled and I supervised the proceedings for the election of officers and the approval of the bylaws. I ran the whole show.

After the meeting I received a lot of congratulations and I went to bed basking in the glow of satisfaction. I really thought I had done a good job because everything had gone as I had planned and everybody seemed happy. I could hardly wait for the morning to arrive to run down to the hospital and tell Fr. Granelli all about it.

The next day, Sunday, as soon as the last parish Mass was over, about 1:45 P.M., I rushed to make my report to the pastor. To my surprise, he received me very coldly, but I thought it was due to the fact that he did not feel well, and I proceeded to give him a glowing report of the successful meeting. He listened to me with an evident air of resignation and neither interrupted nor made any comment. When I finished talking, he raised himself to a sitting position on the bed, and speaking in a sad tone of voice told me bluntly, "Fr. Maestrini, I have to excuse you for you are young and inexperienced, but you really made a mess of last night's meeting. Less than one hour ago a delegation of the members who attended the meeting last night came to tell me that all of them are resigning from the society and will never attend another meeting as long as you are there. They cannot stand your dictatorial way of doing things. You have spoiled everything. You simply don't know how to deal with the Chinese!"

I was flabbergasted! In a humble tone of voice I said, "But last night all of them were very kind to me. They congratulated me a lot!"

"Of course, they did that because they are kind people and wanted to save your face, but they are deeply hurt."

He saw that I was crushed and humiliated and proceeded to give me a long lecture on how to deal with the Chinese. But it was a good lesson and through the rest of my days in China I never forgot it.

I immediately went to work mending fences. Within a few weeks all the young men were reinstated as members, and, with the help of the Lord and of St. Teresa, the association flourished. Most of those young men became my close friends for life and they were the pillars of my work when, a few months later, I became pastor of that parish.

A Slap In The Face!

One afternoon I was alone in St. Teresa's church reading my prayers when a Chinese man rushed into the church screaming and shouting at the top of his voice. Thinking that he might have undergone some serious tragedy, I rushed over to him and tried to calm him down. Finally, in the midst of tears and sobs, I got his story. He was on the verge of despair because his mother had just died and he had no money to buy a coffin. Knowing that according to Chinese filial piety children had the sacred duty of burying their parents in a coffin, I could fully sympathize with him. So I decided to give him enough money to buy a coffin and pay for the funeral, about thirty dollars in all, a large sum in those days. As soon as he received the money, his tears dried up and he ran away almost jumping for joy. That made me a little suspicious, but I thought no more of it.

A few days later, at a gathering of priests, I mentioned this incident and they all burst out laughing. They told me that the guy was a professional impostor who had played the same trick in practically every Catholic and Protestant church in town. I was humiliated and furious and resolved that if I saw the guy again I would teach him a lesson.

Lo and behold! A few weeks later the same guy had the guts to come to the rectory again asking for more money. When I recognized him, I really saw red and lost my temper. Forgetting all my previous resolutions to be patient and understanding, I burst into a violent tirade. That was the worst thing I could have done. In my excitement I mispronounced Chinese words and the poor man did not understand a word of what I was saying. He kept looking at me, smiling and amused at seeing a "foreign devil" get mad. This made me even more furious. Perceiving that I was not getting through to him, I decided to pass from words to action and, with all my strength, gave him a resounding slap on the face. This caught him completely by surprise. He reeled back for a second, then, regaining his composure, with all his strength he punched me in the stomach. This time it was my turn to reel back. As I clutched my belly in pain, I had a last glimpse of him running away at the speed of lightning.

When I reported this incident to my Father Confessor, he wisely said, "You were very wrong in getting angry. You got mad because your pride was hurt. But you should have realized that the poor man did not mean to humiliate you. All he had in mind was to use a clever ruse to get a few meals. You have a beautiful church, a decent house, and you don't need to worry where your next meal will come from. But he has nothing and he felt entitled to a little share of what you have. Next time, try to think the way the poor think in the Chinese way, and you will avoid getting angry and getting punched in the stomach."

I learned my lesson. That was the first and last time I ever slapped anyone!

7

Serving The Poor

My Years At St. Teresa's

When Fr. Orlando and I had arrived in Hong Kong on September 22, 1931, that morning, though still walking on our sea legs, we had been rushed to the cathedral to meet Bishop Valtorta. At the end of that meeting he had taken us aside and, grinning broadly from behind his imposing beard, had confided to us: "Today I am going to sign the contract for the building of a new parish church in Kowloontong and it will be dedicated to St. Teresa of the Child Jesus. Who knows? Perhaps one day you two might work there!" His words were prophetic.

But that first day in Hong Kong we had been too confused and fatigued after the long sea voyage to attach much importance to that bit of information. However, we had been happy to learn about the new church to be dedicated to our favorite saint.

For both Orlando and me, St. Teresa of the Child Jesus, Patroness of the Missions, was much more than just another saint. To us she embodied the very ideal of holiness and of complete dedication to evangelization. She had been our inspiring guide through the long, difficult years of seminary life. Moreover, for me personally, she evoked very special memories. As a young student at the seminary in Rome, I had served at the altar at the ceremonies of her beatification and canonization presided over by Pope Pius XI. These were the first two solemn ceremonies of this kind I had the privilege to witness and both occasions had left unforgettable impressions on me.

When Bishop Valtorta told us of the new church, we never imagined that only one year later I would first become assistant, then pastor, of that parish and that Fr. Orlando would first be appointed as my assistant and that years later he, too, would become pastor (1949-66) and head the parish through phenomenal growth.

My Assignment At St. Teresa's

Bishop Valtorta assigned me as assistant at St. Teresa's parish shortly after it was officially opened on the last Sunday before Christmas 1932. This event was a landmark in the growth of the Church in Kowloon. Only thirty years earlier, in 1902, Fr. Spada had opened Rosary Church, the first Catholic church in Kowloon, in the presence of fifty-two people. When St. Teresa's opened, three thousand persons attended.

I had already worked about one year as assistant to Fr. Spada and probably the bishop thought that Fr. Granelli would be a better training guide for me.

I considered it a great privilege to work under such a man as Granelli. I was sure that I would learn from him what a dedicated priest and missionary is really like.

Let me introduce you briefly to my new parish. The new church was an architectural jewel designed by a Benedictine monk, Fr. I. Gresnit, then professor of architecture at the Beijing Catholic University. It was built at a cost of $30,000 ($150,000 in Hong Kong dollars), which was raised by a committee of Portuguese Catholics under the direction of Fr. Spada.

Designed in the shape of a cross, the church could seat over five hundred people in the central and side areas. The altar, located at the intersection of the two side aisles under a canopy supported by four marble columns, faced the people, a novelty in those days. It was a modest imitation of the papal altar in St. Peter's in Rome. The bell tower—tall, slender, elegant—somehow resembled the famous belfry of St. Mark's in Venice, Italy. The rectory was located in a two-bedroom apartment at the back of the church. The small covered porch of the apartment served as parish office.

St. Teresa's was located at the crossing of Prince Edward and Water-loo Roads, the two principal streets of the fast-developing suburb of Kowloontong, and was surrounded by a large compound planted with trees and flowers. It was an attractive landmark for the entire suburb and very much admired by Catholics and non-Catholics.

The territory of the new parish, carved out of Rosary Church parish, included a large area from the Kai Tak airport to Sham Shui Po, with a population of about half a million Chinese, a few hundred Portuguese, a sprinkling of British and Irish Catholics and quite a few Chinese Catholic families.

When the church was inaugurated, several major Catholic institutions had already been built and were operating in the parish, such as the Maryknoll Convent (a middle school for three hundred Chinese girls), the La Salle College, a high school for five hundred boys conducted by the La Salle Brothers, the Home for the Aged conducted by the Little Sisters of the Poor, and several other minor Chinese schools.

The Pastor: Fr. Andrew Granelli, PIME

Fr. Granelli, then in his mid-forties, was a man of great vision. Tall, large-framed, bespectacled, intelligent, with refined features, sporting a trimmed goatee, he was a man of vision and was endowed with a great sense of humor. His dynamic personality and heart of gold made him a priest loved by all. He had joined PIME after having been a pastor in his diocese of Piacenza in north Italy and had worked in Hong Kong in several capacities since 1925. I had first seen Granelli when I attended the first departure ceremony in Milan soon after joining PIME and had had many friendly conversations with him while I worked at Rosary Church. I admired him highly because he was one hundred percent mission-minded.

A Missionary Parish

At that time St. Teresa's was definitely a "Portuguese" parish because at least eighty percent of the parish population were Portuguese. This created a conflict of goals. The presence of so many Catholic parishioners made our parish just like any other parish in Catholic countries where priests devote all their time catering to Catholics. But Granelli and I had chosen to be missionaries and had dedicated our life to bringing Christ to the non-Christians. Now restricting our activities to catering to Catholics seemed to be almost betraying our vocation. We solved the conflict by dedicating all our energies to making the parish a "missionary parish."

A casual visitor who dropped by the church on any ordinary Sunday might have thought that St. Teresa's was much like any other big Catholic parish in any cosmopolitan city. But that would have been a wrong impression. To us, on the inside, things were quite different. Every activity, every organization, every religious service—in brief, all our work—was definitely oriented toward evangelization. Each activity was intended to motivate and inspire our parishioners to bring the message of Christ to the non-Christians.

We believed that by developing a deeper spiritual life among the parishioners we would stimulate them to bring Christ to the non-Christians. To this effect we organized a variety of activities and religious associations, which included the Children of Mary, the Chinese Catholic Young Men's Society and the Catholic Women's Association, various fraternities, the altar boys, the Ladies' Altar Society, the catechists (groups of people trained for the instruction of catechumens), hospital visitation, the St. Vincent de Paul Society, the teaching of catechism in Catholic schools, and family visitations. All this work kept us busy from morning to night. In those days we did not know what a day off was, much less a vacation. We were laying the foundations of a new parish community and it was thrilling, exhilarating work. I felt completely fulfilled because I could devote all my time to my life's goal: to follow Christ, working for Him among people who did not know Him yet.

By the end of the first year the fruits of our work were very visible. We had a very good, active, cohesive and mission-oriented parish. All the parishioners worked together in a real spirit of unity; souls came to Christ by the hundreds through the schools and through our parish activities; Sunday Masses were increased from two to four and then six, and attendance was constantly increasing; even on week days we had a good number of people attending daily Mass, and all our parish associations were active and flourishing.

My Work As A Pastor

After only eighteen months of hard work at St. Teresa's, Fr. Granelli was exhausted and the doctors ordered him back to Italy for a long period of rest and rehabilitation. The bishop appointed me pastor and gave me an excellent Chinese priest, Fr. Luke Fong, as assistant. Thus, less than three years after my arrival in Hong Kong, I was at the head of a large, fast-growing, multi-national mission parish.

My favorite work was with the poor, especially the non-Catholics who, of, course, comprised the largest part of our parish population. This meant taking special care of widows and orphans, for whom there was no social security of any kind, providing food and clothing for the most desperate cases, finding jobs, arranging free medical care for the sick, pleading with the police for youthful transgressors, helping the illiterate with bureaucratic procedures in government offices, and getting their children admitted to schools.

The St. Vincent de Paul Society, well organized in Hong Kong, helped us a great deal in caring for the poor.[1]

At one time I had over three hundred Mexican women living in my parish. These ladies had married Chinese men in Mexico. In the early thirties when the Mexican government changed its immigration policy and expelled the Chinese from the country, these women, all Catholics, followed their husbands to China. Much to their chagrin, on their arrival they found out that all of the men were already married and their Chinese wives very much alive. They found life in China impossible under such circumstances and took refuge in Hong Kong, where they settled in one of the poorest Chinese sections of St. Teresa's parish.

They had to wait for years before they could be repatriated to Mexico. In the meantime, as they had no skills whatsoever and did not even know Chinese, the parish had to help supporting them until the Hong Kong government came to their assistance. The St. Vincent de Paul Society, as usual, helped us immensely.

Fr. Orlando Becomes My Assistant

By the end of 1934 Bishop Valtorta transferred Fr. Luke Fong to the nearby La Salle College to be chaplain and recalled Fr. Orlando from his work in the Paoan District on the mainland to be my assistant.

It was a real joy to be reunited with my former classmate and to work with him in the same parish dedicated to our favorite saint. We were both temperamentally well suited to working together. I took care of the administration, parish associations, schools, hospitals, confessions and most of the external activities. He did all the fine work of preparing the catechumens for baptism, giving spiritual direction, caring for the sisters and the old people, and supervising youth activities. In a broad sense I did the work of Martha, he that of Mary, and we were happy complementing each other in our respective roles.

We forged ahead with parish work along the lines established by Fr. Granelli and added a few more activities. What pleased me most in those days was the spiritual unity and harmony among all the workers. We belonged to many different nationalities: there were the old, loyal and faithful Portuguese families, such as the Osmunds, the Lopes, the Figuereidos, the D'Almadas, the Alves, the Souzas and many, many more too numerous to mention; there were the British and the Irish, such as Mr. Lawrence A. Barton, Mrs. Clarke, Mr. and Mrs. Francis Soden, Mrs. Patrick Costello, the MacFadyens and many others; there were the growing number of Chinese Catholics from all walks of life—lawyers, doctors, teachers, businessmen—such as the Tangs, the Yeungs, the Chens and the Lums; and, of course, Orlando and I fresh from Italy.

But in spite of the great differences of ethnic backgrounds, culture and education, we were like one heart, working together, praying together with one common goal in mind: to deepen our spiritual life and to bring non-Christians to Christ. It was probably this unity between the clergy and parishioners and our many activities for the poor that made an impression on the people around us, and the number of non-Christians requesting baptism grew constantly.[2]

Shelters For Street Sleepers

Walking through the streets of the incredibly overcrowded Chinese tenement houses in the neighborhood of Nathan Road and Sham Sheui Po, I noticed thousands of people, including whole families with small children, actually living in the streets. They cooked, ate, and slept on the sidewalks. I was told that this was an accepted way of life in Hong Kong and in all the major cities of the Orient.

However, I also noticed that when the cold weather came and temperatures hovered around thirty-five to forty degrees, women and children found lodgings at night, but hundreds of men still slept on the sidewalks. The newspapers daily reported numerous cases of street sleepers who were found dead in the morning because they could not survive in near-freezing temperatures.

On cold nights, as I retired to the comfort of my bedroom, I could not help thinking of the poor street sleepers and I decided something had to be done.

I discussed this matter with Fr. Fong and my good friend and parishioner Mr. L. A. Barton, a true Englishman and a remarkably good Catholic who was very active in all types of parish work. He was a VIP in the financial circles of the Hong Kong government and had a deep love for the Chinese people. I called him my number-two assistant.

We decided to open one or two shelters for street sleepers in the winter and to organize a group of volunteers to run them. We chose the Third Order of St. Francis of Assisi to do the job, as we needed workers inspired by the example of that great saint. Moreover, Mr. Barton was very devoted to St. Francis and so was I, having come from his native land. We proceeded to establish a branch of the Third Order and in a few months over twenty-five men, young and old, mostly Chinese, had joined it. They all volunteered to work for the shelters under Mr. Barton's leadership and my spiritual supervision.

Before winter came we raised the necessary funds, rented two apartments in the heart of the Chinese section of the parish, purchased bunks, blankets, rice bowls, kitchen utensils, pots and pans, and pajamas, too. We hung posters in the streets announcing the opening of the shelters.

We expected the street sleepers to come running to our shelters, but the night we opened, nobody came! All we could do was close the doors and go home crestfallen. We then decided on a new policy and the following night at dusk our Chinese young men, in teams of two, started walking around the streets near the shelters, approaching would-be street sleepers, telling them about the shelters and inviting them to come and spend the night in comfort and warmth.

The street sleepers at first were wary. They were suspicious, mistrustful, and very hesitant to trade the freedom of the streets for the comforts of a shelter. But at last we broke down their resistance and a few men came. They were pleased with our treatment and spoke well of us to their peers. Soon the word spread around and in no time we filled both shelters to their capacity of fifty.

This meant a lot of work for all of us. Every night a team of two men from the Third Order had to be on duty at each shelter. They opened the shelters at 8:00 P.M., welcomed the men coming in from the street and distributed hot tea, a bowl or two of steaming hot rice, and clean pajamas. When the shelter was full, they closed the doors and settled down to spend the night on bunks in the same room with the street sleepers. Early in the morning they collected the pajamas and blankets, again served hot tea and rice and closed the shelters for the day. It was very demanding work but they did it with joy in the spirit of St. Francis.

We ran these shelters for three years but finally had to give them up. The street sleepers were satisfied with the daily bowls of rice we gave them and spent all their earnings as coolies and rickshaw pullers on gambling in the streets. This caused a great deal of noise, shouting and fighting. The neighbors were annoyed and complained loudly to us. We stopped giving out rice and the street sleepers stopped coming. That was the end of our charitable venture.

Many years later, after the war, some Protestant groups again started shelters for street sleepers but they, too, had to close them shortly afterward for similar reasons.

When I read in the papers today about the efforts made in Western countries by city governments to solve the problem of the homeless and street sleepers, I can't help remembering my own experience in this field of social work. I believe now that all over the world, from Hong Kong to Europe and the States, there is a fringe of people who simply have not received from nature the basic gift of being able to run their own lives. These unfortunate creatures are simply incapable of living ordinary lives and cannot adapt themselves to living in shelters just as they cannot succeed in having families or houses of their own. The solution to the problem is not dragging them forcibly into city shelters, but providing them with better psychological care before they reach the stage of being homeless derelicts.

The Employment Agency

One Sunday morning I approached Mr. Barton and, using his nickname, I said, "Brother Leo, can you find a job for A-chun? He is twenty-five years old, has a wife and three children and no job."

"Does he speak any English?" Leo asked.

"No," I replied, "not a word."

"Does he know any art or craft, does he have any skill?" Leo continued, in the hope of being able to help the poor fellow.

"Unfortunately, none whatever," I replied with a note of regret in my voice, "but still the poor man needs money to feed his family."

"I am aware of that, Father, but you also know that there are tens of thousands of A-chuns in Hong Kong! Anyway, tell him to come and see me at the office tomorrow and I will introduce him to some department in the government."

This brief conversation reflected the situation of countless Chinese in Hong Kong: unemployment was the cause of their poverty. This was a chronic condition and practically incurable because the easier it was to find a job, the more people immigrated from the China mainland. It was a Catch-22 situation.

At St. Teresa's we were keenly aware of this problem and we often discussed it with the men of the St. Vincent de Paul Society and of the CYO group. We decided that what we needed was an employment agency. There were, of course, many employment agencies all over

Hong Kong and Kowloon but they charged very high fees and were beyond the reach of the poor people who needed them most.

With the help of Mr. Barton we set up an office in the parish rectory, organized a small group of volunteers to raise funds, bought a couple of desks and file cabinets, employed a part-time male secretary, advertised the new agency in the papers and opened shop. We were confident that requests for work and offers of employment would be pouring in. And the requests came. Day and night a flood of poor, unskilled laborers came pounding at the rectory door, but no employer ever listed even one job with us.

Moreover, we soon learned the difficulty of properly screening applicants. One day a young woman came and applied for domestic work. Without inquiring too much about her background, I proceeded to find a family willing to employ her. When a few days later I succeeded, as she had no phone I immediately rushed to the address she had given us to bring her the good news.

I climbed a lot of dark, filthy stairs in a very poor tenement house and knocked at the door of the apartment she had indicated as her residence. Soon a squeaky door opened just enough to let a ray of light into the windowless corridor. From the crack in the door I saw a row of young ladies lounging around in very scanty attire. Even though I had never seen a brothel in my life, I soon realized this was one. I immediately ran down the stairs as fast as I could, hoping and praying that nobody would recognize me in that environment!

Slowly we came to realize that our plan of running an unemployment agency was good in theory but unrealistic in practice. Chinese are very family-oriented and whenever there was an opening for a job in a shop or business, they immediately recommended their friends and family members. This is why most outsiders had no chance of getting jobs. There definitely was a market for skilled workers, but usually those who had skills also had some money and dealt directly with the professional employment agencies, which were all over town and made good profits. After a little over a month we closed shop. This unsuccessful venture, like that of the shelters, was not a total failure. It brought our parish community more closely together, was an inspiration to all the parishioners, and deepened the concept of Christian charity in the whole parish.

A Spoiled Christmas Dinner

Every year on Christmas day my parents would invite the poorest man in town to our family dinner. One of the men who came most often was a lonely, dirty, desolate beggar, affectionately nicknamed Pius IX because he had been a soldier in Pope Pius IX's army before the unification of Italy. My father always seated him at the head of the table, a place he otherwise never relinquished to anyone else, relative or guest. Our parents carefully explained to us children that Pius IX, the beggar, represented Christ in our midst and that receiving him in our family was like having Christ visiting us.

Through my seminary years, I had always dreamed of renewing this family tradition whenever I would have a church of my own. Accordingly, the first year I was a pastor at St. Teresa's I decided to offer a Christmas dinner to the poorest members of the parish. I submitted my plan to the members of the Third Order of St. Francis and of the CYO. I suggested that, in a true Christmas spirit, they might make a personal contribution to defray the cost of the dinner and furthermore that they might organize the event, distribute the tickets, cook the dinner and serve it . . . and do all this for the love of the Lord. They accepted my suggestion with true Christian spirit and agreed to serve about one hundred people. Naturally, I was very pleased with the success of my proposal because I intended not only to help the poor but also to foster the spiritual growth of the members themselves.

They cooperated with me one hundred percent and carried out the plans as we had agreed, distributing the tickets to one hundred poor people whom I had carefully selected from my parish list as most needy.

Christmas morning at 6:00 I walked, as I did every day, from the rectory to the church. But that morning I noticed a small group of people squatting in front of the parish hall, not far from the church. It was still dark and because I had a lot of things to do I did not stop to investigate. We had Masses every hour on the hour, and heard Confessions during and between Masses, and I had no time to go back to the rectory even for a cup of coffee. I forgot all about that group of early risers in front of the parish hall.

It was about 11:00 A.M. when I heard people quarreling and screaming just outside the church. Immediately a young man from our CYO came rushing into the sacristy and shouted, "Father Maestrini, hurry, hurry! People are fighting! A riot is starting! Call the police!" Alarmed, I rushed out of the sacristy toward the parish hall and saw a motley crowd of beggars fighting and hitting each other, while women screamed and children cowered in fear. I started shouting, gesticulating, ordering them to be quiet, but all in vain. Nobody paid any attention to me and fistfights continued all over the place.

As the crowd was getting nasty, I ran to the rectory to call the police. They came immediately. As good English police do, they started using their rubber truncheons, liberally administering blows on the shoulders, heads and faces of the shouting and screaming beggars. I was disgusted and demoralized. My whole day was spoiled.

What had happened was this: news had leaked out among the beggars and street sleepers in Kowloon that there was going to be a free dinner at St. Teresa's on Christmas day. Some enterprising beggars without tickets had decided to come early and to squat in front of the parish hall's door to make sure that they could get in. Unfortunately, too many had the same idea and by 11:00 there were several hundred beggars obstructing the entrance to the dining room. When the poor families with tickets arrived, the beggars refused to let them pass.

Our CYO men tried in vain to persuade those without tickets to leave. No amount of persuasion could budge the beggars and the fighting started. This is when they called me and I, in turn, called the police. The unpleasant sight of beggars being beaten up and chased away surely spoiled my Christmas.

The following years we organized the Christmas dinner again but took better precautions and, with the help of the Lord, we didn't have any more riots.

Notes

1. The St. Vincent de Paul Society is a worldwide lay Catholic organization, founded by a brilliant French lawyer, Frederick Ozanam, in 1833, to help the poor. I was acquainted with this society from my childhood days. My mother was very active in the work of the society and often asked me to accompany her when she went visiting poor families, distributing food coupons on behalf of the society.

2. Let me share with you some of the outstanding memories of those days at St. Teresa's. Sunday mornings, especially the long, hot months from April to September, were very hectic days. The church opened at 6:00 A.M. and the first Mass was at 6:15. From then on Masses were celebrated every hour on the hour and between the altar, the pulpit and the interminable Confessions we heard during and between Masses, we did not have a moment of rest. Of course, there was no air-conditioning in the church in those days, and very often it was not until after the last

Mass, which began at about noon, that we returned to the rectory perspiring, tired, and exhausted, but happy for the work done for the Lord.

The Holy Week, and Good Fridays especially, were days of great work. On Good Friday the church opened at 6:00 A.M.; at 7:00 we chanted the Hours of the Divine Office; the long liturgical service started at 9:00 and lasted until about 11:00 because of the singing of the Passion and adoration of the Cross. At noon we had the Stations of the Cross in Chinese; at 2:30 the Passion service and the Way of the Cross in English; at 5:00 the chanting of Matins in Latin; at 8:00 P.M. a solemn Passion service and procession with the statue of the dead Christ. When the church was finally cleared at 10:00 P.M. we started decorating it and preparing for the complicated liturgical service of Holy Saturday, which started at 7:00 A.M. the following morning and usually included scores of Baptisms of new converts.

The interior of St. Teresa's Church.

8

Reaping The Harvest

God's Command

"Father, I want to be baptized." These words coming from a non-Christian adult asking for Baptism were music to the ears of the missionaries of my generation. Seeing men and women, young and old, coming to Christ was the fulfillment of our dreams. Humanly speaking, it was also the reward for the sacrifices entailed by our way of life. Even though we knew that the number of Baptisms we administered was in no way the yardstick by which we could measure the success of our work, still it was gratifying to bring non-Christian souls to God.

We were fully aware that many good Christians lived lives of total dedication to the Lord and yet never experienced the joy of seeing the fruits of their sacrifices. We appreciated the vocation of the Trappist monks and of the Carmelite Sisters who were called to serve God in contemplative life and gave up the legitimate joys of the active ministry. But for us called to work in the midst of non-Christian nations, administering Baptism and the Eucharist to new converts always was a great spiritual joy.

During my years in China I had the joy of administering a large number of Baptisms. I will relate here some that took place under unusual circumstances.

School Ministry

Taking advantage of the Hong Kong school system, which allowed different religious denominations to teach religion classes in their schools, I always sought the opportunity to teach religion at the high school level.

In order to understand the situation that prevailed in our Catholic schools in Hong Kong in prewar days, it is necessary to know one of the chief characteristics of the British school system. The British government financially supports private schools, including those conducted by religious denominations. These private schools, in order to get government recognition and financial help, had to comply with basic standards and the legislated curriculum.

The government paid a substantial part of the cost of the school buildings, all the teachers' salaries according to a fixed pay scale, and all the school expenses. The students paid only a nominal monthly fee, which the school collected and turned over to the government. For certain grade levels public exams were held yearly. Students from both the private and government schools had to take them. Results were well publicized in all the city's papers, along with the number of students presented by each school, the number of those who passed, and the number of honors gained. This publicity gave the public a very good criterion by which to judge the merit of each school. Needless to say, our Catholic schools were rated among the very best in the colony, and this is why they were the most sought-after by Christian and non-Christian parents and their children. As the number of Catholics was relatively small, we would not have been able to afford our own schools if only Catholics had attended them, but since they enjoyed an excellent reputation, they were always filled to capacity. In some schools the number of non-Catholic students was as high as ninety percent.

For us Catholics, as well as for Protestants, schools were one of the primary activities of our missionary work because they afforded an excellent opportunity to bring Christ to non-Christians. In Catholic schools there was a daily half-hour religion class, taught by the religious themselves, and all students had to take it. In girls' schools, the sisters invited priests to lecture in order to familiarize the students with the role of the priesthood in the Catholic Church.

No pressure, either directly or indirectly, was exercised on the students to accept Christianity and all, both Christians and non-Christians, were treated the same. Every year many students attracted by the beauty of Christianity asked for Baptism, and many of them also brought their parents to the Faith. This made the teaching of religion in schools a rewarding ministry. Personally, I never felt as happy as when I was teaching a religion class and saw the eager, young students opening their hearts to Christ like flowers to the spring sun.

A Secret Baptism: Mabel Chen

"Father, I want to be baptized," a girl told me one day in 1934, after one of my classes at the school run by the Canossian Sisters in Hong Kong. The speaker was Mabel Chen, a school girl in her early teens. Her typically European blue-and-white school uniform of the Canossian Convent English School was in stark contrast to the Oriental features of her face. Shorter than average in stature, with deep, darting black eyes, she was one of the brightest students in that religion class.

Once a week I traveled from my parish of St. Teresa's in Kowloon by bus, ferry boat, and then on foot up the hill to the Canossian School on the Hong Kong side, about one hour's travel. I taught a half-hour class on religion to the juniors and seniors.

Answering Mabel's question, I said, "I'm very happy to know this, Mabel, but will your parents consent to your Baptism?"

"Oh, no, Father. I cannot tell my parents that I want to become a Catholic. I'm sure they would be mad at me and might even send me to another school. No, I cannot ask for their permission. I want to be baptized secretly."

"This presents a problem, Mabel," I continued. "If you are baptized secretly, how can you practice your religion? How can you go to church on Sundays, abstain from meat on Fridays, and follow other Church rules?"

"Oh, I will manage somehow," she answered, with great confidence in her feminine ability to get what she wanted. "But I want to be baptized soon, because I want to receive Holy Communion."

"And what about your sisters, Frances and Irene?"

"They do not have to know, either."

"I'm sorry, my child, but I cannot agree with you. I am pleased that you want to be baptized, but I don't see why you are in such a hurry. You already have the baptism of desire and, for all practical purposes, you already are a Catholic and a child of God. If your parents found out that you were baptized without their consent, they might take you and your sisters and brothers, too, out of Catholic schools and this would do more harm than good. No, Mabel, I don't think it would be advisable to baptize you now. Please wait for a couple of years until you graduate."

I watched her as she walked back to her class, a living picture of dejection. I felt sorry in my heart, but I was sure I was doing the right thing and I thought no further about this matter.

A few days later, to my surprise, Bishop Valtorta phoned me at St. Teresa's and asked me to see him in his office.

"Why do you refuse to baptize Mabel Chen?" he asked me abruptly.

"How do you know, Bishop?" I replied, astonished to think that a little Chinese girl—and not even a Catholic at that—could go over my head and report me to the bishop.

"She has written to me," the bishop continued, "and wants me to tell you to baptize her. I've talked to her and she seems very determined and eager. She certainly knows what she wants and she is well prepared."

"She certainly is," I said. "But I think there are good reasons for delaying her Baptism," and I proceeded to explain to him the family situation.

"In principle, you are right," the bishop said when I finished talking. "However, there also are exceptions to the rule, and I think this case is an exceptional one. She is so eager and knows her religion so well that she has a right to be baptized, regardless of what the family will do. I believe that in this case a secret Baptism is justified. Go ahead, baptize her. I assume the responsibility."

"If you say so, Excellency!" I said, smiling, as I was very happy that the bishop had given me the green light.

When I gave Mabel the good news, I expected her to jump for joy, but on the contrary, she simply whispered, "Thank you, Father," looked at me for an instant, and ran away. I was a little dismayed at first; then I remembered the Chinese habit of refraining from expressing emotions and I understood. In that glance she had given me, her eyes had said that she was bursting with joy.

A Midnight Ceremony

Even though Mabel was attending classes at the Canossian Convent on the Hong Kong side, she lived with her family a twenty-minute walk from St. Teresa's. As it was close to Christmas, Mabel agreed to be baptized in the church before midnight Mass on Christmas Eve. She was sure that her parents would allow her to attend Midnight Mass as part of her school activities. The problem was to find a godmother who could keep a secret—no small problem even in China! I decided to dispense with a godmother and get a godfather instead. So I turned to my faithful friend Mr. L. Barton, who was always delighted to see Chinese youths joining the Church.

When Christmas Eve came, Mabel arrived punctually at 11:30. She had been successful in persuading her parents to let her go to see what Catholics were doing on Christmas Eve. I asked the altar boys, the church janitor and everybody who was around to leave the sacristy. They were surprised at the unusual request and could not figure out what was happening. After firmly locking the sacristy door, Mr. Barton and I got everything ready for the Baptism and proceeded with the ceremony. As the strains of Christmas carols being played in the church wafted into the sacristy, we were deeply conscious of the beauty and the deep meaning of that hour.

It was because a little child had been born at midnight two thousand years before on the hills of Judea, and because of what He had said and done through His short life in Palestine, that we were now closeted in that room. He had come to teach love on earth, and it was because of love that young Mabel was now ready to fully accept discipleship as His follower at the risk of being thrown out by her family. It was because of love that Mr. Barton was there in his role as guide of the new recruit in the steps of the Lord. I, too, was there because of love. For His love I had left my family and my people, following in His steps to bring His message to the great people of China. That night, in that sacristy little Mabel represented for me the whole of China.

Soon after the Baptism ceremony was over I gave Mabel first Communion, then opened the sacristy door; the altar boys rushed in wondering why I had sent them out. Mabel quietly and unobtrusively left the sacristy and melted into the crowded church. I thought that was the last I would see of her until my next religion class, but I was very wrong.

A Persistent Soul

In the darkness of the early morning hours of the day after that Christmas, at about 5:30, I was awakened by a voice calling me from the street. Unable to recognize the voice, only half awake, I opened my second-floor window and in the faint light of a street lamp I recognized the diminutive figure of Mabel.

"Mabel, anything wrong with you?" I asked with surprise in my voice for being awakened at that unearthly hour after the heavy work of Christmas Day.

"No, nothing wrong, Father," she shouted to me from the street, "but I would like to receive Communion before you open the church at 6:00 so nobody will see me."

"Very good," I said. I was happy to see a new convert so eager to receive the Eucharist and I did not mind the inconvenience.

The following morning at 5:30 Mabel was back again, and again the following day, and she kept coming every day at that hour for over a year and a half. As punctual as a clock, she was at the church door at 5:30 every day whether it rained or stormed, whether it was cold or hot. I gladly adjusted my morning schedule to suit her needs. When occasionally I went on short trips to visit my fellow missionaries on the China mainland, I had to arrange for a priest to replace me and make very sure that he was an early riser who would not let Mabel down.

It was not easy for her to come to receive Communion every day and she had to make a lot of sacrifices. She got up at 5:00 A.M., tiptoed out of the room she shared with her sisters, and slipped quietly out of the house through the back door. Then she walked for twenty minutes along Prince Edward Road to St. Teresa's Church. At 5:30 I opened the side door of the church, and a few minutes later gave her Communion. When at 6:00 I opened the church for the public, she had already disappeared on her way back home, where she could slip unobserved into the kitchen and do her morning chores.

In twenty months, she missed coming to the church only once. That day I wondered whether she was sick or whether her parents had discovered her morning escapade. But she showed up about 3:00 P.M. explaining to me that school tests had prevented her from coming in the morning, and asked for Communion.

"But, child," I said, "you know we cannot give Communion after 1:00 P.M."

"Father, I'm still fasting from midnight. Please make an exception. Give me Communion." And I did. I felt that the Lord authorized me to make an exception to a man-made rule.

When she graduated from the Canossian Convent, she finally told the secret to her sisters and they, too, eventually were baptized. Many years later her parents also joined the Church.

Today, forty-four years later, Mabel is a mature lady who has spent all her adult life in the service of the Church and I am still happy that good Bishop Valtorta authorized me to baptize her under those very unusual circumstances.

An Impromptu Baptism: Mary Fong

One morning in the spring of 1942, shortly after the Japanese occupied

Hong Kong, a Chinese school girl in her middle teens came to see me at the cathedral parish where I was then the pastor. As she entered my office she said, "Shan-fou, my name is Mary. Sister Mary Louise of the French Convent School has sent me to see you. I am a senior and I have studied religion in her class. Now I want to be baptized before leaving for China with my mother. Can you baptize me?"

"Certainly I can," I said, "but when are you leaving Hong Kong?"

"At noon today."

I looked at my wrist watch. It was already 9:00 A.M.

"But, Mary, how can we do it so soon? I have full confidence in Sister Mary Louise, and I'm sure you are well prepared, but is it right to baptize you under these circumstances? You are going to live in a non-Christian village where there is no church and no priest. You will not be able to attend Mass, or receive Holy Communion, or go to Confession. You will have no Catholic friends and you may even be compelled to marry a non-Christian or to participate in superstitious practices. I believe it would be more prudent to postpone your Baptism until you return to Hong Kong after the war."

"Oh, no, Father," she pleaded. "I want to receive Baptism now!" She said it with such determination that I was impressed. She looked very timid and shy, but her determination was unusual in a girl of that age. She continued, "You know, Father, the trip will last several days. We are to go through the war zone. There are soldiers, bandits, thieves every-where. It is a dangerous journey. I may die. No, no, I do not want to wait. I want to be baptized now before I leave."

A Difficult Decision

I admired her faith and determination, but I could not reconcile her desire with the rules of the Church regarding the baptism of teen-age girls in China. In those days, a Chinese girl living on the mainland was totally dependent on her parents with regard to marriage and religious worship. This is why the bishops of China ruled that teen-age girls should not be baptized unless the whole family had become Catholic or there were some guarantees that she would not be compelled to marry a non-Catholic. In the case of Mary the situation was even more serious because she was going to live in a non-Christian village, and conse-quently she would not be able to practice her religion at all.

I knew that under normal circumstances no missionary in his right mind would have baptized her. But were Mary's circumstances on that day anywhere near normal? Certainly not. Did I have sufficient reason to believe that she was in danger of death so that I could dispense with the ordinary requirements of Church law? I surely wanted to baptize her because she seemed so eager and determined, but at the same time I did not want to act in a foolhardy way.

"Sit down, Mary," I told her, "and wait here a few minutes." I went to another room, where I first phoned Sister Mary Louise, who gave me the very best recommendation of Mary.

"Yes, Father," she told me, "Mary Fong is quite ready for Baptism. She is really an exceptional girl. I know that she looks timid and shy, but she has an iron will. I am sure that she will resist any pressure to go against her religion. This is an exceptional case and this is why I sent her to you."

Strengthened by Sister's assurance, I went upstairs to discuss this matter with Bishop Valtorta. He listened to me, understood my hesitation and finally, with a pat on the shoulder, said, "Go ahead, Maestrini. Baptize her. Don't hesitate. She wants Baptism and she has a right to it. The Lord will look after her."

That was what I wanted to hear. Jumping down the stairs three steps at a time, I rushed into the office and told Mary the good news. She beamed with joy.

I gave her some quick advice about how to behave in her new environment, especially with regard to her non-Christian relatives, young people, superstitious village practices, and the like. Briefly I taught her about "spiritual Communion," how to read Sunday Mass in her missal and how to join in spirit in the celebration of Christian feasts. Finally, I asked her to promise that as far as possible she would write to me every month and give me a summary of her daily examination of conscience, so that I could give her some spiritual direction by letter. In turn I promised that I, too, would continue to keep in touch with her and help her in the new, difficult circumstances.

The last obstacle: We needed a godmother immediately. I asked my janitor's wife, who readily consented. Thus all difficulties were overcome and I proceeded to perform the Baptism.

It was 10:30 when we finished. She rushed away to join her mother on the boat leaving at noon for the China mainland. I thought that was the last I would see of Mary Fong.

Three months later I received her first letter. She wrote how, after a long and difficult journey and after escaping death narrowly at the hands of bandits and soldiers, she had finally settled in her native village with her widowed mother. She was attending a local high school and felt very lonely because there were no Catholics around and she did not want to get involved with non-Christian youths. She also confided that she had been beaten up by some relatives because she had refused to participate in the worshiping of village idols, but she had not given in. She included a copy of her daily examination of conscience. Month after month her letters continued to arrive faithfully, and I answered them punctually, giving her whatever spiritual advice I could.

By the end of 1944, her letters stopped coming and I worried whether something had happened to her.

A Happy Ending

A few weeks after the war ended in August 1945, Mary came to visit me at the cathedral. It was indeed a joyous reunion. She immediately asked for her First Communion and I was happy to give it to her. We also made arrangements for her Confirmation. As Hong Kong returned to normal, she came to work for me at the Catholic Center and finally received a scholarship to come to the States. Today she is a professor of Chinese art at the University of California.

9

The Power Of Love

A Dying Girl's Request

One day in the summer of 1938 an elderly Chinese lady came to see me at the mission house. As I did not know her, she introduced herself, saying rather shyly, "Sz Shan-fou, I am not a Catholic. Forgive me for bothering you, but I have an important message to give you."

"Don't hesitate, please. I will be glad to do whatever I can," I said, smiling in order to encourage her and make her feel at home with a foreigner.

She continued, "The daughter of a friend of mine is very sick with tuberculosis and she is not expected to live very long. Her Chinese name is Kwan-chi but she calls herself Teresa. She wants to join your religion, but she is too sick to come to see you. Could you be so very kind as to go and see her?"

Even though the request was rather unusual coming from a non-Catholic, I was all kindness and smilingly replied, "Of course, I will go."

"Very good, Sz Shan-fou, you are very kind. My friend has asked me to inform you that your visit has to be kept confidential. Her husband is very anti-Catholic. He does not like Christians and does not want his daughter to be converted to Christianity. He has told his wife that if he finds a minister in the house, he will kick him downstairs. The best time to see her is in the morning when Mr. Lo is at his office. Please, Shan-fou, be careful." After scribbling Teresa's address on a piece of paper, she left.

I made some enquiries about Mr. Lo and learned that he was a prominent lawyer working in a law firm in downtown Hong Kong.

Teresa was his daughter by wife number two (he had two wives) and lived in a middle-class tenement house on the west side of town. Mr. Lo, with wife number one, lived in an upper-class apartment in central Hong Kong. Teresa's mother had sent me that message because she was eager to please her dying daughter.

A couple of days after receiving the message I went to see Teresa. It was 11:00 A.M. and I was sure that Mr. Lo was at his office in downtown Hong Kong. Without too much difficulty I found the old tenement house in one of the Chinese sections of the city where no foreigners lived. The building, typical of the crowded houses of the less affluent Chinese, was teeming with women and children. They all stared at me with curiosity, wondering why a white man would enter their building. Feeling somewhat uncomfortable under the scrutiny of so many eyes, I climbed the rickety old stairs up to the second floor, praying that I was at the right address and that Mr. Lo would not be there!

I was relieved when Mrs. Lo opened the door, and, recognizing me immediately as a priest, welcomed me. Ignoring the purpose of my visit, she went through the usual exchange of compliments about my kindness and her unworthiness while we leisurely sipped a small cup of hot tea. In the meantime I was wondering where Teresa was. Then finally she led me to a bed at the opposite side of the room and I saw Teresa.

The sight of the girl impressed me deeply. She was lying on a Chinese-type bed of wooden boards with a ceramic brick as a pillow, in a corner of the living room near the balcony. There were no windows in the long and narrow living room. The balcony door was the only source of light and air. Teresa, in her middle teens, though emaciated by her long sickness, still looked beautiful with rich, flowing black hair and bright, intelligent eyes shining out of her pale face.

Speaking in the typical school English of Chinese students, she told me that before she became sick she had attended an English Protestant school in the colony. When the school mistress asked the students to choose an English first name, she had chosen Teresa just because she liked the sound of it. Only later had she heard of St. Teresa of Lisieux and of the Catholic religion. She was enthralled by the life of the young French Carmelite and wanted to become a Catholic like her. She had heard about me from a girl friend who attended school at the Canossian convent and this was why she had asked for me.

I examined her briefly and I was soon convinced that, even though she barely knew the very essentials of Christianity, she firmly believed in Christ and was eager to be baptized. However, since there was no danger of imminent death, she needed more instruction. I could not teach her personally because in the Hong Kong of those days it would have seemed improper for a young foreign clergyman to visit a Chinese girl frequently. So I promised Teresa that I would send a young Chinese lady to teach her catechism and to prepare her for Baptism.

That very day I asked Miss Ellen Chow to visit Teresa and to prepare her for Baptism. Ellen, a recent graduate of the Hong Kong University and herself a convert, was then president of the St. Joan of Arc Association for young Chinese Catholic women (of which I was the spiritual director) and well trained as a religion teacher of prospective converts. She gladly accepted and during the following weeks she kept me informed about Teresa's health and her progress in the study of religion.

Baptism On A Deathbed

One day, about three months later, Ellen phoned me: "Sz Shan-fou, I have just been to see Teresa. She really does not have much longer to live. She is well prepared for Baptism and Communion. Her mother would like you to go there tomorrow morning about eleven o'clock. I also will be there because she has asked me to be her godmother."

When I saw Teresa the following day she looked more emaciated than the first time I had seen her, but she was fully alert mentally and her dark, intelligent eyes were still burning brightly. She was overjoyed seeing me and repeatedly asked for Baptism.

While the disconsolate mother sat sobbing at the other end of the room, Teresa told me that she did not regret dying young. She was eagerly looking forward to meeting Jesus and the Virgin Mary, and, of course, her patron saint, Teresa of Lisieux. As I noticed that she was rapidly growing tired and beginning to talk with difficulty, I quickly baptized her and gave her Holy Communion. As she was praying, welcoming Jesus into her heart, she was radiant with happiness. That first Communion was for her a foretaste of Heaven. When later I left her with a final blessing, her eyes full of gratitude smiled back at me. I will never forget that beautiful smile of dying Teresa.

It is always painful to see a person dying, but it is especially so in the case of a young person and I could not help feeling sad as I walked back to the mission house, about twenty minutes away, wondering how long she would live.

Just as I entered the house I was called to the phone.

"Sz Shan-fou," Ellen said at the other end of the line, "Teresa has just died. It seems that she was just waiting for you to baptize her. She has passed away very peacefully, very calmly, smiling as if she were seeing some beautiful vision."

Sad but resigned, as I knew I had a new friend in Heaven, I thought that was the end of Teresa's case and went back to my room feeling very disappointed that there was nothing I could do to give Teresa a Catholic burial.

An Unexpected Request

Much to my surprise, the following morning, Ellen Chow phoned me again: "Sz Shan-fou, can you believe it? Mrs. Lo phoned to tell me that Teresa's father is very happy you baptized his daughter and would like very much to meet you tonight at the funeral home. Can you go?"

"Gee! This really is a miracle! How do you explain such a change of heart?"

"I don't know and I, too, am baffled, but Mrs. Lo was very insistent. She said that Mr. Lo is really eager to see you."

"Of course I will go. How could I turn him down? Phone her, please, and assure her that I will surely be at the funeral home tonight."

That very evening at 8:00, with some hesitation and apprehension, I gingerly tiptoed into the funeral home where Teresa was laid out. It was a Chinese, non-Christian funeral parlor and, as I had never visited one before, I wondered what I would find.

I pushed the door open and I was almost choked by the smoke and the acrid smell of burning incense sticks. Peering through the cloud of smoke, I saw a spacious, barely lit room with a lot of people milling around, talking excitedly, while a Buddhist monk chanted in a corner and the official "criers" kept lamenting loudly. Everything and everybody seemed strange to me. Looking around, and quite confused, I saw a closed Chinese coffin along a wall of the room and, pushing my way through the crowd, I went in that direction. Soon a short, stout Chinese gentleman, in his fifties, with a round, young-looking face, dressed in a long, silk Chinese robe, came toward me. Bowing obsequiously, and speaking with a slight British accent, he said suavely, "Reverend sir, I am the father of Kwan-chi." I remembered that was Teresa's Chinese name. "I know that you are a Catholic minister and that you have baptized my beloved daughter. I want to thank you from the bottom of my heart." I was perplexed. Was this the rabidly anti-Christian gentle-man who had threatened to kick me down the rickety stairs of his apartment? Before I could recover from my surprise, he added, "Reverend, you have done my family a great favor, but will you forgive me if I ask you for a still greater one?"

Thinking that he was going to ask me to give Teresa a Catholic burial, I replied in earnest, "Of course, Mr. Lo, I will be delighted to do whatever I can."

"You see, Reverend, I cannot understand one thing. I have been told by my wife that my daughter died a very happy death. When I arrived home, shortly after she had passed away, I was very impressed because Kwan-chi had a beautiful smile on her face. She looked as if she were sleeping and having a beautiful dream. In all my life I have never seen anyone looking so beautiful in death. I always thought that Kwan-chi, being only sixteen, would hate to die so young, but I was mistaken. I think that your religion made all the difference to her. If your religion has helped my daughter to die such a happy death, then there must be something in it that I do not know. I want to know more about it! Would you kindly consent to tell me more about your religion?"

"Of course, Mr. Lo. I will be delighted," I answered with unconcealed enthusiasm. "Just tell me when and where we can meet and I will be there. I will be happy to give you all the time you want."

He promised that he would phone me a few days later to set up an appointment. I said a short prayer in my heart for the repose of the soul of Teresa, and left the milling crowd with their burning joss sticks, the melancholic music and the high-pitched laments of the ritual criers. I felt sad that such a Christian girl as Teresa was going to have a pagan burial, but there was nothing I could do. I realized that because of the large family, which included several wives with many children, and because funeral traditions were deeply entrenched in Chinese culture, it would have been improper for me to insist on a Catholic funeral. So I left it at that and went home delighted that Mr. Lo was eager to learn more about Christianity. It seemed that Teresa's long months of suffering were already bearing fruit. A few days later I visited Teresa's tomb in the Chinese cemetery in Aberdeen and blessed it.

Confucianism And Christianity

On a Sunday afternoon, two weeks after Teresa's death, Mr. Lo and I met as dinner guests at the house of our mutual friend Mr. Seu Kon-chi, on Robinson Road. After an excellent and pleasant meal with the whole Seu family, as we leisurely sipped our tea, Mr. Lo turned to me and in a serious tone of voice asked, "Father Maestrini, could you tell me in a few words what the difference is between Confucianism and Christianity?"

For a moment I was perplexed by the unusual request but, recovering quickly and after a brief mental prayer to the Holy Spirit, I began to speak very slowly in order to gain time and coordinate my thoughts.

"Dear Mr. Lo, this is a rather tall order. Literally hundreds of books have been written about Christianity and Confucianism. To tell you the differences between the two in a few words is not an easy task. However, if you are satisfied with the bare essentials, I can put it this way: Confucianism is basically a moral code rather than a religion. The spirit worship practiced by many Confucianists is very much based on the concept of fear and of appeasing the spirits to avoid their revenge. Confucianism does not teach anything about the love of God and the love of men for God.

"Christianity, on the contrary, is entirely based on love. We look upon God as our Father. He creates each one of us out of love to share a life of happiness with Him for all eternity. Obviously, if God loves us, we must love Him in return. Our personal relationship with God is a relationship of love, very much like filial piety. Instead of being afraid of God and trying to propitiate Him, as many Chinese do while worshiping the spirits, we simply love Him as a father and He loves us as His children."

As I was speaking I noticed his small, bright eyes focusing on me and absorbing every word I was saying. When I finished he leaned back on his chair, closed his eyes for a moment, brought both his index fingers to his lips and very, very slowly said, "Do you mean to say, Reverend, that God loves me as His child and I can love Him as my father?"

"That is exactly what I said, Mr. Lo. This is the very essence of Christianity."

"I have never, never heard of such a thing before in all my life," he said, completely stunned.

Good Mr. Seu, himself a convert, had followed the conversation with great attention and was obviously very pleased to see Mr. Lo's interest in our religion. He commented, "Yes, my friend, what Father Maestrini has told you is the real truth about Christianity and this is why I have converted."

"Well, Reverend," Mr. Lo said with eagerness in his voice, "I really must know more about your religion. Will you teach me?"

"Of course, I will be delighted to do so," I exclaimed.

In my mind I could not help wondering about God's ways: this was the same man who only a few months before had threatened to physically throw me out of his apartment and now he was requesting religious instruction from me.

A Chinese Book About The Love Of God

We agreed that Sunday afternoon would be the best time for him to receive instructions. So, the following Sunday at 2:00 I knocked at the door of his beautiful apartment where he lived with Mrs. Lo number one in one of the best sections of town. I brought him a bundle of books in English and Chinese to read and talked to him at length about religion. I visited him again Sunday after Sunday and he listened, enraptured. He never seemed to grow tired of listening to me and reading the books I kept lending him. After a few lessons he was so impressed with Christianity that he told me:

"Father Maestrini, what I have learned so far and what I've read in the books you gave me is so beautiful and interesting that I want to share it with my fellow Chinese. I am sure that by far the bulk of the four hundred million people of China have never had the correct idea of what Christianity really is all about. I have to tell my people. I want to write a book in classic Chinese style and I will call it: *The True Message of Christianity: Love.*"

Needless to say, I was thrilled and heartily encouraged him to proceed with his plan.

For six months I went to his house regularly every Sunday afternoon to teach him religion and to answer his questions. Throughout the weeks he kept on working on his book. Finally one day he told me that his work was finished and that the Commercial Press (the largest publishing house in China) had already accepted it for publication.

It was released to Chinese bookstores at the beginning of 1940 as a booklet of about one hundred pages in paperback and also in a limited, deluxe edition bound in red Chinese silk. I was ecstatic. I sent copies to all Catholic institutions of higher learning in China and sent one copy to Generalissimo Chiang Kai-shek through my good friend Dr. John C. H. Wu.

Soon excellent reviews came pouring in. The President of the Catholic University of Beijing, American-born Fr. Rigney, SVD, defined it as "the best piece of Catholic literature written in Chinese classic style since the writings of Father Matteo Ricci in the 17th Century." Generalissimo Chiang Kai-shek, himself a practicing Christian, praised the book highly and designated it the official textbook for courses on Christianity in all the high schools and colleges in China.

For the first time in the history of the Church in China, Christianity had the opportunity of being presented to the masses of the young, idealistic students of that great nation. I thought then that the conversion of China was only a few years away!

What happened instead was that, shortly afterwards, the Japanese expanded their invasion of China and life was totally disrupted throughout the whole country. China was involved in a life-and-death struggle with Japan and all that was not essential was placed on the back burner, books included. Unfortunately, Mr. Lo's book was one of them.

When at the end of World War II peace seemed to return to China, the communist revolution began and that was the end of religious freedom in China. Today I cannot say if there is even one single copy of Mr. Lo's book to be found anywhere in China.

As for Mr. Lo, I know that he escaped from Hong Kong after the Japanese occupation of that city and went back to China. I never saw him again nor heard from him. I would certainly like to know if he was eventually baptized or not, but I am afraid this is a matter of mere curiosity. I know for certain that he had the baptism of desire and I am equally sure that Teresa arranged things up in Heaven.

About The Chinese Clergy

The love of God that transformed the lives of Mr. Lo and of his daughter Teresa was the same kind of love that motivated young Chinese men to enter the priesthood. Even though this book is not.the place for an essay on Chinese priests, still I cannot avoid reminiscing about at least some of the wonderful Chinese priests of the Hong Kong diocese.

I greatly admired the Chinese priests I met because they had to overcome serious difficulties in order to enter the priesthood. First of all it was not easy for a young Chinese man to embrace celibacy in a society that despised it.

Furthermore, even when Christianity was no longer persecuted in China, still for a young man entering the seminary it meant being estranged from his peers, becoming an oddity in society, almost a traitor to Chinese culture and tradition. While in Christian countries becoming a priest means climbing a step higher in society, on the contrary in a non-Christian society like that of the Chinese, a priest, and a celibate one to boot, was looked upon as a strange person.

Last, but not least, in those days for a Chinese young man to become a priest it meant many extra years of hard study in order to master Latin to the point of being able to read and speak it fluently and to use Latin textbooks all through the eight years of philosophy and theology. It meant becoming very much "latinized" in culture, thinking and behavior. Chinese seminarians were expected to become priests very much like the European missionaries who were their teachers.

But in spite of this hard training, the Holy Spirit produced a good, disciplined, dedicated Chinese clergy and many real heroes among them.[1]

The Hong Kong diocese established its own seminary almost from its very beginning and all the priests I will mention here were the products of that seminary run by the PIME missionaries.

Old Fr. Situ was the Chinese priest who impressed me most. When I arrived in Hong Kong he was almost seventy years old. Of small stature, even by Chinese standards, thin and wiry, sporting a small goatee, he resembled the picture of the Chinese god of longevity. His piety and total devotion to the cause of Christ were an inspiring example to all. He was the untiring assistant to the bishop during the long journeys to the mainland and the religious ceremonies of Baptisms and Confirmations. He spoke perfect Latin and was loved by all.

I worked with old Fr. Peter Lam (ordained in 1902) at both Rosary Church and St. Teresa's. He was a Chinese scholar who had built a high school and the first church in Tamshui, not far from Hong Kong. When I arrived in Hong Kong he was already advanced in years and he struck me as being a holy and zealous priest.

Fr. Francis Chan was one of the most delightful characters I have ever met. He spent the last years of his life as chaplain in the Home for the Aged conducted by the Little Sisters of the Poor and he was idolized by the old men and women of that institution. I can never forget an episode I witnessed. When the Apostolic Delegate to China, Archbishop Mario Zanin, passed through Hong Kong on his way to Beijing, he visited the Home for the Aged. Seeing all the old people gathered in the chapel, he felt that, as the pope's representative in China, he had to give the old people some message from the Holy Father. Not knowing a word of Chinese, but being a former Latin professor, he spoke for about ten minutes in classic Latin about a poem of the French poet Lamartine. Describing the morning rising sun as the symbol of God's love he compared it to Christian charity and spoke eloquently of the charitable works of the missionaries. When he finished, he turned to Fr. Chan and asked him to translate it. Fr. Chan stood up, grinned sheepishly with a broad smile on his toothless mouth, looked the people straight in the eyes and, in colloquial Chinese said: "Hi, friends. This bishop who has just spoken to you is coming from Rome, he says that the pope has sent him, that the pope loves you, blesses you and wants you all to be good Christians. God bless you!" Archbishop Zanin was kind of surprised by the short translation but said nothing. We who understood both him and Fr. Chan could hardly suppress a hearty laugh at the ability of the old man to get out of a difficult situation.

Fr. Luke Fong was my first assistant at St. Teresa's. Even though a young man he suffered from chronic poor health but he, too, was one hundred percent dedicated to working for souls.

Some of the Chinese priests I knew died heroic deaths. Fr. Francis Wong, a dear friend of mine, was brutally murdered by bandits as he worked alone in a remote district during the Japanese occupation. Several of the younger priests of my age were imprisoned by the communists and condemned to working in labor camps for years.

I have always had the highest regard for my fellow priests of the Hong Kong diocese. They were real great men, truly dedicated priests, and their memory a constant source of inspiration to me.

Notes

1. Seminaries in China were identical copies of European seminaries as far as discipline, curriculum of studies and seminary life were concerned. This was the official policy dictated by Rome and we followed it. There is no doubt that humanly speaking it was absurd to try to convert China by means of a Europeanized clergy, but Vatican II was still a long way off.

10

The St. Joan Of Arc
Catholic Young Women's Association

The Canossian Sisters In Hong Kong

The different orders of sisters working in Hong Kong played a very important role in evangelization. I collaborated heartily with all of them as they were great, dedicated women. However, living at the cathedral, very near the Canossian convent, I had, of course, the opportunity of working more closely with them.[1]

The first Canossian Sisters, founded in Italy by St. Mary Magdalen of Canossa in 1808, landed in Hong Kong in 1860. When I arrived, seventy years later, they had developed an impressive network of institutions in the colony, including several of the best and largest girls' schools, two hospitals, one orphanage, an asylum for abandoned babies, a hostel for girls, and a home for the blind. They were then, and still are, one of the major forces of the church in Hong Kong.

Their main English school on the Hong Kong side was Sacred Heart School, which had an enrollment of over five hundred girls, almost all Chinese. It was located at 26 Caine Road, only one short block from the cathedral mission house, and it was part of a very imposing, majestic complex of buildings that also included a Chinese school, the main convent of the Canossian Sisters, the novitiate, and a hostel for girls. Over 125 classes of girls passed through its portals before it was replaced a few years ago.

In 1985, on the occasion of the 125th anniversary of the foundation of the school, Mrs. M. W. Leung Bentley [2] wrote an article for the commemorative issue describing the school building, in which she commented: "It had a fine entrance gate and an open sweep of shallow stone steps leading to the front door and its hospitable portico. The high architectural standards and wide vision of the founders had built the school in such a way that everyone who worked there could breathe clean, fresh air and enjoy the peace and tranquility so essential to spiritual life."

Sacred Heart School was not only the oldest Catholic school in the colony but it was regarded as one of the very best. It always scored high in number of honors and students passing the university entrance examinations.

A small group of Canossian sisters, totally dedicated to teaching, trained their students in the spiritual values of life in addition to the pursuit of academic knowledge. Their work was eminently successful because they not only used efficient teaching techniques but also because the example of their dedicated lives had an all-important influence on the lives of the pupils.

Even though ninety percent of the students were non-Christian, all of them took courses in the Catholic religion and every year a number of them asked for Baptism.

The refrain of the school song composed by Mrs. Bentley well reflected the spirit of the school:

> Come let us form our spirit gay and strong
> For life is great, a gift of beauty rare,
> A wondrous way of winsome grace for us
> To make us joyous, virtuous, nobly fair.

The St. Joan Of Arc Association Is Born

In the fall of 1933, Mother Erminia, the school principal, invited me to lecture on religion to the high school upper classes. I was delighted with the opportunity to teach religion to non-Christians and, in spite of my still very imperfect knowledge of English, I plunged into this new work with all my youthful enthusiasm. At that time I was living in Kowloon, but I did not mind traveling all the way to the Canossian convent in Hong Kong several times a week and prepared my lessons with the utmost care.

It was thus that I entered that promising and fascinating school world, typical of the Hong Kong Catholic Schools of my days. It was a world all its own. The presence of a majority of non-Catholic students who came from different religions such as Confucianism, Buddhism and Hinduism pursuing their scholastic studies in a Christian atmosphere created a unique situation. Religion was not limited to the daily half-hour religion class, but permeated every particle of the atmosphere, physically and spiritually. The somber-looking brown habits crowned by black coifs worn by the sisters were intimidating enough to youngsters coming from non-Christian milieu. The abundance of holy pictures and crucifixes hanging in corridors and classrooms was a constant reminder of religion. However, it was not this vast amount of external religious symbols that influenced the students, but the great example of the totally dedicated lives of the sisters. Their strict life of chastity, protected and nurtured by the practices of a rigorous religious rule, was mysterious and incomprehensible to the minds of young students accustomed to very different sexual views of life. It commanded respect and admiration. This was the school world to which I dedicated a great deal of time during the first ten years of my life in Hong Kong.

One day toward the end of 1934, as I was talking with Mother Erminia, the school principal, and Mother Mary and Mother Angelica, Mother Erminia told me, "The problem here, Father Maestrini, is that we have not yet found the way to keep in touch with our girls after their graduation. At the end of their training here they are practically ready for Baptism, but after they leave this school and fall under the influence of the non-Christian environment of their families, they often marry non-Catholics and forget all about religion. We also lack contact with those girls who were baptized before leaving school. If their parents are not converted, they also return to a pagan environment and gradually drift away from the church. What can we do about this?"

The problem was not new to me and I had already thought about it a great deal. So I had a ready-made solution.

"Well, Mother," I replied, "what we need is an alumnae association. It should be patterned after the Catholic Action groups and should comprise alumnae and other young women, Catholics and non-Catholics, who are serious about doing something worthwhile with their lives. Do you agree?"

A few months later the St. Joan of Arc Catholic Young Women's Association was born with the help of Mother Erminia first and of Mother Angelica later.

It began with only seven members but it soon grew to about twenty and later to over thirty. Most of the members were alumnae of the

Canossian school and were now attending the Hong Kong University. Others were teachers and some were still students in the school. Many lived near the school, some lived far away in Kowloon and in other suburbs, but all came to the weekly meetings regularly.

During the following seven years I dedicated a great deal of time and energy to the association. Even when I was at St. Teresa's Church on the Kowloon side, I never failed to direct the association and to attend the weekly meetings at the Canossian school on the Hong Kong side. It was indeed one of my favorite and most fruitful activities.

I believe that one of the best descriptions of the spirit and work of the St. Joan of Arc Association was written by Mrs. M. W. Leung Bentley in her article for the 125th anniversary commemorative issue.

"I came into the [Canossian] school at the age of seven knowing not a word of English but I had no difficulty in coping with the work of Class 10 which I found both interesting and enjoyable. In the following years I made my way methodically up the School to Class 1 where I gained admission to Hong Kong University. Thus I spent ten uninterrupted years at the school, obtaining a solid understanding of the three R's upon which my subsequent intellectual life was built.

"My connection with the school was not severed by my departure in 1936, for in 1934 Mother Erminia had the help and advice of Father Nicholas Maestrini, PIME, in starting the first Hong Kong branch of the Catholic lay apostolate called St. Joan of Arc's Catholic Young Women's Association. Apart from Nellie and Bonnie Seu (who came from the Holy Spirit School conducted by the Maryknoll Sisters), all its members were either present or past pupils of the Sacred Heart School. The aim of the Association was to train lay Catholics to take part in the apostolic mission of the church: a new movement which was in its infancy.[3]

"Mother Erminia and Father Maestrini were not only far ahead of their time, but they set in motion something that had unforeseen consequences. For the first time girls were welcome to stay on school premises on Wednesday afternoons, the traditional half school day. Girls of different ages were able to meet during those Wednesday afternoons and develop friendly relations among themselves as well as with the nuns who had traditionally held their pupils at arm's length in and out of the classroom. A feeling of comradeship, then of friendship and, most of all, a feeling of belonging to the school, to the church and to each other arose unbidden.

"With weekly meetings on Wednesday afternoons devoted to the study of Catholic doctrine and the intricacies of the spiritual life under Father Maestrini and Mother Angelica (who had succeeded Mother Erminia), we became a close-knit group inspired by the same religious and social welfare ideas that gave meaning and purpose to our school, university, or working lives.

"We ran Sunday schools, evening schools for poor children, monthly retreats, as well as annual week-long enclosed retreats, and taught catechism classes whenever requested. We organized visits to hospitals and orphanages, we held picnics, debates and parties, and we even published the first Catholic girls' magazine, *The Rivulet,* which was placed in general circulation in Hong Kong and was self-sustaining from the start.

"It was a great time to be alive, a time of plain living and high thinking, a time when we felt that all things are possible with God. We thought that we had the chance to change the face of Catholic Hong Kong. Our joint faith and hope and strength engendered a new spirit that spread all over the school so that during the years between 1934 and 1941 Sacred Heart School achieved a reputation, a radiance and a vitality that somehow reflected the spiritual endeavors and discipline so carefully and systematically nurtured by Father Maestrini in St. Joan of Arc's association.

"Our motto was: 'Prayer—Action—Sacrifice' and we believed we really had something worthwhile to live for.

"The Japanese war in December 1941 put an end to it all."

The Motto Of The Association

The words "Prayer—Action—Sacrifice" were not empty words but rather the basic principle that inspired and guided the day-to-day life of the members in all their activities at work, in the classroom or in their family lives.

Prayer: The members were trained to make a daily meditation of at least fifteen minutes, using the Bible or some other spiritual book. At each weekly meeting, two or three members were asked to stand up and give the group a resume of their mental prayers. The exercises of the presence of God, of spiritual reading, of the daily examination of conscience, and of the pursuit of Christian virtues, as taught by St. Ignatius Loyola, were practiced regularly by the members. This high standard of spirituality was not common among young converts, and in order to maintain it the first half-hour of our weekly meetings was dedicated exclusively to developing the spiritual life of the members.

Action: As Mrs. Bentley mentioned in her article, the St. Joan of Arc Association conducted a variety of social and charitable activities. All of them had one aim in common: to bring souls to God through the spiritual growth of the members.

Ms. Margaret Yu[4] recently wrote to me from Vancouver, BC, where she is currently teaching. In answer to my request about what she remembered of the St. Joan of Arc association, she stated, "My sister Josephine and I attended St. Joan of Arc weekly meetings all through the four years of University. As we were not yet baptized because we had to wait for our parents' consent, we did not participate in those activities which required a Catholic presence. But I took an active part in discussions on how to make our work for the church more effective. I read a lot of books on Catholicism, especially lives of saints, no doubt having been stimulated by your weekly sermons to us.

"One day you asked me to read a book on the life of a leader of Catholic Action in Italy, Pier Giorgio Frassati, who died of polio at 29. He was a good mountaineer and the son of an Italian ambassador. He led a most exemplary life which was a great inspiration to all, young and old. You asked me to summarize the book into a pamphlet which you later distributed through the pamphlets racks in all the churches.

"You also handed me some stories of remarkable Catholics in China, written in Chinese, and asked me to translate them into English for publication in *The Rivulet*."

Sacrifice: "Ah-yee, what are you doing writing on your knees? Are you going crazy or what?" asked Ah-yee's mother, an elderly Chinese lady walking gingerly on her small, bound feet as she noticed her daughter kneeling on the floor and using a small tea table as a writing desk.

"No, Mother," Ah-yee answered very calmly, "I am writing a letter and I like kneeling on the floor." The good mother shrugged her shoulders in a sense of frustration and left Ah-yee alone to do what she wanted.

Ah-yee had actually told a small white lie because she did not really like writing letters on her knees. A member of the St. Joan of Arc Association, she had learned that the work for the Lord must always be accompanied by personal sacrifices. Now, as she was writing a letter to friends about spiritual matters, she thought that she would offer to the Lord the sacrifice of writing while on her knees.

Was that "childish" piety? I would rather call it "child-like" piety, the type of piety and mortification that countless saints practiced throughout two thousand years of Christian history, from the hermits of the first centuries to St. Teresa of the Child Jesus in her nineteenth-century convent in Lisieux, France.

Ah-yee was not the only member of the St. Joan of Arc practicing voluntary mortification. They all did it in earnest because they took their motto seriously and regarded personal sacrifice as an integral part of their work for the Lord. Those girls were not novices in a convent. They were recent converts, they were teachers, university students and business women, and some of them belonged to rich families. But they all were seeking something deeper in life than a superficial and materialistic existence, and they found it in the spirituality offered by the St. Joan of Arc Association.[5]

Fifty Years Later

Now, fifty years later, as I am writing this short account of the St. Joan of Arc Association, I cannot refrain from quoting a letter from Mrs. Bentley to me, dated September 1, 1984, commenting on the demise of the association caused by the Japanese war. She wrote:

"Now that we all have time to sit back and think, we are more likely to again need the impetus you once gave us to dedicate what is left of our lives to something more important and elevating than getting on and making money and establishing social status, which seems to be the common aspiration. Nowadays, it isn't at all easy to differentiate between a Christian and a worldling for they both seem to vie with everybody else for the same worldly advantages and selfish gratifications. In fact I have heard priests and nuns extolling the precept of 'Do your own thing!'"

Through the years I have maintained contact by mail with most of the former members of the St. Joan of Arc Association. They are now in their late fifties, but in their letters they still thank Mother Angelica and me for the "impetus" (as Mrs. Bentley called it) that we gave them during their teen years. Of course, during the fifty-odd years from the days of our meetings, not all have developed alike, but all have maintained a strong loyalty to Christ and the church, a life rich in good deeds and a real dedication to Christian ideals.

Today they are scattered all over the world, in the USA and Canada, in Hong Kong and Europe. Most of them have subsequently married and now have children and grandchildren. Several have pursued further studies and have obtained additional academic degrees. Others have continued to serve God and the church through more humble careers such as teaching, editing, and homemaking.[6] One, Rose Yeung Kwok-woon, witnessed to Christ in communist prisons and labor camps for some fifty years.

Twenty-five Years In Communist Prisons And Labor Camps

One day early in 1950, when the communists had already taken over China, Rose Yeung, a member of the St. Joan of Arc Association, came to see me.

"Father Maestrini," she said as if she were talking about some trivial matter, "I want your permission to leave Hong Kong and to go to Guangzhou."

"To do what, Rose?" I asked in utter bewilderment. In those days millions of Chinese were trying to find refuge in Hong Kong and I could not imagine why any Hong Kong Chinese would want to go to China.

"To teach religion and to help the people because the priests are being arrested and sent to prison and the Catholics have nobody to teach them religion."

"But do you realize, Rose, that doing this in Guangzhou now, under the communists, will surely land you in jail before too long?"

"That's O.K. with me, Father. Even in prison I can teach catechism and help others."

I could hardly believe my ears.

In order to fully appreciate what she was proposing to do, I must first give some explanation of the situation.

Miss Rose Yeung was a former student of the Canossian school and a very active member of the St. Joan of Arc Association. I had baptized her several years before. Shorter than the average girl of her age, and sickly, she appeared very frail and diminutive, but her appearance concealed a strong spirit and an iron will.

A teacher by profession, she had spent all her free time helping out in the cathedral parish in Hong Kong, teaching catechism to new converts, helping anyone who needed help. In view of her remarkable dedication to working for the church, I had obtained a scholarship for her at the Grailville College in Loveland, Ohio, which specialized in training girls for the lay apostolate. On her return to Hong Kong in 1948 she had resumed her apostolic activities and kept coming to me for spiritual direction. This explains why she was asking for my "permission."

After the communists completed the conquest of China in 1949, they soon began consolidating their gains. They expelled all foreign missionaries, accusing them of being American spies, and imprisoned most of the Chinese bishops and priests who refused to join the communist-controlled "Patriotic" church. Hundreds of thousands of lay Catholics loyal to the church and to the pope were also arrested. Thousands of them were executed. Other thousands were sent to prisons and concentration camps for a period of reeducation, a.k.a. brain-washing.

This policy was being implemented in south China at the beginning of 1950, and it was then that Rose Yeung decided to go to Guangzhou, the largest city of south China, where the old and flourishing Catholic community was being deprived of all of its priests.

After trying in vain to persuade her not to go, I finally gave her my blessing and she went.

She first worked in a city parish with the Maryknoll Fathers, then, when they were expelled, continued to work with the remaining Chinese priests. By late 1955 she was very well known by the surviving Catholics of that community as a person totally dedicated to working for the church. This was her undoing.

What follows is a summary of the report she wrote twenty-five years later, in 1980, when she was finally allowed to return to Hong Kong.

"I was first imprisoned in December 1955 and held in prison in order to be 'educated.' I had to prove that I understood and accepted Communist ideology. The days were spent in reading, studying and memorizing the works of Mao Tse-tung, of Marx and Lenin, and writing one's reflections on their writings.

"Interrogation sessions were a daily feature of our prison life. Attending these sessions was a real torment and harassment because the interrogators wanted me to give them the names of the people I had helped. One day, as I could not stand this torture any longer, I shouted at the judge that he could do what he liked about ending my life, he could have me shot or executed, I didn't care, but I could not stand the endless questioning any more. The judge was completely taken aback by my outburst. A few days later, when I was again called for interrogation, I was given a different judge.

"I was then confronted with the written confession of a Catholic who accused me of having received money from the former pastor of the cathedral parish, a French missionary, who had been expelled and was then residing in Hong Kong. Of course, the money had been sent to me for distribution to the poor and I had duly distributed it. Receiving money from foreigners, even for charitable distribution, was a crime in their eyes and I was sentenced to a period of 'political education' so that I could eventually be able to see and acknowledge my crimes.

"In March 1957 I was released but placed under constant surveillance. Party cadres often asked me to attend their meetings at which they put pressure on Catholics to accuse their bishop. I always refused to go and this led to my second arrest.

"Late in the evening of February 10, 1958, the police came to arrest me. I was bluntly told to take my luggage, which I always kept ready for such an eventuality, and follow them downstairs. A black limousine took me back to the prison where I had been before.

"I was accused of unlawful parish activities, teaching catechism and helping the poor, and I was detained three months without interrogation. Finally, after a brief questioning, I was detained for three more months and then transferred to a forced labor camp where I met several sisters and lay Catholics. Sister Yeurne was very kind to me and took care of my failing health. When she was released I gave her one of my favorite possessions: one of the two rosaries I had brought with me.

"Because of the delicate state of my health, I was assigned to work in the factory producing 'fuel bricks,' a mixture of coal, mud, and water. Mixing the coal and mud with bare hands would cut the palms of my hands and I would work with only one hand each day, alternating hands to get some relief from the pain.

"In the spring of 1959, I was transferred to another camp in Siu Kwan to do agricultural work, then I passed to a department manufacturing quilts, and later to another department mixing cement. Here a lady officer became very hostile to me because I often received food parcels from my sister in Hong Kong. She took my rosary away from me and also a little golden cross and bracelet. All these items were returned to me later in 1966 when I completed my sentence and was classified as a 'Sun Sung' (a newly born) as a result of their reeducation program of work and study.

"In 1962 I was transferred to the Tea Mountain labor camp. Here I began to suffer from heart trouble and fainting spells. A Catholic girl I had met there kept reporting my health situation to the camp officers, and finally I was transferred to another camp for sickly people. In that camp I was sent to the hospital and I was given nursing duties. This pleased me as I had many opportunities to do spiritual as well as corporal works of mercy. I even gave conditional Baptism to two dying persons. Thank God I was not discovered.

"In 1963 I was sent back to the Tea Mountain labor camp. There I met a Sister who was suffering from tuberculosis. We were in separate rooms and at night I could hear her groaning and suffering. Sometimes I was able to sneak some food to her. Here among my fellow prisoners I discovered some Chinese intellectuals who had been 'sent down' to the countryside to 'learn' from the peasant class.

"When I finished serving my sentence in 1966, I was not set free. I continued to be moved from one camp to another, from one community to another, at the will and caprice of the authorities. I was sent back to do agricultural work and I got sick again. One day I collapsed in a field with an agonizing pain. After being helped back to the dormitory, I fainted. The doctor diagnosed hemorrhage of the stomach and prescribed complete rest. By that time I was eligible to go home and I made many requests to this effect, but all in vain. In 1972 I was assigned to live in a suburb of Canton with two Catholic girls, former prison companions. I was given employment in an agricultural unit.

"Finally, in 1979, exactly 24 years after my first imprisonment, I was rehabilitated and given partial freedom. One day, a certain Mr. Lai from the Religious Affairs Department (the Party controlled bureau in charge of religious affairs) called on me for a talk. He informed me that the cathedral church was now open again and was officiated by Communist priests. He wondered why I did not ask to go there as I had been so active in parish affairs. I refused to go because I did not want to be involved with the Patriotic church.

"I then applied for an exit permit to go to Hong Kong for medical reasons and, at long last, the permit arrived early in 1980."

Back home in Hong Kong after thirty years, Rose was received with open arms by her sister Cecilia, who had been a real angel to her through all the years of her life in communist China. Here she was able to rebuild her broken health, but she has never been her old self again.

In 1982 Cecilia paid for Rose's trip to the USA to see some of her old friends who had moved to the States and to visit Grailville again. She also came to Florida to see me. It was indeed a happy reunion.

Notes

1. The story of the arrival of the first Canossian sisters in Hong Kong is worth telling. On the morning of April 12, 1860, a group of six young sisters of the Canossian Daughters of Charity (popularly known as Canossian sisters) and Fr. Joseph Burghignoli, PIME, arrived in Hong Kong after an exhausting forty-two-day journey by land and sea from

Italy. Much to their surprise, they found no one to meet them at the Hong Kong pier. Speaking only Italian and a little French, they had serious difficulties getting directions to the Catholic mission house half-way up the hill overlooking the harbor.

The mission superior, Msgr. Luigi Ambrosi, and the other PIME fathers were expecting the sisters to arrive late in the fall of that year. Consequently, they were completely taken by surprise seeing the sisters at the door of their house. For several years they had begged bishops and cardinals in Italy to find a religious society of nuns to open the first Catholic girls' school in the new British colony. Most of the religious societies declined the request either because they thought that Hong Kong was too far away or because they believed that the new colony would not amount to anything.

Finally the Canossian Sisters had agreed to send a group of six sisters, but the letter informing Msgr. Ambrosi of the date of the sisters' arrival never reached Hong Kong. This is why when the sisters showed up at the mission house no preparations had been made to accommodate them. There was not even a house ready for them. However, as the priests were very practical men, the first thing they did that day was to prepare a good Italian lunch for the famished sisters.

I summarize here a page from a book by Canossian Sister Lina Riva *(The Governor's Daughter Takes The Veil*, published in 1980 by Canossian Missions Historic Archives, 26 Caine Road, Hong Kong) describing the first day and night of those pioneer sisters in Hong Kong.

While the sisters were enjoying lunch, their first meal on solid ground, one of the fathers went scouring all over the city of Victoria searching for a suitable house for them. By evening they found one not far from the mission house on Caine Road and rented it. It was totally unfurnished.

Hurriedly, the good fathers collected some essential pieces of furniture here and there: four dilapidated beds for six sisters—one had only three good legs, another had loose joints and would collapse at the slightest touch; a couple of very hard mattresses and two or three rickety chairs. There were no pillows and each sister used her own shoes wrapped in her petticoat as a pillow.

In spite of such disastrous beginnings, three weeks later, on May 1, 1860, the sisters opened the first Catholic school for girls in Hong Kong with an enrollment of thirty-two students. The thirty-two students who enrolled that day were English and Portuguese. No Chinese girl applied because in those days Chinese parents refused to have their daughters trained by foreigners, as Mother Riva wrote in her book.

2. Mrs. Bentley's full name is: Man Wah Margaret (Dolly) Bentley, nee Leung. She was born of a large, well-to-do Chinese family in Hong Kong, attended the Canossian school, and later graduated from Hong Kong University. She married a British gentleman, Arthur H. Bentley, and moved to Walton-on-Thames, Surrey, England. She had two children, and after they grew up she taught philosophy, logic, and career guidance in various schools. After a gap of thirty years, she went back to the university and obtained a Ph.D. in philosophy.

3. Here Mrs. Bentley referred to the Catholic Action movement promoted in those days by Pope Pius XI. Catholic Action encouraged Catholics to fully participate in the work of the church.

4. Her full name is Yu Man Sang and she was graduated from Hong Kong University. She is now a professor of English in Vancouver, BC, Canada.

5. I purposely use this old terminology because it better reflects our thinking of those days. Today we would talk of "Christian presence," of the "incarnation of Christ in the local culture," and the like. It seems to me that this new terminology fails to express the real content of the Gospel message, which teaches that the prayers and sacrifices of the worker are indispensable for achieving any truly spiritual success.

6. One of the visible effects of the spirit and the work of the members of the St. Joan of Arc Association after it ceased to exist was the establishment of the St. Joan of Arc School in postwar days. As this school was organized early in 1951, after my departure from Hong Kong, it is not, strictly speaking, an integral part of this book. However, I cannot help writing a brief summary of this activity as a tribute to the brave girls who, on their own, carried on for over twenty-five years the principles of Christian service Mother Angelica and I had instilled in them.

Miss Mary Cheung was an alumna of the Canossian school. She had already graduated when the St. Joan of Arc association was founded. Because she spent a great deal of time abroad, she did not join the association. She followed a banking career both in Hong Kong and in the USA, where she became a bank vice-president. In 1988 she died in a car accident in Scarsdale, NY.

In an article published in the twenty-fifth anniversary book of the St. Joan of Arc School, Mary Cheung summarized the story of the St. Joan of Arc School in these words:

"The outbreak of World War II in 1941 dispersed the members of St. Joan of Arc Association. Those who returned to Hong Kong after the war came together again, but the St. Joan of Arc Association as such was not revived.

"The war years had caused a gap in the teaching of English in the colony because of the Japanese occupation. Thus, immediately after the war there was a great need for night schools for the teaching of English to those who migrated to Hong Kong in search of a better life. Obviously, to be able to speak English was a great asset in Hong Kong as it facilitated obtaining better jobs. The enterprising spirits of Miss Nellie Seu and Miss Ellen Chau (both former presidents of the St. Joan of Arc Association), Lily Lo, Winnie Yu, Bessy Wong and others of the group saw the possibility of catering to this need, and so the St. Joan of Arc English night school was started on borrowed premises in Shaukiwan.

"The school thrived under the able direction of Miss Nellie Seu as Headmistress of a staff of dedicated teachers, several of whom were past members of the St. Joan of Arc Association. On this occasion I particularly want to commend the hard work and sacrifice of these members who, after a hard day's work in their various professions, would travel from Central Hong Kong to Shaukiwan (a distance of over 15 miles) by means of crowded street cars to conduct the night school.

"The school was a success. Later, when a seven-story building capable of accommodating over a thousand students became available for rental, the St. Joan of Arc Association took on the added responsibility of opening a second night school for boys, again under the St. Joan of Arc's name.

"In 1965 I left Hong Kong to live permanently in the USA. When I visited Hong Kong again in 1977 and 1979, I was happy and proud to learn of the achievements of the Sacred Heart School. The small seed of Catholic Action which was cast into the hearts and minds of a small group of students some 50 years before had germinated and grown to maturity to bear a rich harvest.

"To conclude the story I have to add that in 1970 the School was turned over to the Diocese of Hong Kong and was placed under the supervision of Father Joseph Carra, PIME. It still continues today under a new generation of teachers, but the spirit and the school song of the old St. Joan of Arc School remain unchanged."

11

The Beginning Of A Publishing House

The Written Word In China

A great respect for the written word was a characteristic of the Chinese people. Perhaps no other nation in the world had such reverence for the written word as old China.

Chinese characters do not represent a sound as do the letters of our alphabet. They express an idea and are called "ideograms." Some of them are among the earliest written "words" in the world and go back thousands of years. Through the centuries these ideograms have become very complex to write and difficult to memorize. This is why until recently, when the communists introduced a simplified version, only a minority of the Chinese people were able to read and write.

When I arrived in China in 1931, out of a population of four hundred million only forty percent were able to read and write fluently. There were about forty thousand ideograms (or characters) in the Chinese dictionary and they had to be memorized in order to read and write. Many of them gave no indication whatever as to their sound and only an iron memory could retain them. Also, many had twenty or twenty-five strokes and each stroke had to be written in a certain way and in a certain order. This is why reading and writing in China were so very difficult and why those who were able to do so had privileged positions in Chinese society. Learned people were respected more than the rich. It was the reverence in which writers were held that gave China its great writers and poets and one of the richest and most varied literatures in the world.

Lack Of Catholic Books

"Father Granelli, if a Catholic or a non-Catholic Chinese is interested in the Church and wants to read a book on our religion, where can he find one?" I asked my pastor one day at St. Teresa's in Kowloon.

"Nowhere, my dear fellow, or, to be exact, almost nowhere. You see, Maestrini, in China there are no Catholic bookstores because there are practically no Catholic books to sell! Only a few religious orders print some Catholic books, but you have to write to them individually to order one."

I was astonished. Why, in a nation with such reverence for the written word, were there so few books on Catholicism? Little by little, gathering information here and there, I was able to piece the puzzle together. It was a sad picture. There were no Catholic bookstores because there were not enough Catholics to buy books, and there were not enough Catholics because there were no books to make Christianity known. Chinese publishing houses refused to publish Catholic books because there was no market for them and therefore only a few of the major religious orders published books, foremost among them the Jesuits, the Vincentians, the Fathers of the Divine Word (SVD) and the Franciscans.

Furthermore, most of the few books available were written in old, classic Chinese style and only people with a higher education could understand them. They were beyond the understanding of the average Chinese Catholic. Most of these books were written by Chinese religious and were intended for religious. We had no translation of the Old Testament and only one version of the New Testament.

There were a few catechism books, prayer books, some lives of saints and other pious readings. We sorely lacked good literature explaining Christianity to non-Catholics in modern contemporary style for the general public.

Catholic magazines were very few and had extremely limited circulation. *The Kung Kao Po* (*The Catholic Messenger*), founded by Fr. A. Granelli, PIME, a few years before, had a circulation of a few thousand copies.

The situation had to be improved and I decided to do something about it.

The Catholic Truth Society (CTS) Of Hong Kong

When and how was I to begin? I had been in Hong Kong only a couple of years and my primary duties were those of an assistant at St. Teresa's parish. To tackle the problem of the Catholic press in China seemed preposterous, to say the least. However, I decided to make a humble start by distributing Catholic literature in English through pamphlet racks in the churches. There was no Catholic bookstore in Hong Kong and people had no chance to read any Catholic literature. My aim was to begin reaching the numerous English-speaking Chinese.

I needed funds to begin. Through the grapevine I had heard that a few years earlier a Catholic American lady, passing through Hong Kong, had noticed that there were no pamphlet racks in the churches. With genuine American generosity and practicality, she had given one hundred US dollars (about five hundred dollars Hong Kong currency) to Fr. George Byrne, SJ, as seed money for the promotion and distribution of Catholic literature in the Diocese of Hong Kong. Nobody had done anything about it, and the money was still in the hands of Fr. George Byrne, the local superior of the Irish Jesuit community and my father confessor.

I prepared my plans, presented them to Bishop Valtorta, and got his blessing and permission to withdraw the money from Fr. Byrne.

My first step was to get a Chinese carpenter to make the pamphlet racks. What a job! He had no idea of what I wanted and I, with my imperfect knowledge of Chinese, could hardly explain what I had in mind. Finally, after months of waiting, I got my pamphlet racks, self-standing, each with a built-in good, strong money box.

With the collaboration of the pastors, I placed the racks in the vestibules of all the parishes in Hong Kong and Kowloon, six of them in those days. After paying for the pamphlet racks, there was still a balance and I used it to order a supply of pamphlets from the Catholic Truth Society of England, a venerable, long-established society totally dedicated to the spreading of the Faith through Catholic literature. With the pastors' permission I appointed two or three Chinese girls in every parish to take care of the pamphlet racks, to collect the money, to change books, to clean the racks, to keep them orderly.

The initiative was very well received by both English-speaking Chinese and Portuguese Catholics. The people were starved for something Catholic to read and bought the pamphlets eagerly. In spite of the fact that several of the money boxes were broken into periodically, the CTS made a little profit, which was used to expand the work.

My ultimate goal, however, was to reach the non-Christian Chinese masses of the China mainland and to bring them the message of the Gospel through books and pamphlets. For this purpose a publishing company was needed and I decided to establish one along the model of the Catholic Truth Society of England. I asked Fr. Ryan to accept the office of president.

Fr. Thomas F. Ryan was the best-known Irish Jesuit working in Hong Kong. A true English scholar, with several books already published, he taught English at the Jesuit-run Wah Yan College for boys. He also was the editor of *English Review*, published by the Hong Kong Jesuits, and was very prominent in civic affairs. I greatly admired him because of his scientific approach to problems. He would analyze any problem with the typical, unemotional approach of the Anglo-Saxon and then suggest solutions. His Jesuit training had made him a learned and effective leader.

"Father Maestrini, have you even the remotest idea of what it takes to organize a publishing company?" Fr. Ryan asked me when I requested that he accept the presidency of the new publishing company.

"No," I candidly answered. "And this is why I've come to ask your help."

"And what about capital?" Fr. Ryan continued.

"Divine Providence," I answered. "We will begin in a very small way and, with God's help, we will grow as we go along."

"What about the know-how needed to run a publishing company?"

"I will learn," I said confidently, "as others have learned."

"Do you have the time you need for such a task? Aren't your parish duties heavy enough already to take up all your time?"

"Well, yes, but I can cut my sleeping hours, work harder and faster, and take care of the CTS without neglecting my parish duties."

"Well," he said in the end, "you are a very enthusiastic and hard-working young man, Father Maestrini, and I will go along with you. You can count on my help. But all I can do is attend a few meetings because you know that I am fully occupied with my teaching job and my writing duties."

So the Catholic Truth Society of Hong Kong (CTS) was born "on a wing and a prayer." Our first step was to organize a board of directors, and we invited several lawyers, doctors, bankers, and business people from the Chinese, English, and Portuguese communities to join us. I was appointed executive secretary, and so I got my first job in fundraising.

Why China Lacked Catholic Books

The fact that at the beginning of the thirties China was still without an adequate supply of Catholic books was due to circumstances not the fault of the many splendid missionaries who had worked there for over three centuries.

Real missionary work began in China only after the year 1900, when the European powers compelled the country to open its doors to all foreigners. Between the time Fr. Matteo Ricci, SJ, (1552-1610) founded the first modern mission in China and 1900, missionaries were not allowed to enter China officially. Only by defying Imperial edicts did a trickle of foreign missionaries manage to enter the forbidden land. Dodging spies and police, living in hidden places, they still succeeded in establishing the Church secretly in almost every province of the immense kingdom.

Under these circumstances it was obviously impossible to organize a vigorous Catholic press. That there had been tens of thousands of conversions was a miracle.

After 1900 foreign missionaries resumed going to China, but World War I (1914-18) was another setback for the missions because neither European nor American missionaries could be spared for the foreign missions. The real contemporary era of the Chinese missions began in earnest during the early twenties. The first national meeting of all the Catholic bishops in China was only held in 1924.

This is why in the early thirties the market for Catholic books was very limited and, consequently, the Catholic press could not be self-supporting. The whole effort had to be subsidized, but bishops and missionaries preferred spending their meager resources on feeding and sheltering the sick and the needy rather than buying books.

An Illiterate Publisher

After organizing the CTS my first step was to make whatever Chinese Catholic pamphlets existed available to our people in Hong Kong by selling them through our pamphlet racks. After months of corresponding with the few mission presses and perusing their skimpy catalogs, I discovered that there were very few pamphlets written in contemporary Chinese and suitable for general circulation. Obviously the Church in China needed an input of fresh contemporary Catholic literature.

Where could I get funds to subsidize the writing, printing and circula-tion of Catholic books? Where could I find writers and translators? Was there really a market for this type of publication? Would I have the time for this type of work and, most of all, could I become a publisher of

Chinese literature even though I was not yet able to read Chinese fluently? One thing was certain: the need of good Catholic books. Trusting in the Lord, I decided to try.

The question of time was solved by Divine Providence. As the Church in Hong Kong was growing, Bishop Valtorta decided that he needed a secretary. He selected me, not because of any particular secretarial ability on my part but simply because I was one of the few missionaries who was able to type with as many as three fingers! Moreover, Fr. Granelli had returned to Hong Kong after an absence of two years in Italy and his health had improved enough to enable him to take over the parish again. So, in the spring of 1937, the bishop asked me to give up parish ministry and to move to the cathedral to work as his secretary.

He was a very understanding boss and realized that just typing letters was not my cup of tea. He left me plenty of time to dedicate myself to the CTS and to continue my other activities, such as teaching religion in Catholic schools, instructing converts and helping out in parishes.

With the approval of the CTS board of directors, I began to compile a general catalog of all the Catholic books available in Chinese. I began my research work in earnest, corresponded with every Catholic and non-Catholic publisher I could find in China, and in a few months accumulated quite a few catalogs, pamphlet lists, advertising folders, and printed matter from every corner of China. Some catalogs were in French, others in Latin, a few in Chinese, none in English.

This is not difficult to explain: these catalogs were not meant for the general Chinese public, but for the foreign missionaries, who were mostly French, Spanish, Italian and Polish. There were then only a few dozen English-speaking missionaries, mostly Maryknollers, some Columbans from Ireland, and a sprinkling of Canadians.

In all the catalogs from lay publishers, I could not find a single Catholic book. Only the Commercial Press offered a translation of the sacrilegious *Life of Christ* written by the French apostate priest Renan.

The board decided that the CTS catalog would list all the books with their titles in four languages: Chinese, French, Latin and English. I introduced English because none of the existing catalogs had titles or explanations in this language. My contacts with the Maryknoll Fathers had convinced me that they were eager to use Catholic literature in Chinese and I foresaw that they would be our best customers.

Preparing a four-language catalog meant that I had to write the title and a short description of its contents in four languages. Cataloging all the books, grouping them by subject matter, writing the descriptions and such other information as date of publication, language styles used, number of pages, cost, and other information was an immense task. I had no office, no typist, no secretary, and computers were still fifty years away! I did all the work on my portable typewriter, and I had to beg for help from the Chinese priests, the Irish Jesuits, and the French missionaries of the Paris Foreign Mission Society. It took over one year to assemble, correct and review all the materials. The day I brought the manuscript to the printer I was a happy man indeed.

My happiness was short-lived. Little did I know that getting the catalog printed would be a harder task than compiling it. I selected the Salesian Press (a printing school for the training of Chinese orphans, run by the Salesian Fathers) to print my book. I soon found out that the boys who did all the typesetting by hand could not even read European characters, much less understand any European language, and their instructor knew, besides Chinese, only Italian, and a smattering of English. After several weeks, when the first proofs arrived, I almost fainted. There was hardly a word spelled correctly. It was a disaster. I spent more days and months correcting and revising the proofs than I had spent compiling the catalog.

With immense patience (even though this is not my greatest virtue!) and God's assistance, the work was finally completed. One beautiful day, late in 1938, I got the first copy of the printed catalog: three hundred pages crowded with printed matter, listing over one thousand titles. The cover was a good-looking, bright yellow paper with the title in bold characters in four languages: "General Catalog of Chinese Catholic Literature."

Rapid Growth

The publication of the General Catalog marked a leap forward in the growth of the CTS. My task now was to publicize the new book and bring this helpful tool to the attention of all the Chinese and foreign priests, sisters, religious organizations and Catholic schools in China. Not an easy task, especially in view of the fact that the Japanese invasion of China had already started disrupting the mail service with many provinces.

To promote the circulation of Catholic books, I had advertised in the General Catalog that the CTS was willing to function as a clearing house for book orders and subscriptions to magazines from China and abroad—not a small addition to my work.

I could no longer do all the work alone from the little desk in my bedroom and asked the bishop for help. As he genuinely supported my work, he placed two rooms in the mission house at my disposal. And so, for the first time, the CTS had its own office and even a new typewriter.

Now I badly needed a secretary, more specifically a mansecretary. In those prewar days, it was inconceivable for missionaries in China to have a lady secretary. To find a man with a good knowledge of shorthand, secretarial abilities, and a willingness to accept a very modest salary seemed an unattainable dream.

Divine Providence came to my help. One day in 1938 a young man in a British Army sergeant's uniform came to see me. "Father Maestrini," he said, "I work in the British Army as a secretary. I have a lot of free time, and I would be delighted to help you if you can use my secretarial services. I don't need any salary. I would like to do something for God."

These words were like music to my ears. He was God's answer to my prayers. Even though I have now forgotten his name, I still feel immensely grateful. It was he who taught me how to compose and dictate letters in English, how to handle customers, and to cope with the countless details of secretarial work. That humble, unassuming, but very competent young man was really a great benefactor of the Catholic press in China.

We Begin Publishing In Chinese

With the publication of the General Catalog now accomplished, I forged full speed ahead with the plan of publishing books and pamphlets in Chinese. I was greatly inspired by the example of the Protestant missionaries. They had come to work in China long after we Catholics, the number of their followers was half that of ours, yet in the field of Christian literature they were light-years ahead of us.

Several of the major Protestant denominations collaborated in producing Christian literature and founded a joint corporation for the publication of Christian books. Its headquarters were located in a superb high-rise building in the very heart of the business district of Shanghai. Their General Catalog, in English and Chinese, contained over ten thousand titles.

I thought that we Catholics had to do something similar, but the Lord had different plans. World War II and communism destroyed most of our work, but in 1937 and 1938 our hopes were high and our CTS made a lot of headway.

How did we finance our publications? As I had promised Fr. Ryan, Providence came to our help. Besides the meager profits from our pamphlet racks, people who understood our cause helped us generously. Contributions came from many sources without the need of conducting a fund-raising campaign. I want to mention the Sisters of St. Paul of the French convent and especially Sr. Marie Louise Passos, who mobilized her students, Catholics and non-Catholics, to raise funds for the Catholic press. Through several years Sr. Marie Louise continued to secure substantial help for our work.

Now the problem was to secure manuscripts to print. I mailed numerous requests to bishops and missionary societies to send me manuscripts of books in contemporary Chinese. Before too long we received numerous manuscripts of both original compositions in Chinese and translations of European books. With the invaluable help of Fr. Luke Fong, we accepted the most promising manuscripts. I, too, wrote several pamphlets in English and had them translated into Chinese. Some dealt strictly with religious subjects and others with matters of social justice. I always felt a little proud that one of my very first pamphlets was about Chinese communism. While in those days American diplomats in China made great efforts to label Chinese communists as innocent agrarian reformers, we on the spot understood very well that they were all-out Marxists. Later facts proved us right.

I Learn The Science Of Publishing

Realizing that the theological preparation I had received in the seminary could not help me much in the publishing field, I started reading all the books on this subject I could lay my hands on.

I learned some basic lessons that helped me a great deal through all my publishing activities. Let me share with you what I found to be the secret of success in publishing. Whether you publish books for the sake of making money or for the love of God, you need profit to survive and expand. You cannot get into the publishing business with the idea of producing one or two books alone. You have to constantly add new books because it is the new books that sell the old ones. You cannot expect to make money on all the books you publish. If you make money on four books out of ten, you are a successful publisher. Last, but not least, I learned that just as it is not necessary to eat the whole cow to know if the beef is tough, so you don't have to read a whole manuscript to know if it has a chance to sell.

The Goals Of Publishing

As a missionary, my goals in publishing had to be in character with my vocation to bring the message of Christ to China. I was convinced then, as I am today, that the written word is one of the most important tools of evangelization in non-Christian countries. However, in those days practically all foreign missionaries in China dedicated themselves to pastoral work, and the ministry of the written word was neglected. I decided to specialize in that ministry.

My goal, therefore, was to publish books that would present Christianity to the Chinese as the fulfillment and development of all that was good and acceptable in their old religions. I was a great believer in the evangelization methods practiced by Matteo Ricci. He built his ministry on the premise that the basic religions of China had a lot in common with Christianity. Unfortunately, too many of the missionaries who came after Ricci abandoned this approach and regarded most of Chinese culture as the product of the devil's work.

I began writing to people all over China to find competent writers, but with little success. Then I began to look for English pamphlets to translate into Chinese, but found that very few were suitable because, of course, they were all written for Catholics in Europe and the States.

I also ran into a lot of trouble with translators. One translated the sentence "He came from a house with an untarnished reputation" into "He was born in a whitewashed house"! Another translated the title of a pamphlet called "The Spirit of the 'Forty Years'"—dealing with the social teachings of the Church according to Leo XIII's famous encyclical "Quadragesimo anno" ("the fortieth year")--as "The Spirit of Lent" because of Lent's forty days! Not even the diocesan censor noticed the mistake and thus I had several thousand copies of the pamphlet printed with the title "The Spirit of Lent," while the contents were all about the social teachings of the Church in opposition to communist teachings. I had to throw away the whole press run and reprint the pamphlet.

In spite of all these difficulties, we made a start and the presses started rolling. Our books were appreciated and the missionaries, especially the Maryknollers, bought them in large quantities. When the Japanese invaded Hong Kong in 1941 and we were compelled to suspend all our activities, we had already published over a dozen booklets and pamphlets, had a huge stock of publications, and even had a good bank balance.

12

In The Footsteps Of Martyrs

The Haifeng Martyrs

An account of my twenty years with the Chinese would not be complete without a few words about the Haifeng "Martyrs," that is, the victims of the communist persecution of Catholics in Haifeng County in 1927-28.

Since my very first days in Hong Kong, I had heard my fellow missionaries talk about the Haifeng martyrs. Therefore, I was eager to visit that place and to hear that story directly from the survivors. One night in 1936, I took a little Chinese steamboat to Shanwei (Swabue), about two hundred miles northeast of Hong Kong, and twelve hours later I landed there.

Shanwei was, and still is, one of the largest cities of Haifeng County. At that time it also had a flourishing Catholic mission. It is situated on the China mainland along the South China Sea and from time immemorial it has been considered a nest of pirates and revolutionaries. The whole county has been a part of the Hong Kong diocese since our PIME missionaries went to work there in 1860. This was the scene of a bloody communist insurrection from 1925 to 1928.

A Dramatic Rescue

At dawn on December 27, 1927, a British destroyer slowly steamed into the small harbor of Shanwei. What was unusual was that the Catholic bishop of Hong Kong, the Most Rev. Henry Valtorta, PIME, dressed in his clerical black cassock, was on the bridge next to the English captain. What was even more unusual was that the entrance of the destroyer into the harbor caused terror and panic among the citizens and the communist soldiers who controlled the city.

When the ship was near land, a boat manned by a few British sailors with a Chinese priest on board moved toward the nearest pier. Two hours later the sloop returned to the destroyer carrying two Italian priests, two Chinese priests and four Chinese sisters. They had been scheduled for execution by the communist rebels that very day.

The following morning the communist papers reported the rescue under the title: "British interference in the affairs of China." The British papers in England and Hong Kong called it "A humanitarian rescue from the hands of berserk soldiers."

Historical Background

To understand why the priests and sisters were saved from execution through the intervention of a British warship, it is necessary to know what was happening in Haifeng County at that time.

It all started with the first uprising of Chinese communists in 1925, only thirteen years after the overthrow of the Emperor and the establishment of the democratic Chinese Republic. That year two of the major political leaders of that time, Chiang Kai-shek and Mao Zedong, who had been comrades-in-arms at the Chinese Military Academy, broke their alliance. As a result their respective parties, the Nationalists under Chiang and the communists under Mao Zedong, started fighting each other for control of the nation. Their basic difference was about what type of nation China should be. Mao wanted a communist country patterned after the Soviet model, while Chiang wanted a democratic nation patterned after the American and European democracies. The war that ensued between the two political parties was bloody and cruel. It ended seven years later, in 1933, when Chiang crushed Mao's men and compelled him to retreat to the mountains of Yen-nan in the northwest part of China.

One of the areas most affected by that war was Haifeng County in the northeast part of Guangdong Province in south China.

In 1925 the Nationalist government appointed a young man by the name of Peng-pai[1] who had just graduated from a Japanese university, as the head of the Education Department of Haifeng County. What the Nationalist government did not know was that Peng-pai was an all-out Marxist. He soon went into action against the government. Besides spreading Lenin's theories among the hot-headed and rebellious school youth, Peng-pai organized the masses of peasants and farmers who for centuries had been the victims of arrogant and exploiting landlords. Faithful to his Marxist principles, Peng-pai preached hatred of the rich, hatred of religion and of all foreigners—except the Russians, of course. The farmers and students of Haifeng and other nearby counties were soon up in arms against the Nationalist government. They wanted to secede from China and form their own communist state. Civil war flared up and a bloody persecution of landlords, businessmen, Catholics, Buddhists, and anyone who did not join the communists was unleashed and systematically organized.

A *London Times* Report

To give an idea of the violence of this persecution, I will quote a report by the Shanghai correspondent of the *London Times*. It appeared Monday, February 13, 1928, under the title "The Red Terror In South China, Communist Ferocity."

"More detailed accounts have been received of the 'Red' outrages at Hoifung and Lukfung in the Swabue region between Hong Kong and Swatow, where Communists have reigned undisputed since the beginning of December. It is their last citadel in China and they are evidently determined to make the most of it. The details reported by the Swatow correspondent of the *North China Daily News* contain particulars which would be too painful to repeat, but there is every reason to believe in their accuracy. It is perhaps enough to say that conditions at Lingchi, famous for deaths by the thousand, might be regarded now as comparatively mild, with women seeing their babies massacred before themselves suffering death, and corpses rotting in the streets.

"The Communist motto is 'Better 10,000 innocent victims than that one anti-Communist escape.' This principle they are carrying out with a ferocity which has long degenerated to mere blood lust. The whole population is now organized in groups according to age. Those from 10 to 20 are drafted into companies of 'Boys Scouts' with the special duty of espionage, particularly on the doings of their parents and elders in their own homes. Men from 20 to 30 must serve in the communist armies, and for those between thirty and forty other duties are prescribed. Those over forty are designated as "old brains," considered useless burdens on the community, for whom extermination is proclaimed to be the ultimate aim.

"It is the declared policy of the Communists to reduce the population by something like a third so that there may be a better livelihood for the remainder. All title deeds have been destroyed and boundary marks obliterated, thus paving the way for endless litigation when the Communists are evicted. Having been in undisturbed possession for over two months and having been reinforced by 'Red' Russians who escaped the wrath at Canton in December, the Swabue Communists have strengthened their position enormously. They have two fortresses in the mountains well provisioned and armed and reported to be impregnable.

"General Li Chai-sum at Canton has more than once announced his intention of evicting them. The Communists threaten that on the approach of any troops they will kill every man who fails to join them."

Among The Ruins Of The Revolution

In 1935, I visited Haifeng to learn first-hand the story of the martyrs and to familiarize myself with this area of our Hong Kong mission. I then had the joy of spending some time with my confreres Frs. Lawrence Bianchi and Michael Robba, the two priests who had been rescued by Bishop Valtorta seven years earlier. As we traveled from village to village, they showed me the scars of that persecution: burned churches, destroyed rectories, ruined schools and convents, deserted houses.

I will report here what Fr. Bianchi told me when we visited the little village of Ciap-gin.

"This little village," he said when we were passing through the ruins of its outer walls in order to enter the village, "was considered to be fortified because it had a wall surrounding it. The village people, many of whom were Catholics, wanted no part of communism and, trusting in the protection of the fortified wall, defied the communists. A few days later, three hundred Red soldiers and a motley crowd of farmers well armed with hatchets, crowbars and other implements for pillaging besieged it. Resistance lasted only a few days and our Father Francis Wong, at the risk of his own life, tried to mediate an honorable surrender. But all was in vain. On November twentieth, nineteen twenty-seven, the communists invaded the village, massacred more than six hundred people, inserted iron wires through the ears and noses of the village leaders and dragged them through the streets of the city until they bled to death. The rampaging crowd threw others alive into a pool and when they surfaced shot them to death. Many more were bound together, doused with gasoline and burned alive, amid shouts of joy from the spectators."

A Christmas Day In Prison

The climax of my trip was my visit to Shanwei. As we were sipping tea in the small house that served as the rectory, I asked Fr. Bianchi to tell me again the story of their miraculous escape and show me the places where those events had taken place.

"It all started on December thirteenth," Fr. Bianchi said, "as I was in the rectory near the church. You can see it over there," and he pointed to where the little church still stood. "All of a sudden, in the early afternoon, the communist police invaded the rectory. At that moment I was the only priest in the house because Father Michael had gone out to give the last rites to a dying person and Father Wong had managed to escape through a back door before the police saw him. Pointing their guns and daggers at me, the communist policemen demanded that I give them my cache of arms and ammunitions. I told them that I had none and then they accused me of sheltering anti-Bolsheviks in the rectory. They arrested my house-boy, a catechist and four Christians, who were visiting me, brutally handcuffed them and took them to prison. I led the policemen through the church, the house and the convent in order to show them that we had neither arms nor refugees, but they were not convinced and promised to come back again.

"On December twenty-third one of our parishioners, who posed as a communist in order to help us, sent a secret message urging all of us at the mission house to flee because he could no longer guarantee our safety. There were seven of us, four sisters and three priests, and we were under surveillance day and night. It was physically impossible to escape safely. Placing ourselves entirely in the hands of Divine Providence, we said, 'What will be, will be!'

"Events moved fast. At noon of the following day, December twenty-fourth, over one hundred communist soldiers invaded our residence, confined Father Michael and me to one room, the sisters to another, started pillaging the house and convent, handcuffed Father Wong and, in spite of our protests, carried him off to the common prison for criminals.

"Later in the day, the sisters, Father Michael and I were taken away to that small house over there," Fr. Bianchi said, indicating a low building a short distance away, "which was then a very small Chinese inn converted into a prison. We all were placed in a small room, which was purposely kept open to all. As a result we had no privacy whatever. People came in continuously. They watched us, insulted us as if we were their enemies, and vented their rage on us to their hearts' content. Remembering Christ's trial in Pilate's house, we said nothing and kept our peace.

"That evening was Christmas Eve and we badly wanted to celebrate Midnight Mass, perhaps our last Mass on earth! However, the problem was that we had no wine, no chalice, no missal, no vestments, none of the things needed to celebrate Mass, except one large wafer I had hidden in my prayer book. We despaired of realizing our dream. All of a sudden one of our altar boys, by the name of 'Golden Thought,' came to see us. Being only eight years old, he was free to move around the prison. We thought he was sent by Divine Providence and asked him to go fetch a small bottle of Mass wine from the sacristy of the church. We emphasized that his errand had to be kept a secret. Off he went, as proud as a peacock, to do his job. Half an hour later he was back with the precious bottle. But we still needed a chalice and the missal. We decided to wait. Finally, after the evening meal, the guards, tired from the two-day orgy, fell asleep. When all around us was very quiet, Father Michael borrowed some Chinese clothes from a friend who had come to see us and, disguised as a Chinese peasant, managed to slip out of the prison and reach our rectory. He was fortunate enough to retrieve our portable altar and came back to the prison without being discovered.

"At about midnight, as visitors stopped coming and the guards were still asleep, we quietly celebrated Mass. It was the most beautiful Mass of our lives as we anticipated that the next day we would be put to death by the communists. The sisters and two or three lay Catholics who had slipped into the prison to see us received Communion as they, too, were sure that that was the last Communion of their lives.

"Next morning, Christmas Day, all signs seemed to confirm our conviction that it would be our last day. The communists had organized a large parade and demonstration against all Catholics. From early morning, people poured into the city from nearby villages to participate in the demonstration against us. From our windows we could read the signs prepared for the parade: 'Death to the Christian foreign devils'; 'Religion is the opium of the people, down with the Catholic priests.' About ten A.M. the parade started marching under our prison windows and continued until about three P.M. The most crucial moment was at about noon when we saw some of our parishioners, including a young girl, led to the execution place. All of them were shot by the soldiers. I believe they died real martyrs' deaths and that one day they will be recognized by the Church as martyrs and honored on the altars."

"Do you know, Bianchi," I interrupted, "how many Catholics were executed that day?"

"At least thirteen on that day alone in Shanwei. But on the same day many more were executed in other villages of Haifeng County. They all were killed because they refused to give up their religion and accept communism. The total of Catholics killed amounts to over one hundred."

"How come you were not executed that Christmas Day?" I asked.

"We were not killed because the communists wanted more time to organize a larger demonstration and make our deaths an example to all."

"How did Bishop Valtorta in Hong Kong come to know that you and the others had been arrested and that your lives were in danger?" I asked.

"The day we were arrested, one of our parishioners who owned a small boat, seeing us taken to prison, decided to sail the two hundred miles to Hong Kong to inform the bishop. After a stormy trip he arrived in Hong Kong Christmas evening. He went immediately to see Bishop Valtorta and told him what had happened to us. The bishop went immediately to consult Sir Cecil Clementi, the British governor of Hong Kong. The governor, in turn, immediately contacted London by wire and it was agreed that a destroyer of the British Navy would sail that very night with Bishop Valtorta and a Chinese priest, Father Chan, to Shanwei to liberate us. Bishop Valtorta accepted the offer of help from the British government on condition that no force would be used in the rescue operation.

"When the communists saw the British warship steaming into the harbor, they thought the British would immediately open fire and bombard the city. They came to see us and warned us that if the British attempted a landing they would kill us all and escape to the hills.

"What saved us was the fact that the British, smartly, did not use even a show of force. When the sloop from the destroyer came ashore and the communists saw that it carried only a few unarmed sailors and an aged Chinese priest, they were relieved and started negotiating immediately. Father Chan, with his inborn gift of Chinese diplomacy, made no threats and assured them that nothing would happen if they agreed to release all seven of us unharmed.

"The communists did not care about the sisters (worthless women, they thought!) and were happy to get rid of us Italians because of possible international complications. But they strongly objected to releasing Father Francis Wong. The reason was that the arrival of the British ship and our release were a serious loss of face for them. Therefore, they wanted to make Father Wong the scapegoat by submitting him to a people's trial as a traitor and executing him with great fanfare.

"Father Chan was adamant. He proved to them that Father Wong, being born in Hong Kong, was a British subject and therefore they had no right to detain him. Reluctantly, the communists agreed to let us all leave on the British sloop. And so we did!"

"How did you feel when you sailed away from Shanwei and left so many of your Christians behind you in prison?"

"That thought, of course, spoiled much of our happiness at being freed. However, we all realized that nothing would have been accomplished by our remaining there."

"How long were you exiled from your people?"

"It was only a matter of a few months. Nationalist troops arrived a few weeks later and the communists fled to the hills. That was the end of the communist rebellion in Haifeng County."

That visit to Haifeng was very emotional for me. We went from village to village, from church to church, walking many hours every day, in a kind of pilgrimage, reliving the suffering, the torture, the agony inflicted by the communists on the Christians of that area.

I will conclude this chapter by quoting a page from the history of the Diocese of Hong Kong by Fr. Thomas F. Ryan.

"Though the priests and sisters did not gain the palm of martyrdom, there were many others who had every claim to be regarded as martyrs. Two instances can be given:

"One was the son of a village leader, Tsan Ah Kiao. He had grown up during the years of war and village factions, and he became notorious as a fighter. He had his own troop when there was fighting, and in days of peace he was a skilled woodcarver. He was clever, good-humored and generous, and was very kind to the poor and used to get medicines from the missions to give to those who were sick.

"Contact with the mission brought him eventually into the Church and he became a most devoted associate of the missionaries. Because of this, he was sought out by name as the Reds gained control, but for a long time he evaded capture. At last he was taken. His captors then ordered him to raise his hand and cheer for Communism. He cried out instead 'Praised be Jesus Christ!' Then they fell upon him and put him to death with frightful brutality.

"The other was the father of the little boy Golden Thought, who had brought the wine to the priests in prison. As he was a man with some property, he was for that, and for no other reason, condemned to death. The little boy, bright in manner and running about everywhere, made friends with the Communist leaders and because of that they spared the man's life and put him in prison instead. When they discovered that he was a Catholic, he was taken out and executed."

Dr. John C. H. Wu and the author in the late 1930's.

13

East Meets West: Dr. John C. H. Wu

Ningpo, China: March 28, 1899

On the night of March 28, 1899, in Kwei-yun, China, the pregnant twenty-six-year-old wife of banker Wu Chia Ch'ang had a dream. Many years later that son described his mother's dream: "My mother saw an old man with a white beard, leading a young man on horseback as far as the threshold of her chamber. The old man stopped right at the threshold and said to her, 'Madam, this is your son.' Then he left. The horse entered and went directly towards my mother; and, at the same time, the young man was continually somersaulting on the back of the horse, until finally he entered the womb of my mother. This awakened her from her sleep, and early in the morning I was born." The child was given the name Wu Ching Hsiung.

Vatican City: February 16, 1947

"We greet your Excellency as a loyal son of the Church, whose journey to the Catholic faith was illuminated by Dante's *Divine Comedy* and whose thoughts and actions unite in an exemplary way the love of God and the devotion to your native land."

These words were spoken by Pope Pius XII one Sunday at a solemn ceremony in the hall of the throne at the Vatican, when he accepted the credentials of the first Chinese ambassador to the Holy See: Wu Ching Hsiung, also known as Dr. John C. H. Wu.

On that day, physically, I was in Hong Kong, but spiritually I was at the Vatican by the side of the new ambassador, because John Wu was my spiritual son and brother. Throughout the previous ten years I had helped him to grow in his Catholic faith. Now, because of his outstanding witness to Christ, he had been appointed the first Chinese ambassador to the Holy See.

The story of this eminent jurist and scholar and of my friendship with him are an integral part of my life. As a scholar, John Wu opened the door to the world of Chinese classic culture and of Chinese intelligentsia for me; as a convert, he represented for me what every missionary in China, from Matteo Ricci to my days, had dreamed of finding in a convert because of his exceptional zeal and grasp of Catholic doctrine; as a man, he was as close to me as a blood brother because we were bound by the deepest spiritual relationship. As I am writing about my work with the Chinese, I must give some space to the story of John Wu because since the day of our first encounter he deeply influenced all my work and thinking.

"Like A Deer Running After Spring Waters"

At 2:00 on the afternoon of October 25, 1938, I knocked at the door of a modest Chinese apartment on Nathan Road in Kowloon, Hong Kong. A Chinese gentleman with a boyish face, dressed in a long, impeccably cut Chinese silk gown, opened the door and seeing my cassock and Roman collar recognized me immediately as a priest. Before I could even open my mouth, he exclaimed in excellent English, "Oh, Father! You are a Catholic priest. Every priest is welcome to my house. I am greatly honored. Please, Father, come in. I have to talk to you."

With a gesture of his hand and a small bow, he invited me into the dark corridor of a three-bedroom apartment. The second door to the left was that of his bedroom and he motioned to me to enter it. The first thing I noticed, besides the king-size matrimonial bed, was that all the walls of the room were covered with bookcases and filled with books to the ceiling. More books were piled up all over the floor, on the bed, and even under the bed. In the whole room there was no other furniture except a small writing desk near the bed and one chair.

"You see, Father, I live here with my wife and twelve children. We are refugees from Shanghai," he said. Then, pointing to the only chair, he continued, "This is the only chair I have here. Please sit down."

He sat on the side of the bed facing me and without giving me a chance to say a word he continued, "You see, Father, why . . . ?" I do not remember the exact question he asked me, but I do remember that it was about religion. From that moment until 8:00 that evening, he continuously bombarded me with one question after another about points of Catholic doctrine and ascetical life, without stopping, without hesitating, without any effort to find new topics.

Our conversation ranged from basic points of Christian doctrine to the intricacies of Catholic mysticism, from the sanctity of martyrs and hermits to that of St. John of the Cross, St. Teresa of Avila, and St. Teresa of the Child Jesus. His questions came rushing like a mighty waterfall. As I explained things in great detail and expounded on the basic principles of the spiritual life, he seemed like a thirsty "deer at a spring of fresh water" (Psalm 41). He absorbed all I said with real enjoyment, was fully convinced by my explanations, and kept asking for more.

The only brief interruptions came almost every hour when dear, sweet Mrs. Wu, with all the modesty and shyness of a dutiful Chinese wife, slipped quietly into the room, tiptoed to the desk and gently laid on it a fresh pot of hot tea for Dr. Wu. Then she would quietly withdraw without uttering a sound.

At about 6:00 P.M., the two of us had a quick dinner served by the ever-solicitous Mrs. Wu in the kitchen, while we blithely continued our earnest conversation in English. Mrs. Wu spoke neither English nor Cantonese, and I could not converse with her.

"Dr. Wu, where are the children? You told me you have twelve. Isn't anyone home?" I asked during a short pause in our conversation when we were about finished with our meal. All through the afternoon I had wondered where the children might be, because I did not hear a voice, a child's laugh or a scream. The house seemed deserted.

"Oh, no, Father. They are all at home, but my good wife takes care of them."

I was astonished: twelve children ranging in age from a baby to a couple of teenagers crowded into a small three-bedroom apartment, and not a sound!

As soon as the meal was over, we returned to the bedroom study and continued our conversation. When finally I left after 8:00 P.M., tired and exhausted by my talking, I realized that I had not even had time to tell Dr. Wu the purpose of my visit. I wanted to ask him to write an article for our Chinese diocesan paper and I had forgotten all about it.

That conversation was a turning point in Dr. Wu's life, and mine, too. In order to understand why that happened, we have to go back to Dr. Wu's childhood and his religious odyssey.

Childhood In Ningpo, China

Wu Ching Hsiung (later to become known as John C. H. Wu) was born on March 28, 1899, about ninety miles south of Shanghai in Ningpo, "city of peaceful waters." As his family was pagan, it did not occur to the parents that that day was also the liturgical feast day of St. John Capistrano (after whom the Capistrano Mission in California is named) and the anniversary of the birthday of St. Teresa of Avila, born in 1515. Many years were to pass before Wu Ching Hsiung would discover these facts.

Mr. Chia Ch'ang—or simply Master Ch'ang, as he was affectionately called—was the father of the newborn. A successful banker, he had risen from total poverty to considerable affluence and was a man of great spiritual insight. About sixty years later, his son would write of him: "If there was ever a man possessed by the passion for goodness, it was my father. His life motto was: 'Help others even when you have not enough to spare.'"

Strange as it may seem to us Westerners, little Ching Hsiung had two mothers, whom he called, respectively, "The Little Mother" and "The Big Mother." He explained this in his autobiography. When his father was already forty years old and had no children from his wife, she begged him to take a younger concubine for the bearing of children so that the family could continue to exist. Dr. Wu wrote:

"According to the old Chinese ethics, to die without issue was considered as the gravest sin against one's ancestors. This was no doubt bound up with the whole institution of ancestor-worship. So, my Big Mother pressed my father to take a little wife for the bearing of children. So, Master Ch'ang found a poor girl called Kuei-Yuen, which means 'Cassia Cloud,' who was barely 16. He took her home and next year my elder brother was born. In 1894 came my elder sister. I was the last and least of the family. When my little mother died in 1903, I was only four and she was only 30."

The influence of his natural mother was very strong in the physical makeup and in the soul of John Wu. He wrote: "In my physical makeup, there are two strains: one negative, which I inherited from my mother, and the other positive, which I inherited from my father . . . the spirit of my mother helps me to understand Taoism; the spirit of my father helps me to appreciate Confucianism. The Taoist in me looks at the vicissitudes of fortune as the succession of day and night, spring and autumn, in the natural order of things. The Confucian in me urges me on in the cultivation of love, which alone lasts."

It was this little mother who had the dream I reported at the beginning of this chapter.

As Dr. Wu wrote in his biography: "There were quite a few attempts on the part of my elder relatives to interpret the dream. Some said that I was to die young; others surmised that I might turn out to be a revolutionary. But my elder brother thought I was going to be a general. My own interpretation was that I was destined to be a circus actor. However, many years later when I was in Rome, the Gregorian University invited me to give a public lecture on my spiritual odyssey. I began by recounting the dream of my mother, and I continued to comment on it.

"I scarcely believe in the meaning of dreams. However, this dream can serve as a convenient synopsis of my spiritual odyssey. The womb of my mother symbolizes the Catholic Church. The boy is myself. The constant jumping and somersaulting symbolizes all the changes, commotions, and upsets which I had to experience during the long, restless night before I embraced the true Faith. Perhaps the threshold symbolizes the baptism which I received in the Methodist sect. But who could the old man be? Well, for me he represents Confucius and all that is good in the old Oriental culture. As for the horse, I think it represents Providence, because it comes directly towards my mother, in spite of all the movements of the uneasy child."

Master Ch'ang's first wife was the one John Wu called his "Big Mother," and she was the one who really brought him up and educated him. Remembering her, John Wu wrote: "It is not easy for me to write about my big mother. If I am asked who, of all human beings is dearest to me, I would answer without the slightest hesitation that it is my big mother. I've dreamed of her more than of any other person. I wept more tears in memory of her than of anyone else."

In another page of his autobiography, John Wu wrote about his mother: "No mother could be more tender to her own children than she was to me. She loved me, she adored me, she served me like an old maidservant, she waited for me every day to come from school, she made my clothes, she prepared special dishes for me. I do not remember that she ever chastised me or scolded me. How I repent that I was so unkind to her. I often scolded her, kicked her, and threw things at her. Once or twice I was so cruel as to say to her, 'Do you think you could have borne me? No, I am not your son!' She only sobbed and said, 'How I wish I had died before your little mommy, that I might be spared all this!' That touched me to the quick, and I cried and would not stop crying until she retracted that statement and promised to live on. Of course, we were soon reconciled and became better friends than ever."

When the time came to go to school, little Wu immediately revealed both exceptional intelligence and exceptional desire to learn. In his biography he wrote: "When I was 11, which was 12 according to our (Chinese) way of reckoning age, I came across the sentence: 'I was bent upon learning at 15 years of age'; I was so inspired as to write on the upper margin of the page: 'I am bent upon learning at 12!'"

English was then the second language in all the schools in China, and little Wu began to learn it at the age of nine. He wrote: "I loved English at first sight. Later, my interest in it grew by reading the English translations of Chinese classics and essays, which I loved so much."

At fifteen, he entered the junior college in Ningpo, and two years later he entered the (American) Baptist College in Shanghai. Then he decided to join one of his classmates at the University of Tianjin in north China to study law. He passed the entrance examination in early 1916 but soon returned to Ningpo, where he married on April 12.

A Marriage Written In Heaven

I continue from his biography: "My wife and I had never seen each other before our wedding, which occurred on April 12, 1916. Both of us were pagans and brought up in the old Chinese way. It was our parents who engaged us to each other, when we were barely 6 years of age. Although I was engaged not by my own will, I had absolutely no doubt that the one to whom my parents had matched me was destined to be my wife. God has given a good wife to me. In the old days, there were no schools for women, so it was quite natural that my wife did not learn to read. But she was educated in the family tradition, though not through the reading of books. She was taught by her mother how to behave like a woman, how to perform the domestic duties, and the like, with the result that she is full of common sense, which after all is so uncommon.

"As to her religious faith, she was brought up in exactly the same kind of spiritual atmosphere as I was: it was the atmosphere of a simple and sincere natural religion in which both my wife and I were brought up. We even regarded our children as gifts from God."

John Is My Name

Shortly after his marriage he resumed his studies, entering the Peiyang

University in Tianjin. When it was announced that year that the university would be amalgamated with the law school of Beijing University, over one thousand miles away from Ningpo, John and his friend decided to go to Shanghai instead. They entered the Comparative Law School of Shanghai which had been recently opened in that city under the auspices of the American Methodist Mission.

John continued: "In the fall of 1917 I registered myself as John Wu. Nothing could be more casual than the way I came to adopt the name John. In those days, there was a vogue among Chinese students to adopt Western names. Some of us worshiped the heroes of the West such as George Washington, Abraham Lincoln, William Shakespeare, and many others. One day my fellow student Shu and myself decided to pick up some names for ourselves also. My friend chose the name 'Hamilton' because he aspired to be a great constitutionalist and economist.

"As for me, I worshiped so many heroes that I could not decide upon anyone, so I referred to the proper names section of Webster's dictionary. I was running through the section alphabetically, when I came upon 'John.' I felt there was something arresting about it. I read it aloud many times. 'John, John . . .' 'Why,' I said to myself, 'this sounds exactly like my Chinese name Ching Hsiung!' The fact is when my schoolmates called me Ching Hsiung they said it so quickly that the two syllables were merged into one, sounding very much like 'John.' Therefore, this name suited me like a glove. I did not care which John I was following. Anyway, there was John Marshall, John Wesley, John Webster, and the like. So I thought I was in fairly good company. But the interesting thing is that a name that was adopted so casually should have come to stay. From thenceforth I've been known as John Wu, and I hope I shall be John Wu to the end of my life."

Methodist Baptism

Dr. Charles W. Rankin, a Methodist from Tennessee, was the dean of the law school. About forty, a bachelor, he was a true Christian missionary "full of the spirit of love and self-sacrifice." His ascetic life greatly impressed the students.

John Wu's conversion to Methodism came about this way: "Besides the courses on legal subjects, there was a class on religion taught by Rankin. We were required to read the Bible, and I fell in love with it. Also, the edifying example of Rankin made me search for the living source of his spirit of purity and love. The textbook we used on religion,

James Orr's *The Christian View of God and the World*, impressed me
deeply. To make a long story short, thanks to the influence of the Bible
and this book, and to the edifying example of Brother Rankin, I was
brought into my first contact with Christ and was baptized in the Methodist Church in the winter of 1917; and it was only then that I knew that
I was named after the beloved disciple. When, twenty years later, I came
to embrace the Catholic faith, the same name was retained at my conditional Baptism, but only recently have I come to know that John
means 'God has been gracious' which sums up the story of my life."

Ann Arbor, Michigan; England; Berlin

After graduation from law school in the summer of 1920, John Wu sailed
on board the S.S. *Nanjing* from Shanghai to the United States in order to
pursue his post-graduate work at the Michigan Law School at Ann Arbor.
Here he lost his faith.

"I was engrossed in my studies and by imperceptible degrees my
interest and faith in Christianity waned. I ceased to pray and to go to
church. As my own Faith was not firmly rooted, I gradually drifted away
from my first love for lack of a congenial religious milieu. My jurist and
philosophical preoccupations diluted more and more what little faith I
had gotten. I began to look at Christ as a mere man, a human preacher
whose extraordinary personality and lightning-like flashes of moral
insight continued to fascinate me. I adored him in the spirit of hero
worship, which I had imbibed from Thomas Carlyle. As a free-thinker I
no longer cared whether He rose again from the dead, or whether He
actually worked miracles. If He was not God, He was all the more
admirable and worthy of imitation. All questions of dogma were
relegated to the background."

In May 1921, Wu applied for a scholarship at the Carnegie Endow-
ment for International Peace and won it. He chose to go to the University
of Paris. Two years later, in the fall of 1923, he sailed back to the States
to join the Harvard Law School as a research scholar. The following year
he went to Ningpo for a short visit on March 15, 1924, and then moved
with his family to Shanghai.

Heights And Depths

On his return to Shanghai—the Chinese "New York" of those days—he
first took a position as professor of law at his former school and soon

became its principal. In 1927, he was appointed judge of the Shanghai Provincial Court. This prominent position suddenly catapulted him into popularity, money, and a playboy kind of life in the sophisticated society of prewar Shanghai. In the winter of 1929, he went to Chicago, Illinois, as a Rosenthal lecturer at the Northwestern University Law School. Then, in the spring of 1930, he was invited to lecture as a research fellow at the Harvard School of Law.

When he returned to Shanghai at the end of the same year, he decided to practice law. "That was the beginning of the best and worst period of my life—the best materially, but worst spiritually." As he was already well-known, rich clients flocked to his door and overnight he became very wealthy, making as much as $40,000 a month. With money came dissolute living and endless parties with his clients in the Shanghai "flowery houses." He wrote: "Before I realized it, I became a regular playboy. For two and a half years I was out practically every night."

But all this brought him no joy and he felt "utterly unhappy and dissatisfied with myself. . . . The more unhappy I was, the more eagerly I sought after pleasures and the more I indulged in the pleasures, the more unhappy I was. I became prey to a sense of despair." In this state of soul, even natural religious feelings fell into oblivion and the very mention of religion would send him into a temper. This is what happened with his former friend and mentor, Mr. Charles Rankin, whom he called a "bigot" to his face. When another of his closest and dearest friends, Mr. Yuan—a practicing Catholic—made several attempts to introduce the subject of religion, he avoided it, saying, "Let us talk about something more interesting!"

His family life was in a shambles. He began to "loathe the very sight" of his wife and lost all interest in his children.

One day he came across a diary his daughter Agnes was writing for her teachers. He read: "Our family life is simply miserable. For the last few weeks I've not had a glimpse of my father. When I leave for school in the morning, they tell me that father has just gone to bed; and when I return home in the afternoon, they tell me that father has just gone out to seek pleasures. My mother is weeping everyday. Oh, heaven, why should I be born in such a family?"

For the sake of history, it is important to record that thirty years later the very same daughter, Agnes, wrote to her father: "I cannot imagine a better father than you in the whole world." Dr. Wu attributed the change of attitude in his children to the fact that, as he wrote, "With Christ, the home is a prelude to heaven. Without Christ, it is a prelude to hell."

When his eldest son, Tsu-Ling (later baptized "Thomas") confronted him openly about his dissolute living, Wu promised to reform his life but failed to keep his word.

Having discarded the idea of divorce "for my conscience told me it was wrong," he asked his wife for permission to take a concubine. Mrs. Wu flatly refused, but after a lengthy discussion, she promised to let him do so with her consent in four years, when he would be forty years old. John Wu rejoiced, looking forward to having, four years later, a legitimate concubine. However, things did not work out as he had planned: Four years later he became a Catholic. By then the idea of a concubine was gone and he discovered in Mrs. Wu a truly ideal wife.

Politically, he reached the top of his career when in 1933 he became a member of the Legislative Body of Nationalist China, and was appointed Chairman of the General Committee in charge of drafting the Constitution of China. From 1933 to 1936 he drafted the Chinese Constitution and thus had the opportunity of meeting the top intelligentsia of China.

Along with his legal work, he enjoyed philosophizing and writing. Together with a group of internationally known top writers, such as Lin Yu Tang, Dr. Sun Fo, and other famous names, he organized the publication of a high-class cultural and literary magazine in English, for the purpose "of interpreting Chinese culture to the West." The editorial board was officially organized on May 6, 1935, and the magazine was called *T'ien Hsia Monthly*, which means "everything under heaven."

Return Of The Prodigal

As the prodigal son of the Gospel lost every worldly possession and sank into poverty before returning to his senses, so John Wu had to follow the same road of spiritual misery and material poverty to find God again. The "rod of affliction" God used to bring John back to Himself was the Sino-Japanese War.

On the night of July 7, 1937, a minor incident between Chinese and Japanese troops near the Marco Polo Bridge in Beijing became the pretext used by Japan to begin military action in China in order to realize its goals of political and economic expansion. Japan had long ago resolved that Chiang Kai-Shek and the Nationalist government of China had to be overthrown by military action and be replaced with a more friendly and more subservient government. The Japanese army was well-trained and well-equipped. It soon penetrated deeply into China, sowing ruin and destruction everywhere.

Beijing and Tianjin fell to the Japanese the same month, July 1937, and the army continued its devastating march toward Shanghai, over one thousand miles to the south. The battle of Shanghai began on August 13. The Japanese first surrounded that enormous, sprawling city of over twelve million people, cutting off all land communications with the rest of the country. Then they moved into the city, fighting street by street, pillaging, murdering, destroying whatever obstacles they found on their way. However, they did not dare invade the International Concessions, namely, those large areas of the city under the control of such powerful nations as England and France. These privileged areas became a haven of refuge to all those Chinese who could afford to live there.

The battle for Shanghai was hard and bloody, but the city fell by the middle of November 1937. The then capital of China, Nanjing, fell to the Japanese about a month later. Chiang Kai-Shek transferred the seat of the government to Chungking in the far western part of the country. These events profoundly affected Dr. Wu's life.

When the Japanese first attacked Shanghai, Dr. Wu was in Nanjing. As all communications with Shanghai were cut, he spent several anxious and lonely weeks. Finally, through devious ways, paying a lot of bribes, and at great personal danger, he managed to reach the British Concession in Shanghai. There he was reunited with his family. His wife and children had abandoned their sumptuous home in the western sector of the city when it became too dangerous to live there, and had taken refuge in the house of a family friend. However, most of their large properties were lost and John Wu was now a poor man. In the long and lonely hours of his life as a jobless refugee, John's mind turned to God, and through the reading of Newman, T. S. Eliot, and particularly Dante's *Divina Commedia*, he found God again. The incident that determined his conversion was related by him in the preface to his book *The Science of Love*.

"I heard the name of Teresa of Lisieux for the first time in the home of my dear friend, Mr. Yuan Kin-hoang, a most zealous Catholic. In the winter of 1937 I was living in Mr. Yuan's house and I was impressed by the way the Yuans recited their family Rosary. Seeing a portrait of St. Teresa, I asked him: 'Is this the Virgin Mary?' He told me that it was the 'Little Flower of Jesus.' 'Who is this Little Flower of Jesus?' I asked. He looked surprised and said: 'What! You don't even know St. Teresa of Lisieux?' Then he gave me a French pamphlet entitled 'St. Teresa of the Child Jesus,' which contained a short account of her life and many specimens of her thoughts. Somehow I felt that these thoughts expressed some of the deepest convictions about Christianity which I happened to entertain at that moment. I said to myself: 'If this Saint represents Catholicism, I don't see any reason why I should not be a Catholic.' Being a Protestant, I was free to chose whatever interpretation suited my own reason best, and her interpretation was exactly the right one for me, and that made me a Catholic!

"When I confided my decision to Mr. Yuan, he almost fainted with joy, for, as he told me afterward, he had been praying for my conversion for ten years!"

John asked Mr. Yuan to introduce him to a priest and Mr. Yuan selected Fr. Germain, the rector of the Jesuit-run Aurora University in Shanghai. Fr. Germain presumed that Dr. John Wu already knew all about Catholicism and after a summary instruction baptized him in the Chapel of Our Lady attached to the university.

In his autobiography Dr. Wu concluded the story of his conversion to Catholicism with these words: "All my life I had been searching for a Mother, and at last I had her in the Catholic Church, and this in a triple sense. God is my Mother, The Church is my Mother, and the Blessed Virgin is my mother; and these three Mothers have merged into one Motherhood, in which I live, move and have my being."

14

The Kindergarten Of Faith

Faltering Steps

Strange as it may seem, Dr. Wu's reception into the Church was not accompanied by any surge of religious emotion or further progress in the knowledge of Christianity. He wrote in his autobiography: "I did not feel any joy either on the day of my Baptism or at my First Communion. My mind was a blank, feeling neither joy nor sorrow." However, a few days after his Baptism he wrote in his diary: "What joy I feel in my heart! After long years of aimless wondering, I have come back to Christ, this time to stick to Him forever. My pen is too weak to describe the joy of my heart, or rather my heart is too weak to bear the burden of my joy." These words might seem to contradict what he had written earlier, but, as he explained to me, the paragraph above refers to his intellectual attitude towards religion rather than to any heartfelt emotions. His was an intellectual conversion.

His Baptism helped him to better understand the role of the Catholic Church in the world, but his personal life was not affected. In fact, his family did not notice any change in his external behavior. Religion was seldom mentioned in their conversations and very rarely did he attend Mass on Sunday. He did not even read Catholic books. Dante's, Newman's, T. S. Eliot's books, which had helped him so much in his feverish quest for truth, were now gathering dust on his bookshelves. The summary preparation he had received for Baptism did not give him a start in the spiritual life of the soul.

In the meantime, his life as a jurist and a writer was turned completely topsy-turvy by the immense tragedy of the Sino-Japanese War.

As Japan's armies victoriously advanced all over China from north to south, life became more dangerous for Chinese refugees living inside the International Concessions of Shanghai. The Japanese Secret Service saw the Chinese intelligentsia as an obstacle to the control of China and was bent on liquidating them.

The editors of *T'ien Hsia* were obvious targets for liquidation because of their anti-Japanese writings and broadcasts. Consequently many of them escaped to the safety of Hong Kong to continue their work in support of the national government in Chungking. So, by the middle of January 1938, shortly after his Baptism, John slipped away from Shanghai on board a French boat and went to Hong Kong to find a place to which his wife and his twelve children could follow him.

They arrived in February. Most of their luggage consisted of John's books. They all crowded into a three-bedroom apartment near Nathan Road, in Kowloon, trying to adapt to a new a life style.

Gone was their sumptuous home in Shanghai, gone was Dr. Wu's lucrative law practice, gone was the sophisticated life of the international society of the Shanghai Concessions. They were now refugees in a British colony!

They settled down to a new routine of life. The children went to school. John occasionally traveled to Chungking by plane on government duties, but he dedicated most of his time to writing for *T'ien Hsia*. As he wrote later: "In Hong Kong I was reunited with my *T'ien Hsia* friends, and we set up our office and continued our publications. . . . My interest had taken a turn for Chinese poetry. I wrote a long article on 'The Four Seasons of the T'ang Poetry' and contributed my translation of the Taoists' classic, the 'Tao Teh Ching.' From the standpoint of literary output, that was perhaps the most active period of my life."

Even though religion was relegated to the periphery of his life, still he went occasionally to St. Teresa's Church (my former parish) to hear Mass, as he preferred this to Rosary Church even though it was nearer to him.

The "Hound of Heaven" was waiting for him there. Almost one and a half years after his Baptism, on October 15, 1939, John went to Mass at St. Teresa's. When the Communion plate came around, he was so absorbed in his thoughts that he failed to take it from the hands of the person to his right. The pastor, Fr. A. Granelli, noticing his awkwardness, suspected he was a new Catholic and whispered to him, "Please, come and see me after Mass." John did so. He told Fr. Granelli that he was a recent convert, that he had not yet received Confirmation and showed Fr.

Granelli a letter of recommendation from Fr. Germain, who had baptized him. Fr. Granelli immediately phoned Bishop Valtorta and he scheduled October 18, the feast of St. Luke, to give him Confirmation.

I Discover John Wu

"Maestrini," Bishop Valtorta told me the day after the Confirmation of Dr. Wu, "you are always looking for good Chinese writers for the Chinese Catholic paper. Well, I have a good one to suggest to you: Dr. John Wu. I gave him Confirmation yesterday at St. Teresa's. He's a very learned man and quite a writer. Go and see him."

"Fine, Bishop," I replied. "Did you say: John C. H. Wu?" The bishop assented and I continued, "Oh! I now remember. He is the guy who was recommended to me by Father Germain of Shanghai. But he never came to see me and I could not find out where he was. I've been waiting to see him for months. How can I reach him? Do you have his address?"

"Ah, that I don't know. But I will get it for you."

A couple of days later he gave me the address, but no phone number. So I decided to take a chance and visit him at his house for the purpose of asking him to write some articles in Chinese. On October 25 I met him for the first time. I have described our first meeting in the previous chapter. For the sake of history I have to add that I never succeeded in getting Dr. Wu to write extensively for my Chinese paper, but I did gain in him a spiritual son and a loving brother.

Describing our first meeting in his biography, he wrote: "Father Maestrini became my spiritual director and recommended one book after another for my reading . . . practically all the rudiments of my spiritual life were formed in those days and Father Maestrini was the principal instrument that God employed to enlighten me on the fundamentals of the Catholic faith and spiritual life."[1]

The day after our first meeting I returned to his house with a bundle of spiritual books. For months I continued to bring him new books and we spent two or three afternoons together every week talking about religion. He had an insatiable thirst for spiritual things, and so I introduced him to the use of the daily missal, explained to him the liturgy of the Mass and introduced him to meditation and the life of prayer as a means of growth in the pursuit of Christian virtues.

Using the *Manual of Ascetical and Mystical Theology* by Tanqueray as a guideline, we discussed in depth the theory and practice of spirituality. This study opened new spiritual horizons to him. The writings of St.

Teresa of Avila, of St. John of the Cross, and of St. Catherine of Siena became his favorite readings.

But I was not only teaching him; I was learning, too. In our frequent and long conversations, he opened the world of the Chinese classics to me and pointed out the similarities between the Catholic and the Buddhist ascetical doctrines. He was an expert in Taoism and he delighted in explaining to me how the basic teachings of Lao Tze and Confucius are based on the same natural law we Christians recognize as God's Law.

A Convert's Eagerness

John Wu hated to do anything halfway. There was no mediocrity for him; it was all or nothing. As he had sunk to the lowest moral level, so now he strove to rise to the heights of true Christian living. He soon took up the practice of going to daily Mass and Communion. It was not easy in the beginning. His whole schedule of work had to be completely turned around. Owing to the cramped quarters in which he was living with his twelve children, he used to work and write at nighttime up to the small hours of the morning, going to bed at 3:00 or 4:00 A.M. This habit, however, could not be reconciled with attending daily Mass because on weekdays the last Mass was at 7:30 A.M. Slowly, but patiently, renouncing many hours of sleep rather than giving up either his writings or going to church, he made a valiant effort. Every morning he rose early enough to walk over to Rosary Church in time for Mass. Daily communion brought him that deepening of spiritual life and that growth in the love of God he had unconsciously craved all his life.

John Wu was a strange mixture of practicality and impracticality, of speculative thinking and down-to-earth decisions. He attributed his love for speculation to the influence of the writings of Lao Tze, and the practical side of his temperament to the teachings of Confucius. When, after receiving the sacrament of Confirmation, religion blossomed in his soul, it did not remain in the speculative realm. Far from keeping the riches of his newly found faith to himself, he was on fire to share it with others. Christianity is essentially a dynamic religion and John lived it to its full extent.

"Father Nicholas," he told me shortly after we had met, "Christianity is so beautiful that I really want to share it with my family."

"That's fine, John," I answered. However, knowing his outbursts of enthusiasm, I added, "But perhaps, John, it might be better if, for the time being, you limit yourself to showing your family the good example of true Christian living and letting them come to their own conclusions." He followed my advice to the letter. The Holy Spirit went to work, and in a little over one year all the members of his family were baptized. However, their conversion gave me some uncomfortable moments. At the Midnight Mass of Christmas in 1939, I was distributing Holy Communion to a crowded church at the side altar of the cathedral. All of a sudden, I saw the whole Wu family, father, mother and twelve children, including a babe in the mother's arms, coming toward the altar in single file to receive Communion. I shuddered as I was in a serious dilemma. I could not give them Communion because they were not baptized, but I also knew that if I refused and asked them to leave the Communion rail, I would be inflicting on them a severe loss of face.

As I watched them demurely and respectfully kneeling at the altar rail, I made a heroic resolution. Whispering to the Lord, I said, "Lord, you understand! These good people mean no insult or disrespect to you. They do not know our rules. They only mean good. Please, Lord, forgive me, but for the good of their souls, I cannot turn them down!" Then I quietly proceeded to give Communion to each of them, with a prayer that they would soon accept our Faith. My prayer was heard, and thanks to the good example of their father all of them requested Baptism during the next few months.

The Faith Of A Mother

Only a few weeks after that Midnight Mass, in the afternoon of January 22, 1940, I was urgently called to the phone by John Wu.

"Father Maestrini, my little girl Lan Hsien is very sick with pneumonia. She may die any time. My wife has consented to have her baptized. Can you rush over here to baptize her?"

"Of course, John, I will come immediately," I answered with warmth in my voice, but also with much apprehension in my heart. "Lord," I murmured, "is this going to be a test of John's faith?"

I had a good reason to be worried about the sickness and possible death of this child. From my fellow missionaries I had heard that many times, when a family decided to convert to Christianity, it often suffered some serious misfortune. Those prospective converts who did not have a strong faith saw in those misfortunes a "revenge of the spirits" and dropped out of the convert class. Even when misfortunes happened to them after being baptized, some returned to their superstitious practices out of fear of the spirits' revenge. At that moment I was really afraid that if the child died it might mean a serious crisis in the faith of John Wu and his whole family.

As I rushed down the Hong Kong hill and across the harbor to the Wus' apartment, I prayed frantically that John might be spared such a trial. Now, looking back on this event, I believe that the Lord must have smiled on my own weak faith because, as in the case of Lazarus, that sickness was not meant for death but for the glory of God (John 11:4).

When I arrived at Dr. Wu's house, everybody was in tears. Before administering Baptism, I took John aside and said, "John, I am now going to baptize Lan Hsien and we all will pray to the Lord to spare her life, but, if God decides otherwise, we must be equally ready to accept His will."

"Look here, Father," John replied promptly, as if he had read the thoughts of my mind, "I know what it means to do God's Will, and I am ready. I have already told the Lord that even though I love Lan Hsien so very much, still, if He wants her, I will accept His Will and I will not complain. After all, if she dies, what do I lose? Only a few years of companionship here on earth, but in Heaven I will enjoy her company for all eternity."

I am going to quote Dr. Wu's own words to tell the rest of this story as he wrote it in the preface to *The Science of Love*:

"After the Baptism my wife knelt before St. Teresa with the sick baby in her arms, and prayed in deep earnestness. I could not hear her words. When she rose, I asked her what she had said to the Saint. She answered, 'Oh, I just told her that Lan Hsien is too hard to bring up. I'm not fit to be her mother, so I begged St. Teresa to be her mother.' Next morning the doctor came again and, taking the temperature of little Lan Hsien, found that it was a little below 100! It had been 105 on the previous day! Then he examined the lungs and found the pneumonia gone. The only words he uttered were: 'Wonderful! Wonderful!' I told him what had happened and asked him whether he would be willing to certify my story if I were to write it out in detail someday. He said, 'Certainly.' The story is too long to tell here. What interests me just now is the story of the conversion of my wife. It was St. Teresa who confirmed her faith in Christ. So my only function is to teach her Catechisms."

A Fisher Of Men

Dr. Paul K. T. Sih [2] wrote this about John Wu: "In him a personal knowledge of Christ is not a thing to be folded away and secretly treasured, it is to be put to work for others. In his own words, the best way to keep an experience of Christ is to pass it on."

Quoting this statement of Paul Sih, Dr. Wu commented: "It is nothing but the truth. I became a fisher of men, and of women, too, shortly after my Confirmation."

For me, it was real happiness helping him in his "fishing work." I will report only a few anecdotes. A few weeks after we met he told me, "Father Nicholas, I want to introduce you to a friend of mine: Francis Yeh, a colleague at the *T'ien Hsia* office. He is a beautiful soul and I think he should become a Catholic."

"Well and good, John. I will surely pray for him."

"Yes, Father, please do so."

Francis Yeh, also a Chinese scholar from Shanghai, was a refugee in Hong Kong like Dr. Wu. About fifty-five years old, he was not married, but his soul was looking for something more meaningful than just writing articles for a magazine, even a magazine enjoying such high prestige as *T'ien Hsia*. John went to work on him, and in their frequent discussions about life John often introduced the subject of religion, but each time Francis promptly steered the conversation to some other topic. This cat-and-mouse game went on for over one year, and John thought that all his efforts were in vain.

One night as they went for a walk along Chatham Road, they passed in front of Rosary Church. John invited Francis to enter, but Francis refused and said that he preferred to go straight home. John fervently prayed to the Blessed Virgin, asking for the conversion of Francis. For three days they did not see each other again. On the fourth day, Francis went to see John and said, "John, I feel a driving force within me. I want to be baptized as soon as possible."

I did baptize him on February 2, 1940, and we became very close friends. After the war he founded the Catholic Truth Society of China in Shanghai, but the communist takeover and his early death in 1948 destroyed his work. John wrote of him: "He worked for the Church up to the very day of his death."

Mrs. Alice Chow, a divorcee about forty years old, was also working at the *T'ien Hsia* office. One night at a party, right in the midst of a dance, she whispered to Dr. Wu, "John, you have become such a good Catholic now, can you suggest some spiritual books for me to read?"

"Well, what about *The Imitation of Christ* by Thomas a Kempis? I will give you a copy tomorrow."

Later that night, on the way home in a cab, Alice broke down and confessed that, even though a Catholic, she had not practiced her religion for fourteen years. She did not hesitate to tell John that his example of Christian living and his frequent mention of religion at the office had stimulated her return to God. At the suggestion of Dr. Wu, a few days later, she came to see me and made peace with God. She had grown up in Australia, was highly intelligent, well-educated, and a close personal friend of Madame Kung, the sister of Madame Chiang Kai-shek.

After reporting Alice's conversion in his autobiography, Dr. Wu concluded: "Ever since, she has been one of the most devout Catholics I have known." Alice also died shortly after the war.

John, Francis, and Alice became my true spiritual family. More than my spiritual children and dearest friends, they were like brothers and sister to me.

Another dramatic conquest of John's was Mrs. Averil Tong. Early one morning at about 7:30, while in church, as usual, I was urgently called back to the house. Much to my surprise, I found John and Alice sitting in the waiting room with a lady who was obviously distraught.

"Father Maestrini," John said, "Mrs. Tong needs your help. She attempted suicide last night and she is still bent on killing herself. We have spent the whole night with her and finally she has agreed to see you. Please talk to her."

They left and I remained with Mrs. Tong. I am glad to report that Averil Tong never committed suicide. John kept praying for her conversion and even got the Carmelite sisters to pray especially for her. A Carmelite nun who at that time was seriously sick offered her life for the conversion of Averil. Finally one day Averil asked for Baptism. She is still alive while I am writing these pages, and she is still a close and dear friend.

Witnessing To The Faith

John Wu's desire to share his faith with others was always discreet and profoundly wise. It tended to assume different aspects according to different circumstances.

He told me the following episode. One day, on one of his trips to Chungking, he was attending a meeting of top government people. Seated around the table were several of his former "playmates" from the old days in Shanghai. During a lull in the business at hand, the conversation drifted to women and sex. John did not join in the talk and felt very uncomfortable. Noticing this, a much-decorated general and old friend, turning to John, said, "John, are you always as naughty as in the old days? You should go to number two on X street. There is a 'flowery house' as good as any one we had in Shanghai. The nude girls are really top!"

John could not stand it any longer. He slowly rose to his feet while fumbling in his pocket for his rosary beads. Then, dangling the beads in front of all, slowly and calmly he said, "Look, friends. I want you all to know that I have changed. Now I am a Catholic and I don't enjoy scurrilous talk anymore," and sat down. The men froze. No one made any sarcastic comment and the conversation returned to the business at hand. When the meeting ended, several people congratulated him on his courage to stand up for his faith.

Forgiveness

Early one morning, at about 9:00, I went to see him at his house, as I expected that he would be back from church at that time. He came in more than one hour late, and when he saw me he told me the reason for his delay: "You see, Father, yesterday a gentleman came to apply for a very important position in the government as there is a vacancy to be filled. I know that he is not qualified for that position and turned him down as gently as I could. But he got mad, called me all kind of names, and left in a rage."

"What has this to do with your being late this morning, John?"

"Well, on my way to Mass I remembered Jesus' words about making peace with your enemy before presenting your offering at the altar, so I went directly to his house to apologize and make peace. I wanted to let him know that I was not offended by his insults, and I asked him to forgive me for making him mad."

"You did that!" I interrupted, not believing my ears, as I know how difficult it is for Chinese people to apologize.

"Yes, Father Nicholas, I apologized. He was shocked and asked why I was apologizing. I told him that as a Catholic I am supposed to be at peace with everybody and I wanted to remain his friend even though I could not give him that position. He was so surprised that he asked me to tell him more about my religion, and now he is thinking of becoming a Catholic. I think, Father Nicholas, that before too long you will have another Baptism to perform." The gentleman later went to Chungking and was baptized there a few months later.

A Test Of Faith

The very purpose of life is to love God more than anything else in the world. This is why sometimes God puts us to a test. John's test came in a way completely unexpected by me.

After much pressure from me, at last John wrote an article in Chinese on the spirituality of Christianity for our Chinese diocesan paper. Much to my surprise, when I submitted the article to the diocesan book censor, a Chinese priest appointed by the bishop, he refused to give me permission to print it. He explained to me that even though the article was excellent, it used typical Buddhist terminology to express such Catholic concepts as penance, self-denial, and mortification. Even though those Buddhist words expressed our Catholic thoughts correctly, they were never used in Catholic writings. The reason was that the uneducated readers might interpret such usage as an endorsement and an approval of the Buddhist religion.

With much hesitation, I went to see John and told him the situation. He became enraged. "How can a priest who has never attended a university, and has never studied Chinese literature in depth, dare to criticize my writings?" I was shocked and surprised by his violent reaction and tried to calm him. But his pride as a scholar had been deeply wounded, and he felt terribly hurt. Even though I endeavored to pacify him, he kept on raging and finally said, "If this is the position of the Catholic Church toward my writings, then I will have to review my own position toward the Catholic Church."

I was flabbergasted and realized that this was a temptation of pride, which he had to win. Patiently I sat down on the only chair in the room and told him that I was determined not to leave his house until he changed his mind and resolved to go to Confession. For two hours I talked to him, explaining the basic principles of humility and the necessity of forgiveness. Sometimes he seemed convinced, but a few minutes later he was again in a rage.

After about two hours, God's grace won. John knelt down in front of me, right in his bedroom where we always had our conversations, and said, "Father Nicholas, I know I am a sinner. Forgive me. I want to make my Confession now!" From that day on, John's faith never wavered again.

Notes

1. For the sake of history, I have to mention the fact that in his auto-biography Dr. Wu gave a slightly different version of our first encounter. He wrote: "As I came out of my first visit to the Bishop, my eyes were attracted by the books exhibited in some glass cases. Just as I was looking, a young priest came out from his office and asked me: 'Are you Dr. Wu?' 'Yes—I said—but how do you know me, Father?' He told me that he had received some letters from the Jesuits in Shanghai inquiring about me." Dr. Wu wrote his biography twelve years after our first meeting and it is not surprising that the details of our first encounter escaped him. However, I remember that event most clearly and my version is the correct one. John was correct when he wrote that I had placed some bookcases with English and Catholic books in the vestibule of the mission house in Caine Road and that my office of the Catholic Truth Society was just next to the entrance of the house. Whenever Dr. Wu came to see the bishop, he invariably looked at the bookcases, as he was naturally fond of books, and often purchased some. However, our first meeting took place at his house, as I described above.

2. Dr. Wu's godchild and a famous writer. For many years he was professor at St. John's University in Brooklyn, New York.

15

Plans For The Evangelization Of China

The Science Of Love

One day in March 1940, the publication manager of the *T'ien Hsia* magazine in Hong Kong told Dr. Wu, "John, we are badly in need of a major article for the April issue of *T'ien Hsia,* and there are only fifteen days left before going to press. Can you write one?"

"About what?" John replied in surprise.

"About anything you want, provided, of course, it is within the guidelines of our editorial policy."

"Can I really have a free hand and write about anything I want?"

"Of course you can."

"Consider it done," John said. "I will bring over the manuscript to you before the deadline."

That day John Wu went home in high spirits. For quite a few months he had toyed with the idea of writing about his newly found faith. But he did not feel ready yet to write a book, nor could he think of a subject for an article. The request from his fellow editor of *T'ien Hsia* gave him the final push he needed. Yes, he would write an article about his favorite topic: the love of God as lived and practiced by St. Teresa of Lisieux.

He phoned me immediately to give me the good news. "Father Nicholas, you have been urging me all along to write something about Christianity. Well, I have just committed myself to writing a long article for *T'ien Hsia* on St. Teresa of Lisieux. I will need your help, and I count on you."

That very afternoon, I was at his house. He had already decided on the title—"The Science of Love: A Study in the Teachings of St. Teresa of the Infant Jesus." Alice Chow and Francis Yeh also came along, rejoicing at the good news and offering their collaboration.

During the following weeks, as John wrote this 10,000-word article, I was with him practically every day. He wrote and rewrote every sentence and consulted me about points of doctrine. Francis Yeh and Alice Chow, both excellent scholars, were often consulted about the use of English words. John, however, did all the writing. He worked into the wee hours of the morning without stopping. When finally the manuscript was ready, he proudly walked over to the *T'ien Hsia* office to deliver it. He was a happy man. We celebrated this event with a friendly dinner because we all felt as if we had gone through labor pains.

The gist of the article is this: At the spiritual school of St. Teresa, Dr. Wu discovered the Catholic concept of life, namely that life is neither a mere bargain with God nor a dry series of "don'ts" with heavy sanctions. Rather, it is a relationship of love, a loving surrender of the creature to its Creator, a falling in love of man with God, and, to express it in John's own words: "a kiss for a kiss, or rather a small kiss for a big kiss between the soul and his Redeemer."

The article has passages of unsurpassed beauty. It is neither an abstract study of the mystic's concept of life nor a dry analysis of a religious system, but a deeply moving interpretation of the way of Christian love. This inspired essay is Dr. Wu's song of gratitude to the mercy of God, who raised him from the depths and darkness of atheism to the heights and radiant light of Christianity.

A Successful Publication

T'ien Hsia gave the CTS permission to publish John's article in booklet form and we decided to have two editions: one in paperback, the other printed on deluxe paper and bound in red Chinese silk. This latter was especially intended for distribution in the United States.

The book was an instant success. Within a couple of years it was translated into fourteen languages, including Chinese, French, Italian, German, Hindu, and Telegu. I prepared the Italian translation, which was published by our own PIME press in Milan, Italy.

The Science of Love claims a special place among all the writings of Dr. Wu. It is also his very first writing on a Catholic subject after his conversion to the faith. To my knowledge, it is also, in the history of the Church, the first book on a Christian subject written by an Oriental scholar in a Western language—at least in modern times.

The Sunday Missal

In the early forties, about three hundred years after Christianity had been brought to China, there was not yet a Sunday missal in Chinese for use by China's three million Catholics. There was a Chinese edition of the Daily Roman missal in old Chinese classic style, published by the Paris Foreign Mission Society. But it was a bulky, expensive book, difficult to follow and not very practical for the average lay Catholic. It was used almost exclusively by Chinese priests and sisters.

I have always considered the use of the missal on the part of the laity as an indispensable means for an intelligent participation in the liturgy and consequently for the growth of a truly Christian spirit. This is why for years I had dreamed of publishing a Sunday missal in popular modern Chinese language, but I had never had the opportunity to do so for lack of funds and of competent help.

While teaching John Wu how to follow the Mass, I noticed that he cherished the liturgy and that he found it a valuable help in his spiritual life. I soon realized that in John Wu I had at last found the man to write a new modern translation of the Sunday missal.

I spoke to him about this plan and he enthusiastically volunteered to do the writing. In those days we did not yet have a complete translation of the Bible in Chinese, and the translation of the scriptural readings used by the daily missal was poor. I asked him to do a new translation of all the prayers and of the liturgical instructions contained in the missal and to improve the translation of the readings from the Old and New Testaments.

To facilitate the use of the missal by the laity I wanted to have it printed in two colors, but the CTS could not afford the extra cost. I then wrote a begging letter to Fr. Steadman of the Confraternity of the Precious Blood in Brooklyn, NY, whom I knew through correspondence. Much to my surprise, he volunteered to pay the total cost of the entire edition of 10,000 copies. He sent me a shipment of thin Bible paper (which we could not find in Hong Kong) and a check in the amount of five thousand American dollars, a very large sum of money in those days. Thus, through Chinese and American collaboration, the CTS was able to publish the first Sunday missal in modern Chinese.

Again I asked the Salesian press to print the missal and this time Brother John and his Chinese students did an excellent job. The missal was beautifully printed in two colors on thin paper and clothbound. It sold then for one Hong Kong dollar (twenty cents U.S.), all over China.

In spite of the raging Sino-Japanese War, orders came pouring into my office. The publication of the Sunday missal was a significant event in the history of Christianity in China and one of the first fruits of the conversion of John Wu.

Preparing China For Christ

The period of time from the end of 1938, when John Wu received his Confirmation, to December 1941, when the Japanese invaded Hong Kong, was a time of tremendous spiritual growth for John Wu. He felt that bringing others to the knowledge of God was an integral part of Christian living. Francis and Alice, moved by the growth of John's spiritual life and by his example, also became more and more involved in bringing the faith to others. All three of them were part of the elite social circles of Chinese society and had close contacts with the leading personalities of the Chungking government. It was in this environment that they exercised their successful ministry and brought many non-Christians to the faith.

Because of our close friendship, we shared our experiences, our hopes and our efforts. Through them I discovered a new aspect of missionary work: the ministry to the intelligentsia of China. They formed a distinct class and had their own needs and characteristics. At that time our three Catholic universities in China (Shanghai, Tianjin and Beijing) were in Japanese-occupied areas. Their work was very much curtailed and any contact with Nationalist China was strictly forbidden. Consequently, except for some exceptions in Chungking, there was no Catholic ministry to the Chinese intellectuals. The work of my three friends was really providential.

Through our frequent discussions about making Christ known in China, we came to the conclusion that a lot of preparatory work among the intelligentsia was needed before the real evangelization of China could be successful. We felt it was necessary to create a favorable attitude toward Christianity among the intellectual leaders of the country in order to influence the whole nation. History teaches that it is scholars and writers who mold the public opinion of a nation.

In those days a very peculiar situation existed in China with regard to Christianity. Even though President Chiang Kai-shek and his wife were practicing Christians, and hundreds of prominent leaders in all walks of life knew Christianity well, having studied in Protestant American universities, Christianity was not making great inroads. We felt that the

Chinese intelligentsia had to be stimulated in order to become more interested and more active in promoting Christianity. We were convinced that China needed groups of highly educated Christians who through their writings, speeches, and good example would make Christian ideas and values filter down from the speculative realm of the intellectual circles to the level of the man in the street.

We realized that personal ministry alone was not sufficient to influence the attitude of the intellectual classes toward religion. We needed books, books that would emphasize all that Christianity has in common with Chinese culture and religion. Our goal was to show convincingly how Christianity is the ultimate fulfillment of Chinese religions. As John Wu put it: we needed teams of scholars to "baptize" Chinese classics and show how their teachings prepare the way for the coming of Christianity.

Books are the tools of the intelligentsia and we needed plenty of them in Chinese. But there were none. Catholic writers had never been seriously stimulated to either try to produce original books presenting Christianity to the Chinese or to translate important Christian literary works from Western languages into Chinese. The reason, of course, was that there was no market for this type of literature and no money to invest in this activity.

We realized, of course, that giving precedence to works of charity (schools, hospitals, outpatient clinics, and other institutions) was a form of religious activity in full conformity with the Gospel and that the Church in China had made much progress even without an adequate supply of books. In those days there were in China over three and one half million converts, scores of Chinese bishops, 2,500 Chinese priests, 5,000 Chinese sisters, three universities and thousands of schools, outpatient clinics, hospitals and convents throughout China. But, still, the Church had not made much of a dent in the evangelization of Chinese culture. We felt that the work of pre-evangelization of Chinese culture had yet to be started.

Even the Protestant denominations, which had much larger budgets and much better mass media, had not fared much better. The Protestant Chinese literature was strictly Bible-oriented and not too concerned about Chinese culture.

A Great Plan

One day John, Alice, Francis and I, during one of our frequent conversations on the evangelization of China, agreed that a step in the right direction would be translating into Chinese classic books about Christianity from Europe and America. These books, we felt, would introduce Christianity to the Chinese intelligentsia. Francis Yeh, the most practical and down-to-earth of the group, with his usual humor and powerful laugh, said, "Well, if there are no Christian books in Chinese, let's begin translating books from other countries and publishing them!" We agreed with him and immediately started formulating plans to this effect.

We decided to compile a list of outstanding Catholic books by the best European and American Catholic writers and to arrange for their translation into Chinese. The list covered every aspect of Christianity, such as theology, spirituality, arts, science, history. We selected books by English and American authors to be translated first. Because America and England were the most popular and respected nations in the China of those days, books from these two countries would more likely be accepted and read.

Long and complicated negotiations with the Commercial Press of China led to the signing of a contract for the publication of manuscripts that would be prepared under the supervision of the Catholic Truth Society. The CTS would select the books to be translated and pay for the cost of translation. The Commercial Press would take care of the cost of publication and of circulation. This was to be a non-profit venture, and the income from royalties would help the CTS to pay for the cost of translations. The initial capital for this venture was to be raised by the CTS among its Hong Kong friends.

We chose *The Spirit of Catholicism* by Carl Adams as the first book of the series. The second was *Isabella of Spain* by the famous historian Walsh. Chesterton's and Belloc's books and many others were to follow later. We secured the services of a competent translator and before too long we had the complete translation in Chinese of Carl Adams' book. We gave it to the Commercial Press and were already halfway into the translation of Walsh's books when the Japanese attacked Hong Kong on December 8, 1941. Our plans went up in smoke. Through the following four years of war we were separated. Dr. Wu, Francis, Alice and their friends escaped to free China while I remained under the Japanese in Hong Kong. There was no time to think about books when our very survival was at stake.

After the war we did revive the plan, but John went to Rome, Alice and Francis died shortly afterward and the Chinese government was again engulfed in war with the communists. That was the last nail in the coffin of our great plans for the evangelization of China.

16

1937: A Disastrous Year

A Cholera Epidemic

The year 1937—the "Year of the Ox," according to the Chinese calendar—was a disastrous one for Hong Kong. A cholera epidemic and then two violent typhoons hit the colony. Worst of all, the destructive effects of the Sino-Japanese war began to be felt in Hong Kong too.

The cholera came first. In China, cholera was always regarded as one of the worst scourges afflicting men.[1] The Chinese did not know any' medicine or effective remedy to stem the course of this disease; the only remedy they knew was to run away from it. When cholera broke out in one Chinese village, most of the people would run to other villages, often spreading the epidemic.

In Hong Kong, however, things did not happen that way. Energetic countermeasures put into effect by the government helped contain the disease. The first to die was a young Chinese man returning to Hong Kong from Guangzhou. (This was no surprise because according to official statistics cholera was prevalent in central China during the decade 1930-40.) Cases reported to the medical authorities grew steadily and corpses of people struck down by cholera began to appear in the streets. Fr. Ryan wrote: "The disease appeared suddenly and spread rapidly. It took the medical authorities completely by surprise, and though energetic measures were taken to deal with it and to give attention to the stricken, over a thousand people died."[2]

From the very beginning Bishop Valtorta was on the front lines of relief work. Realizing that government workers were few and overworked, he offered the services of volunteer sister-nurses to the authorities, but the offer was declined. When, however, the epidemic grew beyond measure, the government asked Bishop Valtorta for help. Five volunteer sisters and one priest were placed immediately at the disposal of the authorities. They did great work and when the situation returned to normal their assistance received official recognition.

In addition to this hospital work, according to Fr. Ryan, "the moral help given by priests was an important factor in limiting the progress of the disease, for they checked the panic which was rising in some of the more densely populated areas of the city, and induced the people to keep calm and take the necessary precautions against the spread of the disease."[3]

Bishop Valtorta set the example. Defying the risk to his own health, he constantly visited the overcrowded Chinese hospitals to console patients and give moral support to the sisters working there. He urged pastors to help widows and orphaned children. The St. Vincent de Paul Society, under the direction of the pastors, raised and distributed funds to the families of the cholera victims.

In his report to PIME's headquarters, Bishop Valtorta quoted a remarkable case. A young Christian fisherman was hit hard by the first typhoon of that summer and lost his boat and house. As if that misfortune were not enough, he suddenly became sick and his wife realized it was cholera. Penniless and in a state of desperation she brought him to the government hospital and begged the sisters for help. As the poor man lay in bed in a comatose state with all the signs of imminent death, the sisters took the young wife and the two little ones to pray in the church. A recent convert to Catholicism, the young woman prayed aloud with all her faith: "Lord Jesus, don't allow my husband to die. Now we have no house, no work. How can I raise these two creatures by myself?"

Echoing the mother, the children, five and six years old, also prayed: "Sacred Heart of Jesus, please let our father live, please, please!" The fact is that in spite of the totally negative medical prognosis, the young man survived and was later able to reestablish his business.

Bishop Valtorta concluded the report by writing: "A miracle? I do believe so."

The Health Department ordered widespread inoculation, and this, along with the charitable assistance of Catholic and Protestant organizations, reduced the terrible effects of the scourge to a minimum. Official statistics recorded about one thousand deaths, but adding unreported deaths and deaths in villages outside Hong Kong, the real figure was certainly many times that given by the government.

All of us priests and nuns were inoculated and none of us contracted the disease. Even the sisters who had direct contact with sick patients in the hospitals suffered no casualty. And, tragic as the whole experience was, it did not disrupt life as much as the typhoons did.

Typhoons: The Second Scourge

"Father Spada, what is a typhoon?" I asked my old pastor the first summer I was in Hong Kong. In the next twenty minutes I got an earful of stories of the devastation caused by these tropical storms. Basically typhoons are not different from hurricanes, which occur along the eastern coast of the USA, except that they are more numerous (sometimes over twenty of them in a year) and less seasonal. Typhoons can occur at any time of the year, although August, September and October are the peak season. The word "typhoon" probably comes from the Cantonese word "tai fong," which means "strong wind."

I went through several minor typhoons during my early years in Hong Kong, but two "biggies" came in 1937. The first came on September 2, packing winds of 164 miles an hour, and the second, almost as strong as the first, arrived during the night of October 3-4.

In those days radio was still in its infancy and very few Chinese owned radio sets, so the Hong Kong government informed the people of the impending threat of a typhoon by means of conventional signs displayed in different parts of the city. These signs were hoisted high on top of the tallest buildings and were visible to a large part of the population. Signal number one (in the shape of a T) meant a typhoon watch; there was a typhoon heading toward the colony. Number two meant a typhoon alert, meaning that the storm had come within a radius of three hundred miles. Numbers three through eight indicated the direction from which the typhoon was coming. Numbers nine and ten indicated that the center of the storm was over the colony.

The center for tracking typhoons along the China coast was located in the Jesuit Astronomic Observatory of Zi-ka-wei near Shanghai, almost midway along the coast from north to south. In my days the observatory was directed by Jesuit Fr. F. Gherzi and subsidized by the Chinese government and shipping interests. In spite of limited equipment, Fr. Gherzi is credited with saving the lives of hundreds of thousands, if not millions, of people from Thailand to Korea, not to speak of thousands of ocean liners, cargo ships and other vessels sailing in the west Pacific.

Usually, when typhoon signal number one was hoisted only few people paid attention and began the necessary preparation because very often the storm changed course. However, when number two was hoisted everyone was concerned. Windows were boarded up, food and water stored, schools closed down, junks and small boats hurried to their shelters as people sought the safety of home or shelter. During such "alert" periods the ferry linking Hong Kong and Kowloon was always jammed with people either returning to their houses on the other side of the harbor or trying to escape to a safer place. I remember several such trips across the harbor with a very rough sea on overloaded boats, with all the passengers, including myself, praying with all our hearts to make it home safely.

When the barometric pressure fell very low as the center of the storm approached, the sky assumed a dull gray color, and a sense of impending disaster pervaded the air. The winds began to increase in violence, the roaring of the sea rose in volume and rain fell in sheets and buckets. As the fury of the winds grew, trees were uprooted, roofs flew away, chimneys were smashed, windows and doors were blown inward, everything not solidly anchored became a projectile carried away by a tremendous force. People cowered in their houses, in semi-darkness during the day because of the boarded-up windows or in darkness at night as electricity went out. After a few hours of this infernal racket, rain and wind would suddenly cease. The sky would become more luminous and a great calm spread over the city. You knew then that you were in the very eye of the storm, and that the worst was still to come.

Within fifteen or twenty minutes, the wind, rain and noise gradually started all over again, ever increasing in violence. The hours passed slowly and agonizingly. The stifling heat was always intense because the windows were all boarded up. The light was poor. All you could do was listen to the terrific roar, in fear that at any moment the roof would be blown away or a window would cave in, or even that the house might be washed downhill in a mud avalanche caused by the torrential rains.

When the worst of the typhoon itself finally passed, mud slides and flooding continued because of heavy rains. It usually took two or three days before life could return to some kind of normal pace. In every storm those who suffered most were the boat people who lived on junks and the squatters who lived in shacks on the hills. Unfailingly they were the worst of the casualties.

I weathered the typhoon of September 2 in comparative safety, watching through cracks in the boarded-up windows of our sturdy mission house the incredible spectacle of the harbor in turmoil, and praying for those in danger of losing their lives. It seemed that all hell had let loose. During the worst three hours of the storm more than forty boats of all sizes were snatched from their anchors or piers and tossed away at the mercy of furious winds. They were smashed, then, on the beach or grounded in shallower waters. All the strength of their powerful engines working at full steam could not save them. Among the grounded ocean liners were the Italian *Conte Verde* and the Japanese *Asama Maru*, two of the larger ships calling at Hong Kong. Even the powerful tug *Kau Sing,* especially built by the port authorities to save people in case of storms and fires at sea, sank, a victim to this typhoon.

Most of the buildings in the colony were strong enough to withstand the fury of the storm, yet not a single one failed to suffer damage. Even in our mission house, a four-story, reinforced concrete building, several windows caved in. One of our priests was hit full in the face by a flying window pane, suffering serious injury.

In the Chinese villages surrounding the city, small houses were destroyed by the hundreds, and with them chapels and mission buildings. Giant trees were uprooted, entire groves devastated, cars and people blown into the sea. Along low coastal areas powerful waves raised by the high winds and extraordinary tides swept inland through city streets and villages, overturning and devastating everything in their path. At the height of the storm, a crowded tenement burst into flame. In spite of the superhuman efforts of the firemen, people died by the hundreds. Even the corpses lined along the road were washed out to sea by a powerful wave and lost forever.

The boat people suffered the heaviest casualties. Fishing fleets were entirely wiped away. The typhoon came so fast that they had no time to return to their shelters, and bore the brunt of the storm on the high seas. The government estimated the number of deaths at sea at over fifteen thousand. But the people on the land did not fare much better. Thousands more lost their lives in houses blown away, mud slides, floods, etc. Financial losses were in the scores of millions of dollars.

On October 4 we had the second typhoon. This one hit the northern area of our diocese on mainland China, and the widespread destruction again affected tens of thousands of our poorest people along with many church buildings and institutions. The storm disrupted communications so extensively that news of the damage suffered by our houses on the mainland did not reach Hong Kong, only a couple of hundred miles away by sea, until the end of the month. The reason was that communications by sea were already impossible because of a Japanese blockade and because most of the overland route had been washed away by a terrifically high tide, which swept over all the low lands.

The War Is Felt In Hong Kong

When the Hong Kong papers reported the clash between Chinese and Japanese troops near Beijing on the night of July 7, 1937, we in Hong Kong were not too concerned. Nobody foresaw that the clash was the beginning of a conflict that would engulf both nations, changing the course of history and the lives of billions of people. My own life, too, was deeply affected and disrupted by the upheaval.

For a true understanding of the causes of the Sino-Japanese war, one must have at least a summary idea of the events that led up to it. Here I will limit myself to reporting briefly those facts relating to the effects of this war upon us in Hong Kong.

When, after the July 7 incident, the Japanese army defiantly entered Chinese territory from the Manchurian border and marched toward Beijing, the world realized that Japan meant business. Their ultimate goal was the occupation of China, and the overthrow of the Nationalist government in order to establish a puppet regime at the beck and call of Japanese interests.

I cannot give here a detailed account of the Japanese rapid advance on Chinese soil during that first phase of the war. However, a brief outline may help the reader to better grasp the magnitude of the havoc, the sufferings, the anguish, the disruption of the lives of hundreds of millions of Chinese caused by this unexpected, unjustified and unprovoked military aggression. The major facts of the first fifteen months of the war are these:

Four weeks after starting its aggressive march from the Manchurian-Chinese border on July 7, the Japanese army occupied Beijing and Tianjin, the two largest cities in north China. Then several army columns marched over a thousand miles southward, defeating the Nationalist army in severe battles and, in November, occupied Shanghai, the largest city in China. Five months later, in December, they occupied Nanjing, the capital.

Chiang Kai-shek moved the seat of the government to Wuhan, over a thousand miles to the west, in central China. Relentlessly, the Japanese pursued him there, too, continuing at once west toward Wuhan and south toward Guangzhou. Both these cities fell to Japan the following October (1938). Again Chiang moved the capital further west, this time to

Chungking in the mountainous and remote Sichuan Province.

In the meantime other military units moved southward toward Guangdong, the virtual capital and largest city of south China, the rice bowl of the country. Besides following the overland route from the north across central China, the Japanese decided to also attack Guangdong from the east. In September 1938, in preparation for this attack, several army and navy units landed on the Chinese mainland in Bias Bay, about fifty miles north of Hong Kong, and marched directly east toward Guangdong, crossing most of the territory of the Hong Kong diocese. A month later, in October, Guangdong fell to the Japanese.

Besides these land operations, the Japanese took over the major Chinese railways from Beijing to Wuhan and Guangdong. They enforced a sea blockade along the China coast from north to south, depriving Chiang of much-needed supplies from abroad and devastating the lives of millions of fishermen along the coast. They totally destroyed the budding Chinese air force and civilian airlines and thus gained complete control of the air. Unopposed they carried out thousands of air raids on military and civilian targets, bombing large and small cities, harbors, rivers, and villages indiscriminately. Their purpose was to break down whatever resistance there was by creating confusion, panic and despair.

Yet, in spite of the enormous losses of territory and human lives, China neither surrendered nor even dreamed of asking for peace. With traditional Oriental patience millions of people fled to unoccupied territories while those who had to remain in occupied zones resorted to non-violent resistance. Even though there were Chinese who collaborated with the Japanese, Japan never succeeded in organizing a Chinese puppet government that could effectively control the occupied areas.

When on July 7, 1937, the shooting war started along the Chinese-Manchurian border, nobody in Hong Kong paid much attention. There was no formal declaration of war and everybody thought that it was just another incident between the two countries. Even the Chinese population was not stirred up. The newspapers reported the bare facts, and the usual war rhetoric did not impress anyone. Beijing was two thousand miles away!

However, when the modernly equipped Japanese army crossed the border into China a few days later, marching on Beijing, the British colony began to take notice. Chinese public opinion was electrified and solidly unified against this new and unjustified Japanese encroachment on their territory.

By the time the Japanese started marching south toward Shanghai, after conquering Beijing, the effects of the war were being felt more and more deeply in Hong Kong. Wave after wave of Chinese refugees escaping the Japanese advance began to arrive by plane, train, ocean liner, junk, and even on foot. Their harrowing stories confirmed the press reports of the cruelty of the invaders, the devastation of property and the terrible sufferings of millions of people. We missionaries soon became involved in relief work for the refugees.

The Story Of Chen Pak-To

Here is just one case out of the millions of tragedies inflicted by the war, the case of just one young boy whom I met one day on the streets in downtown Hong Kong. At first glance he looked like any other of the thousands of homeless urchins, roaming the streets of the large metropolitan areas, eking out a miserable existence by stealing and begging from foreigners and from Chinese shopkeepers. But a closer look revealed that he was different. His darting, intelligent eyes and his refined manners made him seem an oddity in that environment. As I walked along the oceanfront in central Hong Kong on an errand for the bishop, he recognized me as a priest because of my Roman collar. A little shyly and hesitatingly, he left his gang and approached me. Speaking in a heavily accented Cantonese dialect he said, "You are a priest, aren't you?"

"Yes, son, I am," I responded, surprised. "But how do you know that I am a priest?"

"Father, I am a Catholic, too. The missionary in my village dresses like you. All my family is Catholic."

"But where are you from? What are you doing here in Hong Kong going around with that gang?"

"Father, all my family have been killed. I escaped by a miracle."

Looking more closely at him and noting the pathos in his eyes, I said, "Son, come along with me to the mission house and tell me your story." As we walked along, he unburdened his soul to me and I felt in my heart all the horror and cruelty of that tragic war.

His name was Chen Pak-to. He had two brothers and one sister, and came from a well-to-do family in a provincial town of the Anhui Province, north of Shanghai. Life used to be peaceful and serene in the Chen household as father ran the family business and mother, with the help of a couple of servants, took care of the brood of growing children. There were a lot of Catholics in the quaint little town and even a resident missionary. Missionary nuns ran a small elementary school for Catholic children. Chen Pak-to had learned his religion at the knees of his pious mother but it was at the school that he had later learned his catechism and had become an altar boy.

At fifteen he had gone to the local high school and was planning to enter a university later. The ebb and flow of the turmoil in the Chinese nation as it developed from an old-fashioned empire into a modern, democratic nation had been hardly noticed in the happy childhood of Chen Pak-to. The provincial governors in the Anhui Province had changed, the warlord and generals had succeeded one another, small local armies had come and gone, but life had continued to be peaceful and serene in the Chen family.

Then one day early in the fall of 1937 there had been ugly rumors of invasion. A Japanese army column was marching toward Shanghai and, after badly beating the Chinese Nationalist Army, had proceeded to occupy the Anhui Province. Chen Pak-to's town had gone into panic and many had run away, but the Chen family had decided to stay and take refuge at the Catholic mission. For weeks in advance of the marching army, a series of Japanese air raids had hit civilian targets indiscriminately, killed hundreds of people and thoroughly disrupting their centuries-old way of life.

The dispirited Nationalist garrison assigned to defend the province had melted away before the onslaught of the Japanese armored column. Many Chinese soldiers, seeing the futility of resistance, had lain down their arms and run for their lives. Before long Japanese tanks had entered the town. Japanese soldiers, drunk with victory, had roamed the streets pillaging, raping, beating up people, burning shops and houses. The Chen family had found refuge at the mission house, but when a few days later they returned home they had found their shop burned down and their house pillaged. A well-to-do family, they had become penniless.

As Mr. Chen had rummaged through the ruins of his shop to salvage whatever could be salvaged, he had been surrounded by a group of soldiers and ordered to follow them as a coolie to carry their goods. He had refused and was killed on the spot as a lesson to other reluctant recruits. The broken-hearted family had buried him quickly and decided to separate: Mrs. Chen, with her daughter and the youngest son, had decided to return to their native village to live with some relatives, while Pak-to with his younger brother would follow his school and move west to free China.

Migrating schools were a common phenomenon in those days. Large numbers of school youngsters and teachers, rather than submit to Japanese rule, marched out of the occupied areas, carrying on their shoulders school desks, blackboards, laboratory equipment, school supplies, etc., in order to continue their education in free China.

The long march of Pak-to and his school was not different from that of hundreds of other high schools, colleges and even universities. Teachers and students, boys and girls, carrying their school equipment on their shoulders, marched hundreds of miles pursuing the dream of living and studying in free China. On their long trek to freedom they were often attacked by Japanese soldiers or strafed by Japanese planes. But they kept going, greeted as heroes by village people, spending cold nights in the open air, eating whatever came their way in order to survive, occasionally finding refuge in a Catholic or Protestant mission, or some abandoned pagan temple. Many died of starvation, cold or sheer exhaustion, but the survivors kept on marching, the torch of freedom burning brightly in their hearts.

It often happened, as it did in the case of Pak-to, that once they were settled in a city in free China, the Japanese would occupy that part of the country also, and the poor students would have to start all over again continuing westward.

On one of these marches toward the west Pak-to's brother had died of exhaustion and fatigue. Pak-to had buried him and continued on with the school. A few weeks later another group of migrating students from the Anhui Province had caught up with him and he had learned that his mother and sister, on the way to their native village, had died in a Japanese air raid. Being now completely alone in the world, he had lost interest in the school and decided to go to Hong Kong in search of freedom. He had left his teachers and classmates and, on foot, begging, stealing, starving, occasionally obtaining a ride in some truck, he had traveled south over one thousand miles until he had crossed the border at night and took up street living in Hong Kong.

When he finished telling me his story I was almost as emotionally drained as he was. At the mission we fed him a good meal. Then we found a place for him to stay with a Catholic family and enrolled him in a Chinese school. He remained with us four years, until Hong Kong itself was invaded by the Japanese in December 1941. Then, again on foot, alone, he resumed his trek toward unoccupied China and freedom.

He never came back. To this day we don't know what happened to him. He probably died in the midst of his journey toward freedom, somewhere on the road. His memory has always remained in my mind as a symbol and an example of the immense tragedies of that cruel war. What the Chinese people suffered through eight long years at the hands of the Japanese invaders can never be adequately expressed in words.

Notes

1. Speaking of cholera in China, my friend Dr. John C. H. Wu told me that in 1945 when he attended the conference for the foundation of the United Nations in San Francisco, as a delegate of the Chinese government, he was present at a meeting between our President Harry Truman and Syngman Rhee of Korea. As Mr. Truman was insistently urging Syngman Rhee to form a coalition government with the communists, Mr. Rhee exclaimed: "Mr. President, the Communists are like cholera. In my country, when cholera breaks out in a village, you run fast. You cannot compromise with Communists as you cannot compromise with cholera." Syngman Rhee reflected the wisdom of centuries. Truman did not understand and the communists took over half of Korea at the cost of many lives.

2. Ryan, p. 213.

3. Ibid.

17

1938:
The War Comes Closer To Hong Kong

An International Committee

"Maestrini," Bishop Valtorta said to me one morning in the late summer of 1938 as I reported to him for work, "this afternoon there is a meeting at Bishop Hall's house. We have to organize a War Relief Committee. Get ready to come with me."

Bishop Hall was the Anglican bishop of Hong Kong and an outstanding figure in the life of the colony. We all respected and admired him for his broad views and his deep sense of religion combined with tact and kindness.

Refugees from war-torn China were arriving in great numbers and this was creating a serious problem for the colony. As the overcrowding increased so also did disease and famine. In the summer of 1938 Hong Kong experienced the second-worst cholera epidemic in its history and thousands of people died.

In the meantime the Japanese invading forces continued their march to the south toward Guangzhou, about two hundred miles by air from Hong Kong. Everybody feared a further swelling of the refugee population and the colony's government appealed to all charitable associations to join in relief work. Bishop Hall, after consulting with Bishop Valtorta, convened a meeting in his house of all representatives of the major religions in order to coordinate relief work.

It was a memorable meeting. All the leading religious personalities of the colony were there, including Buddhists and Parsees. All agreed to join hands and work together for a more efficient and better-coordinated relief work in both the colony and the China mainland. When the time came to elect officers, Bishop Hall stood up, eulogized Bishop Valtorta for his charity and his ability, and nominated him Chairman of the Joint Relief Committee. There were no other nominations and Bishop Valtorta was elected unanimously.

Let me remark that if something of this nature were to happen today, we would not be surprised. However, that was 1938. Regrettably, coexistence among the various Christians denominations in the colony had often been marred by strife and rivalry. We Catholics had never worked closely with other religious denominations, even though we had very friendly relations with most of them, especially the Anglicans. When our Chinese friends were facing danger, we set aside all of our theological differences and historical rivalries and joined hands in a common effort to make our relief work as effective as possible.

Bishop Valtorta soon appointed a Catholic committee of the most influential Chinese and English Catholics. Its purpose was to coordinate Catholic relief work with the General Committee, formulate plans for the housing of refugees and organize soup kitchens, distribution of blankets, food, medicines and bandages. Before the end of that summer there were already half a million refugees in the tiny colony and the population had grown to over three million. In a surprise night raid the police discovered that the number of street sleepers had increased by over twenty-five thousand new arrivals.

The Japanese Landing Near Hong-Kong

In the morning of October 7, 1938, Hong Kong awakened to find that the Sino-Japanese war had suddenly arrived at its border. Screaming headlines in the morning papers announced that during the night Japanese naval forces had made a surprise landing in Bias Bay on the China mainland. That was only fifty miles north of the colony. As there was no opposition, in the afternoon of the same day an armored column began marching east toward Guangzhou. This meant that it was going to cross the area of our diocese on the China mainland.

It just happened that that very week was the week for our annual retreat and all of us, Chinese and Italian priests, from Hong Kong and the mainland were making a retreat with Bishop Valtorta at the mission house. The news of the invasion came as a terrible shock to us and left us bewildered and dismayed. All our mission districts and parishes in

Haifeng and Huiyang Counties were right in the path of the invaders. Thus, thousands of Catholics and prospective converts, our hospitals, our schools, all of our institutions were left unprotected and at the mercy of the invading army. Being fully aware of the destruction and casualties that had devastated Catholic and Protestant missions located in the path of the Japanese invaders in other parts of China, we feared the worst. This calamity was affecting not only the bishop and the pastors of those areas, but all of us. Our missions, our Christians, our work, our houses, our own Chinese people were going through suffering and devastation and we could not be with them.

Adding to our pain and the frustration we all experienced at being so far away at such a critical time was the lack of news. October 7, 1938, was one of the saddest days of my mission life.

The bishop canceled the spiritual retreat and told all the pastors of the invaded areas that they were free to return immediately to their parishes if they could find any transportation. They all rushed out at once, hoping to reach their parishes ahead of the advancing Japanese forces. A few hours later they all returned crestfallen to the mission house because no means of transportation were available. The border was sealed and all travel by sea or by land had been suspended.

We all had to settle down to a painful period of anxious waiting. Relief work took up all of our time because a new large wave of refugees soon began arriving. October 7, 1938, was the beginning of a long, painful period in the history of the Hong Kong Diocese.

Life In Occupied Areas

At the end of that month our priests were finally able to travel back to their parishes on the mainland.

On the evening of October 27 we bade a tearful farewell to Frs. Michael Robba, Lawrence Bianchi and Raphael Della Nina. Later in the night they left Hong Kong on an old Chinese junk bound for Haifeng County, about two hundred miles northeast of Hong Kong. They faced a very dangerous journey because of the Japanese blockade and because they had to sail across Bias Bay, where the Japanese were still landing troops and supplies. The Japanese had threatened to sink any boat that came too close to their ships. Furthermore, bands of pirates were preying on the few lucky boats that survived the blockade.

The following day we also bade farewell to another group of Chinese and Italian priests who left on foot to reach their posts in the Huiyang area. Because there were neither buses nor trains available they decided to walk the 150 miles to their destinations. Their journey was risky. They first had to walk about forty miles to cross an area of free China infested with bandits and thieves. Then, once they reached the Japanese-occupied territory, they had to deal with the Japanese authorities to secure travel permits through occupied China. These permits were not much of a protection from other Japanese units, roving soldiers and bandits, but one could not travel without them.

For two painful weeks after their departure we received no news. The bishop and all of us were on pins and needles not knowing what had happened nor how much our missions had suffered.

Finally, on November 14, some refugees brought us letters from both Haifeng and Huiyang. All our priests had arrived safely.

Fr. Mike Robba, a delightful man with a great sense of humor, wrote from Haifeng proudly informing us that he had scored a great victory. He did not mind the three long days of uninterrupted navigation in the rickety, overcrowded old junk. He did not mind the dangers from the Japanese, the weather and the pirates. He was happy because he had succeeded in smuggling ashore a barrel of sacramental wine . . . probably the first imported wine to enter south China after the Japanese occupation! Passing on to more serious things, he reported the loss of over a dozen churches and chapels, burned down or bombed. Life was continuously disrupted by daily Japanese air raids and the phenomenal growth of banditry, but his parishioners were alive and he was happy.

Fr. Poletti sent us news from Huiyang. In spite of the risks their overland trip had been uneventful. All of them had reached their destinations safely notwithstanding blistered feet and aching legs. He wrote:

"Thanks to God almost all our Christians are safe but unfortunately they are now scattered all over this county. They live with relatives or hide in the woods because their towns and villages have been bombed, burned or totally destroyed. Most of our churches and chapels have been destroyed, too. There is one village where the church was not destroyed, but all the houses were demolished. In Huichou, the seat of the county, there are hardly any houses left standing. The beautiful public reading room built by Fr. Pilenga was destroyed and the books burned. Only our Catholic hospital with four Canossian sisters is still standing and functioning. It is the only hospital for hundreds of miles around and does a terrific job assisting the sick and wounded.

"In the midst of great devastation we have had truly heroic examples of faith and courage. When the Japanese arrived in my village of

Tamtong, my catechist, Wong, a man of great faith and courage, was able to gather together in the Church all the women of the village, Catholics and non-Catholics, and saved them from being raped. He was arrested five times by the Japanese but managed to escape or get released. Unfortunately he was not successful in his effort to save my house. It was sacked and burned. I have lost everything I had except the clothes I have on my back.

"Thanks to God, nowhere in our churches was the Holy Eucharist desecrated. At Tamtong a young boy managed to distribute Holy Communion to those who were in the church and finished just as the soldiers reached the door. In another village a young man hurriedly gathered some people in the church and distributed Communion while the soldiers were only half a mile away and bombs exploded all around.

"Life here is very difficult. To travel from one village to another is almost impossible because of thieves and bandits. Almost every night there are armed robberies. Under these circumstances it is impossible to harvest the rice crop and people face a great famine. Shops are closed and there are no groceries available. All our priests are working hard encouraging and consoling our folks, relieving so many miseries, distributing whatever medicines we can get, praying and suffering with our people."

The Japanese invasion of south China in October 1938 was only the prelude of worse things to come. The Japanese, unable to maintain the occupation of large areas because of lack of personnel, and unable to appoint effective puppet regimes to run the occupied areas, began the disastrous policy of playing "cat and mouse" with the Chinese people. They would occupy a city, burning and destroying it, keep it for a few days, then leave and move to some other nearby area to do the same. This kept the poor people on the move all the time and left them without a local police force to control the mobs and the bandits. The Chinese officials and the policemen who survived the Japanese onslaught were always the last to return, if they returned at all, because they were invariably the first target of Japanese spies and collaborators.

The city of Huichou (population circa one hundred thousand) experienced this disastrous policy. The Japanese occupied it first on their march from Bias Bay to Guangzhou and they practically destroyed it. The homeless and frightened people scattered in the countryside. A few weeks later the Japanese abandoned it and most of the people came back. With immense patience, the distraught people began salvaging what could be salvaged. They stretched canvases between the remaining standing walls to replace the burned-out roofs, sold or bartered whatever household wares and bric-a-brac they had for a little rice and vegetables, and went around scavenging for pieces of wood to start fires for cooking. The same happened again and again after every bombing. The incredibly patient people would come crawling back after each air raid or period of occupation. With bare hands they cleared the debris of the ruined walls, stretched canvases, burned joss sticks to their ancestors, prayed for a better future. Their enduring patience and tenacity were not merely the result of Oriental fatalism, but rather the fruit of the sterling qualities of their character and self-discipline.

In spite of daily air raids, the poor people resumed, ever so slowly, some kind of normal life, but schools remained closed, bandits multiplied, public transportation was non-existent, trade was stifled, fields could not be cultivated and people suffered and died in great numbers.

When, after several months of hard work, the city had been partially rebuilt and life had returned to some normalcy, Japanese troops returned. The whole cycle of destruction and rebuilding would start all over again.

The Effects Of The War In Hong Kong

The explosions of Japanese bombs in Bias Bay were not heard in Hong Kong, but their closeness sent shivers through the three million people in the colony. From October 7, 1938, on, our life was never the same again. The first effect of the invasion was, of course, a surge of refugees, who strained our relief organizations. Bishop Valtorta and Bishop Hall immediately convened a meeting of the General Relief Committee and every church, every organization, every volunteer group was mobilized. The committee decided that it could not limit its assistance to those lucky enough to escape to Hong Kong. It also had to do whatever it could for the famished and homeless thousands of victims of Japanese aggression on the China mainland.

All of our parish organizations pitched in to do relief work. The first goals were the distribution of food, medicines, bandages, and blankets to the refugees. Then we began to man soup kitchens, supervise temporary refugee camps, find schools for the children, and scan the area for jobs for adults.

A joint expedition of Catholic and Protestant clergymen was organized to bring food and medicines to the China mainland. A large chartered passenger boat loaded with all kinds of goods left from Hong Kong for Guangzhou. For two weeks Catholic priests and Protestant ministers lived together in close quarters helping thousands of displaced, wounded, homeless people on the mainland. It was the first time that Catholic priests worked so closely with Protestant ministers and this close communion brought about an increased respect and love for each other. It was real, down-to-earth ecumenism in the true bond of Christian charity. I volunteered for that joint expedition but Bishop Valtorta told me in no uncertain terms: "I need you here. You stay with me." And that was the end of that.

The Relief Committee made an attempt through government channels to establish a neutral demilitarized zone near Hong Kong to be supervised by neutral foreigners. However, neither the Chinese nor the Japanese governments wanted to even discuss the plan and our efforts failed.

The Influence Of A Bishop

Frantic activities due to the war situation did not distract us from our main goal: the spiritual growth of the community. Bishop Valtorta organized a "League for the Sanctification of the Clergy," to offer prayers and sacrifices for the spiritual growth of the priests. To this end special religious practices were observed every Thursday before the First Friday of the month. Priests celebrated the Mass of Christ the High Priest, sisters in their convents offered special prayers, and the faithful participated in such devotions as the holy hour for the specific purposes of the league. On that day the bishop, in the very early hours of the morning, would journey to the Carmelite Convent in Stanley. It was a tedious trip of over fifteen miles by bus, but Bishop Valtorta liked to celebrate Mass in the sisters' chapel and to pray with them for the spiritual growth of the clergy of his diocese.

He often preached the monthly day of recollection to us Chinese and Italian priests in Latin. Being a fine Latin scholar and a deeply spiritual man, he always did an excellent job.

Besides praying, preaching and promoting the growth of the spiritual life of his clergy, Bishop Valtorta set an example of a very austere life. He had no regard for human comforts nor did he even care for his own health. His quarters in the bishop's house consisted of only one medium-sized room, which served the dual purpose of private study and bedroom. His bed, three wooden boards without any mattress, was relegated to a corner of the small balcony, which he had enclosed with windows. The other furniture consisted of only a desk, a chair, a bookcase and a worn-out easy chair on which he did most of his reading, praying and thinking.

The long cassock he constantly wore throughout the day was greenish in color rather than black, because of old age, and was often covered with patches. He consumed a minimum of food, certainly less than an ordinary Weight Watchers portion. He never complained about food and ate whatever the Chinese cook served to the community.

He worked hard from 5:30 in the morning until late at night. There was no air conditioning in Hong Kong in those days and throughout the long, hot summer he spent sleepless nights because of the heat and humidity. My own bedroom was next to his and I would hear his alarm clock go off regularly at 5.30 A.M., then the light in his room would come on and shortly afterwards I would hear him tiptoeing to the chapel for his hour of meditation.

He never took a day of vacation, never did anything for his own pleasure, never went to a play or a movie. His life can be summarized in three simple words: prayer, work, fasting.

As his secretary for many years I watched him very closely. His austerity and total dedication to mission work and to the welfare of the poor impressed me deeply. He believed that he, his men and the church buildings were there for only one purpose: to serve the poor. With such an example before us we all felt inclined to take our spiritual life very seriously.

Statistics

Statistics are not a valid yardstick for measuring spiritual growth. However, they do at least indicate the level of religious activity. Considering the prevailing war situation, the statistics of the Hong Kong Diocese for 1938 are an impressive testimony to the work done by the clergy and the sisters.

In that year there were over 36,000 baptisms of adults and children, including emergency baptisms in death-impending situations. For the first time the number of Communions distributed reached one million. Over 16,000 students, mostly non-Catholic, attended our Catholic schools. There were 60 Italian and 20 Chinese diocesan priests, 16 parishes and 306 churches and chapels. In the field of social work the diocese conducted or supervised 15 orphanages and homes for the aged with a total of 400 beds, one leper hospital, and ten outpatient clinics, which treated over 80,000 patients free of charge yearly. The Catholic Truth Society distributed over 30,000 pieces of literature in Free China.

18

1939-1941: Under War Conditions

Negotiating With Bandits

During three painful years from 1939 to 1941, in spite of war raging near and far, the Church in Hong Kong grew and made steady progress. Crosses and suffering brought us closer to one another and to God. Catholic refugees arrived from China in unprecedented numbers. New converts in the colony increased the Catholic population of our parishes, and also the number of students in Catholic schools. New and flourishing Chinese Catholic organizations came to life.

In the meantime, Japan, after its rapid conquests of 1937 and 1938, let the war enter a stalemate that lasted practically until the counterattack of the Allies in 1944. During this stalemate period Japan withdrew military forces from some areas, only to return intermittently. The bombing of cities, railroads, and waterways to destabilize the area and prevent military buildup of the national forces continued unabated.

One day, much to our surprise, we learned that the Japanese had abandoned Bias Bay as suddenly as they had invaded it. They continued to withdraw their troops from the area bordering Hong Kong. In a few days all the territory of the diocese was again free China. However, constant air raids and rising banditry still made normal life impossible.

Taking advantage of the lull in the war, Bishop Valtorta decided to visit the areas that had just been evacuated by the Japanese. But these areas were controlled by bandits now and one could not go anywhere without first obtaining the bandits' "kind permission." Frs. Poletti and Pilenga in the Huichou area and Frs. Robba and Bianchi in Haifeng County went to work contacting the various bandit chiefs of the area along the bishop's planned route in order to get permission from everyone and "protection troops" (bandits) to accompany the bishop.

The negotiations were long and detailed and were conducted with "serious face" by both sides. There was something ludicrous, but at the same time humorous, in having priests personally negotiating with bloody murderers. It was even more humorous to see a Catholic bishop, a successor of the Apostles, traveling with an escort of bandit troops, but it was the only way to travel and Bishop Valtorta did not hesitate to submit to the situation. Because of the lack of normal means of communication, the long trip was one of the most difficult and fatiguing Bishop Valtorta ever undertook. It was also one of the most consoling and rewarding. The bandits, who had their own honor system, kept their word and not a single incident marred the three-week trip.

"I am very tired but also very happy," he told me the first day after his return when I was in his room briefing him about the events of the last several weeks. "You know, Father Nicholas, I was able to distribute all the thousands of pounds of medicines I'd brought with me for the various hospitals and outpatient centers. None was lost. Even in large cities where, before the war, the non-Christian community usually ignored my visits, this time people came in large numbers to visit me and thank me. In Huichou, the mayor organized a public reception to thank me for what the Church had done for the city. The hospital of the Canossian sisters and our parish church and rectory have been the center of relief work throughout the Japanese occupation. Of course, all the merit goes to our good priests who live there under very trying circumstances. God bless them. I'm happy because, after so many years of work the Church at last begins to be recognized and appreciated. Too bad that it has taken a war to bring the love of Christ to the attention of the non-Christians. The Lord surely knows what He is doing."

For months afterward he talked about that dangerous trip, which somewhat resembled St. Paul's journeys—floods, robbers, false brothers, hardships, sleepless nights, hunger and thirst (2 Cor. 11, 26).

A Disastrous Air Raid

One victim of the hardships of those days was Fr. Ambrose Poletti, who contracted a severe typhoid fever. For several months he lingered between life and death in the Huichou Hospital. However, the solicitous care of the good sisters, especially of the superior, Mother Maria Biffi, kept him alive and returned him to good health by the end of the summer. During his stay in the hospital, Huichou was bombed more than a dozen times but the hospital was never attacked.

The morning of January 8, 1941, was a typically cold, crisp winter day in Huichou. Soon the hospital started humming with life as sisters, nurses and patients entered another day of intense relief work. As the sky was cloudless, they wondered whether the Japanese would come for the nth time to bomb the city. Throughout the almost daily raids the hospital had escaped direct hits. People began to think that it was a safe refuge, that the Japanese would not dare bomb a property marked with a huge Red Cross on the roof. Hundreds of people had come to live near the hospital and every time an air raid alert sounded hundreds more sought shelter there.

However, things were to be different on that fatal eighth of January. Only a few minutes after the air raid alarm sounded, a squadron of silver-winged planes appeared at the horizon and flew directly over the hospital, releasing a string of bombs. For a few seconds it seemed all Hell had broken loose! When the dust settled a few minutes later the devastated area resounded with the heart-rending cries of the wounded and dying. Survivors began to crawl out of the ruins, but Mother Superior was nowhere to be seen. Rescue workers found her later, dead, right on the threshold of the hospital, where she had tarried to urge some latecomers to hurry inside. Several hundred refugees died on that day and the hospital, a total loss, was never rebuilt. It was the end of an institution that had been a beam of light and comfort to so many for scores of years.

The Devastation Of War

The Huichou hospital was only one of the scores of mission buildings destroyed by Japanese bombs. However, these losses were insignificant compared to the thousands of homes, public buildings roads, bridges and boats lost in the entire area of our mission. Thanks to God none of our priests or sisters, except Mother Biffi, were killed, even though many narrowly escaped death.

In 1941 Father Poletti was able to get a letter through to Italy; it was published in PIME's mission magazine. He summed up the feelings of our missionaries in these words: "This year I went through all kinds of dangers and many times I came close to losing my life. The continuous tension and the uncertainty of the future is enervating. My continuous worries about my scattered, starving, homeless folks is a constant cause of exasperation. In spite of all this I have lost neither courage nor the

love for my work. I never felt so close to my parishioners and I have
never loved them as much as during these days of danger and tribulation.
I would be happy to die for them. But I also have to confess that when
bombs are falling all around and the earth shakes from the explosions I
cry, 'Lord, the spirit is willing but the flesh is weak.' As long as this
painful situation continues I would never leave this place for all the gold
in the world.''[1]

We Become Enemies

Through the latter part of the thirties, European politics began to interfere with our work both in Hong Kong and in China. Bishop Valtorta was
Italian; two thirds of the diocesan priests, about fifty, working in Hong
Kong and on the China mainland were Italian; over eighty Italian sisters
were conducting a vast array of educational and social activities in the
colony. Thus, when Mussolini signed the anti-Comintern pact with
Germany and Japan against England, France and China in 1937 we
technically became enemies of both England and China. However, our
long-established tradition of abstaining from political activities had
earned such a good record for us that it saved the situation. Our relations
with the British government of the colony, with our Chinese priests and
friends, and with the Chinese government did not suffer in the least, and
we continued going about our work without hindrance of any sort.

Both the people and the government were aware of the fact that as
missionaries we were interested in the work of God, not in politics. As a
matter of fact, practically since the beginning of the colony in 1842 the
Catholic Church in Hong Kong had been founded and staffed by Italians.
As a result, until the mid-thirties, the Catholic Church was known as the
Italian mission, the Italian convent, the Italian nuns. Within the narrow
circles of the colony, "Italian" and "Catholic" were practically synony-
mous. Nobody quarreled with it, nobody took offense. Regardless of our
nationality both clergy and sisters kept the law, collaborated with the
government and abstained from politics. Thus mutual respect for one
another grew throughout the years.

According to our missionary training we regarded the mission assigned to us as our God-given fatherland. We lived in it and served it
with loyalty and devotion. This enabled us to continue our work for God
and the poor while enjoying the freedom, the confidence, and the respect
of both the British and Chinese people.

This does not mean, however, that we did not share the sufferings of those tragic months and years with our own friends and relatives in Italy. Regardless of individual political inclinations, we all suffered at seeing Italy siding with Japan against England and China, and condoning the wanton Japanese aggression against our friends the Chinese.[2]

The Effects Of The Italian War

The day Italy declared war against England, the governor phoned Bishop Valtorta to see him in his office. There, with extreme kindness, he expressed his embarrassment at having to limit the number of Italian priests in the colony.

"Your Excellency," the governor said, "has a Vatican passport and therefore there is no problem whatever as far as you are concerned. Please feel absolutely free to continue to move around and to do your great work as you wish. With regard to the Italian sisters, we have decided that since they do such invaluable work for the children and the poor of the colony, it would be against the interest of the people to ask them to leave the colony. Moreover, we know that they have never been involved in politics and therefore all of them can stay and continue their work as before." This was music to the bishop's ears as he had worried a great deal about what would happen to our numerous schools and hospitals if the sisters had to leave.

"With regard to the priests," the governor continued, "we have decided that their number in the colony must be reduced."

"How many will you leave me, Your Excellency?" the bishop asked.

"Well, since you have some Chinese priests available, do you think you could replace some of the Italians with Chinese priests? Would Your Excellency be satisfied if we let you keep one Italian priest for each parish?"

"Yes," Bishop Valtorta answered eagerly, as he had dreaded leaving the parish without pastors. "It is very generous of your government to do this and I am most grateful. However, may I ask for one exception, if at all possible? Besides one Italian priest for each parish, could I also retain my personal secretary, Father Nicholas Maestrini, and the two men in charge of the administration office, Father E. Bruzzone and Brother Mario Colleoni? They are practically irreplaceable at this moment."

"By all means, Your Excellency, we would never want to deprive you of such help. Please include their names in the list of priests you wish to have remain in Hong Kong. By the way, the only restriction we have to impose on the Italians remaining in the colony is that they personally report every week to the Police Station and that they place all their outgoing mail in a special box in the Central Post Office for censorship."

When Bishop Valtorta came back to the mission house that morning he was radiant. He had obtained from the governor more than he could ever have expected and the continuation of religious activities in the city was assured.

A few days later the Italian priests who had no parishes left the colony. Some went to Macao, where the good Portuguese bishop had offered them hospitality, while others chose to go to the China mainland and joined our confreres there.

Trouble With The Law

For me life continued on an even keel as my time was taken up between my duties as secretary to the bishop and my publishing work for the Catholic Truth Society. As the Sino-Japanese war was in a kind of stalemate, postal communications with free China were still functioning and I was able to continue corresponding and mailing books to China. As the number of books we published increased, so did my work. The booklets we published were very popular with our missionaries in China and I had more correspondence, more books to mail and more books to order for our customers than ever before.

However, I found the governor's restriction about placing our outgoing mail in the special box for enemy aliens very annoying as it caused additional delays. In those still youthful years I was intolerant of restrictions I judged superfluous and irrelevant. Without consulting the bishop or the CTS Committee I decided to open a kind of branch office in nearby Macao. I entrusted a load of books to a Chinese friend who was going to live in Macao and he promised that he would mail the books to China as I transmitted orders to him.

I soon found out that even my business letters were delayed by the censors. That was too much for me. I wrote to my friend that in order to avoid the special censorship, I would sign my letters with my Chinese name, Sz Shan-fou, and would mail them in the regular mailbox. Being fully aware that I was planning to circumvent the law, I took special precautions to ensure that they did not end up in the mailbox for enemy aliens. Needless to say, I was quite proud of my resourcefulness and kept it a secret from everybody. Then, all of a sudden, I found myself in deep trouble!

One morning about 10:00 Bishop Valtorta received a call from the governor's office asking him to see the governor at 11:00 A.M. on a very urgent matter. Living under war conditions, the bishop was quite apprehensive and before leaving asked me to say some special prayers as he had been called to the Government House.

By 1:00 P.M. the community had already finished its noon meal and everybody left the dining room. I lingered on waiting for the bishop to return to make sure that he would have something warm to eat. When he returned he came straight to the dining room still in his street clothes. I noticed immediately that his usual smile was gone and he seemed to be in a rage. Trying to ignore these danger signals I said cheerfully, "Hi, Bishop! How did your meeting with the governor go?"

"Sit down, you idiot! I have to talk to you. You really have put me and yourself in real trouble!" I was dumbstruck, as he had never addressed me that way before. Moreover, I could not think of any wrong I had done even if my life depended on it. The bishop shouted to our houseboy, who had appeared from the kitchen, to bring him something to eat, and then, sitting down, brusquely motioned to me to take a seat in front of him.

"How stupid can you be, Maestrini?" he started with a voice still quivering with rage.

"But what have I done, bishop?" I asked in the most innocent and disarming tone of voice I could muster.

"What have you done? And you still have the guts to ask me this? Well, let me tell you: The governor, the head of the police and a lot more people are all mad at you and have decided to expel you from the colony. Do you realize what kind of mess you have put me in?"

"But why, Bishop?" I asked again in pained surprise.

"Because you have written to your friend in Macao that you are going to send letters to him signed with your Chinese name without mailing them through the special Post Office Box for enemy aliens. This is why! They have in their hands your stupid letter and the governor showed it to me."

"Oh, that's it!" I exclaimed, and this time I was surprised because I had entirely forgotten the matter. It suddenly dawned on me that I had really done something very wrong and that I had betrayed the trust the British authorities had placed in the bishop and in me.

Humbly, I murmured, "I am sorry, Bishop, I am really sorry."

"Well," the bishop continued in a mollified tone of voice, "I have been able to persuade the governor to forgive you and to let you remain in the colony. It took me more than an hour to convince him to do so. I had to use all the arguments I could think of to make him change his mind. At the end of the conversation he told me: 'Bishop, you surely know how to argue a case. To listen to you, one would say that Maestrini is right and I am wrong, But here is his letter in black and white proving his guilt.'

"I told him that you are a very impulsive young man, that you may act stupidly but are not bad and would never do anything against the government. He has agreed to place you in my personal custody and I have guaranteed that you will never do such a stupid thing again. But watch out, Maestrini, the police have their eyes on you now."

Then, as he saw me crestfallen and humiliated, he added in a more conciliatory tone: "Remember, I am your bishop and your friend. Keep me informed of what you are doing. Consult me when you have any doubt. It may save both of us lots of trouble."

Notes

1. Missioni Cattoliche, 1941, p. 188.

2. The situation changed for the worse when Italy went to war against England on June 10, 1940, and we Italians in Hong Kong overnight became "enemy aliens." In order to understand the abnormal situation in which we Italian missionaries in Hong Kong came to find ourselves it is necessary to briefly recall the major political events of World War II in Europe as they affected us in the British colony.

After the years of chaos and confusion that followed World War I, Hitler became Germany's political head in 1933 and, in order to reestablish the nation's prestige wounded by the defeat of World War I in 1918, he embarked on a policy of expansionism. He first occupied the Rhineland in 1936, then annexed Austria in 1938, and in the same year, taking advantage of an undecided British foreign policy, dismembered Czechoslovakia. The Nazi-Soviet non-aggression pact (August 1939) freed Germany to attack Poland. Britain and France, who had guaranteed Polish independence, declared war on Germany. In the spring of 1940, mobile German units staged blitzkrieg attacks and conquered Denmark, Norway and the low countries, and occupied France. British, French and Polish troops (350,000) were evacuated at Dunkirk.

In Italy, Mussolini rose to power in 1921 as the head of the Fascist Party, which then represented a coalition of conservative forces bent on saving the country from revolution and communist domination. It soon turned into a benevolent dictatorship bent on bringing order to Italy and on consolidating its position within the European community. He did succeed and was universally acclaimed as a great leader. In 1931, the tenth anniversary of his rise to power, university students in the USA elected him "Man Of The Year."

However, in the second decade of his government he went sour. Misunderstood by Britain, scorned by France, Mussolini broke a centuries-old tradition of political alliance and collaboration with both countries and, ignoring the feelings of the Italians, turned to Hitler. In 1936-39 he helped Franco's Spain to foil Stalin's plan for the establishment of a communist government in that country, in 1937 completed the conquest of Abyssinia, annexed little Albania and established the Italian Empire with King Emmanuel III as Emperor. In November of the same year he signed the German-Japanese anti-Comintern pact. His purpose was to save Italy from isolation and gain some advantage from the impending war between Germany and England.

When in the fall of 1939 Hitler invaded Poland, Mussolini remained on the sidelines, but when in the spring of 1940 the reports of German victories in France and Scandinavia shook the world, he wanted to become part of history and to intervene in the war before it was too late. Then, without even consulting his ministers and disregarding the feelings of the nation, he declared war on Great Britain and France on June 10, 1940.

19

On The Eve Of The Hong Kong War

Religion And Politics

In 1941 war engulfed Europe, and US intervention became more and more probable. In China, the Chungking government turned desperately to the USA for help. Chiang Kai-shek was waging two wars at the same time: one against the Japanese invaders to control their expansion, the other against the communist army which, instead of fighting the Japanese, was setting up its own government on Chinese soil in opposition to the Nationalist government.

America was the only possible source of help. Moreover, America was the nation most respected by China in those days. Madame Chiang Kai-shek, all the cabinet ministers and many high government officials were graduates of such famous American universities as Harvard, Yale and Columbia.

Since its very beginning the Nationalist Party had looked at the USA as the model democracy after which to pattern the rebuilding of China. Now that democracy in China was seriously threatened, they were turning to the USA as their only hope and the last source of help.

Unfortunately they found a deaf ear in the White House. Roosevelt had placed China at the bottom of his list of priorities. He certainly was a great president but he understood very little of the Orient and of Orientals. According to Theodore H. White [1], Roosevelt regarded China merely as a springboard for an attack on Japan in case of war against that country. However, since Japan was not yet at war with the USA, Roosevelt paid little attention to China and regarded Chiang as a "petulant nuisance." He appointed General Joe Stillwell ("Vinegar Joe") as head of the US forces in China in spite of the fact that the good General knew nothing of China and Chinese politics. Stillwell failed to understand Chiang Kai-shek, and Chiang understood Stillwell even less.

The Nationalist Public Relations Office in Chungking sent out frantic appeals to all loyal friends of China abroad to make every possible effort to alert the American public to the sufferings of China at the hands of the Japanese, and to exert pressure on Roosevelt.

All of us foreign missionaries in China felt empathy for China because it was the victim of unjustified aggression. Moreover, we identified the interest of Christianity with that of a free China, and felt a righteous indignation at the arrogance and cruelty of the Japanese invaders. I thought that as a missionary it was my duty to help China. I didn't regard helping my adopted country as political work, but as part of my Christian work.

The opportunity to do something concrete to help China came through Fr. Charles Meeus, a young Belgian missionary attached to a Chinese diocese in north China. He had been requested by his Chinese bishop to go to the States to seek help for the refugees. On his return to Chungking he passed through Hong Kong. He had read Dr. Wu's booklet *The Science of Love*, knew my name and so came to see me. He was young, handsome, dynamic and a real charmer. My close friends John, Alice, Francis and Averil loved him and we had several meetings discussing what we could do to make China's plight known to the Catholics in the States. After lengthy discussions, we decided that the Catholic Truth Society should publish a book on the real situation of China and of the Church, and the disastrous effects of the Japanese invasion.

We asked the best Catholic writer in Hong Kong, Fr. Thomas F. Ryan, SJ, to write a book on the situation in China and he enthusiastically agreed. It was entitled *China Through Catholic Eyes*. [2]

Fr. Meeus put me in touch with Msgr. Edward A. Freking, National Secretary of the Catholic Students' Mission Crusade at Crusade Castle in Cincinnati, Ohio. Being a man of extraordinary intelligence and exceptional missionary zeal, Msgr. Freking heartily approved of our idea. He promised to buy a substantial number of copies and to promote circulation of the book to Catholic school students.

An Important Document

Dr. Wu, on one of his trips to Chungking, spoke about our initiative to Madame Chiang Kai-shek and she readily agreed to write the preface to the book. I quote it here almost in its entirety. Coming from the pen of the Chinese First Lady, it is a great testimonial to the esteem Christian missionaries enjoyed among the leaders of China.

"For the last four years China, with a population equal in number to all the members of the Catholic Church in the world, has been fighting a war of resistance against Japanese aggression.

"To the 400,000,000 Catholics scattered throughout the world, therefore, it must be a vital concern how your missionaries in China are meeting this challenge under the rough frown of war.

"The following pages will depict in brief China's present progress, and from them you will also obtain an insight into the terrific suffering which millions of our people have endured. They have been stripped of all material possessions, yet they have retained an unconquerable spirit.

"No account of China's resistance is complete unless it records the worthy part missionaries have played whether at the front, in the rear, in Free China, or in Japanese occupied areas. They have not accepted the facile passivity of inaction; on the contrary they have hurled themselves unsparingly and with consecrated zeal into the task of alleviating pain and misery, both physical and spiritual.

"For example, the saintly Fr. Lebbe, until his death, led his group of workers into the very jaws of cannon-fire to succor the wounded in the battlefield, and eventually sacrificed his life for the people he loved.

"Large numbers of Catholic missionaries, at the risk of their own lives, have protected refugees and preserved the honor of the hordes of terrified and helpless women who ran into their compounds when the Japanese military approached. Others devoted themselves to the rescue and care of innocent and bewildered children caught in the whirlwind of war. Still others with undaunted courage continued educational work amongst the stricken and destitute.

"All these missionaries have throughout kept their banners flying, and their spirits vibrant in the midst of the charred ruins of their missions. The memory of their colleagues killed and wounded by Japanese bombs and machine-guns must serve as an ever-present reminder of the threat of death overhanging them. In all that they are doing they have shown the quality of mercy which blesseth him that gives and him that takes. In deed and in spirit, their all-embracing charity is like manna dropped in the way of starved people.

"Chungking, Szechwan. May, 1941 Mayling Soong Chiang [Madame Chiang Kai-shek]"

China Through Catholic Eyes

The first part of the book presents a panoramic view of China from its earliest days. Fr. Ryan described a country whose civilization "is the oldest that exists in the world today." Reviewing briefly the history of China, he spoke at first of its old religions, its ancient culture, its great philosophers and writers and the characteristics of its people. Then he described modern China's struggle to pass from a strictly closed civilization and a monolithic structured government to a modern democratic nation.

He devoted a whole chapter to the new constitution of the Chinese Republic (drafted by Dr. John Wu), which was then in the final stages of official adoption by the government. Ryan described this document as "an ingenuous application of democratic principles to the conditions and mentality in China" and "a practical medium for putting democratic power into practice."

About the rising communist power he wrote: "There is in China a Communist army which has shown itself, in spite of promises and engagements, hostile to the State and hopes one day to threaten its supremacy. The Government will not bow to the Communist army, and while it is determined to do everything possible to avoid Civil War, it is ready to face this extremity if necessary rather than allow any minority to challenge the supreme authority of the State."

Then he presented a powerful picture of the Chinese spirit of resistance, of the heroism of its soldiers and of the struggle against insurmountable odds to bring China into the twentieth century.

In the second part he traced the origins of Christianity in China from the days of the Nestorians (seventh and ninth centuries) to Archbishop John of Monte Corvino[3] and to St. Francis Xavier and Matteo Ricci, SJ, in the sixteenth century. After giving a sweeping view of the stunted growth of Christianity in China during the last three centuries characterized by struggle, bloody persecutions and thousands of martyrs, he then described the terrific progress made by the Church after the establishment of the Chinese Republic. In a little more than thirty years (1911-41) the Catholics had grown from an insignificant hidden group to over three million. It was a mature church with scores of Chinese bishops, over two thousand Chinese priests, 2,500 foreign missionaries, three Catholic universities, over 600,000 Chinese youths studying in Catholic schools and thousands of churches scattered throughout the country.

In a final appeal for a true understanding of China, he continued: "The bonds of sympathetic affection between the Catholic Church and China are stronger than they have ever been. China needs to be understood in the world today for, if the world only knew it to the full, the world needs China, this power of strength that wants only peace and may soon be the greatest force for it in human history. China needs to be understood, and the Catholic missionaries, men of every nation, spread through every section of the country, seek nothing from China but are anxious to give it God's greatest gift. Living with the people and for the people, these missionaries one and all cry out: Let China live; help it to live its life in peace. Their confidence in China is boundless; their affection for its people is born of intimate acquaintance. They ask for the people of China, sympathy; for its suffering, help; for its cause, understanding; for its treatment at the bar of the nations' judgment, justice. And the Catholic Church in China and beyond it commit the cause of China and the future of the people of China to the blessing of the omnipotent God."

An Ill-Fated Edition

Fr. Ryan and I worked closely with the printer to produce a beautiful edition. It was richly illustrated with pictures from all over China and fine line drawings especially made by Chinese artist Wong Wing Kit. The first cloth-bound edition of three thousand copies was released early in July 1941 and was soon out of print because of large orders from the States and also from Ireland and England.

Msgr. Freking was very pleased with it and ordered five thousand copies. We rushed immediately into a second edition. After many difficulties I had the five thousand copies ready, crated and safely loaded on board the SS *President Harrison* of the President Line, bound for the States. It left Hong Kong on December 5. We had pinned a lot of hope on that shipment and when the ship left we drew a breath of relief.

A few days later, on December 8, the Japanese invaded Hong Kong and our lives were changed dramatically. During the tragic weeks and months that followed the occupation of Hong Kong I forgot all about our precious cargo on its way to the States.

About one year later I received a secret message from our PIME priests in Macao that a bank there had received $5,000 from the States for me. Only then did I remember the shipment of books to Msgr. Freking; I had assumed that they had arrived safely. The message scared me. If the Japanese learned that I was receiving money from the States, they would certainly execute me as a spy. Through a reliable friend I sent a hurried note written in Latin to my fellow priests in Macao asking them to leave the money in the bank and, for God's sake, not to mention the matter to anyone.

When the war ended in 1945, I learned from Msgr. Freking that the precious crate of books had never arrived. It had been lost on December 7 when the Japanese seized the *President Harrison* and its cargo. The President Line informed Msgr. Freking of the tragic end of their ship and the loss of its cargo. Msgr. Freking then, in cooperation with the Society for the Propagation of the Faith in Boston, proceeded immediately to print an American edition of the book in April 1942. It was from the proceeds of this American edition that he sent me that sum of money.

Today it is not easy to find a copy of that book. When the Japanese occupied Hong Kong, I destroyed all the copies we had. The copy I have used in writing this book was kindly placed at my disposal by the Maryknoll Library in Ossining, New York.

My Favorite Ministry

My favorite ministry has always been spiritual direction. It was especially so during those war days when unusual hardships and sufferings brought many souls closer to God.

Spiritual direction can be defined as a highly personal and individualized guidance by means of which a counselor, more properly called a spiritual director, endeavors to help a person develop a higher spiritual life and strive toward Christian perfection. Spiritual direction is very different from spiritual counseling. Counseling is, generally speaking, of a temporary nature and is used mostly in cases of emergency or special need. On the contrary, spiritual direction requires a stable relationship between the director and the directed, a complete openness and voluntary obedience on the part of the disciple, regular encounters and frank discussions of everything affecting the life of the spirit.

Spiritual direction is one of the choicest and most spiritual ministries because its immediate goal is leading souls to God. According to St. Francis de Sales and many other spiritual writers, spiritual direction is a very effective means of spiritual growth, a useful remedy against spiritual illusions, self-deceptions and other pitfalls of the spiritual life.

As I could not have a regular parish assignment on account of my work as secretary to the bishop, I had to find different ways to be active in the ministry to non-Christians and in the spiritual care of souls. Through writing and publishing books for non-Christians, I fulfilled my primary missionary duty of bringing the knowledge of Christ to them. Through spiritual guidance and counseling I fulfilled my primary desire to minister to souls and to help them to grow in the love of God.

My favorite work was spiritual direction of sisters, priests and lay people. To this I added vocational guidance, that is, helping young people to find out if they had a true vocation and nurturing it through spiritual growth.

Spiritual direction is fascinating work; it involves a great deal of time, a few joys, many disappointments and occasionally, believe it or not, some bodily risks.

At one time I was preparing a girl to enter a convent as she showed definite signs of a true vocation. Her father, although a practicing Catholic, was violently opposed to her entering a convent and refused to give his consent. However, as the young lady was over twenty-one years of age, I told her that if she wanted to dedicate herself to Christ, she had to disregard her father's opposition.

The day before she was due to enter the convent, the old gentleman made a terrible scene, accusing the girl of cruelty, lack of love for the family, etc. He also threatened very seriously to jump out of the window if she carried out her intentions. The poor girl was distraught with fear and her heart was torn between the desire to follow Christ and the fear, of causing her father's suicide.

I counseled her at length and prayed a lot, but, knowing human nature, I was convinced that his threat was an empty one. I advised her that she was free to do what she wanted but if she was sure that God was calling her then she had to follow the Gospel's advice and enter the convent. She decided to do so.

The day she entered the convent I was uneasy and prayed very specially for the old gentleman, hoping that he would not do anything drastic. Thanks to the Lord, he did not jump out of the window and died many years later in his bed. Today, almost fifty years later, this good sister is still alive and active and I still correspond regularly with her.

On several other occasions, irate parents threatened to punch my nose if I encouraged their children to enter a convent or a seminary, but thanks to God I was never scared by these threats and my nose is still intact.

As a rule I always was extremely cautious and never encouraged anyone to enter religious life unless I could see positive signs of a true vocation. I believe that out of the many boys and girls who asked for my spiritual direction I persuaded at least 90% not to enter religious life. In every case, their supposed vocation seemed motivated more by a desire to escape difficulties than by a sincere wish to follow God. I am grateful to God that almost all of those whom I encouraged to enter religious life have persevered to the end. Many are already dead, but some are alive, still living fruitful lives in the service of God.

A Very Special Soul

The departure of many Italian priests from Hong Kong because of Italy going to war with England (June 1940) brought me an increased workload in the field of spiritual guidance. Some of the priests who left Hong Kong asked me to take care of their spiritual children and I did this as diligently as I could.

One of the fondest memories of this period of my life is that of my relationship with Anthony Hwang. At that time he had just finished High School, had been baptized by my dear and close friend Fr. Ottavio M. Liberatore, and had already applied to enter a Benedictine monastery in northwest China.

Anthony had been extremely well prepared by Fr. Liberatore and was already living an intense spiritual life of communion with God. Highly intelligent, gentle, soft spoken, endowed with very refined manners, he was a perfect Chinese gentleman of the old school, in spite of his young age, besides being an extraordinarily good Christian. His spirit of self-restraint and penance, his zeal, his dedication were an example and an inspiration to me. I always looked forward to our meetings with great joy.

I made final arrangements for his admission to the monastery and was able to solve a few difficulties for him as I was a personal friend of the founder of that monastery. Finally, through the help of Dr. Wu, I was able to purchase a ticket for his air trip to Chungking, not an easy thing then.

In those days there was only one daily flight of the China Airline linking Hong Kong with Chungking in free China. As the plane had to fly over Japanese-occupied areas it could fly safely only at night. It used to leave Chungking Airport after dark, arriving in Hong Kong late in the evening. Then it would leave Hong Kong about 2:00 A.M., circle over the city to get above the surrounding hills, and then fly straight to Chungking to arrive there at dawn if it wasn't attacked by Japanese planes. All in all it was a risky journey for young Anthony and I was very worried. The day before he left Hong Kong he came to attend my Mass, and I gave him Holy Communion thinking that probably that was the last time I would see him. I also gave him a farewell letter containing such spiritual advice as a father would give to his son. That night I knelt for a long time in my room praying for him.

A few weeks later I received news that he had reached the monastery safely. Then the Japanese occupied Hong Kong and I no longer heard from him. For years and years I kept praying for him every day, always wondering if he was still alive. More than fifty years passed before I saw him again for the first time as an elderly Benedictine monk. He came to visit me here in Tequesta, all the way from Oregon City. It was quite a reunion. He showed me the letter I had given him the day he left Hong Kong.

On The Eve Of The Hong Kong War

On Sunday, December 7, 1941, everything seemed to be normal in Hong Kong. The British took part in the Sunday parade at the Anglican cathedral and then went to Happy Valley for the horse races in the afternoon. Chinese shops were open and did business as usual. The middle-class Chinese went to the beautiful beaches and the rest of the population lolled either at home or in the streets, enjoying the beautiful warm day. We priests had our busy morning church services as usual and prayed for the refugees and the victims of war. I had a late evening dinner with Dr. Wu, Averil, Alice, and Francis and nobody talked of war.

As I walked back home from the ferry on the Hong Kong side I noticed the usual crowds of British hanging around the Hong Kong Hotel, but the streets were deserted and silent. Everything seemed normal. Hong Kong was peaceful, serene and as self-complacent as ever. After all, who dared to attack Hong Kong and draw the ire of the British Empire?

Only after the war did we learn that the situation was not as peaceful as it had seemed. Early that day, the Hong Kong military command had received intelligence reports of the presence of large contingents of Japanese troops along the Hong Kong border with China. That afternoon General Maltby had called up the Civil Volunteer Company to report to their barracks. But the civilians in Hong Kong had been told nothing of these events and most of the three million people of the colony went to bed that night blissfully ignorant of the catastrophe that would befall us all within a few short hours.

Notes

1. Theodore H. White, a graduate of Harvard, was at that time in charge of the *Time* office in Chungking. In his fascinating book *In Search of History* (published by Warner Books) he gave a first-hand account of the relationship between Chiang Kai-shek and Stillwell. Even though White's judgment of Chiang is certainly biased by his empathy for Mao, his report on the Chiang-Stillwell relationship is a graphic account of the tragic mistakes that ultimately led to the loss of China to communism.

2. I am sure that today I would have wanted the title to read *China Through Christian Eyes*, but that was 1941, long before Pope John XXIII and the ecumenical movement. At that time Christian denominations worked very independently of each other.

3. A village in central Italy, not far from Perugia, Umbria.

20

The Seventeen-Day War: Hong Kong Surrenders To The Japanese

Monday, December 8, 1941

On the morning of Monday, December 8, 1941, the sun rose over Hong Kong in a cloudless, brilliant blue sky, the air was crisp but not cold, and the hills gleamed a luscious green in the morning light. The usual sounds of the city waking for a normal business day were all around. Rhythmic screaming of street vendors, screeching brakes of buses carrying morning workers to their jobs, heavy shutters being raised—all these sounds wafted up from the city below to the balcony of my room in the mission house as I looked out on the morning scene. It was one of those mornings when a thirty-three-year-old man in the full vigor of manhood feels happy to be alive and grateful to the Lord.

After rising at 5:30 as usual, I leisurely performed my spiritual exercises (it was the Feast Day of the Immaculate Conception) and at 7:00 I started on my twenty-minute walk to the Holy Spirit School conducted by the Maryknoll Sisters on Caine Road. At the door of the convent Sr. Amata,[1] a young nun from the USA, welcomed me with her usual kind smile and greetings. Then she ushered me into the small school chapel crowded with Chinese high school girls, all members of the Children of Mary Sodality and all recently converted to the Faith.

I began the celebration of Mass, they sang beautiful hymns and I preached a carefully prepared homily. I felt very inspired by the sight of those eager young faces relishing their new faith.

At exactly 8:00 I was pronouncing the words of the Consecration when suddenly there came the drone of dozens of planes overhead, followed by a series of explosions. "Another nuisance air raid rehearsal," I thought, trying to concentrate on the celebration of the Mass. But the first explosions were immediately followed by others, telephones started ringing, nuns began shuffling in and out of the chapel whispering to each other, and the girls were becoming restless in their pews.

"What's happening?" I wondered, as fear crept into my heart. As my back was turned to the congregation (this was the way we celebrated Mass in those days), I could not get any idea of what was happening. I tried to continue to concentrate on what I was doing. At Communion I was shocked to see every girl rushing out of the chapel as soon as she received the Sacred Host. I was perplexed by this unusual behavior.

As soon as I finished Mass and returned to the sacristy, Sr. Amata rushed in, pale and frightened, and said, "Father, the Japanese are bombing Hong Kong. You had better rush back to the cathedral immediately!" So that was it. What we thought would never happen was actually happening. War had come to Hong Kong.

A Terrible Day

Even though I knew that during an air raid no one was supposed to walk in the streets, I felt that I had to hasten home immediately. I rushed through deserted streets, my heart heavy with fear and uncertainty. Those few bombs from the sky would wildly change the course of my life . . . and of Hong Kong, too. The war was no longer hundreds of miles away. It was here, all around me, in the very streets of Hong Kong. We were in the front line. There was no way to hide, to escape from the tiny colony. What was going to happen to us? Nobody could tell. But certainly, no matter what the outcome of the war, I felt that tragic days were ahead for all of us.

When I arrived at the mission house I found hopeless confusion there. The usually quiet entrance hall was full of people coming and going, young mothers with their screaming broods begging for shelter, others begging for food, others just idly watching the commotion. The bishop, pale, with anguish written all over his face, was trying to comfort, to reassure, to promise shelter to all.

In the midst of all that confusion, old, diminutive A-wong, our faithful houseboy, kept on calmly cleaning the large bay window facing the mainland, the direction from which the Japanese were attacking Hong Kong. I gently tried to persuade him to stop working there and move away from the window. Unperturbed, he replied, "Shan-fou, it does not matter. If the Lord wants me to die I will die anyway," and calmly resumed his work. I envied him his serenity.

About 10:00 A.M. the chief of police phoned the bishop and told him that all the Italian priests in the colony had to gather at the mission house by 4:00 P.M. with one small suitcase each. The chief explained that we would be taken to a concentration camp for our own safety. The order was definite. This time there was no pleading with the governor, no exceptions. Poor Bishop Valtorta was floored. It meant that all his parishes would be without priests or greatly understaffed, and this at Christmas time!

In the meantime, from radio bulletins and local papers, we learned about the simultaneous Japanese attacks on Pearl Harbor, the Philippines and Malaya. The world seemed to be coming to an end.

The hours passed slowly as we suffered great mental anguish. To leave our work, our parishioners, our catechumens, and our churches would have been painful at any time but to do so just when war was coming and when our people would need us most was unbearably painful. Thank God, that first day the Japanese concentrated on making headway overland through the New Territories and did not bomb the city again. We got busy bidding a tearful farewell to our people, phoning those whom we could not visit, and giving last-minute instructions to those who came to say goodbye.

We Go To Jail

At 4:00 P.M. all fifteen of us gathered in the entrance hall of the mission house. Shortly afterward a police van showed up. We had just time to kiss the bishop's hand and receive his blessing before being herded into the van. We were no longer free! We were prisoners! It was a terrible sensation. It seemed nonsensical that because thousands of miles away a dictator spurned by England had decided to go to war against that country, we must now lose our freedom and be jailed by our friends. We tried to console each other, thinking of Christ, who also had gone to jail, and we prayed the rosary.

Our first stop was at police headquarters, a real bedlam that afternoon. Serious-faced British and Chinese policemen were coming and going, prisoners were constantly brought in and out, and orders were barked over loudspeakers. The typical orderly atmosphere of a British police station was gone.

We were herded into one corner of a large room and told to stay there under the supervision of two Chinese policemen. There we remained for three hours, without food or drink, anguished in mind and distraught with fear and uncertainty. As darkness fell all the large windows were sealed shut and covered with blankets because of the very strict blackout rules. Only a few dim lights were allowed inside.

At 7:00 P.M. we were joined by a few lay people of other nationalities, ordered to march outside and unceremoniously pushed inside a military truck, all in absolute darkness. A few orders and counter-orders were given, and two soldiers were stationed on the running board on each side of the driver. Their task was to peer through the darkness and direct the driver, because the truck could not use headlights and, of course, there were no lights in the streets. I will spare the reader the details of that two-hour trip, fifteen miles from police headquarters to the Stanley Prison on a moonless night, on twisting, tortuous country roads and up and down hills overlooking sheer cliffs. The truck proceeded at a turtle's pace, the two men on the running boards shouting orders to the driver while we inside prayed for our lives.

Finally, about 9:00, we reached the Stanley Prison. In complete darkness we passed through the heavy gates, which clanged shut behind us. We passed through several buildings where prisoners were shouting and screaming, and finally stopped in front of an empty dormitory building.

"This is your camp, gentlemen," a soldier barked. "Get yourself a room and make sure not to use any lights."

"What about dinner?" some hungry soul asked.

"It's too late now. We'll see about it tomorrow." They locked the door and there we were, hungry, frightened, disconsolate prisoners of war. With the help of flashlights and candles (brought along to say Mass) we explored the large, empty building. Each of us chose a cell (all had iron bars at the window) and, ignoring the growling of empty stomachs, stretched out on thin mattresses for our first night in prison. Thanks to God, the building was immaculately clean. Prison personnel had done a very good job of cleaning it in the few hours before we arrived.

The Japanese Advance On Hong Kong

Most people today have only some vague idea of what happened at Pearl Harbor the morning of December 7, 1941. Beyond that, they know very little of the Far East War (1941-45) and of Japanese wanton aggression in Southeast Asia. In this chapter I limit myself to giving a brief account of the Seventeen-Day War and the surrender of Hong Kong, as these events played a very important part in my twenty years with the Chinese.

All the books I have read about the Hong Kong War agree on three points.

The first point is that the British were not prepared for a massive attack, especially one coming from the mainland. As far back as 1933 the Chiefs of Staff in England and Gen. Hastings Ismay had proposed the demilitarization of Hong Kong because the colony, a mere patch of four hundred square miles, was of little strategic importance. To defend it would mean condemning it to death with all its military personnel and the civilian population. As late as 1940, just before he ended his term as governor of Hong Kong, Sir Geoffrey Northcote recommended the withdrawal of the British garrison for the same reasons. But the War Office in London did not heed him. Rather, it followed the advice of the influential Britons in Hong Kong who firmly believed that the colony was an impregnable fortress and that Japanese threats were only gestures.

On January 7, 1941, Winston Churchill wrote in a memo: "If Japan goes to war with us there is not the slightest chance of holding Hong Kong or relieving it. It is most unwise to increase the loss we shall suffer there. Instead of increasing the garrison it should be reduced to a symbolical scale. We must avoid frittering away our resources on untenable positions. Japan will think long before declaring war on the British Empire, and whether there are two or six battalions at Hong Kong will make no difference in her choice. I wish we had fewer troops there but to move any would be noticeable and dangerous."

However, at the insistence of his advisors he later changed his mind to please them. In September 1941 he requested the MacKenzie King government in Canada to send at least two battalions (about two thousand men) to help defend Hong Kong. They arrived in Kowloon on November 16, 1941, under the command of Brigadier Gen. Lawson. They disembarked with much fanfare and were received with great enthusiasm.

Tim Carew, in *The Fall of Hong Kong*, reported that British Capt. C.M.M. Man of the Middlesex Regiment and his wife, watching them land, said, "Our joint impression was firstly one of relief that at long last we had some reinforcements for what was a pathetically under-strength garrison. Our second reaction was that the Canadians appeared fit, over-confident, and unusually well-equipped by our standards. I remember overhearing one Canadian just off the ship saying, 'When do we get to grips with the Goddamned little yellow bastards?'[2]

The second point is that the fortifications on land were totally inadequate. The construction of three defense lines (called Maginot Lines) across the New Territories to prevent an invasion from China had been started, but never completed. Only in the fall of 1941 did the commanding officer of the military garrison, Major Gen. C. M. Maltby, rush his soldiers to resume construction, but still they were never properly finished.

The military personnel in charge of defending the colony—British, Canadian, Indian punjabis and rajputs and civil defense volunteers, including Portuguese and Chinese companies—totaled at most about ten thousand men. The Japanese had sixty thousand experienced combat soldiers massed at or near the Hong Kong border. Moreover, they had a large, modern air force in Canton, less than two hundred miles away. The British air force in Hong Kong consisted of only eight old warplanes. The Navy had only a few small units.

The ammunition available was old and limited. Some of it was left over from World War I. One Hong Kong resident wrote that for every "bang" (shell) fired by the British the Japanese answered "bang, bang, bang": three to one. Defense plans, though revised after the arrival of the Canadians, concentrated more on an attack from the sea than on an invasion by land.

The third point is that British intelligence was very poor. It had reported that the Japanese military equipment was inadequate and old-fashioned, that the Japanese soldiers' night work was poor, that the cream of the Japanese army had been lost in the war with China and that therefore the Japanese army was ineffective. This misinformation, coupled with the traditional complacency of the British brass and the top civilians, was the ultimate cause of the loss of Hong Kong.

The Attack On Hong Kong

On December 7 (on the Far East calendar) British patrols discovered a large concentration of Japanese soldiers near the Hong Kong border. They immediately alerted Gen. Maltby, who was attending the morning service at the Anglican cathedral in downtown Hong Kong. Gen. Maltby did not inform the civilian population but proceeded to call up the civilian reserve. He manned all the fortifications around the island and the mainland, and waited.

The Japanese strategy for the occupation of the Far East was to deal a

mortal blow to the American Pacific fleet, seize all the foreign colonies
in the Pacific Ocean from Hong Kong to the Philippines (Indochina,
Malaya, Indonesia, etc.), secure for itself oil sources in the Pacific and
wait for America to surrender. The keys to success were surprise and
speed. They almost succeeded.

The morning of December 8 (again according to the Far East calendar)
at exactly 8:00 (simultaneously with the attacks on Pearl Harbor and the
other Pacific targets), the Japanese Army crossed the Shum Chun River
along the Hong Kong-China border and began their advance into the
New Territories. Twelve bombers and thirty-six fighter planes bombed
the Kai Tak Airport and the Sam Shui Po barracks where the Canadians
were housed.

Ellen Field[3] in *Twilight in Hong Kong* wrote:

"I was asked by the loud crump of falling bombs. I opened my
eyes believing that some kind of maneuvers had started. I made for the
nearest window. The shutters gave way, hurling me out over the rail.
Several aircraft were circling Kai Tak airfield from which a black cloud
of smoke was rising, even as I watched, I saw the cloud suddenly become
laced with flame. I saw sticks of bombs dropping and craters opening up
in the runways, already strewn with burning planes.

"The enemy aircraft were circling Kai Tak, apparently without finding
opposition. A black pall hung in the sky, and every now and then there
would be the sudden crump of bombs and the boom of A.A. guns. As yet
we had heard no air raid siren, so clearly we had been taken completely
off guard.

"That initial attack by the enemy lasted just under an hour. It was
almost 9 o'clock before the noise of aircraft engines suddenly died away
and then, shortly afterwards, the sirens sounded for the first time—giving
the all-clear. A few minutes later, over the radio, came an announcement
signed jointly by the Governor and the G.O.C. It said: 'Great Britain and
America are at war with Japan. We have been attacked by enemy aircraft, and the population is urged to remain calm. The situation,' it
further claimed, 'is under control.'

"Like most Europeans in the Far East, I had always thought of the
Japanese as an inoffensive and obsequious race, and it was not easy to
accept the idea that they might dare to invade a British Colony. Yet now
the evidence was there before my eyes, in the fires that were burning all
over Hong Kong and in the great clouds of smoke that were blotting out
the sky. They had dared, all right."

Provided with excellent maps of the New Territories prepared at leisure by their spies through the years, and guided by Chinese fifth columnists[4] three full regiments (nine battalions) began to advance in two columns along the eastern and western borders of the New Territories. Avoiding the main roads, which had been made impassable by a British demolition squad, they moved rapidly along narrow paths through the hills. By 4:00 P.M. that same day, overcoming strong British resistance, they scaled the top of the Tai Mo Shan (at three thousand feet, the highest point in the New Territories).

The British, punjabis and rajputs put up a violent resistance and caused many casualties, but they were out-gunned and out-numbered.

The Japanese night work was superb. Using hidden paths through the hills, they moved to the back of the British line and, in spite of fierce bombing and even bayonet attacks, compelled the British to withdraw, with heavy losses on both sides.

In the meantime Japanese air raids by large bomber formations started coming over Hong Kong and Kowloon at all hours of the day and night. The Japanese literally applied the famous Douhet theory practiced by the Germans, maintaining that continuously repeated, concentrated air attacks have the most effect on the morale of the enemy."[5] But, as Hitler's blitzkrieg strengthened England's will to resist, so the Japanese bombings made the Hong Kong military forces more determined to prevail. Unfortunately the odds against the British were too high.

Key position after key position along the twenty-two-mile-long and sixty to eighty-mile-wide corridor of rugged terrain from the Chinese border to Kowloon was lost, in spite of heroic fighting. By the evening of the third day the Japanese forces were in the suburbs of Kowloon. The fifth day they completed the occupation of the mainland part of the colony.

Under cover of darkness, the valiant British men who remained crossed the harbor and regrouped on the island. The war bulletins of the Hong Kong governor, Sir Mark Young, were vague and rhetorical and nobody informed the British and Chinese people in Kowloon of what was happening. Wild rumors were circulating about the impending arrival of the Japanese and many people escaped to the island using whatever means of transportation they could find to cross the harbor. The majority, however, learned the reality of the situation too late, when Japanese soldiers knocked at their doors. Hell broke loose! Looting and raping by Japanese soldiers and a few Chinese traitors terrorized the population.

Life At Stanley Concentration Camp

In contrast with the tumultuous situation prevailing in Hong Kong, our life at the Stanley Prison was characterized by boredom and mental anguish. The guards were kind and cooperative, and the food, the same as that served to Chinese prisoners, was adequate for us. A large yard enclosed by high walls was placed at our disposal and we were even given a few books from the prison library. The Maryknoll Fathers came to visit us a couple of times and brought cigarettes. The Carmelite sisters, whose convent was not far from the prison, sent promises of prayers and spiritual encouragement.

We set up an altar in a cell, celebrated daily Mass, and prayed countless rosaries. But our souls were in agony. We had no radio, no news whatever of what was happening to our beloved Hong Kong, to our churches, our Christians, all the people we had to leave behind. Only through rumors whispered by the guards did we learn that the Japanese were advancing and that Kowloon was lost.

Surrender Demanded

The War Office in Tokyo had given the Japanese commander of the invading forces, Lt. Gen. Sakai, ten days to complete the occupation, of Hong Kong. It had taken five full days to occupy the mainland, and time was running out. On the morning of Saturday, December 13, Sakai sent a small handful of officers on a small boat flying a white flag, to bring the following message to Sir Mark Young:

"Since our troops have joined battle I have gained possession of the Kowloon Peninsula despite the good fighting qualities of your men, and my Artillery and Air Force, which are ready to crush all parts of the Island, now await my order. Your Excellency can see what will happen to the Island and I cannot keep silent about it. You have all done your duty in defending Hong Kong so far, but the result of the coming battle is plain, and further resistance will lead to the annihilation of a million good citizens and to such sadness as I can hardly bear to see. If Your Excellency would accept an offer to start negotiations for the surrender of Hong Kong under certain conditions, it will be honorable."

Sir Mark Young replied: Nothing doing! Then Sakai ordered a merciless two-day blitz, bombing military and civilian targets. He hoped the attack would destroy the defenders' morale, thus making possible the invasion of the island on Monday, December 15. But Hong Kong forces kept shelling the Japanese positions and when Monday came Sakai was not ready. He wired Tokyo for an extension and was given up to January 1 to complete his job. On December 17 Sakai sent another peace mission to Sir Mark Young, asking again for surrender. The answer was: "The Governor and the Commander-in-Chief, Hong Kong, declines most absolutely to enter into any negotiations for the surrender of Hong Kong and he takes this opportunity of saying he is not prepared to receive any further communications on this subject."

G. B. Endacott described what followed the governor's refusal:

"On the 18th the bombardment intensified still further, and all indications pointed to the imminence of an assault. The Central District was shelled again, and the Colonial Secretariat building damaged. The Asiatic Petroleum Company's oil storage tanks and a neighboring paint factory had been set on fire and for some days a pall of dense black smoke covered the northeast of the island making a perfect cover for the attackers. The shoreline was again heavily shelled until hardly a pillbox remained, and the road was blocked with debris. It came as no surprise when that night the Japanese mounted their assault and carried the war to the island."

The attack began at 10:00 P.M. at the narrow Lyemoon passage between Hong Kong and the mainland, about a mile wide. The military installations in that area had been destroyed by bombs. The punjabis assigned to that area put up heroic resistance. However, by midnight the Japanese had already landed six battalions. At 1:00 A.M. the division commander, Lt. Gen. Sano, came ashore on the island. Leaving pockets of resistance behind, the Japanese made for the top of the hills from which they could control the city at their feet.

For five days a fierce battle raged all over the island with major casualties on both sides. By the evening of December 24 the entire island was practically under Japanese control, even though they refrained from entering the Central District to avoid house-to-house fighting.

The Stanley Peninsula where we were remained a bastion of resistance. This peninsula consists of a thickly populated isthmus about a thousand feet wide at the narrowest point. This isthmus joins the peninsula to the Hong Kong island. The fishing village and our internment camp were right on the isthmus. Fort Stanley was about a mile south on the slopes of the hill facing the ocean.

On December 23, after the Japanese had occupied the top of the hills overlooking Stanley, we began to hear the whining of shells passing over our heads. The Japanese kept hitting the fort. We were fully aware that if

the Japanese decided to send their infantry to scale the hill and occupy
the fort they would first have to raze our building and pass through our
camp as it was right in the middle of the narrow isthmus. That would
have meant certain death for us. We prayed and prayed and prayed to
be spared.

On the evening of December 24 the Japanese unleashed a vicious
attack, supported by tanks, against the Stanley village and were practically at the door of our prison building. Thinking that the following day,
Christmas, would probably be our last day on earth, each of us celebrated
Midnight Mass in the middle of the night by the light of a candle. The
whining of bombs and the furious explosions all around us were our
Christmas music. I will never forget that Christmas Eve and Midnight
Mass. The beautiful words of the liturgy about heavenly choirs and
angels and peace seemed so ludicrous within those prison walls with
bombs flying overhead and people being killed all around us.

We could not help thinking that, after all, we were not the only ones to
suffer. All the three million people of the colony were no better off. That
night, for the first time in the history of Catholic Hong Kong, there was
no Midnight Mass in any of the churches of the colony. The curfew and
the strict blackout made it impossible. Only a few Irish Jesuits celebrated
midnight Mass in British military barracks and at the Hong Kong Hotel.

Christmas Day: Hong Kong Surrenders

On that fateful Christmas morning, December 25, 1941, a gray, dull
sky reflected the feelings of misery and desolation of the people of
the colony. Its defenses were in shambles but still there was no hint of
surrender. Hong Kong's leading local paper, the *South China Morning
Post*, came out with an upbeat editorial:

"Hong Kong is observing the strangest and most somber Christmas in
its century-old history. For the first time in years the streets lack stocks
of ready-to erect Christmas trees; when people knocked on shop doors or
stood in lines yesterday they were not seeking gift trinkets but bread or
rice. Friends remembered to toast one another, in moderation, and at city
hotels, which were crowded. All were cheerful in the knowledge that, for
all their present hardships, they would not go either hungry or thirsty this
Christmas."

There also was a Christmas message from Governor Young:

"In pride and admiration I send my greetings this Christmas Day to
all those who are working so nobly and so well to sustain Hong Kong

against the assault of the enemy. Fight on. Hold fast for King and
Empire. God bless you all in this your finest hour."

I leave it to the pen of Ellen Field to summarize the pathetic story of
the surrender:

"The dawn of Christmas Day found our soldiers tired and exhausted
and desperate. The Japanese sent another surrender request which the
Governor still rejected. He reported to London: 'Stout fighting is going
on. Enemy working towards center of town. All in very good heart and
send Christmas greetings.' But this was a last gesture. The Japanese
began their final attack. They made rapid progress along the North Shore
and came within shooting distance of H.Q. Our main forces were now
completely out of touch with an isolated force still resisting in Stanley
Peninsula, which had only eight mobile guns left with about sixty rounds
per gun.

"At 3:15 P.M. the G.O.C. and the Naval Commander advised the
Governor that no further effective military resistance could be made; and
so the white flag was raised. The silence of defeat descended upon our
island."

This is how Ted Ferguson described the effect of the surrender on the
Hong Kong people:

"The impending enemy occupation caused a frenzy in Victoria.
Mothers created hiding places for young daughters in cellars and upstairs
closets; the prices of black-market Japanese flags sky-rocketed; embas-
sies and colonial government staffs darted from room to room, burning
documents in wastepaper baskets; Chinese lawyers, doctors, and other
professionals put on coolie outfits and disappeared into slum areas.
The guests at the Hong Kong and other luxury hotels worried about the
Japanese getting hold of liquor. Hundreds of bottles were smashed in the
streets, and champagne and Johnnie Walker used to flush toilets. So
many bottles were emptied on bar floors that alcoholic rivers ran through
some lobbies."

It was not until 6:00 P.M. that the guards of our prison camp informed
us of the surrender. Far from rejoicing, we were completely dejected and
were as much saddened by the loss of Hong Kong as the British. Our
future under the Japanese was a frightening prospect but that evening we
did not have much time to think about the future. In spite of the surrender, bombs continued to whine overhead and explosions kept occurring
on the hillside below the fort. We could not understand why. At about
10:00 P.M. some Japanese officers in fatigue uniforms, dirty, disheveled,
still half camouflaged with tree branches, appeared at the door of our

building. They informed us that the next morning we would be sent home. But in the meantime the bombing continued. Finally, about midnight, it ceased. We later learned that the fort commander, Brigadier Gen. C. Wallis, at first refused to surrender when General Headquarters raised the white flag, and waited until he received written orders from Gen. Maltby to capitulate. He signed and surrendered to the Japanese on December 26 at 12:41 A.M.

Silence descended on the martyred colony: the silence of complete exhaustion. We, too, slept for the remainder of that night. It was the first night in a week we slept without being awakened by bombs.

Notes

1. Sr. Amata died here in the States in the spring of 1988.

2. Unfortunately, only a little over a month later the "little yellow bastards" killed more than half of the Canadian contingent.

3. Even though married to a British gentleman who was interned as a war prisoner, she claimed Irish descent and avoided being interned. Thus she remained free in Hong Kong to the end of the war and did terrific work for the war prisoners, among whom were her husband and her father.

4. Members of a clandestine, subversive operation working within a country to further the enemies' political aims and military invasion. This term was very commonly used, especially in Europe during World War II.

21

After The Surrender

Destruction And Death

In the early hours of December 26, 1941, the sun rose over Hong Kong in a brilliant blue sky, the quiet waters of the Pacific around the Stanley Peninsula shimmered in the morning light; the verdant hills were aglow with the thousand colors of tropical vegetation, but an ominous silence reigned supreme: the silence of death. Where, only a few hours before, barrage after barrage of exploding shells punctuated by desperate cries of the wounded and dying had prevailed, now life seemed extinct. Even the birds, frightened by the bombing of the previous days, seemed to have deserted the peaceful blue sky.

At the Stanley Prison all of us internees were greatly worried, not knowing what the day would bring. The British and Chinese guards had disappeared, breakfast did not come, and we timidly ventured into the yard to explore what was happening. Nobody was around. At about 9:00 A.M. we finally heard the raspy voices of Japanese officers shouting orders. Before long a Japanese military truck showed up. None of the soldiers spoke English but somehow we were made to understand that we had to climb aboard, which we did eagerly.

If our previous trip from Hong Kong to Stanley at night had been a nightmare, the return trip from Stanley to Hong Kong was probably even worse, though for different reasons. This time we traveled in an open truck, and what we saw was frightening and heartrending. Of course, no effort had been made as yet to clean anything up. Anyone who has never seen the sight of a conquered and devastated city the very first day after a ferocious battle can never be able to visualize the gloomy horror, the wanton destruction, the grim desolation of the scenes we saw.

The fifteen-mile road to Hong Kong passed through some of the areas where the battle had been fiercest, such as Stanley Village, Wong Nai, Chong Gap, Happy Valley and Wanchai. The carcasses of burned trucks, cars and even tanks were strewn all along and littered the side of the road and the slopes of the hills. In the street there was filth everywhere, glutted or broken mains gave off a dreadful stench, almost all the buildings still standing were pockmarked by shell splinters, and some buildings flew the Rising Sun, others plain white sheets. Bodies of dead soldiers in uniform and of civilians lay in the most grotesque positions and were strewn all along the road. Some seemed still to be alive, but no one bothered to help them. Collapsed buildings were reduced to mounds of debris, with pillars contorted and sprawling in all directions. Some rag-covered Chinese crawling here and there in terror at the mere sight of a Japanese military truck gave us an inkling of the fear that dominated the city.

However, the most painful, humiliating, heartrending scenes we saw were those long lines of British and Canadian soldiers, bedraggled, disheveled, their faces stained with blood and mud, bound by coarse ropes one to the other like pigs, crouching along the curbs of the streets. They were at the mercy of the Japanese soldiers, who watched them with fixed bayonets on their guns, cursing, shouting, kicking anyone who moved. To see those valiant boys who had simply done their duty now being treated like animals brought tears to our eyes. Yet there was nothing we could do for them.

What I saw during that trip made me realize in no uncertain terms that the Hong Kong we had known no longer existed. Whatever life there could still be would be agony. The following days and years proved that my forebodings were correct in every respect. I must confess that at that moment I conceived such profound dislike for the Japanese and their brutal, unjustified aggression that it bordered upon hatred. I had to struggle hard to contain it within the limits of the Christian duty of forgiveness.

After a one-hour trip we were literally dumped on the front lawn of a second-class Chinese hotel in the Wanchai District. Nobody gave us any instructions and we were simply abandoned there under the hot sun. Japanese and Chinese collaborators with the arrogant air of new bosses came and went, but nobody paid any attention to the funny-looking group of fifteen young white men in long, black gowns with collars backward.

Phones were not working so we could not reach the bishop. We waited and waited and waited. Some of the more humane Chinese recognized us as priests and begged us not to move, not to go anywhere because there was looting all over and the streets were not safe. Hesitantly we sneaked into the hotel, managed to get some tea and a little food, and returned to wait outside. We had no place to sit but on our suitcases. The afternoon dragged on slowly. Finally we were able to learn from some Chinese people that the bishop was alive, that the cathedral, the convents of nuns and the largest churches had been damaged, but not seriously. That was a big relief; not all was lost.

Late that night the Chinese manager of the hotel came out to tell us that he had received orders to assign rooms to us. He proceeded immediately to do so.

The hotel was only a twenty-minute walk from the cathedral, but we remained in it three days. On the fourth day, having seen no Japanese, and having received no orders from anyone, we quietly walked away and returned to our own respective residences. Of course, we left to the Japanese the privilege of paying the hotel bill!

The Church Under Fire

As we walked back to the mission house, I could hardly believe my eyes, seeing misery and devastation everywhere. The exterior of the mission house had not suffered much damage, but we soon began to hear stories of what had happened during the seventeen days of our internment in Stanley. Fr. T. F. Ryan summed it up in these words:

"The invaders left death and destruction in their path. Shelling and bombing were continuous, and soldiers and civilians suffered alike. Every day one heard of deaths of relatives and friends, families made homeless by the destruction of their homes, and of ruin and suffering. Among the Catholic population the Portuguese suffered heavily because of the many Portuguese volunteers who, after covering themselves with glory in the fighting, died in the conflict.

"A good deal of damage was done to Catholic buildings. The cathedral was struck by shells; St. Joseph's Church, too, was heavily damaged; the Canossian Hospital at the foot of Peak Road was struck and set on fire and completely destroyed. Almost all the buildings suffered some damage, and it would be a long time before they could be repaired."

Buildings had suffered some damage, but thanks to Divine Providence the hundreds of sisters and the tens of thousands of people who had taken refuge in our Catholic institutions had not been molested by the Japanese. Even the Carmelite convent in Stanley, where twenty nuns, alone and defenseless, could have been easy prey for marauding soldiers, was safe. Mother Superior told the bishop that when, in the heat of the battle for Stanley on December 24, Japanese soldiers came to the door ready to enter the convent by force, she had gathered all her nuns dressed in their white habits in the parlor behind the double iron grille and had placed the elderly nuns in the front lines with the young ones hidden behind. After explaining to the commanding officer that the convent was a holy place and that no man could enter, as an exception she let him come inside and gave him a "Cook's tour." It did not take long for the officer to be convinced it was a holy place. Not only did he tell his soldiers to leave but he also placed the convent under the army's protection and nailed an official seal of the Imperial Japanese army on the convent door to prevent other military units or hunting soldiers from harassing the sisters.

The same thing happened to all of our convents and churches, which were crowded to capacity with tens of thousands of women and children. Following the order of Bishop Valtorta, every Catholic property and institution, including churches, rectories, parochial halls, classrooms and every building the church owned, was used to shelter, feed and protect people, especially the elderly, women and children.

I gained an idea of what had happened in our institutions all over the colony when I returned to the cathedral. Every priest's room, including mine, every nook and cranny, even the stair landings in the house, the church and the sacristy were crowded with people, especially old ladies, young women and children. They were sleeping on the floors, using Chinese chattees (earthen pots used as charcoal burners) to cook their rice. The bishop, with the help of only one Chinese priest and one Spanish priest, was supervising everything from distributing rations to assigning sleeping places.

A few hours after I returned to the cathedral, I went to visit the nearby Canossian convent. That also was a sight I will never forget. As I wrote in a previous chapter, the Canossian convent was a huge complex of multi-storied buildings with hundreds of rooms and classrooms covering an area of several square acres. Even there every nook and cranny of the buildings, including the covered verandas, was filled to capacity. There were probably close to twenty thousand refugees. Later I was told that the same was true at St. Paul's convent, almost as large as the Canossian convent. There was no doubt that on this occasion, thanks to Divine

Providence, the church in Hong Kong really had done a magnificent humanitarian work. I estimate that all of our Catholic institutions combined saved at least tens of thousands of women from being raped by Japanese.

The Rape Of Hong Kong

The raping and looting of the vanquished by the victors is an evil almost as old as the world itself. The history of mankind has recorded happenings of this type in every culture of the world. Hong Kong was no exception, and suffered the full brunt of Japanese soldiers' greed and lust. The code of the Japanese armed forces officially condoned looting and raping as a reward to officers and soldiers for good fighting. Japanese soldiers had very little else to look forward to in the military service. The food was traditionally poor, the pay insignificant, and discipline very strict. So, when such occasional bonanzas came along, soldiers and officers indulged themselves to their hearts' content. About the rape of Hong Kong and Kowloon, Ted Ferguson wrote:

"After their Japanese commanding officers officially declared all Chinese females to be prostitutes, soldiers strode into private homes demanding "fa ku niang" (flower girls), the Cantonese euphemism for whores. Some houses were entered and the same women assaulted so often that their husbands or parents agreed to let them become personal flower girls for Japanese officers. That way, the girls got less abuse and their families were assured a steady food supply."

Very often raping was accompanied by murder—murder of parents and especially mothers who tried in vain to shield or protect their daughters. Often, too, murder of the raped girls themselves would occur when, wounded and exhausted by savage attacks, they were of no further service to the men.

What made the indiscriminate raping of women heinous to both Chinese and white people was the callousness of officers and soldiers who regarded this as legitimate sport. Perhaps the cause of this behavior may be attributed to the fact that in Japan prostitution is considered a normal occupation, without the stigma attached to it among the Chinese and white people. In Japan it is not uncommon for a young girl to become a prostitute for a few years in order to support her parents or merely to earn money. She will then get married and lead a faithful life.

Besides raping, there were numerous cases of other wanton atrocities, the worst cases happening in hospitals. I will quote only the story of

what happened at St. Stephen's Hospital, which was under the care of
Dr. George Black, one of the oldest and most respected doctors in the
colony. Here is a summary from Tim Carew's book:

"Black looked out of the front door. About two hundred Japs were
advancing towards the hospital. Squaring his shoulders, he strode
forward to meet them.

"'This is a hospital,' said Black with dignity. 'You can't come in
here.'

"The two leading Japs nudged one another and laughed. Then one of
them, with his bayonet fixed, advanced grinning on the doctor, took
deliberate aim and shot him through the head.

"A single Jap voice called out, 'Banzai!'

"Then there were no more voices, only the jostling movement of
urgent and heated bodies as the Japs surged forward. Colonel Black's
body was bayoneted a dozen times as he lay on the floor, blood welling
from the wound in his head. Captain Whitney started bravely forward
and brought down a Jap with his revolver before he received six bullets
in the stomach. As he fell, a press of bodies bore down upon him: the
bayonets rose and fell again. . . .

"The nurses could only stand helplessly and watch the slaughter of the
defenseless wounded men. The Japs ripped bandages from torn bodies
and from the stumps of recently amputated arms and legs. They plunged
their bayonets into the men in the beds. One nurse, flinging her body
across a patient was bayoneted with the man in the bed; it took the
Japanese a long time to get his bayonet out of their bodies. In the space
of thirty minutes fifty-six wounded men had been hacked to death. A few
patients managed to hide under beds and in dark corners while the orgy
continued."

Ted Ferguson added that the nurses, after being compelled to help
cremate the dead, were taken away. A Canadian priest, Fr. James Barrett,
the Catholic chaplain, asked to see them but was not allowed to do so.
Months later at a war crime trial he testified that when he saw them the
next morning they walked and talked like zombies and they admitted that
"they had experienced dreadful things during the night."

Similar atrocities were committed at other hospitals on both the Hong
Kong and Kowloon sides. There were only a few exceptions, such as St.
Albert's Hospital.[2] There, on Christmas Day, a group of rowdy soldiers
faced the matron, Mary Currie, tall and stately, at least four inches taller
than the leering officer who confronted her. Without even speaking he
kicked her in the shin with his heavy military boot. Mrs. Currie, hiding

the excruciating pain, looked at the diminutive officer with profound disdain and said aloud, "I thought the Japanese were civilized."

An English-speaking Japanese officer interfered, barked some order to his men, and told Mrs. Currie, "Japanese soldiers are civilized."

"It certainly does not look like it," Mrs. Currie replied. "If you want to see how *civilized* [and she put emphasis on that word] people treat their wounded, come and see."

She escorted him to a cot where the body of a mutilated Japanese soldier lay in a bed under snowy white sheets, bandaged and evidently having been treated with the same attention as the wounded British soldiers.

"We could not save him," Mrs. Currie said, "but we did the best we could for him."

Tim Carew concluded, "There was no brutality in St. Albert's Hospital after that."

Looting And Atrocities

Thanks to Divine Providence, our Catholic institutions were spared looting. However, all over the colony there were widespread cases of looting both during and immediately after the fighting during those few days when neither British nor Japanese were in control. As I did not witness these tragedies myself, I will quote here J. B. Endacott's report:

"Sporadic looting had occurred during the battle but with the cessation of the fighting it appeared on a greatly extended scale. The homes of those absent were stripped. The fuel problem became acute, for rice must be cooked, and wooden furniture became more marketable as fuel than serving its original purpose. Looters were liable to be summarily shot on the roads, and it is surprising that they still continued to take the risk. John Stericker in his *Tear for the Dragon* has described conditions at the lower Peak Tram Station where the Japanese tied Chinese looters to a tree by their necks and hands, in groups, and left them to strangle, while others were strung up and hanged from lamp-posts. He also tells of looters having their hands pierced by bayonets and being thrown into the sea with their hands threaded together. Other observers have also left accounts of Chinese looters being tied up and tortured.

"Japanese soldiers also operated on the streets and showed a particularly keen interest in watches; they would innocently ask the time from a passer-by and the victim, glancing at his watch to oblige, was forthwith relieved of it, and report had it that an ambition to have the whole of the arm straddled with watches was not uncommon among the Japanese soldiery.

"The evidence shows beyond doubt that the Chinese were treated badly in many instances, and quite at variance with Japanese propaganda which stressed the theme of 'Asia for the Asians.'"

A comic episode was that of a small-sized Japanese sentry in the luxury neighborhood of the Peak who appeared on duty wearing a beautiful, costly fur twice his size!

The Positive Side

In the midst of so much horror and so many atrocities, there were also accounts of heroism and charity worth remembering:

The Chinese emerged from their seventeen days' ordeal of fire with no little credit, and all eyewitness accounts pay tribute to their discipline and good humor in the face of danger. "There was no panic at any time, the proverbial patience of the Chinese was fully demonstrated, and their unruffled calm in moments of danger and alarm won the unstinted praise of those not ordinarily given to praise," wrote Fr. Ryan.

"The Chinese were orderly, there was no panic," wrote another observer, and another commented on the orderly processions into the air raid shelters, saying, 'The public shelters were filled to an unbelievable extent with Chinese who remained good humored and placid.'

"The reaction of the local Chinese community to the British defeat was one of numbed surprise and sullen acquiescence in the new conditions, accompanied by a grim determination to survive; and, of course, to the very poor, immersed in the problem of getting two meals a day and a bed-space, it mattered little who won. The mass of the Chinese had tried to continue their normal jobs, leaving the fighting to those whose business it was."

Camps For Prisoners Of War

All the British, Canadian, Indian and Portuguese men found in military uniforms were rounded up on December 26 and herded into several hastily prepared POW camps. To report the horror stories as well as the acts of kindness that accompanied this operation is beyond the purpose of this book, but I cannot refrain from reporting two happenings.

The Japanese commander of the Sham Sheui Po Camp was an extremely cruel and sadistic man who caused immense suffering. He enjoyed torturing and tormenting his prisoners. After the war, the war crimes tribunal condemned him to death for his inhuman behavior. At the other extreme, the whores of Wanchai's Red Light District were most remarkable in their kindness. Tim Carew wrote:

"The legend of the Angels who appeared before the Tommies at Mans, France may or may not be true; the Angels of Wanchai wore, not white robes and wings, but gaily colored cheongsams, slit to the thigh. These were the 'dahnhomers' who came to the battered soldiers of Hong Kong with water, looted cigarettes, beer, bandages and food. Many of these Angels of Wanchai—loose women, amoral women and even diseased women—risked brutal beatings by the Japanese to take parcels to the men behind the wire who had no one else to cherish and comfort them."

Unfortunately we Italian priests could do nothing for the POWs. Not even the bishop was allowed to visit them. Technically we were "allied" with the Japanese and could not show sympathy for the "enemy." Needless to say, for us the enemy was the Japanese and certainly not our British and Portuguese friends languishing in those camps, whose only guilt lay in having done their duty.

The same situation prevailed with regard to our British and American civilian friends. They were left free during the first few days after the surrender, but on the morning of January 4, 1942, a cold, drizzly day, all British, American and Dutch residents were ordered to report to a parade ground bringing only an overnight bag. That was the beginning of four painful years of internment. They were never again to return to their homes or to recover their valuable possessions.

That day several thousand such persons milled around in the open air under the rain, and the Japanese did not know how to organize them. Finally they were divided into groups according to their height and were marched into several buildings in different parts of the city, under unsanitary conditions, with hardly any provisions made for food and other necessities. It was a very grim sight to see our friends reduced to such a state.

After several days they were taken by sea to Stanley. The prison and several other buildings in the village were surrounded by barbed wire and changed into a concentration camp. Only the traditional British spirit of accepting challenges helped most of the internees to survive the ordeal until the end of the war.

As in the case of the POWs, we could not even say farewell to them. The fact that they were ordered to bring along only an overnight bag led them to believe that they would be detained for a few days at the most. It was a cruel trick of the Japanese officers, who would use the beautifully furnished British and American villas for their own billets and did not want the owners to take away anything!

One group of lively, young Maryknoll priests managed to come to the mission house before they were interned, to say hello to Bishop Valtorta. When they were leaving, some of my confreres and I accompanied them to the door. I envied them. I would have preferred going with them to the concentration camp rather than living under the Japanese. As the Mary-knollers left, they turned toward us and shouted, "Long live America. See you next July fourth!" We did not know then that July 4 would come around four times before we could see them again.

On the occasion of the internment of the British, the *Hong Kong News* (the Japanese paper printed in English) wrote: ". . . the vaunted supermen of the white race have melted like butter. In eighteen days of conflict it was all over, a horrible muddle of inefficiency and helplessness which has bequeathed a miserable aftermath." Their arrogance was unbearable indeed!

Notes

1. Whether the Japanese did it out of humanitarian feelings or to preserve it for their own use is a judgment I am not competent to make.

2. This hospital was the spacious house of studies of the Spanish Dominican Fathers on May Road, which had been converted into an emergency hospital during the hostilities.

3. The beautiful story of efforts made by a few white people to succor and help the POWs can be read in the books of Ellen Field and J. B. Endacott.

22

Misery In Occupied Hong Kong

Life In Chaos

To return to our houses was certainly a relief after the bombing in Stanley and the confinement at the Wanchai Hotel. The actual fighting was over and we were unhurt and in good health. There was a lot for which to thank the Lord.

However, the chaotic and heart-rending conditions prevailing all around us made life agony. It is impossible to describe the tragic changes wrought within Hong Kong by seventeen days of war. From the height of the terrace of the mission house I looked down at the city below: the central district of Victoria, the harbor, the Kowloon Peninsula, the faraway hills. The scenic view had not changed. Most office buildings were still there, the Peak above us and the hills on the far horizon. But what a change in the lives of the million and a half people living within that area! Where before there had been a prosperous city living with law and order, now there was nothing but chaos, misery and despair. Life seemed an unbearable task. Nobody had a job. Banks, offices, factories, post offices, shops were closed. Public transportation was suspended. Schools were closed indefinitely, and no one knew if and when they would reopen under the new masters. Bereavement, desolation, uncertainty about the future, starvation, fear of rampaging soldiers, and unabated misery reigned supreme. Facing the specter of unemployment and starvation, people felt hopeless and helpless.

Increasing the misery of the people was the fact that the Japanese seemed to have no plans for administering the colony. Hong Kong was in a unique situation compared to other Chinese cities occupied by the

Japanese. In other cities such as Canton and Shanghai, the leadership was changed but the main structures of city government remained the same, and life went on. But in Hong Kong, the colony's government was completely wiped out overnight and there was no one ready to replace it. For several days Hong Kong remained in the hands of military officers who did not have the vaguest idea how to run a city of one and a half million people. This added untold misery to the life of the population.

I Am Jobless

I, too, was one of the million jobless people. The bishop no longer needed me as secretary because there were no letters to write and no secretarial work to be done. The Catholic Truth Society could not function any longer because there was no mail service. There were no religious classes to teach because the schools were closed. As normal living was turned totally upside-down there was not even pastoral work to be done because people were afraid to venture out of their houses and nobody was coming to church. However, I believed that once a priest, one is a priest forever, and that the priesthood is not a job but a way of life. Therefore I felt that this was my hour of opportunity, the hour when I could follow in the steps of Christ more closely than ever by consoling, helping, assisting people in need. I had a million and a half of them around me.

I began helping the refugees in the mission house. Little by little they began returning to their houses and a lot of them needed help. Dr. John Wu and Francis Yeh were among the refugees at the mission house. Dr. Wu had had no news of his family in Kowloon and I somehow managed to put him in touch with them. At the Canossian convent there were also many people who needed help of one kind or another. I tried to help them in whatever way I could. But exercising charity is never easy; doing it in wartime under a foreign power is even dangerous. Very soon I was in serious trouble.

Among the refugees in the Canossian convent was the wife of the Finance Minister of China, Mrs. O. K. Yui, who had taken refuge there incognito, dressed as a servant woman and sharing the same hardships as everybody else. For her own safety, the sisters treated her like any other refugee. However, the very efficient and highly organized Japanese Secret Service knew her whereabouts and kept close watch on her.

I had already met Mrs. Yui on several occasions, so when Dr. Wu, who was a close friend of hers, asked me to see if she needed help, I went to see her several times at the convent. Unaware that there were spies even among the refugees, I volunteered to carry messages for her to people outside who were planning her escape to free China. I also brought food and other things to her. I thought that nobody would know what I was doing, but the Japanese did learn about it from their spies. One day when I returned home from the convent, Bishop Valtorta called me to his room and, with an anguished tone of voice, said, "Maestrini, you are in serious trouble. A friend of mine who has some contact with the Japanese has warned me that the Japanese know all about what you are doing for Mrs. Yui. If you do not stop helping her immediately, the Japanese are going to put you in jail. Please, do not go to the Canossian convent for any reason, and for at least three months do not even show your face in the streets."

I was totally devastated. Now I really was grounded and jobless. For a few days I stayed close to home and avoided any public contact with important people, even with John Wu. As things settled down and people resumed coming to church, I started doing whatever ministry work I could at the cathedral and spent most of my time praying, reading and studying. After a couple of weeks the bishop informed me that Mrs. Yui had left the Canossian convent and had arrived safely in free China. I then gradually resumed my activities at the Canossian convent and was even bold enough to venture around in the streets. Convinced that the Japanese had too many other problems to worry about to spy on an insignificant, little Italian priest, I resumed as normal a life as was possible under those circumstances.

Life Under The Japanese

The Japanese declared Hong Kong a "captured territory," and it was placed under their sovereignty to be used as a strategic base for war purposes. Lt. Gen. Rensuke Isogasi was appointed Governor of Hong Kong. On the day he took office he issued a message to the people of Hong Kong calling Britain "public enemy of mankind, whose loss of Hong Kong was a matter for rejoicing." He called on the Hong Kong people to "help achieve victory in the Greater East Asia War, to eschew 'easy practices' and to elevate the life of the place to Japanese levels in the light of 'the Kingly Way,' as set out in the Confucian classical writings."

A civilian form of government was organized with a Court of Law (Japanese military style) and a new police force. The Chinese community was represented by a Consultative Commission, which had no executive power. Public utilities were gradually restored but soon deteriorated because of lack of maintenance. Mail service was resumed but only with Japan, occupied China and Macao. The rest of the world was inaccessible to us by mail, cable or phone. We received only news from Japanese agencies.

All government and private cars were confiscated soon after the invasion and later shipped to Japan. Public transportation was reduced to a few run-down buses and ferries. Walking was officially encouraged as a way to better health, and Japanese shops did a brisk business selling us their bicycles.

Hospitals were few and poorly equipped. Doctors were scarce and medical supplies from Japan were at a premium. Cholera broke out in 1942 and 1943 and inoculation was compulsory. There was an anti-spit campaign to teach people not to spit in the streets and even a "rat week" in 1945 to help wipe out the invasion of such rodents that occurred due to general unsanitary conditions. The bureaucracy became unbearable, as the Japanese suffered from a real mania to have everything and everybody registered. Not only did every person need an identification card to move around and to get food rations, but every piece of property, every business, every street vendor, every activity, every change of address, even every radio set, had to be registered. To make matters worse, regulations controlling registrations changed constantly. Endless queues for registration and for food rations became a nightmare.[1]

Famine was widespread. There were no jobs due to lack of industry and commerce because the Japanese wanted to keep Hong Kong as a war base. There was no food; supplies could not arrive from China because of the war or from abroad because there were no ships. An American journalist who was allowed a few months of free time before being interned in Stanley reported that every night about two hundred corpses were picked up, people who had died of starvation. Merely by walking the streets one could see lots of people everywhere barely able to walk, wide-eyed, soulful, helplessly looking for assistance, despair in their eyes. But the Japanese did not care; they only wanted to reduce the population of the city in order to get rid of a big burden.

Fear also became pervasive. In spite of a few exceptional cases of kindness, Japanese soldiers, policemen and secret police agents were generally a terror. They not only indulged in arbitrary shooting and bayoneting of harmless Chinese civilians for minor offenses but also tortured and terrorized them for sport. Surprise arrests of suspected spies were frequent, day or night. It was not enough to keep the law in order to avoid trouble. A mere suspicion that one knew or might be associated with a suspected spy could land one in jail for weeks or months, without explanation or trial. Soldiers and officers generously administered kicks in the shins, blows with rifle butts and vicious slaps under the slightest pretext.

Japanese sentries were posted at street corners all over town. All who had to pass in front of them had to bow with joined hands, no matter what they were carrying. If one did not do it properly, according to Japanese style, one would be promptly kicked in the shins, or slapped in the face.[2]

Severe famine, constant fear and miserable conditions of life all joined together to cause a great exodus. In less than two years over one million people left Hong Kong for the interior of China. The main reason: survival.

The Great Exodus

In December 1941 Hong Kong and Kowloon (not including the New Territories) had a population of over one and a half million. By August 1945 the population was estimated at less than five hundred thousand. That meant an average exodus of over thirty thousand people a month, although registration to obtain exit permits was a long and painful nightmare.

Soon after the Japanese occupation of Hong Kong people began to leave for China. Traveling meant facing terrible dangers and discomforts because of the complete breakdown of all transportation services by land or sea. The Japanese, however, favored this movement in order to reduce the problem of controlling an overpopulated city in a war base. They opened a Repatriation Bureau to issue exit permits and secured a few old river steamers to carry people from Hong Kong to mainland China.

With their mania for registration and paperwork they required a strict scrutiny of one's life before permits were issued. Endacott wrote:

"Many preferred to leave secretly via the underground, provided they could pay the required protection money to the guerrillas. The story of repatriation is long and complicated, since the regulations frequently changed and scarcity of transport caused delays. Bureaucratic controls made the process of leaving a protracted one, involving long queues for the necessary exit permits, for the required vaccination and inoculation certificates, and for certificates of health from the Anti-epidemic Bureau, all of which had to be produced before the passage tickets could be bought. As tickets were available only one day before sailing, their purchase normally entailed queuing for about forty-eight hours and since the number sold bore little relation to the available accommodations, passengers usually had to go to the wharf the previous night to ensure getting on board. They were searched on the quay and their luggage examined, an arbitrary process of emptying everything on the ground, leaving them to retrieve their possessions as best they could. It all required monumental patience and persistence."

Dr. John C. H. Wu's Escape

When the Japanese attack came, Dr. Wu was living with his twelve children and his wife (who was expecting their thirteenth child) in a small apartment in Kowloon. As Dr. Wu was an important official in the Chungking government he was wanted by the Japanese. The day the Japanese reached the periphery of Kowloon, John's family urged him to escape to Hong Kong, as the island was supposed to be able to withstand a Japanese attack. Dr. Wu wrote that at the idea of leaving his family he "tasted something like death."

But his eldest son, Thomas, then twenty-four years old, insisted, "Daddy, you simply cannot afford to fall into the hands of the Japanese. In going to Hong Kong you still have a chance to escape. I shall take care of the family, which would be safer without your presence. Go in peace and trust everything to God."

Dr. Wu continued: "I still shillied and shallied, but the rattle of the machine guns came nearer and nearer. So Thomas caught me by the arms and dragged me to the ferry just like a policeman dragging along a criminal. I caught the last boat."

In Hong Kong he took refuge in the mission house with Francis Yeh and remained there through the painful days of the Japanese attack. I met them both at the mission house when I returned from Stanley. They could not go back to Kowloon because there was no ferry service.

Suddenly on January 9 both Dr. Wu and Francis Yeh received an official order to report to the Japanese Military Headquarters at the Hong Kong Hotel downtown. The Japanese knew where they were and no escape was possible.

Dr. Wu wrote: "On January 8 I asked Father Maestrini to offer a Mass at the altar of St. Joseph, and to beg the great Saint to guide us in our dealings with the Japanese. Francis and I received Holy Communion and prayed ardently for protection and guidance. At ten o'clock we went to the Hong Kong Hotel. A Japanese officer who spoke Chinese fluently, came to talk to us. I asked him what he wanted to see me for. He said in a roundabout way how desirable it would be for China and Japan to make peace. I said, 'I certainly love peace more than you do. It is most easy for Japan to make peace with China.'

"He pricked up his ears and asked, 'How?'

"'Oh, it is very simple,' I replied, 'Withdraw all your troops from China, and there will be peace.'

"He said, 'But we cannot withdraw our troops. If we do, your troops will follow us to Japan.'

"I answered, 'As to that, I can guarantee that China has never wanted war. It was your honorable country that started it. We have always been on the defensive. If you withdraw your troops, I cannot imagine that our troops will ever invade Tokyo.'

"I was as polite as I could be, but evidently he did not like my logic. After a few moments of ominous silence, he said, 'You will stay here!' Addressing himself to Francis, he said, 'You, too!'"

So Wu and Yeh were confined to a room and forbidden to have any communication with outsiders. When the bishop and I did not see them returning to the mission house, we began to worry. There was nothing I could do because, as I said before, I was not allowed to leave the house, but the following day the bishop began making the rounds of Japanese offices. With typical Oriental nonchalance he was referred from one office to the other and only after several days did he finally learn that they were being held incommunicado at the Hong Kong Hotel. I then managed to sneak some spiritual books to them, including Karl Adams *Christ Our Brother* and a Chinese prayer book.[3]

The bishop got busy seeing what he could do to get Dr. Wu and Francis Yeh released. Realizing that he did not have much influence with the Japanese, he turned to Sir Robert Kotewall, a mutual friend of his and of Dr. Wu. Sir Robert was then a very influential person as he was "collaborating" with the Japanese in order to protect his friends. Being held in very high regard by the Japanese, he succeeded in obtaining Dr. Wu's release.

"On the morning of the 30th we heard a loud knock on the door, louder than any we had heard," wrote Dr. Wu. "I was really frightened this time. I thought that was the end of us. On opening the door, we saw a Japanese officer solemnly announcing to us the coming of the bishop. The bishop? Did he come to administer Extreme Unction to us? But the bishop was smiling, he told us that Sir Robert Kotewall had kindly undertaken to bail us out, and that we could return home this morning! That was heavenly!"

They lost no time and an hour later John was reunited with his family. Everyone was alive and well. He had come home just in time to greet his thirteenth child, who was born the following morning.[4]

Even though released from internment at the hotel, Dr. Wu was confined at home and could go only to the nearest church once a day. In the meantime the Japanese made several attempts to secure his collaboration.

The following episode illustrates the risk he ran by remaining in Hong Kong under the Japanese:

"In the spring something happened which really vexed me. The Japanese municipality was organizing a 'representative council,' composed of 'leaders' in all walks of life, such as banking, law, medicine, journalism, culture and education. An officer approached me and showed me the list of the names. My name headed the list as representing 'culture'! Well, I thought, this is a greater calamity than the war itself! I said to the officer, 'I appreciate the Mayor's good intentions. Please convey my thanks to him. But as to being a member of the representative council, I think you know as well as I do that I am an officer of the Chinese Government. After all, China and Japan belong to the same civilization, and the foundation of that civilization is loyalty. Without loyalty there can be no talk of culture and education. Please ask the Mayor to cancel my name!' My name was canceled and the Japanese respected me all the more!"

Wu soon came to the conclusion that he had to escape, but he worried that this might cause trouble for Sir Robert. Friends assured him that Sir Robert was too important to the Japanese for them to do him any harm, so he got in touch with the underground to arrange his flight to free China. The occasion came when the Japanese ordered that all laborers from Shanghai and other parts of Japanese-occupied territory should go back to their native places, traveling on land, because there were not sufficient boats. Dr. Wu recounted that this "furnished a golden opportunity for us to escape. Francis Yeh and I registered ourselves and all the members of our families as laborers under assumed names such as 'King Ah-pao,' 'Wang Ah-mao,' 'Chang Hsiao-ti,' 'Li Mei-mei,' and so forth. We dressed ourselves in the shabbiest clothes you can imagine. I shaved off my beard, which I had grown during my imprisonment. But Thomas was frightened while we were still planning our exodus. He said, 'Daddy, do you realize what you are doing? Can we seriously hope to break the net of secret intelligence for which the Japanese are so famous? You are running into death! If you are prepared to die, we are willing to die with you. If you are not, don't try.'

"'I am!' was my answer. As I look back upon those days I still tremble. But I did not feel any danger then!"

One more problem worried him. Was he telling a lie to pretend to be returning to Shanghai while on the contrary escaping to free China? In his mind he was convinced that anything built on a lie could have no good results.

"So I went to confession to a Chinese priest," he wrote. "I exposed to him the whole situation and asked his advice: 'Father, whatever you will say, I will obey.'

"'Go ahead!' he said. 'It would glorify Christ and His church by showing to the world how patriotic a Catholic can be!'

"I pricked up my ears at those words and said, 'Is this Christ talking?'

"'Yes,' the voice came from within the confessional, 'it is Christ talking!'

"'Then, Father, will you follow me with your prayers?'

"'Certainly. Our Lady will never forsake you!'

"'But Father, is it a lie to say that I am going to Shanghai?'

"'Well, you are going to Shanghai by way of Chungking!'

"That settled the matter for me. Running into death or running into life, I had Christ to back me up."

That day he did not know that he would indeed return to Shanghai one day, but only on his way to Rome to become the first Chinese Ambassador to the Holy See.

The night before leaving he composed a little poem for the Japanese officer in charge of his case. Among other things he wrote: "Excuse me for going away without saying Goodbye! Loyalty requires the skipping of minor courtesies." He left the note on a table inside the house as he was sure the Japanese would break in.

The morning of May 2, after attending Mass at St. Teresa's, his favorite church, he and his wife and thirteen children (John Jude was then only three months old), Francis Yeh and a few other friends, twenty persons altogether, all dressed as the poorest of the poor with old, patched-up clothes, climbed into a borrowed truck and began traveling west. Shortly afterward, four Japanese policemen stopped the truck and climbed on board. Everybody was terrified, shuddering at the thought of what might happen if the Japanese discovered that they were leaving town without a permit. John Wu took out his rosary beads and began to pray. Impressed by his piety, and thinking they were only beggars, the Japanese did not even bother to question them. After about ten miles of driving in silence, the Japanese ordered the truck to stop, said a raspy "Arigato" ("Thank you"), bowed and left. They had only wanted a ride.

"We continued our journey, but when we reached Sa Tou Ku, it was already eventide," he wrote. "We waded over to the boat, but the boatmen said we could not start for the other shore because the Japanese would machine gun any vessel sailing in the dark. So we had to spend a night in the boat, and we had a good showerbath as it was raining. As soon as dawn came, we sailed toward Ch'i Ch'ung. From Ch'i Ch'ung we walked to Ping Shan. When we reached Ping Shan, it was late in the afternoon. I kissed the ground with tears of joy, because that was the beginning of Free China."

Free China! Oh, the feelings, the ecstasy of being free again! The first part of their dream had now come true and all of them were safe and sound, including the baby. They had managed to cross the Japanese lines because the underground organizations that had helped them to escape knew the points where the Japanese did not man frontier posts.

From Ping Shan the group of weary "laborers" moved northwest. They still had over seven hundred miles to travel, mostly on foot, to reach their destination. Now they did not have the Japanese to contend with, but bandits and guerrillas were active in the region and there were still many dangers. Being dressed as very poor people, however, they did not attract the attention of bandits. With his characteristic humor, John wrote: "The bandits evidently were frightened away lest we should borrow money from them."

The Wu party attended Mass in every church they could find on the long trek, and marveled at the universality of the Church.

At last, on June 12, forty-one days after leaving Hong Kong, they reached Guilin, one of the largest cities in central west China. A few hundred miles from Chungking, Guilin was a hub of Chinese resistance, acting as an American forward base. The twenty "laborers" were welcomed by hundreds of high-ranking Chungking officials and friends who had preceded them there, and also by the jovial Msgr. Romaniello,[5] then superior of the Guilin Maryknoll Mission.

The good monsignor composed the following little poem to welcome John home to free China:

Touchdown

Doctor Wu, you are so true
To the spirit of fighting men.
Whiskers long: from a lion's den,
Hidden with Mary's mantle of blue,
You led your brood of five and ten,
Over water, road and fen,
Into the land of free men.
That is why I rejoice with you.

John Wu and his family were among the fortunate ones who lived to tell the story of their escape from Hong Kong. However, about two million people left Hong Kong and only God knows how many of them died along the way in search of freedom. Fatigue and deprivations took a tremendous toll. Their number is certainly to be counted in the tens of thousands, innocent victims of mankind's greed.

For John and his family, this dangerous trip was not only the highlight of those war years, it was also an occasion for them all to grow in their gratitude to God.[6]

John wrote: "The more I think of that experience, the more I marvel at the goodness of God. All our children, except John Jude who was only ' three months old, keep vivid memories of the exodus, and whenever we talk about it at our family Rosary, our talk becomes a chorus of praises to our all-merciful Father and to the Blessed Virgin, the Mother of good counsel. I can find no better words to describe our feelings than verse four of the Psalm of the Good Shepherd:

"'Though I should walk in a dark valley, I will fear no evils, because Thou art with me. Thy rod and Thy staff: these comfort me.'"

Notes

1. G. B. Endacott described in detail this registration mania: "The Japanese administration was intensely bureaucratic, and every activity was regulated and supervised, although this did not always make for efficiency and consistency of action. Everybody had to have a pass to move around. Laws issued on March 28, 1942 for the control of Hong Kong affairs strictly controlled people entering, leaving or residing, also the importing or exporting of goods and the setting up or conducting of any business; people had to make a full report of themselves, or if there

were any change, to apply to the Gendarmerie Headquarters in quadruplicate. The local population had to register their requirements for water, gas, electricity and telephones. All house owners had to register their property, and get permission to undertake repairs. Doctors, lawyers, herbalists, hawkers and market stall holders had to supply particulars and register. All religious bodies and schools had to supply information and register. All house property had to be re-registered for tax purposes. Changes of address and the possession of radios had to be registered with the gendarmerie for security reasons, and registration was, of course, essential for rice rationing. The tally of registrations could be greatly expanded, and it created massive requirements for queuing for forms, permits and licenses and filling them in. Moreover, as noted, regulations and orders were amended from time to time making for wearisome repetition. The Japanese patiently explained the orders and their need, and induced the district bureaus and Chinese councils to urge Chinese to cooperate, but no wonder that there was little enthusiasm and orders had to be amended and simplified, and periods for registration extended. The Hong Kong News regularly complained about the apathy of the Chinese in complying with these demands. This weight of bureaucratic interference in daily life naturally created bribery and malpractice among the officials and the Chinese."

2. Once, passing in front of a sentry, I only took my hat off instead of stopping and bowing to him with joined hands. The sentry stopped me, shouted at me and tried to slap me, but I avoided the slap by quickly drawing back my face.

3. It was through this prayer book that John came to know about St. Jude. "When one is in distress, prayer becomes such a real thing. On January 16 I discovered in the book a prayer to St. Jude, 'the patron of hopeless cases.' I said to Francis, 'Read this prayer. It seems as though it were specially written for us!' He said, 'Let us then start a novena in honor of St. Jude.' We turned the wardrobe into a kind of altar, and every day we recited the prayer together with the Rosary. Sometimes I would imitate the celebration of Holy Mass, with Francis as the server. We succeeded in memorizing many prayers and ejaculations.

"One day I was praying alone to St. Jude. A thought came to my mind: my wife was going to give birth to another boy, and I was going to name him after St. Jude. Somehow I was sure it was going to be a boy."

4. "I went to Mass the next morning to offer my thanksgiving to God and to satisfy my thirst for Holy Communion. After my return home, Father Maestrini called on me and we had a most joyful time together. It was not so much a conversation as a duet of praises of the wonders of God and His Providence. As we were still talking we heard the cries of the newborn baby in the next room! It was a boy. In half an hour, the doctor gave orders that we could come in. I asked the Father to baptize the baby right away. This he did. As it was the feast of St. John Bosco, he suggested christening him John. I explained to him about my commitments to St. Jude. The good Father said, 'Then why not call him John Jude?' I agreed."

5. Msgr. Romaniello later became the famous "noodle priest" of Hong Kong.

6. This is what happened in Hong Kong after John's departure:
"How narrow the escape was in reality can be gathered from some of the facts we came to know only afterwards. On May 3, the day after our escape, a couple of Japanese officers came to our house and knocked at the door. Receiving no answer, they broke in. They immediately sent out telegrams to Macao and Kuang Chow Wan to have us arrested. But they did not imagine that we had taken the land route. Then they approached Sir Robert Kotewall. Sir Robert said, 'I only guaranteed that they are good men. I did not say that they would not escape. Furthermore, I am in Hong Kong, and they are in Kowloon. How was I to know that they were running away? If there is any negligence, it is on the part of the military authorities in Kowloon.'"

The Hong Kong cathedral and its belfry in 1931.

23

Wartime Pastor: The Beginning

I Am A Pastor Again

One morning in May 1942, Bishop Valtorta told me: "Maestrini, I would like you to take over the cathedral parish. Father Spada is seventy-six years old and his health is failing. Conditions in the parish are now so different from before that he would like to retire. Please do me this favor and take over this parish."

Good Bishop Valtorta did not really need many words to convince me to accept. First of all, the ultimate dream of every priest is to work as a pastor, and I was no exception. After almost six years of desk work as secretary to the bishop and executive secretary of the Catholic Truth Society, I felt a deep craving for pastoral work again. I thanked the bishop for the appointment, and Fr. Spada was relieved to relinquish the job. For me, on the contrary, only thirty-four years old, this appointment was a welcome challenge and I accepted it with enthusiasm.

The cathedral parish was the oldest and most populous parish on the island, and included in its territory all the overcrowded central district of the city of Hong Kong. Before the Seventeen-Day War the cathedral had on its register over one thousand families, boasted several large Catholic schools with thousands of students, included one Catholic and several city hospitals, and about half a million non-Catholics within parish bounds. Due to historical circumstances, at least two-thirds of the cathedral's parishioners were Portuguese Catholics. As I have already explained, long before Chinese were converted to Christianity in significant numbers, the Portuguese from Macao had made up the bulk of the Catholic population of the colony. The cathedral parish remained the bastion and stronghold of Portuguese faith and Catholicism up to December 8, 1941.

The Seventeen-Day War, as it changed everything else, also completely changed the makeup of the cathedral parish population. The Portuguese community, which had prospered under the open-minded British rule, became outcasts under the new bosses. Because Portugal was a neutral nation in the war, the Hong Kong Portuguese could not be interned as enemy aliens but, being "white," they were ostracized. All Portuguese businessmen, bank, and government employees were now jobless and there was no future for them. This is why, as soon as communications with Macao resumed, the Portuguese began to leave Hong Kong in droves. Their exodus depleted the Catholic population of the cathedral. When I took over the parish, almost ninety percent of the Portuguese had already left for Macao. The Chinese parishioners numbered less than one hundred families.

Reorienting The Parish

In a previous chapter I wrote that since my seminary days I have always regarded the priesthood essentially as a life of service to God and to the community as the people of God. However, as a missionary priest my service had to be, first of all, oriented to non-Christians because that was my specific calling in life. To be a missionary priest now meant to me to serve my parishioners with a view to involving them in bringing the message of Christ to the non-Christians. Even though we were twenty years before Vatican II, I was already fully convinced that the Church is "missionary by nature" and that a parish in a mission country must be primarily a missionary parish. War or no war, to follow in the footsteps of Christ through evangelization was my primary duty and that was what I set about to do.

My first task was to reorganize the Chinese parishioners and make them more aware of their duty to share the faith with non-Christians.

The basic problem was how to reach non-Christians. From the human point of view, war days seemed the worst possible time to talk about religion to non-Christians, as they were totally absorbed in the problem of immediate survival. But calamities, whether personal or communal, are a double-edged sword: they alienate some people from God but also draw others closer to Him. Among the half million non-Christians of my parish, in spite of famine, fear and misery, there certainly were souls seeking God and we could reach out to them.

Obviously, I could not go around Hong Kong ringing handbells and preaching Christ on street corners. The Japanese would have arrested me in no time. First of all I had to pull together the remnants of the cathedral's Chinese Catholic community by giving them the best possible service. In this way I hoped to stimulate them to reach out to non-Christians and speak with them about Christ.

The first thing I decided to do was to restructure Sunday services. Until that time only the 6:15 A.M. Mass had had the homily in Chinese, because that Mass was intended for the Chinese Catholic servants of Portuguese families. At all other Masses the homily was in English for the benefit of the Portuguese and of the English-speaking Chinese Catholics. But under these new circumstances, I introduced the homily in Chinese at all Sunday Masses except one in English. In normal times my second step would have been to organize charitable activities to help Christians and non-Christians. Under the changed conditions of those days, though, this was impossible. The physical and social needs of the poor were immense, but there was practically nothing we could do to respond to them. People needed relief from famine, from fear, from unemployment; they needed transportation, protection, security. The traditional Christian method of bringing the message of Christ to non-Christians through works of charity could not be practiced in those days because everything was strictly rationed and controlled by the Japanese authorities. Supplies could not be obtained from anywhere. But I still had freedom to do spiritual work and I decided to devote all my time to it.

The bishop assigned Fr. Felix Shek, an elderly and holy Chinese priest, as assistant to me and we worked well together. We started to make Sunday services more attractive with homilies tailored to the new circumstances. We added some exterior signs of joy, such as music, altar boys, more flowers, candles, etc. Then we introduced para-liturgical services, such as novenas, holy hours, Way of the Cross, etc., because people felt a need to pray together. All this was meant to offer inspiration and consolation. Recalling the liturgical training I had received at the seminary in Rome, I made every effort to involve the people in the liturgy of the Church by the recitation of the communal prayers, singing, etc. The annual Forty Hours Devotions were especially favorite times. On these occasions the main altar under the big dome of the church was richly decorated with quantities of flowers and candles. The solemn services helped to relieve, for a few hours, the pain and sorrow that dominated every moment of our dreary lives. These were moments of peace and serenity in the midst of the turmoil of the war and they strengthened our faith. We also began to make family visitations, urging people to attend church frequently and to talk to non-Christians about Christ.

We could not give away much in the way of food or money but we did try to help in at least the most desperate cases. Little by little our efforts began to bring results. More parishioners began to attend services regularly on Sundays and weekdays. Some fallen-away Catholics came back to the Church, and people from neighboring parishes also started to attend some of our services. The empty seats in the large naves of the cathedral began to fill up. Most consoling of all, the number of non-Christians asking for religious instruction grew considerably and that meant a great deal to me as a missionary.

A-Chan: A Valiant Woman

A-Chan was only forty years old but her wrinkled face and emaciated body made her look over sixty. She was a widow with four small children ranging from two to seven years of age. A mere four feet nine inches tall, she was all fire and zeal for God.

"Sz Shan-fou," she said to me the day I baptized her, "now that I know that God loves me, I want to work hard to bring at least one hundred people a year into the Church. I want to do this to thank the Lord for making me a Christian." She kept her promise. She was constantly looking for every conceivable opportunity to interest people in God. Then she introduced them to Fr. Shek or to me for religious instructions. Most of them ended up embracing A-chan's faith. Through the war years she brought more converts to me than anyone else in the parish.

She never asked for help for herself or for her children, but I knew that she was barely eking out a living by peddling Japanese cigarettes curbside in downtown Hong Kong as I had seen her there myself many times. But I was curious to see where she lived.

"Where do you live, A-Chan?" I asked her one day.

"I'm ashamed to tell you, Sz Shan-fou," she replied. "My house is too poor for Shan-fou to see it."

I insisted and she added, "I live with my children in a corner of the roof."

I could not figure out what she meant by "living in a corner of the roof," so I decided to pay her a visit.

The address she gave me was a crowded tenement house in the poorest section of central Hong Kong. After climbing what seemed endless flights of stairs I finally emerged from the poorly lit stairway onto the sun-drenched roof. Threading my way through walls of shirts, trousers, and underwear hanging to dry in the sun, I finally discovered her "apartment." It was indeed a corner "apartment" on the roof! The ceiling and walls consisted of a rotting canvas stretched between three wooden poles nailed to a corner of the low parapet. Another piece of canvas hung in front and served as a door.

The inside, a tiny area about ten feet by ten, contained only a bamboo mat rolled up on the floor (obviously her bed and her children's bed), a typical Chinese earthen pot for cooking her meals, and a couple of rusty pots and pans. Two old, patched suitcases served as a closet. A tiny kerosene lamp was all she had for lighting.

I had never seen such extreme poverty. After that visit I resolved to help her and her children to survive through the war. I scrounged, I begged, I borrowed money to help them, and with the help of Divine Providence I was able to assist her until the war ended. After the war she continued her work for God and souls for many years until I finally lost touch with her.

The Real Cross: Famine

In spite of all the spiritual activities in the parish, neither my parishioners nor I could be oblivious to a very earthly reality: hunger. I have already mentioned this subject in a previous chapter, but here I want to add some further details to illustrate the tragic condition inflicted on us by the Japanese invasion. Those who have never experienced hunger for an extended period of time will find it difficult to appreciate the unrelenting physical and mental suffering caused by prolonged famine. It is, I believe, one of the most cruel forms of torture man can endure. It is pervasive; it affects the whole being: mind, body, emotions, will to work, outlook on the future, ability to think and to judge, in short, all human activities of mind and body. The mind cannot be compelled to concentrate on any subject: at all times it thinks food, it sees food, it smells food, it craves food. Food becomes an obsession that leaves one no peace, day or night. And the worst part is that there is no relief. Even if one manages to get a slightly better meal than usual, one cannot help thinking: tomorrow, the day after, and the next day after it will be the same all over again: gnawing stomach pains, mental anguish, living agony.

Under those circumstances there were no social activities, no parties, no recreation whatever. However, I did manage to get one party going. A Chinese friend came back from Macao and brought me one pack of Camel cigarettes. I must confess that at that time I was smoking, even though there were no cigarettes to buy except cheap, evil-smelling Japanese cigarettes. Bad tasting as they were, they were a little help to forget hunger. To get a whole pack of American cigarettes seemed a gift from Heaven. I would not have enjoyed smoking them alone and therefore I suggested to some friendly smokers that we celebrate the event with a party, and so we did. One day we met at my friend's house for lunch. The meal consisted of boiled turnips, boiled rice, one small fish for ten people, some Chinese vegetables and a dessert of grated turnips with a little sugar. After the scrumptious meal, each received one cigarette and we started smoking. The cigarettes tasted just heavenly. But we had just lit the cigarettes when the air raid alarm sounded. In terror, we rushed to the air-raid shelter and the party was over!

A few months after the surrender, the ample reserves of food stored by the British for a prolonged siege were exhausted. It is alleged that part of the food and other goods stored by the British were requisitioned by the Japanese for their own armed services, but most was privately sold for the personal profit of the officers and it ended up in the hands of Chinese. For us in Hong Kong widespread famine then began. No food supplies arrived by sea because of the presence of Allied submarines along the China coast. Chinese farmers were reluctant to sell goods to Hong Kong because they were paid in military yen, which were worthless. Thus the trickle of food from mainland China was first used for the thousands of Japanese civilians and the families of the military. Whatever was left was far from enough for the needs of the population which, during the first two years, still hovered about one million in the city alone.

To make matters worse, whatever little food was available was also extremely expensive. People had no money because there were no jobs. There was no industry and, especially, no import or export business, the mainstay of the Hong Kong economy.

Seeing daily so many people slowly starving to death, knowing my complete inability to help them, was my greatest suffering as a pastor. It surely made me suffer more than did my own stomach's growling in search of a square meal. Out of the countless cases of people I actually saw die of starvation I will mention but one case.

Kong-chi and Kong-tak were two brothers, fifteen and seventeen years old respectively. They had never known their father. Their mother, a professional streetwalker in the last stages of her livelihood, was not able to support them. The tragedy was compounded because Kong-chi was seriously handicapped. He had been born with a deformed body and could not coordinate the movement of his arms and legs. He was fairly intelligent but thin and undernourished. With the help of the St. Vincent de Paul Society, he had attended St. Joseph's Catholic School and had learned some elementary shorthand and typing. However, because of his handicap he could not move around without the help of his younger brother, Kong-tak, who was tall and sturdy but slightly mentally retarded. He had learned to carry Kong-chi on his shoulders and took him wherever he had to go, the two forming an inseparable team.

A few months before the war I had hired Kong-chi to do clerical work for the Catholic Truth Society at the recommendation of the St. Vincent de Paul Society. It was pathetic to see Kong-tak every day, climbing the stairs leading up to the mission house, carrying Kong-chi on his shoulders. He would go straight to my office, dump his brother on a chair in front of a typewriter, and then sit in a corner until Kong-chi had to be moved again. The salary I paid them was the only income they had.

When the Japanese attacked Hong Kong and I was interned in Stanley, the two boys became unemployed and penniless. When I returned I looked for them, but they had moved and I could not get their address. After several weeks I discovered them living in a cheap little apartment on the second floor of a small house on Caine Road, not far from the cathedral. In the midst of the confusion and utter poverty of those days and the lack of employment, there was no way for me to employ them or to find a job for them. I did, however, occasionally send them some money through their mother when she came begging at the cathedral. But what I could give them was not enough to keep them alive. Whenever I passed in front of their house I invariably saw poor Kong-chi sitting by the window, lonely and disconsolate, the picture of misery, growing paler and thinner by the week. Looking from the window was his only recreation. After a few months, I no longer saw him at the window. I inquired of the neighbors, who told me that both brothers had died of starvation. I am still haunted by the memory of that young face at the window silently imploring help . . . and I could give none.

We "Eat" The Belfry And Golden Articles

In 1888 when Bishop T. Raimondi, PIME, and other PIME missionaries built the cathedral in Hong Kong, they faithfully followed the Catholic tradition of adding a belfry. Next to the church's main entrance they built a 150-foot-high, imposing bell tower housing a set of melodious bells imported from Italy. The belfry was to be a visible and highly audible symbol of the presence of Christ in the midst of "pagan" Hong Kong.

Little did they know that fifty-four years later those bells would be requisitioned by the Japanese and melted into arms and ammunition to kill the Chinese. Also, they never foresaw that the wooden structure supporting the numerous bells would one day be quite literally converted to rice to save many people from starvation.

During the occupation, cooking fuel was a rare and expensive commodity in Hong Kong because there was no coal, no gas, nor firewood. Anything that would burn well enough to cook a meal was at a premium. Once the bells were gone, the belfry was useless, but the tons and tons of wooden beams were a fortune in those days. Bishop Valtorta, with the full consent of the community, decided to demolish the belfry and sell the beams as firewood. The proceeds of that sale gave us and many of our poor people "daily rice" for many months.

When the money from the sale of the belfry was exhausted, there was nothing else to sell but the few gold chalices and other valuable religious articles that had been donated to the parish through the years. They were kept in a safe in the bishop's office. Every three or four weeks, when he was alone, good Bishop Valtorta would open the safe, and with much hesitation choose a golden paten, or the gold cup of a chalice or a ciborium, to be sold. After he had made his choice, he would carefully hide it under his cassock and slowly walk downtown to sell it ounce by ounce to a Japanese shop, after endless haggling about the value. Then, pale and haggard, he would return to the cathedral and give all the money to the administrator, Fr. E. Bruzzone. In those days, selling gold involved a great deal of personal risk because of the many spies and robbers, and Bishop Valtorta preferred to risk his own life rather than endanger any of his priests.

A Visit From Robbers

Because of famine, robberies were more frequent than usual, and we did not escape them. One night a couple of thieves robbed the cathedral's sacristy, stealing all the chalices, ciboria and other articles kept there for daily use, including my personal silver chalice—my parents' gift for my First Mass.

We all regretted the loss but, thinking that the theft was due to famine more than to greed, we replaced the sacred vessels with some spare ones stored elsewhere, and forgot all about the theft. However, I did regret the loss of my own chalice because of its sentimental value.

In spite of our tolerant attitude, my good sacristan, A-Chun, was furious. The thieves had robbed "his sacristy" and he had lost face. He swore to catch the thieves and punish them. He was sure that the thieves would return to steal what they had left behind, and therefore he sacrificed the comfort of his bed at home and went to sleep in the sacristy every night. I told him that it was unnecessary, but his thirst for face was too strong and he did not listen to me.

Several weeks after the robbery, we in the mission house were awakened by shouts and screams coming from the street below at about 4:00 A.M. We all rushed down to the door and saw A-Chun standing triumphant and unhurt over the bodies of two rag-covered beggars writhing in pain. He had floored them with an iron rod. The Japanese police came and took them away. A-chun had regained face!

Again we forgot the robbery but the police did not. Probably because foreigners were the victims, the police wanted to show their ability and really pursued their investigation of the matter. A few days after the robbers' second visit, we were called down to the police station to identify what remained of our stolen articles. All we saw was a mass of melted-down metal. The only vessel still absolutely intact was my First Mass chalice. I thanked the Lord and was very happy to take it home, and I am using it to this day.

A Painful Job: House Rector

Lack of the bare necessities of life, especially food, was of double concern to me because, besides being pastor, I also had the unenviable job of rector of the mission house. This meant that I had to provide food, staff, service, etc. for the fifteen or so priests, Chinese and Italian, living there. Once the Japanese occupied Hong Kong several of our Italian priests had been compelled to leave their parishes on the mainland and return to Hong Kong.

Trying to provide two meals a day for fifteen hungry men in a time of rations and famine was a nightmare, but actually getting our scanty allowance of rice, flour and oil from the Japanese was even worse. I will spare the reader a description of this chapter of my life, save to state that I survived this ordeal because a good lady from South Africa, stranded in

Hong Kong, volunteered to stand in line daily for hours to get our rations of oil, flour, eggs and other foodstuff. To us she was simply known as Terry. Middle-aged and single, she was devoting all of her life to serving the priests and the Lord. Day in and day out, under rain or sun, often under air raids, she never failed to get our rations. I regard her as one of the greatest benefactors of my life.

Meat, fish and vegetables were not rationed, but were extremely expensive and available only at a large public market in downtown Hong Kong, quite a distance from our house. I often had to go personally to buy these commodities in order to save money. Needless to say, what we were able to afford was not much and the twenty-two hungry priests found the portions totally inadequate for their appetites. While good Fr. Ed Bruzzone, the administrator, complained that I was spending too much money, the other priests complained because I did not give them enough to eat. In those days I was certainly not the most popular guy in the mission house! Bishop Valtorta, however, was an outstanding exception. He never complained, never grumbled, never even tried to supplement the meager portions I served to the community. I believe that his death in 1951 at only sixty-eight years of age was very much due to the sufferings and deprivations he underwent during the war.

Volunteer Helpers

Thanks to Divine Providence I found generous people to help Fr. Shek and me in the parish work. Tall and elderly Mrs. Pat Costello was Irish kindness and goodness personified. Having lost her husband shortly before the Japanese attack, she was trapped in Hong Kong by the war and found refuge in the hostel for women conducted by the Canossian sisters. She had little to do in those war days, and gladly volunteered to help me with church work.

Sheila X was a different case. When spring came, I noticed a blonde, white girl loitering alone every morning in the public gardens just opposite the cathedral. That was no place for a lonely girl to spend her time, and her behavior indicated that she might be mentally disturbed. I asked Mrs. Costello to approach her and see if we could help her.

The next day Mrs. Costello had a long conversation with her and then reported the situation to me. Her name was Sheila. She was Irish, Catholic and only twenty-seven years old. Her sister had left Hong Kong just before the war and now she lived alone. During the fighting days in Kowloon she had been raped under tragic circumstances. With no future and her little supply of money fast dwindling, she was thinking of suicide, as religion did not mean much to her. However, she was willing to accept help. I ran over to the Canossian convent and begged Mother Wilhelmina, the directress of the hostel, to squeeze in one more bed. That very night Sheila was welcomed as a roommate of Mrs. Costello. The two became inseparable. They looked very much like mother and daughter and spent most of their time cleaning, decorating the altar, and taking care of church vestments.

Other friends who helped me greatly were Mr. and Mrs. Poon Cheung and their large family. Through all my years as pastor they were my trusted advisors and confidants. They ran a candle-making business from their apartment at St. Joseph's Terrace, a stone's throw from the cathedral. They belonged to an old Catholic family and had lived in the parish for years. Kind, gentle and wise, they and their large family were great spiritual leaders and were active members of almost every parish association. Refusing to leave Hong Kong for the safety of the mainland, they dedicated themselves to helping the poor and supporting the church.

One night they were instrumental in saving my life. I was coming home from family visitations after dark but in bright moonlight when all of a sudden I noticed that someone was following me. Looking back I was dismayed to see two Japanese in military uniforms. I started to walk faster and they did the same. I broke into a run and they, too, started running after me. Frantic with fear, I rushed up the seventy steps of the stairs leading from Caine Road to the cathedral. At the top of the stairs, instead of going toward the house door, I ran in the opposite direction, leading them away from the mission house. Running desperately along the side of the church, I outdistanced them and fled uphill through the narrow, tortuous streets above the cathedral. Still the Japanese were in hot pursuit. At a fork in the alley before reaching the Wah Yan College building, I turned downhill on a side street, and the pursuers, not seeing me, kept going up. I then realized that they had lost me! I happened to pass in front of the Poons' house, and through the cracks of a window I saw a light still burning. After I pounded furiously on the door for what seemed an eternity, Mr. Poon at last opened the door and I fell exhausted into his arms. As I began to catch my breath I told them my story in whispers. Immediately we blew out all the candles and remained very, very quiet for over two hours. When we were sure that the soldiers had gone their way, Mr. Poon accompanied me down to the cathedral and the safety of the mission house.

24

Nearing The End Of The War

Help From Heaven

In the fall of 1943, one of my parishioners, John Chan, said to me, "Father, have you heard that Pope Pius XII has recently consecrated the world to the Immaculate Heart of Mary, in order to solicit Mary's intercession for world peace? I heard this in a church in Macao. Some friends told me that many parishes there are also making such an act of consecration to Mary."

"That's beautiful, John," I replied, "but, no, I have not heard anything about it. You know, we get no news from Europe. I would really like to know what the pope has actually done. When you go to Macao next time, please ask some priest there to give you more information about this and possibly get literature."

A few weeks later he brought back to me a Portuguese magazine containing an article about the solemn consecration of the world to Mary, performed by Pius XII in Rome. The magazine also reported that the pope had urged every parish and every family in the world to consecrate themselves to Mary as an act of filial devotion to God. I showed the article to Bishop Valtorta and suggested consecrating the cathedral parish to the Immaculate Heart of Mary according to the Holy Father's wish. The bishop encouraged me to do so and we planned the ceremony together.

The following Sunday, Fr. Shek and I talked about the intended consecration at every Mass and the people responded to the Holy Father's invitation with real enthusiasm.

The date for the official consecration of the parish was set, and we began the spiritual preparation for this event. Naturally we wanted to make this an occasion for individual spiritual growth instead of just another religious ceremony. On the day we had set, the bishop himself presided over the ceremony. We had an extraordinary attendance in church. Then, responding still more fully to the pope's suggestion, many families requested individual consecrations of their own households. This consisted of placing a holy picture of Mary on a kind of family altar, which was intended to become the visible center of the spiritual life of the family. Further, the family would solemnly promise to pray together daily, to live a true Christian life, and to help each other to grow in the love of God and neighbor.

Usually a little celebration would be planned in connection with the ceremony and close friends and neighbors would be invited to participate. Almost every family in the parish held such ceremonies and I attended every one of them. Those wartime parties usually consisted of plain Chinese tea, a few Chinese cookies of the cheapest kind, and turnips. Turnips were the cheapest and most easily obtained vegetable in those days. They were served roasted, boiled, fried, in every way under the sun. The remarkable thing is that although since childhood and to this very day turnips are the only vegetable I detest, in those days of famine, even turnips tasted good to me.

The Horror Of Air Raids

On the last Sunday in October 1943 we celebrated the solemn Feast of Christ the King with a Eucharistic procession in the cathedral compound. We felt that a solemn celebration of this feast would help all the Catholics of Hong Kong and Kowloon to better realize the role of Christ in the world. For the first time in the history of the Church in Hong Kong, the cathedral was literally filled with Chinese Catholics.

For us Chinese and Italian priests who had spent so many years in Hong Kong working toward this goal, it was a red-letter day, indicating the unmistakable success of our policies and of our long years of work. However, that day was to go down in history as the beginning of the most painful and catastrophic period in the history of Hong Kong.

About 4:00 P.M., as the sun began to descend in a cloudless sky in the west, the cathedral compound was crammed with people and the procession was reentering the church. Suddenly we heard the drone of approaching planes, and soon twelve bombers appeared from the east flying at a rather low altitude. We assumed they were Japanese planes and did not pay much attention. Then all of a sudden the air raid siren started screaming and we realized that this was the first air strike by the Allies. Before we could take shelter the planes were over Wanchai, a little more than a mile distant by air, and we could see bombs falling to the ground. From the cathedral compound we watched, horrified, a string of violent explosions ripping through the heart of the city, blowing buildings sky-high. Terror-stricken, we dispersed, running helter-skelter to wherever we could find some shelter. The procession ended in total confusion.

It was then almost two years after the beginning of the war in the Pacific. The Allies were finally taking the offensive and had come to bomb Japanese military installations. Unfortunately that first surprise air raid intended for the Japanese arsenal and barracks caused over ten thousand civilian deaths. Most of the bombs fell over the densely populated Wanchai area.

After that first air raid I became extremely scared of air strikes and I did not have a single day or night of peace until the end of the war, two years later. Only cloudy and rainy days gave me some relief. We were sure that the American planes would not come in bad weather as there was no reliable radar yet. I used to pray for rainy days as one would pray for one's own life. For over two years I slept every night completely dressed, ready to jump from bed and run for the shelter down in the basement.

During daytime air raids I rushed over to the Canossian convent (about a four-minute run) where there was a good basement under a multi-storied building. There I shared my fears with some of the nuns (the brave ones did not bother to come down to the shelter) and the little orphaned Chinese girls who, like me, were praying, shuddering and crying to the accompaniment of the explosions and the rattling of anti-aircraft guns.

I'm sure that many of my readers have never lived under the daily threat of air raids, and will smile with sympathy at my childish behavior. I can only say as an explanation that that was the way I felt and I could not help it. The bishop and many of the other priests were not terrified by air raids as much as I was, and sometimes did not even go down to the shelter.

On some rare days, when I was caught by surprise and could not get over to the convent, I ventured to watch the bombing of Kowloon from the balcony of my room. Once I saw an American plane, hit by the flak of Japanese anti-aircraft guns, spinning down in flames right in the middle of the harbor. It was a horrible scene. We learned later that the

American pilot survived the crash, was captured, paraded in the streets of Hong Kong as a criminal and, finally, shot.

From October 1943 to the end of the war we had literally hundreds of air raids. The worst day of air strikes was in the fall of 1944 when air raids started at sunrise, about 6:00 A.M., and continued at intervals of fifteen or twenty minutes until sunset. That was a day of terror but, as usual, Providence looked after us and I am still alive to tell the story.

It is important to remember that it was the Japanese who (long before Hitler's blitzkriegs), in the war against China, developed and perfected the use of planes to bomb military and civilian targets. Now, under the almost daily bombing by the Allies, the Japanese began to experience what they had so wantonly inflicted upon others. Unfortunately it was the innocent civilians who paid the price. Whenever an air strike took place, there was a conflict of emotions in our hearts. We wanted the Allies to blast the Japanese out of Hong Kong, but the price we had to pay for it was indeed high.

A Vow To St. Jude

In 1944, as the air raids became more and more frequent, we all began to realize that the cathedral, the mission house and most of our parishioners who lived nearby were in a particularly dangerous situation. We were only a mile away by air from the Japanese arsenal and their military headquarters, obviously legitimate targets for the Allies' bombing. I decided to turn to St. Jude, the saint of impossible causes. Therefore I suggested to the congregation that we make a vow, namely that if the church and most of the nearby houses escaped being bombed, we would erect an altar to St. Jude after the war. All agreed and with the consent of the bishop we made a public vow.

Through the grace of God this prayer was fully answered. Even though bombs fell all around us, neither the church nor the nearby houses were ever hit. A couple of incendiary bombs did fall on the wooden roof of the cathedral, but did not explode. We discovered them long after the end of the war when workmen inspected the roof and found the unexploded bombs. St. Jude really heard our prayers and, after the end of the war, we built the altar we had promised.

The Suffering Of Fear

As I have mentioned before, besides famine, fear was the most devastating factor in our lives those days: fear of air raids, fear of starvation, fear of forthcoming battles, fear of the Japanese military in general and especially of their secret police. We had good reason to fear them as the following episode demonstrates.

One morning in 1943, at 7:30 A.M., four Japanese men in military uniforms suddenly appeared at the door of the mission house. In their militant rude and arrogant tone they ordered the frightened Chinese doorkeeper, A-Wong, to take them to the room of one of our Italian PIME priests, Fr. A. Pulit. They forced open the door of his bedroom and gruffly asked the surprised and still half-sleeping man, "Are you Mister Pulit?"

"Yes," he answered.

"Well, get dressed and follow us. Hurry! You don't need to take anything. Move! Come with us."

While a couple of soldiers remained in his room to watch him dressing, the other two wandered along the corridor, followed by a timid A-Wong.

"Whose room is this?" they asked, stopping in front of a closed door. It was my bedroom.

"This is Sz Shan-fou's room," A-Wong whispered, and added, "he is in church now for the morning services."

"Go and fetch him immediately," they ordered.

When I heard that they wanted me I was really frightened. With an earnest prayer to our Blessed Mother I rushed up to my room and found the two policemen already inside tinkering with my radio.

"Whose radio is this?" they asked gruffly.

"Mine," I replied, forcing myself to look unconcerned.

"Has it been castrated?" (This was the term used to indicate that the short-wave section had been removed by an authorized Japanese shop. This regulation had been imposed by the military authorities to prevent the public from listening to American and British short-wave broadcasts.)

"Yes," I answered.

"Show us the papers."

Even though I had had the radio officially "castrated" and I knew I had the papers, I was nonetheless shaking with fear. I fumbled for the documents in my drawer and, with a forced smile, handed them over to the two grim policemen. They examined the papers carefully, nodded that everything was OK and left satisfied, while I was still shaking in my boots.

I followed them into the corridor and watched helplessly as they took Fr. Pulit away. Where were they taking him? Why? What wrong had he done? What was going to happen to him? We could not get an answer to our questions. Even the bishop who, later that day, visited several Japanese offices asking for some explanation was rudely rebuffed and told to mind his own business.

Exactly twenty-seven days later, the formerly robust and sturdy Fr. Pulit, now thirty pounds lighter, showed up at the mission house, thin and wobbly, still shaken by his ordeal. His crime? He had been seen talking to a gentleman suspected of being a spy. Actually it turned out that neither Fr. Pulit nor the other person had done anything wrong. But nonetheless, on mere suspicion he had to endure twenty-seven days of solitary confinement in jail, where he was served only one bowl of rice twice a day.

A Secret Burial

One day in the early summer of 1942, a parishioner, Mr. Seu Kon-chi, came to see me at the parish office. He was about sixty-five years old, retired and a well-to-do stockbroker. A short man with a round, young-looking face and bright, shining eyes, he was not only my parishioner but also one of my dearest and closest friends. He had a large family. Two of his daughters, Nellie and Bonnie, were very active members of the St. Joan of Arc Association.

Speaking slowly and fighting to hold back tears, he said, "Father Maestrini, I have decided to leave Hong Kong tonight, taking the night boat with all my family. I cannot carry any Hong Kong currency with me. Will you keep this bundle of notes and bury them for me?"

With those words he handed a brown paper bag to me and continued, "There are one hundred notes of one thousand dollars each in Hong Kong currency, one hundred thousand dollars in all [about $25,000 US]. But don't worry, if the money is stolen or destroyed it does not matter. If it is saved, I will come back to get it at the end of the war."

I knew very well that it was forbidden under penalty of death to keep any Hong Kong currency. But I could not say no to my good friend and, disregarding the danger, I accepted the bundle with the intention of burying it. In those days, it was a common practice to bury things for safekeeping. I placed the half-opened paper bag on the top shelf of the closet in my bedroom, but did not get around to burying it! For months, whenever I opened the closet, I saw all that money and each time promised myself I would bury it soon. But I never carried out my resolution. The day the Japanese came to arrest Fr. Pulit, they also inspected my room, as I mentioned above. Suddenly, right after they left, I remembered Mr. Seu's money and I almost fainted! If the Japanese had only opened the closet door, they would have seen the large bundle of Hong Kong dollar bills staring at them from the top shelf of the closet. I cursed my stupidity and thanked our Blessed Mother Mary for saving my life.

Immediately I ran over to the nearby seminary and told my predicament to the rector, my good friend Fr. Alfred Feroldi, who readily volunteered to help me. We placed the money in a large glass jar, sealed it carefully with candle wax and, that very night, under cover of darkness, dug a hole in the ground at the foot of a wall in the courtyard of the seminary building and buried the money. That secret burial was a providential move.

Salvation From The States

About the end of 1944 the diocese was at the end of its financial resources. We had sold the wood of the bell tower and what little gold we had in chalices and religious articles, and now there was nothing else to sell. It was impossible to appeal for help to our headquarters in Italy or to get any money from abroad. The diocese owned a few apartment houses, which had been bequeathed to it through the years, but these were worthless at that moment. Nobody wanted to invest in buildings that any day could be destroyed by Allied planes. We could not borrow from banks because we had no collateral. We really were at the end of our resources.

One day, the bishop, Fr. Bruzzone and I were in the administration office at the mission house discussing what could be done to solve the crisis. The bishop turned to me and said, "Maestrini, you have the five thousand dollars you received from the States in Macao. Why can't we use that?"

"But, bishop," I mildly objected, "that money belongs to the Catholic Truth Society. Can we ethically use it?"

"Listen, young man," he said "survival is the supreme law. Let's make a deal. The diocese sells to the CTS a town house in Kowloon, which we received as a bequest some time ago, and the CTS pays the diocese five thousand dollars. After the war, if the house is still standing, the CTS can sell it and get its money back. If the house is destroyed, it can still sell the lot and the diocese will make up the difference."

I saw Fr. Ed's and Brother Mario's faces light up and I, too, began smiling. It was an excellent solution. A sum of $5000 in those days under the Japanese was a huge amount and we could live on it for at least one year. Smilingly I told the bishop, "Whatever you say, bishop, it surely is OK with me." I gave a letter to the bishop for our priests in Macao authorizing them to withdraw the money, while Fr. Ed and Brother Mario got busy finding out how we could safely communicate with Macao without passing through Japanese mail censorship. In those days a letter by mail from Hong Kong to Macao, a distance of only forty-odd miles, took about three months. Many sisters were in the same situation as we and could also get funds from Macao if only we could find a way to avoid the mail.

At the request of Fr. Ed, a young Chinese man, captain of a barge carrying goods between Hong Kong and Macao for the Japanese, came to our rescue. He had been a student in our Catholic schools and, out of compassion for our situation, agreed to carry our illegal mail—at no charge. Before long we had part of our money, as we had decided to get it by installments, and at last our financial problems were temporarily solved.

In Danger Of Death

Both we priests and the sisters took full advantage of the providential good will of this young man—I have now forgotten his name—and an active correspondence ensued between us and Macao. Every two or three weeks there was a bundle of mail being exchanged. We sent requests for money and other goods to Macao and they sent us large sums of Japanese yen. This exchange went on for several months until one morning in May when a person, who refused to give his name, called Fr. Ed on the phone and told him in whispers: "The barge from Macao has arrived, but by no means come to get the mail today. Someone has betrayed the captain and the Japanese police have arrested him and confiscated all the mail."

Fr. Ed gave me the bad news immediately and I almost fainted. In sheer terror, my legs shaking, I could barely reach the bishop's room to give him the message. He, too, was frightened. His already pale face turned completely white and he stammered with difficulty, "Pray, Maestrini, for God's sake pray!" Then he rushed to the chapel, where he remained for a long time.

Our fears were more than justified. The bishop, the sisters, Fr. Ed, Brother Mario and I were guilty of crimes punishable by death. Hong

Kong was at war, and the war was turning sour for the Japanese. To send letters or communications to people outside the city, bypassing the military censorship, was a crime punishable with death. To convert foreign money into yen on the black market was also a crime punishable by death. We were guilty of both crimes.

To make things worse, the Japanese had the irrefutable evidence of our crime in their hands. We were sure they would come any moment to take us to jail and to try us at a military tribunal. The death sentence was a certainty. I never prayed so hard in all my life as I did those days, but even prayer could not allay my fear. During the day, every noise sounded to me like the heavy footsteps of the military police coming to pick me up. At night, I could hardly sleep, dreading the knock at my door, which would signal the end of my days. I divided my time between the church and my room.

In spite of this interior agony, the days went by slowly and the Japanese never came to arrest us. To this day we do not know why they did not. Through the grapevine we learned to our dismay that the captain had been condemned to death and was to be executed on August 16. But Japan surrendered on August 15, and a few days later the captain walked away from prison a free man.

The Japanese And Religion

Our status as Italian citizens in Hong Kong again became critical when Italy signed an armistice with the Allies on September 8, 1943. Overnight we technically became "enemy aliens" again. For a few days after September 8 we were left in suspense and did not know what would happen to us. Finally at the end of September the Japanese military governor called the bishop to his office and informed him that the military government did not plan to intern the Italian priests and sisters, since they regarded us as dedicated religious people who had to remain at our places and continue our religious work.

We were relieved and happy at the good news. Not only could our religious activities continue but we were also pleased to know that we had earned the esteem and respect of the military. In all honesty, though, I must admit that if they had read our hearts and had known what we all thought of their cruel practices, they would very probably have shot us. But we kept our thoughts to ourselves and behaved as good citizens, not meddling in politics and totally concerned with our religious work.

In fairness, I wish to emphasize that through the four years of occupation the Japanese military and civilian authorities maintained a strict hands-off policy with regard to religion, whether Christian or non-Christian. They simply were not concerned with religion and totally ignored churches, pagodas, temples, etc. The sufferings we did endure were due to the unjustified occupation and we priests and sisters suffered like the rest of the population.

The Last Months Of The War

The winter, spring and early summer months of 1945 were the most painful of all. As the American navy moved north from the South Pacific and was approaching Japan, scoring great victories in the Philippines, Iwo Jima and Okinawa, the tension in Hong Kong grew. Food became scarcer and more expensive, electric power was poor and the service irregular, the yen decreased in value by the week. The Japanese attitude became more arrogant and irritable and air raids became more frequent and devastating. Foreigners were regarded with even greater suspicion and hostility. The Japanese, sensing our joy at news of Allied victories, told us over and over again: "We know that the Americans will land one day in Hong Kong, but you will not live to see that day. We will kill you all before the Americans land." We were sure that was no idle threat.

All through those months the Japanese were making preparations to defend Hong Kong inch by inch. They kept on digging tunnels on the side of every hill around town, including the central district of the city, working at it day and night. The dull explosions in tunnels were heard continuously during the day and the night. Every thud increased my fear and gloomy forebodings. When Germany surrendered on May 7, 1945, our hidden joy for the Allies' victory was much dimmed by the realization that an American attack on Hong Kong was coming closer and closer.

The Japanese never reported their losses in the Hong Kong papers. The official war bulletins called their defeats "strategic retreats" and we were never sure of what was happening.

At the beginning of August a rumor was spread around town that the Japanese had proposed peace under certain conditions and that the Allied Supreme Council had rejected the proposal, insisting on unconditional surrender. This was sad news for us because we were sure that the Japanese military would never agree to unconditional surrender.

From friends who had hidden radios and could listen to Allied broadcasts, we heard rumors that the Americans had dropped a new kind of

bomb on Hiroshima on August 6. But not until after the bombing of
Nagasaki on August 9 did the Japanese publish a communique in the
Hong Kong News, tersely stating: "The Americans have dropped what
seems a new kind of bomb on Hiroshima and Nagasaki. They did considerable damage."

On August 10, rumors of an impending surrender became more
insistent, but they were only rumors. In the meantime the Japanese kept
on furiously digging tunnels day and night. Finally, on the evening of
August 14, there came an official bulletin informing the Hong Kong
population that the Japanese Emperor would make a broadcast at noon
the following day.

Our hopes were raised but the doubt still persisted: Was it going to
really be a surrender or a new declaration of war to the bitter end?

That night I went to bed fully dressed, as usual, for fear of air raids.
The dull thuds of explosions continued through the night but suddenly
ceased about 4.00 A.M. A ray of hope crept into my heart: Was it true?
Could the Emperor's speech really be a surrender?

The Glorious End

The morning of August 15, feast of the Assumption of the Blessed Virgin
Mary, as I was going from the sacristy to the main altar of the cathedral'
to celebrate Mass, a dear friend of mine, Mr. Lipton Chuang, approached
me and whispered in my ear, "Fr. Maestrini, I have just heard a short-
wave broadcast. The war is really over. The Emperor will announce the
surrender of Japan in a broadcast at noon today. Blessed be God!"

Joy overcame me. I felt as if I had been born again and was beginning
a new life. After years of looking death in the face, now I could think of
living and working. I celebrated that Mass as if I were on cloud nine.
Never have I celebrated another Mass with equal joy. At age thirty-
seven, after almost four years of prolonged agony, my parishioners and I
could at last look forward to living again!

Living again! Getting rid of the heartbreaking fear, forgetting the
constant pain of hunger, seeing my parishioners returning to a normal
life, resuming my missionary work under normal circumstances . . . only
a few hours earlier all these things had seemed only a dream, and now
they were about to come true.

After Mass I passed on the information from Mr. Chuang to the bishop
and all my confreres at the mission house. At noon we were all crowded
around a small radio. We patiently listened to the Emperor's broadcast in

Japanese, and when finally a recap was given to us in English, we embraced each other, we shouted, we cried out for sheer joy.

Long before peace came, a Chinese friend of mine who was a doctor had confided to me that he had a bottle of Remy Martin brandy hidden in his house and that, if peace ever came, we had to drink it together to celebrate.

That afternoon I went to see him and for two hours we talked and praised the Lord and sipped brandy! It was the first hour of relaxation we had had in four years and we enjoyed it to the full extent. I must confess that I went home slightly tipsy, and that night I paid for it with a terrible headache. But it was worth it!

25

Liberation

Numb Relief

A sensation of numb relief was the reaction of the people in Hong Kong when they awakened in a free Hong Kong on the morning of August 16. The nightmare of the war was over and the fear of famine, air raids and impending battles was gone. These were now but memories of yesterday. However, there was no jubilation in the streets, there were no parades and public rejoicing. Everyone was too weak and exhausted even to celebrate. We were just happy to be alive and to have survived a terrible ordeal.

Days of uncertainty and calm waiting followed. At first we were apprehensive about a bloody revenge on the part of the Chinese. In view of the tremendous sufferings the Japanese had inflicted on the Chinese, both in Hong Kong and in China, one could logically have anticipated a bloodbath. On the contrary, the Chinese behaved with restraint, dignity and a maturity in full keeping with the tenets of their Confucian tradition. I was amazed. There were only a few thousand Japanese soldiers and civilians scattered in the midst of half a million Chinese, yet not a riot, not a single attack. Some looting occurred, but mostly of Japanese food storages and rich Japanese dwellings. The Japanese soldiers, though still armed, kept a very low profile. They lost their arrogance so suddenly that people pitied them.

For almost two weeks the date of the official surrender of the Japanese remained in a kind of limbo. Chiang Kai-shek, as Commander-in-Chief of the China theater of war, wanted to be the one to receive the surrender. London objected and finally it was agreed that British Rear Admiral

C. H. Harcourt, still in the Philippines with a mighty fleet, would come to Hong Kong to accept the Japanese surrender on behalf of both Britain and China.

In the meantime, the highest surviving British official in the Stanley internment camp, F. C. Gibson, took things over. The Japanese command allowed him as former colonial secretary to form a temporary city government. A few days later, Mr. Gibson, together with top bankers and former directors of public utilities, set up an office in downtown Hong Kong and began reorganizing the government, the police force and public utilities, which were barely functioning. Law and order prevailed throughout this period of waiting. At 11:00 A.M. on the morning of August 30 the British fleet, under Rear Admiral Harding, arrived with units of the American Navy. For all of us who had endured four years of war and famine there could have been no more glorious sight than the arrival of the victorious British fleet and American Navy. Shortly after they docked, the Union Jack flew once more on the Peak, signifying to all that Hong Kong was free again and that new life was dawning at last.

The following day the Japanese were ordered to report to designated locations in order to be interned while waiting for repatriation. Everything proceeded smoothly and there were none of the indignities, the hatred and the fear that had prevailed when the Japanese had interned the British.

The arrival of the British not only meant freedom, it also enabled us to catch up with four years of world news. We knew nothing of the real nature of the atomic bomb, of technical progress in so many fields, of radar, or even what a jeep was, much less of the events of the war in Europe. Learning all of this was an exhilarating experience.

Obviously throughout the four years of war I had worried about my family in Italy. For four years I had not heard from them or about them because Hong Kong had been isolated. With three younger brothers of military age and two aging parents I was anxious to know first if they were still alive, and then how they had fared through the war in Italy. Shortly after the arrival of the British fleet I received a cable from them, sent through Vatican City, informing me that all of them were safe and sound. About a month later I received a bundle of letters totaling over two hundred pages. It was the war diary my mother had faithfully written for me through every day of the four long years of war. In it she gave me all the news about the occupation of Perugia by the British armed forces, and of my three brothers who had seen action on the Italian, the Abyssinian and the Albanian fronts. All of them were home, safe and sound. I really celebrated many Masses in thanksgiving to God.

A New Beginning

One evening early in September 1945, Fr. Bernard F. Meyer of Maryknoll asked me, "Father Maestrini, why don't we start a Catholic Center and a serviceman's club in downtown Hong Kong?"

It had been a hot, sultry day and after our evening meal almost all of us at the mission house had gone up to the rooftop terrace hoping for a kindly evening breeze. Fr. Meyer, an American from Iowa,[1] had just been released from the Stanley camp a few days before. He had declined to be repatriated to the States, preferring to stay in Hong Kong in order to continue his work for China. After his liberation from the Stanley internment camp he and Fr. Do Hessler[2] had come to live at the cathedral in order to recuperate from their ordeal and to spend some time with Bishop Valtorta and me, as we had been close friends for years. I had published all of Fr. Meyer's numerous religious books and catechism manuals in Chinese. Meyer and I worked well together because I greatly admired his extraordinary qualities as a man, as an American, and as a missionary, and he, too, appreciated my spirit of initiative and action.

The thought of opening a Catholic Center right in the business district of Hong Kong had been a cherished dream of mine for years, but the high cost of rentals and the poor financial condition of the mission had always made it an impossible dream to realize. That evening, Fr. Meyer and I were resting our hands on the low wall of the terrace, in a moment of leisure, looking at the city at our feet. Beautiful Hong Kong was still there; though thousands of buildings were in ruins and countless others were pockmarked by shells, scarred and defaced, Hong Kong was still beautiful, the true "Pearl of the Orient," just beginning to wake up after a long, dark nightmare. Our conversation continued.

"Gee! I would surely love it, Father Meyer," I said, "but how can we do it? This is a dream I have had for years. Where can we find the money and the personnel in our present situation?"

"But now is exactly the right time," he insisted. "Look at those beautiful buildings along the waterfront—Kings Building, Queens Building, the Hong Kong Hotel! In a few months they will be bubbling with new life. Hong Kong is going to rise from its ashes, but now those buildings are empty. The British people from Stanley are too weak and sickly to return to business immediately. I know that they are preparing to leave for England in a few days, as soon as the government can provide a boat. It's quite possible that we could rent a couple of floors of office space now for a song. Why not try it?"

"Great! I think you are right, Berny. Why not try? I am game if you are."

Buoyed up by my enthusiasm and with typical German fondness for detail, he continued talking at length, going into the most minute aspects of the plan. It was late in the evening and I was bleary-eyed for need of sleep when we retired to our rooms. We had agreed that in the morning he would go downtown to explore the possibility of renting office space. And the next morning at 9:00 he was already knocking on doors in downtown Hong Kong, still a skeleton city.

He came back to the cathedral at noon looking radiant. He took me aside and, babbling with enthusiasm, eyes sparkling, he said, "Father Nick, we are in luck! I spent a couple of hours with the British President of the Hong Kong Land Company, which owns most of the buildings downtown. We know each other from our Stanley days. He has shown me several empty offices. The two I like best are two floors in the Kings Building, the second and the fourth floors. Each floor has eight thousand square feet. You can use the second floor for a chapel and for the Catholic Center activities. I can have the fourth floor for the Servicemen's Club. If we do not hurry up we will lose this opportunity. The rent is stiff—ten thousand Hong Kong dollars [$2,000 US] per month for each floor, but I think we can manage."

"How?" I exclaimed. "We are broke. Everybody in Hong Kong is broke.[3] There is no money around. How can we pay the rent?"

"Just think, Father Nick," he said with unlimited self-confidence, "we only need help for the first month. Then I'm sure that our activities will generate enough cash to pay our rent as we go along. Now I can hold religious services for the Army and Navy people and pick up some collections. I will beg from my friends, too. I'm sure that I can put the Servicemen's Club on a self-supporting basis in one month. You, also, only need the first month's rent, then you can operate a small chapel, hold Sunday services, and get the Sunday collections. You can hold concerts, sell books and religious articles and do a lot of things to raise funds. We really can swing this, Father Nick. Why not try? Are you with me?"

"One hundred per cent, Berny," I answered as I was encouraged by his appraisal of the situation, and added, "After all, what is ten thousand dollars? God can still perform miracles."

Soon after lunch we had a long talk with the bishop. He was enthused with the plan but, not surprisingly, he was hesitant at first as the rent seemed an insurmountable obstacle. However, when we explained to him our practical plans to raise funds to pay the rent, he was convinced of Meyer's good business mind and of my abundant energy and said, "Go ahead. God bless you, but remember, the diocese has no money. I give you my blessing but financially you are on your own." Then, turning to me, he said, "I know now that I am going to lose you as my secretary, but," he added with a smile, "you are a bad secretary anyway and I think I will survive."

The next morning Fr. Meyer and I went to explore our new domain in the Kings Building. I will never forget the impression of desolation I had on that first visit. There still was no electricity and the dark corridors and rooms of the immense building were depressing. Stairs, corridors, offices had only whatever little light could filter through the dirty windowpanes. Doors were missing, windows were broken, and dirt, dust, and cobwebs were everywhere. There was not a stick of furniture. My heart sank. Did we have to pay $10,000 a month for that dirty place? Wouldn't the Hong Kong Land Company do anything to put the building back in order?

"No," Fr. Meyer said, "if we want it we have to take it as it is, but don't worry, Nick. This is nothing. A good cleaning, a coat of paint, a few boards and nails, and a bunch of cleaning and scrub women are all we need to get the work done. We'll have the place in tip-top shape in no time."

Encouraged by his optimism and realizing the potential for good of a center for Catholic activities right in the heart of the richest business district in the Far East, I kept up my enthusiasm.

The St. Nicholas Club, as the Servicemen's Club was going to be called, was going to be used as a "home away from home" for the British and American servicemen who were pouring into Hong Kong and had no place to go in their free time. Fr. Meyer planned to serve good, wholesome, home-cooked food. There was room for one hundred people.

The center would have a large room with a seating capacity for two hundred people, a chapel for fifty people, several large, private offices, a large showroom for books and religious articles, and plenty of storage space for the Catholic Truth Society's stock of books. All of this right in the very heart of town! That very morning we signed the application for rental and the closing date was set for September 20, when the first month's rent was due.

Goodbye To The Parish

As soon as we started working on the new venture, I realized that my new job would require my full time and this was not compatible with parish work. I loved my parish ministry intensely and my heart was torn between the two. I decided in favor of giving my full time to the Catholic Center because I knew that if I did not do it, there was nobody else to take up that work and the diocese would be deprived of a tremendous opportunity for missionary work. The Catholic Center meant bringing Christ to the business center of Hong Kong. It meant a rare opportunity of limitless contact with non-Christians and of witnessing to Christ in a totally non-religious environment. On the contrary, the parish could dispense with my services because our priests were returning from Macao and the bishop would have no difficulty in finding a substitute for me. He encouraged me to take up the center's work and so, with great regret, I resigned from the parish as of the end of September.

Providential Help

While we were waiting for the day to sign the rental contract I kept praying and thinking: Where on earth can I find $10,000 cash? My prayers were heard and Divine Providence came to my help in an unforeseen way.

One morning, shortly after we had committed ourselves to renting the floor space, my friend Mr. Seu Kon-chi suddenly appeared at my parish office, smiling and jovial as in former days. I had not seen him for over four years.

"Sz Shan-fou, I am back!" he blurted out, bubbling with joy as soon as he saw me at my desk. "All my family is back with me. We are all safe, thanks to the Lord."

We embraced each other and then he told me about his family's adventures on the China mainland during the four years of war. At the end of the conversation he casually mentioned, "By the way, what happened to the money I asked you to bury for me?"

"Of course, I buried it as you told me to do and it is still safely underground." I did not tell him about my stupidity in keeping the money in my room before burying it.

"Well," he said, "I could use it now."

"By all means," I said, "today I will dig it up and bring it to you."

With the help of Fr. Feroldi, I had no difficulty in locating the exact spot where we had buried the money in the dark of night almost four years earlier. This time we dug it up in full daylight without fear of going to jail. The jar was intact, the wax seal still holding, and when we opened it the bank notes inside were as crisp as the day we had put them in. That evening I went to Mr. Seu's house and gave him the precious bundle.

Next morning he came to church and after Mass gave me an envelope, saying, "Sz, Shan-fou, this is a little something for your kindness to me," and placed a thick, sealed envelope in my hands. Later, when I opened it, a cascade of $100 bills spilled out of it. I counted them: exactly $10,000!

A Dream Becomes Reality

On September 20 we signed the lease with the Hong Kong Land Company, paid one month's rent, and took possession of our valuable premises: a complex of sixteen thousand square feet of office space, with dirt all over, broken floors, windows with broken panes, ill smelling and deserted. Fr. Meyer went to work immediately on the building while I did the necessary desk work preparing for the organization of the Catholic Center. With his uncanny ability of being good at everything, Fr. Meyer seemed as much at home doing carpentry work as writing books or directing an army of Chinese workers on a building project. He recruited a number of women and got them to work scrubbing, dusting and cleaning. Then he got hold of carpenters, electricians and painters, all eager to work for a living, and in a few days both the second and fourth floors were completely transformed.

We needed furniture. He went scavenging empty offices in buildings vacated by the Japanese and found a number of chairs, tables, sofas, etc., But how to transport them? Providence again helped us. Fr. John Chatterton, the Navy chaplain with the British fleet, a very pleasant and charitable man, came to the mission house to visit the bishop. Fr. Meyer and I approached him, told him our plight, and he immediately put us in contact with Captain O'Connell of the HMS *Resource*. All our troubles were solved. The good captain, also a very charming person, placed at our disposal both trucks and sailors, to collect the furniture, to transport it to our offices, to get food supplies for the St. Nicholas Club and to help us with the endless details of this big operation.

In the meantime, Brother Mario helped me to organize the Catholic Center. The Royal Navy sailors helped us to partition the large hall and build an attractive little chapel. We dedicated it to the Immaculate Heart of Mary as a token of gratitude.

Fr. Meyer had secured for us enough bookcases, sofas and curtains to make the conference room look like a pleasant lounge where soldiers, sailors, shoppers, tourists, and business people could come in to rest, read and visit the chapel. We even managed to get showcases for our religious articles shop and scrounged around for all kinds of books, new and used, medals, rosaries and church artifacts to sell.

I selected a room near the entrance door as my office and furnished it with one old desk, one chair and one old typewriter: enough to do the necessary work. I was able to hire an excellent secretary, Miss Aurea Baptista. She was experienced, mature, and had executive ability. I had known her for a long time as she was the organist at the cathedral and a prominent leader in the Portuguese community.

On October 4, the Feast of St. Francis of Assisi, we had the official inauguration of both the Catholic Center and the St. Nicholas Club. Gen. Festing, the newly appointed Commander-in-Chief of the Hong Kong Military Administration, who was a practicing Catholic and daily communicant, came to the dedication with some of the top brass of the armed forces. They regarded both the St. Nicholas Club and the Catholic Center lounge as a great service to the men of the armed forces. That very day the bishop blessed the new chapel and opened the religious articles shop. It was the official beginning of the St. Nicholas Club and of the Catholic Center. Both activities were blessed by the Lord and through the following years both rendered great service to the Hong Kong community.

The chapel was an immediate success. I celebrated daily Mass there every morning at 7.30 A.M. with Gen. Festing as my altar boy. All through the day, especially during the noon hours, people came to pray.

The religious articles shop was the solution to our financial problems. People were eager to buy anything religious. I began frantically ordering supplies of religious books and religious articles from England, Ireland and the USA. As fast as they arrived, the people gobbled them up. After I made the first rental payment with the donation from Mr. Seu, I never had any difficulty paying the rent with the cashflow from the religious articles shop.

The St. Nicholas Club proved a real boon to servicemen. Typical American and British home-style foods were served for a reasonable price and were very much appreciated. The club, especially at meal times, was always full. On some days as many as fifteen hundred meals were served. Many people from the armed services came to enjoy the club's good food, to spend a quiet moment in the chapel, and then some time in the center's lounge.

The center soon developed a number of activities that were of service to the community and also provided a source of contact between Catholics and non-Catholics. Fr. Ryan, in his history of the Church in Hong Kong, summarized the work of the center in these words:

"The Catholic Center fully lived up to its name, because within a very short time a great many Catholic activities were united in it. It had a much frequented chapel where, in addition to morning Mass, there was evening Mass for the armed services every Sunday. This attracted a large attendance of the lay Catholic population. The large meeting room of the center, in which a lending library was also housed, was constantly in use for various religious, cultural and social gatherings. In those early months after the war, when distractions were few in the Colony, lectures were frequently offered in this hall and were very well attended. The newly formed St. Thomas More Society, another product of the Stanley internment camp, also held its meetings there."

The Catholic Center and the St. Nicholas Club had another unforeseen effect. I can categorically state that if PIME and I are in the States today it is very much due to the American youth I met in those days. In my preface to *Forward With Christ*, which I published here in the States in 1953, I wrote:

"As director of the center I had an opportunity to meet many American Catholic young men serving in the Army, the Navy, the Marines and the Air Force. This was my first contact with American youth and I quickly learned to admire them. Their sound Catholic education, their magnificent spirit, their generosity, and the high level of their moral standards made a favorable and lasting impression upon me. They made me feel that the nation from which these clean cut and vigorous Catholic boys had come must be a nation destined by God for high and noble achievements."

It was due to my high regard for American youth that, when I was assigned to develop PIME in the States, my first resolution was to recruit and train young American men for the missionary priesthood.

A Stormy Beginning

Hong Kong needed a diocesan paper in English. I'd had this conviction since my earliest years in Hong Kong. Now, in the whirlwind of changed life and innovative thinking of the post-war period, this need became imperative. The English-speaking Catholic population was about to grow by leaps and bounds. Along with peace, Portuguese, European and

American Catholics were returning and becoming even more numerous than before. Also, the English-speaking Chinese population would grow as a result of the growth of our Catholic English schools.

Furthermore, Hong Kong was a missionary diocese. The Catholic population had to be well trained and fully knowledgeable of its religion as well as of its responsibility to share its faith with the non-Christian world all around. In my life I have always believed, as William Barclay put it: "In the last analysis religion is never safe until a man can tell, not only what he believes, but why he believes it. Religion is hope, but it is hope with reason behind it."[4]

I knew nothing about organizing and running a diocesan paper. Nothing! But, "I will learn, I will experiment, and with the help of God I will succeed," I told myself, and I started.

Today, looking at this venture in retrospect, I would not blame anyone who criticized me. One might even call such self-confidence presumptuous, but God certainly helps those who trust in Him.

The bishop gave me his blessing and repeated his usual warning, "Remember, Maestrini, financially you are on your own." All the priests I consulted fully agreed on the need of such a venture and all promised their collaboration in promoting the circulation of the paper. Fr. Ryan, with his typical businesslike, Anglo-Saxon mentality regarded my plan as amateurish, but did not entirely discourage me. So in December 1945 I decided to start the publication of a diocesan paper in English.

Learning By Trial And Error

In the beginning I was both editor and publisher of the paper, but I made it my first order of business to hire a lay editor. Because the paper was intended for lay Catholics I believed that a lay Catholic editor would communicate more easily than I with the targeted audience, being better able to understand their needs. I remembered that shortly before the war I had read an article about The Grail, a movement of Catholic lay women founded in Holland and gradually spreading throughout the world. Thinking that an Australian editor might demand a lower salary than an English or an American one, I wrote to The Grail in Australia asking for a qualified Grail member to come to Hong Kong to work as editor for our paper. I knew that negotiations would take a long time and as I felt there was no time to waste, I decided to make a start in the meantime, with the first issue scheduled for publication on the first Sunday in March.

Selecting a name for the paper was my second concern. Since we were living in a pluralistic society, I wanted the title to be as ecumenical as possible so as to avoid alienating non-Catholic readers or making the paper seem exclusively denominational. After much discussion and consultation with others, we settled on *The Sunday Examiner*.

To find a printer was the third important step. The war had ended only three or four months before and most of the old English printing firms were not ready for business yet. The few that were functioning were charging exorbitant prices, which I could not afford. Prewar paper stocks were dwindling and new stocks had not yet begun to arrive. It was almost a hopeless situation. I turned to my old friend Brother John, Director of the Salesian Printing School. His staff consisted of only a dozen or so Chinese students and the school had only a few old printing machines. The students could neither read nor speak English though they did all the typesetting by hand. Brother John, a native of Malta, also had only a grade-school knowledge of English, but he was a good teacher and I hoped he could print the paper for me.

In order to get Catholic news from abroad, I subscribed to *The Catholic Register* of Denver, Colorado, and *The Tablet* of London. For local news I depended on my fellow priests, and every pastor promised to appoint a parish correspondent. I hired a Chinese lady to take care of circulation records, and I was in business.

We decided to publish the paper once every two weeks in an eight-page tabloid size containing both local and worldwide news of religious importance, and a magazine section.

A Disastrous First Edition

About the middle of February I gathered up some news clippings from old Catholic papers, along with several religious magazine articles, and took them all to Brother John. I asked him to set up in type everything I brought him, in column format, so that I could prepare the page layout. Three days before the publication date, I went to pick up the galley proofs to correct them and do the layout. When Brother John showed the proofs to me I almost fainted! Thinking that I had given him too much material for one issue, he had set up in type only one third of all the articles I had given him! As I remonstrated with him for not carrying out my orders, he calmly remarked: "Well, after all, the articles I discarded are not very interesting." He spoke as if he were the editor and I the apprentice. I was furious!

Sitting down at a small table right in the printing room, I started correcting the proofs and I was dismayed beyond words. There was not even one correct line. However, as I was committed to publishing the paper within forty-eight hours, I had to get it printed, no matter the cost. Settling for a four-page edition, I worked for hours alone in the dim light of the printing room, correcting proofs and preparing the layout. I asked Brother John to get his students to work extra hours and by a miracle of Divine Providence I got the paper printed in time for distribution to the churches on Saturday morning.

From the point of view of a publisher, it was a shameful first edition. The layout was unbalanced, there were typos throughout, and the whole paper was a disgrace. To this day I am ashamed of it, but it was a beginning, anyway.

The following Monday I went to see my friend Mr. Noronha, owner of the professional and highly respected Noronha Printing Company. I pleaded with him for help and, being a good Catholic and an old friend from my days at St. Teresa's, he agreed to print my paper for a price that I could afford. From the second issue on the paper came out regularly, professionally laid out and printed. Probably because there was so much eagerness to read and so little reading material, the paper was a success and before too long was self-supporting.

The Catholic Truth Society Revived

The centuries-old Catholic dream of the conversion of China never came so close to being realized as during that first year after the end of the war. China came out of the war fully victorious and with a new prestige of being one of the superpowers, a position it had never enjoyed before in world opinion. Because of the Christian leadership of President Chiang Kai-shek, of his wife, and of most of the foreign-trained government officers and intelligentsia of China, Christianity was no longer regarded with suspicion. Moreover, the fact that all Christian missionaries, Catholic and Protestant, had loyally suffered with the Chinese people for eight years and helped millions of victims regardless of creed had greatly impressed the Chinese people.

The Catholic Church, in particular, enjoyed an excellent reputation then because many dioceses had been completely entrusted to Chinese bishops and Chinese clergy. This wise policy of Rome was beginning to remove from the Church the stigma of being a foreign religion. The threat of Mao Zedong's communist armies winning the civil war seemed remote and everybody was confident that Chiang Kai-shek, with his much superior forces, would squelch them again as he had done before.

Realizing this new and extremely favorable situation, I decided to resume at full speed the work of publishing Chinese books. This time I had no financial problems. The house the diocese had given the Catholic Truth Society in exchange for the $5,000 from Msgr. Freking was still standing and in good shape. It had even escaped bombs and looting. I put it up for sale and in a few days I got all of our money back with profit.

With this capital at my disposal I was able to pay for Chinese writers and in no time new booklets on religious and social questions started pouring out of Chinese presses. At times I had as many as a dozen new booklets being printed by Chinese printing presses all over town. Postal communications with China were good, my fellow missionaries and their parishioners were starving for Chinese literature, and I was happy to supply them with it.

The bishop assigned Fr. John Chen to help me with the Chinese Catholic monthly, the *Kung Kao Po*. I hired an excellent lay Catholic, Mr. Yam Hin-peng, as editor, and resumed regular publication. The circulation shot up immediately.

Good News!

It was in the early months of 1946 that a missionary of the Paris Foreign Mission Society from northwest China, passing through Hong Kong on his way back to France, came to see me. He had bought our booklets in prewar days and, having corresponded with me, wanted to meet me personally.

"Father Maestrini," he said in French as soon as we were seated in my office, "for a long time I have wanted to see you and tell you personally how much good your publications are doing. Let me tell you my experience. You remember that before the war I bought many of your books. Well, what I did not tell you then was that I became the butt of the jokes of my confreres. They spent whatever money they had buying rice for their folks. I, too, spent money on rice and medicines, but I also spent some on your books and I gave away rice and books. I felt that I had to feed body and soul together. Well, the war came, France was occupied by Hitler, and we French missionaries were interned by the Chinese. All of our mission districts and parishes remained without priests for several years. Unfortunately, without religious assistance and under the pressure of their peers, many of our Christians abandoned their faith and returned to their pagan way of life. When, after the war, we returned to our parishes and made a survey of the situation, we found that many Catholics had defected. My mission district was the only exception: none of my Catholics had abandoned their faith. The only reason which could account for the difference was that through the use of literature my folks were better instructed in the Catholic faith and had stronger convictions. My policy of feeding body and mind had paid off."

Needless to say, his words were music to my ears and did a great deal to strengthen my conviction about the effectiveness of the apostolate of the written word.

Notes

1. I consider Fr. Bernard F. Meyer of Maryknoll a truly great missionary and one of the dearest friends I ever had. A short sketch of his character and of his activities will help the reader to better evaluate the great work he did for Hong Kong and the missions in China.

Bernard Francis Meyer was born on February 16, 1891, in Brooklyn, Iowa, into a family of German background, and grew up on his family farm in Stuart, Iowa. This first period of his life left an indelible mark on his character and he preserved many of the admirable qualities of people accustomed to working the land. Life on the farm was hard and young Bernard combined school work and farm work as a matter of fact. Full of energy, he was always doing something useful, always active and eager to learn. It was here he developed one of the basic principles that governed his life: "I can do anything that anyone else can do." For Bernard Meyer this was not a boastful statement but a simple truth.

He graduated from the local high school in 1909, decided to become a priest and entered the college-seminary in Davenport, Iowa. Three years later, in 1912, after graduating with honors, he began his theological studies at the Sulpician Seminary of St. Mary in Baltimore. It was here that he discovered the foreign missions through reading the glorious saga of the missionaries' work in the Far East, and avidly read Field Afar (the magazine of the newly founded (1911) Maryknoll Mission Society. He was deeply impressed by the fact that while there was a large number of American Protestant missionaries, Catholic ones were extremely few in those days. Even though he cherished the idea of being a parish priest, his heart "was secretly throbbing to larger things and wider issues," as his biographer wrote. In the fall of 1914 he joined twelve other seminarians at Maryknoll, was ordained a priest on December 2, 1916, and was one of the first group of Maryknollers to land in China, on October 25, 1918.

With the group assigned to work in southeast China he proceeded to Yangchun, where for a few months they had a veteran French missionary, Fr. Gauthier, to help them learn Chinese and guide them in the first steps of missionary work.

The first few years in China were hard, but Bernard showed that he was possessed of every spiritual, psychological and physical attribute for success. As he had done on the farm back in Iowa, so now he could not resist the impulse to "fix things," and fix things he did, both physically and spiritually. These were the first years after World War I and a new air, a new spirit, a new desire for change was breathing through China. Bernard got down to work, experimented with new methods in teaching religion, opened schools, hospitals, founded a school to prepare catechists, built churches, organized out-patient clinics, made friends, attracted countless Chinese to Christ and baptized them. He even started a mass conversion in an area that for centuries had been irresponsive to the work of the missionaries. He was too active, too valuable to remain in the same place too long. He was a pioneer and was assigned to open up one new area after another for missionary work.

His mind was too active, his perception of the Church's needs too keen, to allow him to limit his interest to just one particular parish or district. He recognized that there were activities that no one particular parish priest could undertake because they were beyond the purpose of a pastor's work. One of these needs was providing books to teach religion, especially a catechism and a teacher's manual, to enable teachers and catechists to do their all-important job. So, in May 1941, he asked for a one-year leave of absence from his mission in Guilin to go to the Maryknoll house in Hong Kong to write these books. He asked me to publish them and we worked together like brothers. The result was the publication of a large teacher's manual in letter-size format and over five hundred pages.

He was in Hong Kong when the Japanese occupied the colony and was soon interned with the British and the other Americans at Stanley concentration camp. When the Americans were given an opportunity to be repatriated, Fr. Meyer and Fr. Don Hessler, also a Maryknoller, rather than leave the three thousand British internees without religious assistance, refused to be repatriated and chose to remain in the camp. It was a truly heroic choice worthy of great priests.

To complete this story I must add that in 1947, when his work in Hong

Kong was completed, he was assigned to work with the French Missionaries in Guangzhou (Canton).

In May 1950, his advanced state of arthritis and other physical ailments compelled him to return to the States, where he spent his time lecturing and writing books until he died at Maryknoll headquarters in 1973 at 84 years of age.

2. Fr. Don Hessler, a Maryknoller from Detroit, Michigan, also became a very dear friend of mine. He arrived in China shortly after I did and through casual encounters we became fast friends. I fully shared his deep spirituality, his intense love for people and his ideas about missionary work. Shortly after the war ended, he fell seriously ill and returned to the States. Years later he was assigned to work in the Yucatan Province of Mexico, where he is still living.

3. In those early days after the war everybody was practically penniless because the currency then used, namely the Japanese military yen, was declared worthless.

4. Barclay, St. John, p. 160.

26

1946-1947: Years Of Growth

Rebuilding And Planning For The Future

Ordinarily, one of the great joys of youth and adulthood is the ability to plan, to establish goals and to work toward achieving them. For many of us in Hong Kong, the year 1946 was a time of youthful enthusiasm, of planning, working, achieving goals. China was emerging from eight years of war, uncertainty and destruction. The Chinese were finally able, to look to the future and to plan for growth and development. For us missionaries it was an especially exciting year because it seemed that at long last all the circumstances were favorable for a full and systematic evangelization of the Chinese masses. It was a year of hope, of growth, of blossoming life.

Today, looking at it in retrospect, we must thank God for keeping the future hidden from our eyes. Had we known what was going to happen to us and to our plans within two short years, 1946 would have been a year of mourning, frustration and despair. In fact, all of our work and plans made that year for the evangelization of China came to nothing. They were totally destroyed when communism came to power.

The First Catholic Press Convention In China

The Catholic press in China was still in its infancy because the country, since the establishment of the Republic in 1911, had been continually torn by internal wars and the war with Japan. Therefore the Chinese Catholic press had never been seriously developed.

The few existing Catholic publishers were all very small unbusinesslike undertakings belonging to different religious orders. With the traditional lack of collaboration among religious orders (typical of pre-Vatican days), and lack of business methods, every religious society acted independently with regard to both production and circulation of books. Now that at long last China was unified, the time seemed ripe to begin coordinating the work of the Catholic press.

The virtual head of the Chinese Church of those days was the apostolic delegate (the pope's representative), Archbishop Antonio A. Riberi, a Vatican career diplomat residing in the then capital of China, Nanjing. I had met him when he passed through Hong Kong on his way to China and I was on very friendly terms with him. So I wrote to him to suggest organizing the first convention of all Catholic publishers in China in order to promote the growth of the Catholic press and to coordinate the circulation of Catholic books. He welcomed this initiative and invited me to proceed with plans for the event to be held in Shanghai.

The preparatory work of contacting all the religious orders active in the publication of books and periodicals took several months. A publishers' convention had never been organized before in China and religious superiors were skeptical of even accepting the invitation. Finally, as I kept stressing that it was the apostolic delegate who wanted the convention, I had a list of about a dozen participants. The convention was set to open in September 1946 under the chairmanship of Archbishop Riberi in Shanghai.

I arrived there by boat a couple of days before the beginning of the convention and went to stay at the Franciscan Procuration (mission house). This large residence in the heart of the city served as the hub of the far-flung Franciscan missions all over China. The superior of the house was an Italian Franciscan, a former Count from Milan, endowed with extraordinary intelligence and worldwide culture.

The day the convention opened in the presence of the apostolic delegate he asked me to chair the meetings. There were about a dozen delegates, all elderly clergymen, Chinese and foreigners of different nationalities. Unfortunately, most of them were more interested in the techniques of printing than in promoting Catholic literature. However, speaking Latin, English, French and Italian we managed to understand each other and work together.

Our situation was a peculiar one because out of the twelve or so delegates none of them had executive power to make decisions on behalf of their respective religious societies. In a religious orders the real executive is the provincial superior but the delegates at the convention were only men in charge of the printing presses of their respective orders and lacked the authority to make decisions.

In spite of this serious handicap, the meeting proved to be very successful. Archbishop Riberi gave the keynote address and I spoke at length about China's need of a vigorous Catholic press. We all achieved a better awareness of the importance of the Catholic press as a missionary tool for the evangelization of China. We decided to start searching for Catholic writers and to encourage them to publish books through secular publishers whenever possible. Moreover, we decided to keep the channels of communication open with one another, to place more emphasis than in the past on publications of a social nature, in addition to devotional publications, and to promote the use of modern Chinese literary style rather than the old classic style.

John Wu, The First Chinese Ambassador To The Vatican

The evening of September 11, 1946, while in Shanghai for the Catholic Press convention, I went to see Dr. John Wu at his house. It was our first meeting since his escape from the Japanese in Hong Kong in May 1942. Only three days before this meeting, the Chinese government had officially announced that China had established diplomatic relations with the Vatican and that President Chiang had personally appointed Dr. John Wu as the first Chinese ambassador to the Holy See.

This event brought great joy to all of us missionaries. Forty-six years earlier, during the Boxer Rebellion, we were still being hunted like wild animals; now the president of the nation, himself a Christian, acknowledged the Holy Father as the spiritual leader of the Chinese Catholic Church. It was an historical gesture that boded well for the future of the Church in China.

An Inspiring Example

The evening I went to John Wu's house for dinner I found his house full of important visitors: Archbishop Yu Pin, two priests, a Shanghai banker and several other distinguished people.

During a pleasant after-dinner conversation we began to notice small children peeping into the room, then disappearing. Dr. Wu became slightly restless and finally he told us frankly: "Gentlemen, nine o'clock is the hour of saying the rosary with my family and the children cannot go to bed unless we have said the rosary together. Will you kindly excuse me and I will join you later."

The archbishop said, "Dr. Wu, may we join you in the rosary?" Of course, all agreed and soon Mrs. Wu and twelve children (ranging in age from two years to twenty-five) filed into the living room. Only Mrs. Wu sat, with her youngest child on her lap, while Papa Wu and the children and the guests knelt down to say the rosary.

It was not a short rosary. At every mystery Dr. Wu gave a short explanation to his children, in Chinese, of course, and added some pertinent advice. At the end he asked the archbishop to say a few words and then the family withdrew while we continued our conversation.

The Book Of Psalms: A Best-Seller

In the long history of countless translations of the Bible into different languages the world over, Dr. Wu's translation of the Psalms is certainly something unique and worth telling.

Back in 1938, while Dr. Wu was experiencing the excitement of his newly found Catholic faith in Hong Kong, he translated into Chinese a few of his favorite Psalms. When he happened to meet Madame H. H. Kung, a devout Protestant very fond of the Bible, he showed her his translation as a matter of conversation. She liked John's work and, wanting to share it with her sister, Madame Chiang Kai-shek, sent her a copy. In turn, Madame Chiang Kai-shek showed it to the president, Chiang Kai-shek, who also greatly liked the translation. In the summer of 1940 during one of his visits to Chungking, Dr. Wu had several meetings with President and Madame Chiang Kai-shek and gave them his translation of several Psalms. Dr. Wu related in his biography that on September 21, 1940, Madame Chiang wrote to him: "For many years, the Generalissimo has been wanting to have a really adequate and readable Wen-li (literary) translation of the Bible. He has never been able to find anyone who could undertake this matter. Many leading Christians to whom he has spoken of this matter assured him that the word of God is so wonderful that the truth shines through even a bad rendition in Chinese. But we feel that this is dodging the question for if, in spite of the bad text, some have found comfort and understanding, how much more powerful the Bible could be as an agent to enlighten men's hearts and minds, if a really clear and readable translation could be had!" The letter ends up by saying that I should take up the job and that "the Generalissimo would gladly ginance the undertaking of this work."

At that time China was so deeply involved in the war and Dr. Wu had so many duties in the legislative Yuan (Chinese Parliament) that he neglected this matter. But in 1942, after his escape from Hong Kong, when he arrived in Guilin he saw Madame Chiang and she brought up the matter of the translation again. It was agreed that Dr. Wu would soon begin the translation of the entire book of Psalms and would be placed on the president's payroll. John requested a very modest salary, hardly enough to keep body and soul together for his large brood, and Madame Chiang almost doubled it. Thus he was able to dedicate himself completely to the new task.

While still in Hong Kong John had told me that when he translated anything from a foreign language, especially the Psalms, he would read the translation to his wife, who was completely illiterate. If she understood it at first reading, then he was satisfied, but if she did not understand it he would continue to work on it, writing and rewriting, until she could understand it easily. John's reasoning, of course, was that if his wife understood it, everybody else would also be able to understand it.

In his biography, he called this period of life in Guilin "the poetry of life." Even though living with his brood of children in a decrepit, leaky hut with mud floors, he spiritually felt on Cloud Nine, reveling in the beauty of the Psalms and feeling very much inspired by them. This perhaps is not much of a surprise if we remember that Chinese poetry, like the Psalms, is full of symbolism, of figures of speech, of vague sentimentalism to a far greater extent than Western poetry. Hebrew poetry is really much closer to the Oriental mind than to our more prosaic Western way of thinking.

In 1944, while John was in Chungking for a meeting of the legislative Yuan, the Japanese army marched westward to occupy Guilin. Their purpose was to destroy the powerful American air base there, which had been organized and run by the famous Flying Tigers of Chennault. John, frantic with fear for his family's welfare, did everything possible to catch a plane to rejoin them in Guilin, but he was unsuccessful. This was providential. The Japanese advance was very fast and his family managed to get the very last train out of Guilin. Mrs. Wu and each of the twelve children were actually thrown on board the train through the windows by the sturdy Thomas Wu. The only thing they could salvage besides the clothes they wore was the manuscript of Dr. Wu's translation of the Psalms. Dr. Wu joined them later in free China and finally all moved to Chungking.

After the war ended, Dr. Wu's translation of the Book of Psalms was published by the Commercial Press. Shortly after publication, Mr. Wong Yuan-wu, general chairman of the firm, informed Dr. Wu that his book was the best seller they had ever had. In his biography Dr. Wu wrote: "I suspect Our Lord has a special predilection for things of humble origins. The version was born in a pigsty. The popularity of that work was beyond my fondest dreams. Countless papers and periodicals, irrespective of religion, published reviews too good to be true. I was very much tickled when I saw the opening verse of the first Psalm used as a headline on the front page of one of the non-religious dailies. They arranged the ten words in such a way as to surround my picture like a crown on the head. Thus was 'the uncrowned king' crowned! The words, if rendered back into English, would read as follows:

'Happy only is the gentleman who does good,
God will shower on him infinite blessings!'

"From this you will see how little accurate my version is. But I did not publish it as a literal translation, only as a paraphrase. My chief object was to interest the Chinese public in the Holy Scriptures."

An American Lay Missionary In China

At 7:30 on the morning of January 5, 1947, I was at the Kowloon dock waiting for a passenger ship of the US President Line to tie up at the pier with nine hundred Protestant missionaries on board. Passenger liners from the States to Hong Kong had just resumed regular service and this ship was carrying the largest contingent of missionaries ever to come to work for Christ in China after the war. In the midst of the nine hundred Protestant missionaries there was a young American Catholic lady, Mary Louise Tully, from Grailville, Ohio, coming to China as, I believe, the first lay Catholic missionary from the States. It was an historical moment. Here I have to retrace my steps in order to explain how that event came about.

At the end of 1945 I had contacted the Grail in Australia about sending one of their members to Hong Kong to work as editor of our diocesan paper. A few months later, the Grail replied, saying that they had forwarded my request to the Grail's president visiting in Loveland, Ohio, as that branch of their organization was interested in sending lay missionaries to China. I did not like the idea of an American girl on my staff at the center, as I was convinced that she would find it very difficult to adapt to our environment. However, I decided to wait for the American Grail to contact me.

In the meantime, Bishop Valtorta decided to go to Italy for health reasons and to visit the States on his way to Europe. When he arrived in the States, coming fresh from the Chinese theater of war, he was very much sought after by journalists for interviews, and several articles about him appeared in various Catholic papers. Dr. Lydwine Van Kersbergen, president of the American Grail, saw his name in the paper and, remembering my letter forwarded to her from Australia, invited him to Loveland, Ohio, to discuss the feasibility of sending lay missionaries to China.

The end result of that meeting at Loveland was that one day in October I received a short letter from Bishop Valtorta in Grailville. He informed me in very few words that a certain Miss Mary Louise Tully would come to Hong Kong on the first available ship to work with me at the Catholic Center. He asked me to make all the necessary arrangements to provide for her salary, room and board.

I must confess that when I read that letter I hit the ceiling! How did the bishop dare to make arrangements concerning my work without consulting me first? Moreover, I did not want an American blonde floating around my office because in our Chinese environment it would have been embarrassing. Visitors would certainly misunderstand the presence of a Western girl working closely with a priest. Furthermore, I had serious doubts about her fitting into our work: could a highly trained American college graduate get along with the Chinese girls working in my office who had at best a high school education? Would she be satisfied boarding with a Portuguese or Chinese family? Would her salary break down the precarious finances of the center?

I was really on the verge of writing to the Grail to cancel the arrangements. However, before writing I prayed a lot about it. As my anger subsided I began to see things more clearly. I realized that, after all, the bishop had visited the Grail, had met Miss Tully, and so had more information than I had. It occurred to me then that he might be right. Therefore I decided it was better to obey and wait and see. It was the wisest decision of my life.

A few days later I heard from Miss Tully and her letter resolved all my doubts and worries. She sounded so ready to learn, so willing to follow directions, and so eager to work that I began to look forward to her coming.

I went to meet her at the dock accompanied by my secretary, elderly Miss Baptista, and a couple of Chinese girls from the office staff. We all gave her a hearty welcome and accompanied her to the hostel for Catholic young women at the Canossian convent, where she would stay until we made final arrangements. Later that day I sat down for a good talk with her and soon realized that her coming was a blessing for the work of the center and for the missions in China.

Her story was very simple. After graduating from St. Teresa's College, in Winona, Minnesota, Miss Tully had been seriously pondering how she could best serve the Lord as a lay person when she heard about the Grail and its goals. Attracted by the new idea, she had decided to devote her life, as a lay person, to the pursuit of the goals of the Grail. After a period of training at the Grail headquarters in Holland she went to Grailville, Ohio, waiting for an opportunity to go to the foreign missions as a lay missionary.

According to the Grail's thinking, this meant that she had to go as a lay person and find work to support herself. This, of course, was quite in contrast with the practice of religious orders and foreign mission societies. We missionary priests and nuns went to the missions as members of a religious society and the society provided all the basic necessities of life so that we did not have to go hunting for jobs or worry about room and board.

A Revealing Conversation

Here are the salient points of my first conversation with Miss Tully.

"How are you planning, Miss Tully," I asked her, "to do your work as a lay missionary?"

"My program is simply to live according to Christian principles a God-centered life in all daily relationships, jobs, and responsibilities: at the office or the hostel, at picnics, at recreation, in dealing with printers, missionaries, celebrities, coolies, table companions, fellow workers and fellow parishioners.

"I believe that if you try living a Christian life, your companions whether in a newspaper office or anywhere else will come rather quickly to know your manner and purpose of life without your needing to say much about it. This is natural. If your whole life were centered in the motion pictures, people around you would be certain to get some ideas about movie life from your conversation. If you were passionately fond of roller-skating, you would very soon take some of your companions skating with you. So, we hope, if we are sufficiently convinced that God is really the beginning and end and joy of all life, our conviction will be contagious and, with God's help, it will spread to others."

"What do you mean by a God-centered life?" I asked, to test her.

"I think, Father, that we have to learn from the children of this world. If one is convinced that a dollar in the pocket is a man's best friend, he will be an apostle of his belief and will probably spend his life seeking dollars and turn many of his companions in the dollar-seeking direction. But if one believes that the Christian Faith is the greatest treasure, he must spend his life seeking that treasure and sharing it."

Fully satisfied with her answer I continued, "Are you planning to learn Chinese?"

"Yes, I think that my position at the Catholic Center will give me many opportunities to do useful work while learning Chinese customs and the Chinese language. Before I can be effective in bringing the knowledge of Christ to China, I must know the country well. I would like to take regular lessons in the Chinese language."

"Would you like to live with a Chinese family?"

"Yes, I would be grateful for that opportunity. I presume that Chinese girls at the center act and talk more or less like office workers anywhere, and perhaps they even imitate the office mannerisms that they see in American movies. But I'm sure that at home they must relax and be themselves. I can get to know their culture better by living with them."

"You are correct. I will make arrangements for you to live with a Chinese family. What salary do you expect?"

"Father, I would like to have the same salary as the other Chinese employees, and perhaps just a little more to help me pay for Chinese lessons."

We decided on $300.00 ($50.00 US) a month. Half would go for board and lodging and the rest for Chinese lessons, transportation, clothing and incidentals.

I was very pleased with that conversation and I was even more pleased when I saw Miss Tully at work in the following weeks and months.

She fitted in beautifully with the other twenty-five ladies on the staff. Unassuming, always eager to take the last place, charming with all whether they be VIPs or coolies, old or young, rich or poor, always ready to help anyone in need, she won the hearts of everybody on the staff and of everyone she met.

"Sz Shan-fou," a Chinese girl of the staff said one day with indignation in her voice, "Miss Tully always comes last. She always wants to be served last at table, she always takes the last place in the chapel, her salary is even less than what I get, and yet she works more than anyone else. I think you are unfair. She is American, she is a university graduate, she is so good. It is unfair. She ought to come first in everything."

Rather than being offended I was truly pleased by these remarks and I tried to explain to the young lady that if Miss Tully wanted to be the last I had no right to interfere with what she wanted. With regard to her salary, I said that I paid Miss Tully what she had asked me to give her and that she refused to accept more. I don't think I was very successful in convincing the young lady. She was a new Catholic and she could not grasp the deep spirituality of Miss Tully's true Christian way of life. The fact is that all the time Miss Tully worked at the Catholic Center as part of a staff of Chinese, Portuguese, young and old, men and women, she never had the slightest quarrel with anyone.[2]

The Catholic Center Staff

By the beginning of 1947 our activities at the Catholic Center had grown so much that the staff had been increased to twenty-eight. I do not remember all the names but I have to write a few lines at least about some of those wonderful people who made the work of the Catholic Center a success.

I have already mentioned Fr. John Chen, a good writer and devoted priest whose dedication to work was an inspiration to all. There was also quiet, unassuming Mr. Yam Hin-ping, who was not only an employee but a real friend, and also an excellent writer. Miss Aurea Baptista was tops as stenographer and as an executive assistant. Forever smiling, endowed with a contagious laugh, she was a tremendous help in giving the staff a sense of family.

Other important additions were:

Fr. A. Boerio, PIME, medium height, with a round, friendly face, came from the PIME Mission of Henan Province in central China. After working there for thirteen years he had to leave for reasons of health and was assigned to Hong Kong to work with me at the center. Being fluent in Chinese, he was a great help in the Chinese department and a valid assistant in helping me with correspondence with missionaries all over China.

Mrs. Mary Lyons, a wife and mother, relinquished an excellent job with one of the leading shipping lines in Hong Kong to come to the Catholic Center to work as manager of the Catholic Book Store and religious articles repository. With an uncommon talent for business and total devotion to her work, she made the Book Store a success and the main financial source of revenue for the upkeep and running expenses of the Catholic Center. She worked there until she reached retirement age.

Marie Tsang, May Wong and Marie Vieira, also excellent workers, were employed in various departments and dedicated most of their lives to working for the Catholic Center. Both Marie Vieira and May Wong remained there until they retired a few years ago. Marie Tsang married many years later and moved to Australia.

Frank Lai, my faithful storekeeper and dear friend, was a tremendous help as he had developed an uncanny ability to keep accurate records of all the movement of new and old books as they were printed, sold, sent out on consignment or returned. With the help of a simple Chinese abacus he kept track of the tens of thousands of copies we handled every year. He married charming Hortense Wong, also a member of our staff, and after I left Hong Kong they moved to Newport, Gwent, in Great Britain, where they still live. They now have many children and grand-children.

I cannot conclude this chapter without mentioning old Mr. Noe Botelho. A retired clerk from a British firm, he came to work for me at the Catholic Center as general supervisor and troubleshooter, at no salary. Totally devoted, modest, hard-working, he was able to handle all kinds of jobs without ever hurting anyone.

Dear old Mr. John Gutierrez was also another excellent retired worker who came often to help me at the Center. He was my right hand in organizing the Hong Kong Diocesan pilgrimage to Manila on the occasion of the International Eucharistic Congress in 1937.

The Chinese Businessmen's Catholic Club

The story of the two years of growth (1946-1947) would be incomplete without a mention of the opening of the Chinese Catholic Club for Catholic businessmen. A Catholic Club for men had already existed before the war and had met at the mission house. It had included both Chinese and Portuguese but never flourished because it did not have its own quarters.

In the fervor of the after-war reconstruction period, and in the certainty of the growth of the Church in Hong Kong, I felt that this valuable association had to be reorganized and relocated downtown. In order to grow and develop they needed space of their own. By the end of 1946 I gathered a fairly large number of Chinese Catholic businessmen interested in the project and after lengthy discussions we decided to establish a Chinese Catholic Club for businessmen in the central district of Hong Kong. We found an office with several thousand square feet of space in a building only a couple of blocks from the Catholic Center and we rented it.

The purpose of the club was to encourage social intercourse among the Catholic businessmen for the purpose of strengthening their faith and to promote Catholic business practices, to nurture mutual welfare and to provide healthy recreation and sports among the members. The club flourished from the very beginning and is still going strong in the eighties.

Notes

1. From "The Shield" magazine of Jan. 1950.

2. Miss Tully at work. I am now quoting excerpts from an article Miss Tully wrote for a Catholic magazine after one year of work at the Catholic Center.

"How long have you been here?" asked my talkative fellow passenger on the Hong Kong-Kowloon Ferry. She was a gray-haired, elderly Englishwoman whom I had never met before. "Two years," I answered. "You from England?" "No, I'm from America." "Oh! Well, I suppose you'll be going back soon. You must have made a fortune by now—all the foreigners do." I answered, "No, I'm not planning to go back. I didn't really come out to make a fortune." She looked surprised. "Why not? You look intelligent enough." I tried to control a smile; I am not always told that I look intelligent! But she wasn't being funny. She was only one of many Westerners who have let me know that making a fortune is the only sensible occupation for an intelligent person in the Orient.

Young women who had been trained for the lay apostolate work and who had the intention of living in China as wholehearted Christians could be of great influence, by praying and working together with the Chinese, trusting God to use them as instruments in building up the Catholic lay apostolate in China.

That was more than one year ago, and my experiences during this time have convinced me that there is, definitely, a field here for the Catholic lay apostle. Since I arrived, I have been employed at the Catholic Center in Hong Kong.

As you can guess, my position at the Catholic Center gives me the opportunities to do useful work while learning Chinese customs and the Chinese language. This is ideal because I know that before I can help in the lay apostolate in China I must know the country well. I've been taking lessons regularly since I arrived, and I am learning to talk in Cantonese about most everyday affairs.

My experiences in getting acclimatized have not been without their humorous side. In the first home where I stayed, I noticed that the family cat seemed to have an extraordinary devotion to me. As soon as I would sit down at meals, the cat would walk round the table until he came to my stool, and there he would settle down. After a few days I began to understand why: he had discovered the very first night that I was quite inexperienced with chopsticks and under my place at the table he could expect to find the best pickings! As the days went by, I grew more skillful, and the cat showed a growing lack of interest in me.

I have not been lecturing or teaching classes. If someone comes and says to me, "I want to become a Catholic; will you instruct me?", I answer, "With pleasure." If someone comes and says—and this is a more frequent occurrence—"I don't want to become a Catholic and I don't want instructions and I don't want to talk to a priest, but I want to ask you what is the meaning of this," I talk about whatever the inquirer wants to talk about—if I know something about it; otherwise I help to find someone who does. And it is surprising how the inquirers do come.

A teacher came to me and said—these are her actual words—"Can you teach me how to be happy? I have been watching you for a long time, and you are always happy. And in my heart I am always sad . . ." Others express similar ideas in different words. More attractive than the idea of happiness seems to be the idea of purpose, which my Chinese friends are able to sense in the Christian way of life. Time and again, conversations have run like this: "You seem to have some purpose in what you are doing. I don't. I am just living from day to day. I wish I knew what life is for, anyway. Do you know?

It is hard for us to realize what it can be like to be twenty years old and never once to have heard the Gospel. One day I was reading with a Chinese girl the account of the Last Judgment as it is given in St. Matthew, where it is foretold that Christ will say: "Come, you that have received a blessing from my Father . . . for I was hungry and you gave me food, thirsty and you gave me drink; I was a stranger and you brought me home . . ." "But," she interrupted in bewilderment, "how can I do it? When have I ever seen Christ?" We turned the page (we were using Monsignor Ronald Knox's translation) and there we read: "Whereupon the just will answer: 'Lord, when was it that we saw thee hungry, and fed thee, or thirsty, and gave thee drink?'" We had to laugh, because my friend had asked exactly the question our Lord had prophesied. Then, seriously, we read on: "And the King will answer them: 'Believe me, when you did it to one of the least of my brethren here, you did it to me."

In this Gospel passage, a whole new outlook on life was revealed to this Chinese girl. The same girl was thunderstruck when she heard the Gospel reading for the 12th Sunday after Pentecost. It is the parable of the Good Samaritan. She was so amazed that I had to ask: "Have you never even heard that before?" "No," she said, "never." Now she is taking a medical course at a university so that she can give practical help to the sick poor—for in them she now sees Christ in need.

The author assisting Bishop Valtorta at the blessing of the Catholic Center.

27

1948-1949: Two Critical Years

The Communist Party's Rise To Power

German sociologist Max Weber wrote: "What is rational from one point of view may very well be irrational from another." This statement certainly applies to the different ways different people regard the growth and final victory of the Communist Party during the years 1937 to 1951. Today, from the point of view of hundreds of millions of Chinese, the communist victory is an unparalleled triumph, while from the point of view of other hundreds of millions of freedom-loving Chinese, and of Western friends of China, the communist rise to power is regarded as the greatest tragedy in that nation's history.

Even though I will deal more extensively with the subject of communism in chapter 29, I cannot fail to give here a short resume of the political events in China from 1945 to 1950. These events completely destroyed my cherished plans of working in and for China and permanently altered the course of my life. The number of people whose lives have been altered by communism in China runs into the hundreds of millions and I am one of them. Looking at communism from the point of view of its victims, I cannot fail to regard it as the greatest catastrophe which ever befell the Chinese people.

By August 15, 1945, when the Japanese surrendered, the Communist Party had increased from forty thousand in 1937 to over one million and effectively controlled about one-third of China's territory with a population of ninety million people. Chiang Kai-shek, the legitimate president of China, could not tolerate such a state-within-a-state and started fighting the Communist Party and its armies. President Truman and

General George Marshall arranged a truce in the vain hope that they could bring the two parties to work together. Truman failed to realize that there cannot be any compromise with communism. Chiang Kai-shek, under pressure from Truman, reluctantly agreed to the truce. The communists eagerly accepted it because it served their purpose as they needed time to transport the vast supply of Japanese arms and ammunitions (donated by Russia) from North Manchuria to the China border.

When the truce was over, and the communists had fully armed their men, war flared again. The situation of the two contestants was uneven. The Kwomingtan, Chiang Kai-shek's Nationalist Party, had now been in power for twelve years, had lost its revolutionary fervor, was divided by cliques and weakened by corruption. On the contrary, the Communist Party was a young party, afire with revolutionary spirit, ruthless in its methods, always ready to eliminate dissenters by execution. Constant brainwashing and forced education of the liberated (subjugated) people was the major weapon in forcing them to submit to its rule. The communist army, called "The People's Liberation Army" (PLA), was strictly disciplined and controlled by the Party. For every three or four soldiers there was a political spy. On the contrary, the Nationalist army had a low morale, incompetent leadership, and was no match for the communists.

While we in Hong Kong were busy rebuilding a new life, preparing and planning for the future, civil war between communists and Nationalists broke out in earnest in China in the summer of 1946. It remained at the stage of guerrilla warfare through 1947. For us in Hong Kong it was far away, up in the north, and we were confident that Chiang would finally prevail and save China from the scourge of communism.

In the middle of 1948 the Nationalists' situation deteriorated and the communist army boldly moved to conquer the whole of China. The people were tired of war and of the Kwomingtan and many thought that anything would be better than what they had. They accepted communism passively, only to find out too late their dreadful mistake. Youth, always ready to accept revolutionary ideas, looked upon the Communist Party as the party of a new China, free from corruption, where justice would prevail. Nationalist soldiers, eager to go home and be through with the war, attracted by false communist promises, began to desert en masse by the hundreds of thousands. Only after their desertion did they come to realize their mistake: most of the officers were executed and the soldiers were considered a kind of second-class citizens.

That summer there was a disastrous two-month battle in the Nien area in the north. Over half a million Nationalist soldiers were besieged in a six-mile area by three hundred thousand men of the communist army. The tragic outcome was that about two hundred thousand Nationalists were killed, and the survivors surrendered on January 10, 1949. That was the beginning of the end. That same month Beijing and Tiangin surrendered. In April the communist army stormed across the Yangtze and occupied Shanghai, and in October reached Guangzhou in the south. Then the Chiang Kai-shek government fell and many of the Nationalist leaders fled to Taiwan. The "liberation" of China was completed. The suffering of the people began in earnest.

The China Missionary Bulletin

When Fr. Meyer and I opened the Catholic Center, we were thinking mostly of the needs of the Hong Kong Diocese. We never dreamed that only three years later Divine Providence would use the center for an international role. This role was publicly acknowledged by Cardinal Spellman of New York when, during one of his visits to the colony, he called the Catholic Center "A lighthouse of truth in the gathering darkness which surrounds us."

This international role came about in different ways, one of them being the publication of the *China Missionary Bulletin*. In 1948, as the communists extended their occupation of north China, people again began to escape from the Mao "paradise" to the safety of Hong Kong. Only ten years before, in 1937, the Japanese invasion had compelled people to escape. Now the communist "liberation" had the same effect. This time, however, Catholics and Catholic institutions felt especially threatened by the Red army because of the well-known anti-religious attitude of the communists. At the beginning of their conquest the communists used a policy of tolerance toward Catholic and Protestant missions, but as soon as they subjugated the whole country they threw out their mask and started a methodic persecution of all religions.

One of the first Catholic activities to move out of Shanghai was the *China Mission Bulletin*. Fr. Francis Le Grande of the Scheut Fathers, a truly apostolic soul and a dear friend of mine, had started publishing the magazine soon after the end of the war, with the blessing of Archbishop Riberi. It was a monthly publication of about one hundred and fifty pages each issue in English and French, and was the only Catholic cultural mission magazine in Asia. Its goal was to help missionaries and lay Catholics to become better aware of the growth of the Church in China, its needs and its problems, and to serve as an open forum for the discussion of mission methods, strategy and plans.

One day early in 1948 I received a wire from Fr. Le Grande asking me to take over the publication of the magazine and to produce it in Hong Kong because Shanghai was no longer safe. He had decided to remain behind the Bamboo Curtain and therefore needed someone else to continue the publication of the magazine. I wired back accepting the task and set up an office at the Catholic Center to begin publication of the magazine in Hong Kong. Fr. Leo Bourassa, a Canadian Jesuit working with Fr. Le Grande, came from Shanghai to take care of the French section of the magazine. Fr. Tom Bauer of Maryknoll was assigned to edit the English section. They were co-editors and I was the publisher. Both were wonderful men. Old, refined Fr. Leo was soft-spoken, calm and kindness personified. Fr. Tom was younger, energetic, strong-willed, a real executive.

In order to easily distinguish the Hong Kong publication from the previous one, we changed the title to *China Missionary Bulletin*. It was a great and stimulating venture of a truly missionary nature and the three of us worked together like brothers, in complete harmony. I was proud to add this new publication to our other activities in the publishing field. The new magazine, like its predecessor, continued to be very well received in mission circles all over the world and it grew in circulation. It was published until 1951, when religion in China had to go underground and Catholic missions were closed.

The Catholic Welfare Committee

Soon after the end of the war in 1945, Fr. Frederick MacGuire, short, lean and dynamic, was appointed executive director of the Catholic Welfare Committee in Shanghai for the distribution of relief supplies donated by American Catholics. In 1948, when the Liberation Army was approaching the city, he was ordered by the New York office to move out in order to continue relief work for the benefit of the still-unoccupied parts of China. Fr. MacGuire and I had become close friends during my visit to Shanghai in 1946, as we thought alike in many matters. He asked me for space at the Catholic Center to set up an office for his work. Partitioning a section of the lounge at the center, I arranged office space for him and provided him with secretarial help. Thus he was able to continue his relief work. Early in 1950, when the communists completed the occupation of China, his work came to an end and he was called to Washington, DC, where he organized the Foreign Missions Secretariat and became its first executive director.

Archbishop Riberi's Branch Office

On February 23, 1947, the Apostolic Internuncio (Ambassador) to China, His Excellency Antonio Riberi, paid an official visit to the Hong Kong Diocese. Solemnly received by a large number of dignitaries, clergy, laity and the band of St. Louis Industrial School of the Salesian Fathers, he proceeded to the cathedral, where he celebrated a Solemn Pontifical Mass. Later he paid an official visit to the Catholic Center, where we held a reception in his honor. He was deeply impressed by the work of the center. Two years later, when the communist army was marching on Nanjing, where he resided as the Vatican's Ambassador to China, he decided to remain at his place as most of the other diplomats did. However, knowing that by remaining behind the Bamboo Curtain he would be isolated from the rest of the world, he had to make provisions to continue to help the bishops and laity who remained in free China. Therefore he asked the Secretary of the Embassy, Ohio-born Msgr. Martin T. Gilligan, to go to Hong Kong and set up a temporary office there at the Catholic Center. I was very happy to be of help to him and I set aside another section of the lounge as an office for him.

Thus the center became also a small extension of the Vatican for the care of the missions in free China. Unfortunately this arrangement did not last long. By the end of 1949 the Peoples' Liberation Army had completed the "liberation" of China and this brought to an end the work of both Msgr. Gilligan and Fr. MacGuire, as well as of the activities of the Catholic Truth Society in mainland China.

The Growth And Decline Of The Catholic Truth Society

Until early in 1948, in spite of the looming threat of the communist occupation, our publishing activities grew at a furious pace. We recognized the handwriting on the wall and realized that there was not much time left for us to work. We wanted to send as much literature as possible into China before it was "liberated." The CTS had published several pamphlets condemning communism as an atheist organization bent on the destruction of religion, but when, at the beginning of 1949, we realized that the end was near, we changed tactics and limited ourselves to publications dealing strictly with religion.

The communist takeover happened just when the prospects for the future of our work had seemed brightest. In 1949 I met and became a friend of Mr. K. V. Li, who was General Assistant to the Chief Executive Officer of the Commercial Press. This great and famous firm, the largest publishing house in China, had weathered the Japanese war and had expanded to the whole of China again. Mr. Li was a new convert and was ready to use his knowledge and expertise to facilitate the publication and circulation of Christian books in order to give his fellow Chinese a fair chance to know the true nature of Christ's message. However, even before I could get a manuscript ready to be printed, the communists took over Shanghai and that was the end of our hopes.

The Bishop Returns From Europe

On Sunday, September 7, 1947, Bishop Valtorta returned to Hong Kong from Italy on a hydroplane of the British Overseas Airways, which had just begun service between Hong Kong and England. It was the first time that one of our missionaries traveled from Europe to Hong Kong by plane. Even though the trip took five full days, it seemed an extraordinary feat. It had taken me thirty-one days by ship from Venice to Hong Kong. Today it takes only sixteen hours by plane, but in those days long-distance commercial aviation was in its infancy.

A large delegation of Catholics met the bishop at the airport and a Chinese gentleman, Mr. Peter Shek, presented him with a brand-new Austin car as a token of gratitude on the part of the Hong Kong Catholics. For the first time the bishop of Hong Kong had a car and, as he did not yet have a new secretary, I became his official driver.

A public reception was held at the Catholic Center welcoming him back and the large hall was filled to capacity. The bishop was deeply moved by the warmth of the reception and spoke at length about his trip through the States and Europe. His health had greatly improved and he was eager to get back to work. He surely had plenty of it to do.

Only one year earlier, in 1946, when we celebrated the twentieth anniversary of his consecration as a bishop, the whole diocese was in bad shape after eight years of war. Now the Catholic institutions in the colony were springing back to new life and were flourishing. However, the part of the diocese on the China mainland was still in a shambles. Most of our missionaries had been compelled by the war to leave their mission districts, and most of the churches, chapels, schools, etc., had been pillaged or destroyed. Almost every mission house had to be rebuilt. Guerrilla warfare between Nationalist and communist troops continued to increase in frequency and viciousness. At the reception the bishop announced that thanks to the generosity of American and European Catholics he had brought back some funds and that the work of reconstructing the churches on the China mainland would start soon. It was a beautiful dream that never came true. Just a little over one year later the communists took over and all we had rebuilt was confiscated and used for the benefit of the Communist Party.

The Growth Of Missionary Work

The coming of Miss Tully to the center brought me not only much needed help in the editing of the *Sunday Examiner* but it also offered a great opportunity to expand our many activities.

We soon began to formulate plans to develop the work of the lay apostolate in China. This work had to be done by the Chinese themselves according to their culture and mentality. Therefore, foreign members of the Grail could only train Chinese workers, set an example of Christian living and then let them take over. The Grail intended to use their presence in Hong Kong as a springboard for more direct lay missionary work in China proper. For this purpose Grailville offered us several one-year scholarships for Chinese girls to go to the Grailville College in Loveland to be trained in the principles of spiritual life and lay apostolate. The plan, of course, was that these Chinese Grail-trained girls would form the nucleus of the movement and in turn would train others in China. The presentation of Christ's message to the whole of China required looking far beyond the narrow limits of the British colony to the entire Chinese territory. Therefore, besides sending Chinese girls to Grailville, we also needed more Grail members from the States and Australia to come to Hong Kong to learn the Chinese language and way of life. Later these Grail members, with the Chinese girls trained at Grailville, would go to the China mainland, and especially to Chinese universities, to get degrees in order to recruit more lay apostles among the university professors and graduates. We felt that because the cultured classes could set a more influential example in Chinese society, we had to aim at them as our first target.

Little did we know that all of these elaborate plans were simply to go up in smoke—thanks to Mao Zedong.

My First Visit To The USA

August 21, 1948, was going to be the seventeenth anniversary of my departure from Italy and my farewell to my parents. Both they and I were obviously eager to see each other again. After the bishop returned from Italy, it was time for me to take a few months off to see my family. The work at the center was proceeding smoothly and Bishop Valtorta was glad to let me go. On his advice, I decided to go to Europe via the USA in order to visit the Grail in Loveland as well as the Grail houses in England and Holland for the purpose of formulating plans for the lay missionary work in China.

I sailed from Hong Kong early in March and, for economic reasons, I traveled on a cargo ship that carried only twelve passengers. It took eighteen days to sail from Hong Kong to San Diego, California. We traveled under a constantly overcast sky without ever sighting land. I was alone practically all the time because the other eleven passengers slept most of the day and danced most of the night. It was a miserable trip and I spent most of the time locked up in my cabin writing letters on my portable typewriter.

As soon as I set foot on US soil in San Diego, I fell in love with this great country. It really was love at first sight! After a short visit to Maryknoll in Los Angeles and San Francisco, I traveled by train to Santa Fe, New Mexico, to see my old friend Fr. Don Hessler of Maryknoll, who was there recuperating from an illness. He, too, was an admirer of the Grail and still is a great believer in the lay apostolate. We had long and serious conversations on this subject. Through him I met Archbishop Edwin V. Byrne of Santa Fe, one of the great American missionaries. It was this chance encounter with Archbishop Byrne that enabled me several years later to secure a mission district in his diocese for PIME.

From New Mexico I hurried on to Loveland. The Grailville of those days simply defies description. Even if I wrote a whole book about it, I still could not do it justice. The external appearances were simple enough: a two-story, large, rambling country house in the midst of lush, green meadows and fields, typical of the fertile Ohio valley, a huge barn and other smaller buildings scattered nearby constituted the Grailville College campus. However, the people, the spirit, the lifestyle were something unique. I will not even attempt to describe it because it was something so unusual, so refreshing, so brimming with life, so different from any other place that it could not be appreciated unless one had seen it.

The US leader of the Grail then was Dr. Lidwyne Van Kerbergen, a graduate of the Nimegen University and a member of the early nucleus of the Grail, trained by Fr. Van Ginneken himself. Her vision, her intense spiritual life, her knowledge of spiritual things and her ability to handle young women were unique. The staff was formed by a group of the most intelligent, intensely religious and yet broad-minded people I have ever known in my life. Most of them had university degrees. There was nothing pietistic about them, only solid Christianity lived 100% daily.

The student body changed yearly and it was made up of well-educated young women from all over the States who came to Grailville in search of a full and true Christian way of life that would give meaning and purpose to their existence.

Half a dozen or so families, all Grail-trained members, lived in close proximity to the college. They had fully embraced the Grail's ideals and strived to forge a life style in full accordance with the Gospel's principle of Christian living. It would take far too long to list even the names of the Grail staff and of the families. We all became close friends and their example greatly inspired me and influenced my life. Three years later, when I returned to work in the States, they were very instrumental in helping me develop PIME in this country.

At Grailville I had extensive conversations with the staff about the concept of developing the training and work of lay missionaries. This led me to write an article on this subject, which was published in America magazine in the fall of 1948.

In collaboration with the Grailville staff, we prepared a program for a special one-year training course for lay missionaries, to start the following October. I promised I would return to Grailville on my way back to Hong Kong to inaugurate this course.

From Loveland I went to La Grange, Illinois, to meet Miss Tully's parents. I was fascinated by them—tall, lean, almost ascetic-looking, Mr. Tully was a retired banker, the founder of the St. Thomas More Catholic Books Association and a member of the Board of Trustees of Notre Dame University. A soft-spoken, highly intelligent man, he was also a brilliant executive. He had a rare ability to analyze situations and to find solutions. Mrs. Tully was a delightful lady, courteous, compassionate, widely read. She could talk intelligently about almost any subject.

I also paid a visit to Mr. Jim Doyle in Milwaukee, Wisconsin. He had met Bishop Valtorta in 1946 during a retreat at the Divine Word Provincial House in Techny, Illinois, and had become an ardent fan of the venerable missionary bishop from Hong Kong. Bishop Valtorta asked me to pay him a visit, which was the beginning of a lifelong friendship.

Finally, after a visit to the Grail in Brooklyn, I sailed on the SS *Mauretania* to Ireland. I had discovered Ireland through my numerous Irish friends in Hong Kong and, having read so many books about that country, I craved to see it. I landed in Cobh and traveled on a small train to Dublin, where old Mrs. Pat Costello, of the Hong Kong war days, was my hostess. I found Ireland one of the most charming and pleasant countries in the world.

After crossing to Britain by ferry, I traveled to London by train. Food was still rationed then and I shortened my visit there, but even though I found England quite different from Ireland, I enjoyed its charm.

After a brief visit to the Grail house in London I hurried to Amsterdam to visit the international headquarters of the Grail. Miss Rachel Donders, the International President, came to meet me at the boat and drove me to their headquarters, where I spent a couple of the most remarkable days of my life in almost continuous meetings about the problems of the lay apostolate, formation and support of lay missionaries. From there at last I took a train to Italy via Paris.

I Rediscover My Family

Since my departure from Italy, my dad had always dreamed of coming to meet me at whatever Italian port or frontier railroad station I would arrive on my first return to Italy. Coming from France, the frontier station was Bardonecchia on the French-Italian border. The night previous to my arrival in Italy, as the train traveled through France, I could hardly sleep because of excitement. When daylight finally came, we were still on French soil and the day was rainy and gloomy. As we approached the Italian frontier the train entered the long tunnel under the Alpine Simplon pass and half an hour later we emerged on the Italian side of the Alps: the most marvelous sunshine and the bluest sky I had seen in seventeen years welcomed my first return home.

Slowly the train descended from the height of the Alpine pass to the valley below and at 9:00, perfectly on time, we pulled into Bardonecchia. As the train came to a stop I saw all my family lined up on the platform, eagerness and anticipation showing in their eyes. With no difficulty I recognized my aging parents and I felt an indescribable thrill when I was at last in their arms. But at first I did not recognize my sister and my brothers, whom I had left when they were very young. I found them now very grown up, married and veterans of many years of war on the different Italian fronts.

I will not take space here to describe this meeting with my father and mother as these matters of the heart defy description. It will suffice to say that we soon got into our car and started on our five-hundred-mile trip through north and central Italy to Perugia, where we arrived late that same evening.

During that three-month vacation, I spent most of the time with my family, visiting relatives scattered all over Italy, getting acquainted with them again and meeting with new family arrivals. It was the first time in seventeen years that I experienced the warmth of family life and I really enjoyed it as I discovered that blood really is thicker than water.

But it wasn't all fun. I did some work, too, renewing my contacts with PIME and making useful connections for my work in Hong Kong. I visited Dr. John C. H. Wu several times at the Chinese Embassy to the Vatican and I enjoyed seeing the high esteem in which he was held by Church dignitaries.

The three-month vacation soon came to an end and I had to bid farewell to my family. This parting was especially painful because my father was then seventy-five years old and definitely in failing health. I had the feeling that that was the last time we would see each other. He passed away only three months later on January 17, 1949, of a stroke. He was very proud of having a priest son and he enjoyed talking with me about theology and the modern trends of the Church. He especially felt the full impact of my absence because out of the eighteen years of my priesthood I had actually spent no more than a few weeks with him. But, as usual, he faced the cross bravely and did not say a word to keep me even one day longer. My mother naturally again shed many tears but she, too, was proud to see me dedicated to my work.

28

The Work Continues To Expand

The Legion Of Mary

"Maestrini," Bishop Valtorta said one morning in 1948 after my return from Europe, "Father Aidan McGrath[1] is coming to Hong Kong to organize the Legion of Mary. I told him that you would be glad to let him use the Catholic Center as his headquarters and that you will help him. The Legion of Mary could really be a terrific help in Hong Kong and I would like to see it established in every parish. I know, you scoundrel, you love the Blessed Virgin and I count on you to help Father McGrath do a great job here."

Needless to say, I was delighted with this new assignment because I believed in the Legion of Mary as a powerful instrument for spiritual progress. For the benefit of those who are not familiar with the Legion of Mary, I will introduce it here briefly.

The Legion of Mary is an association of lay Catholics founded in Dublin in 1921 for the spiritual growth of its members and the general intensification of Catholic life. It achieves these goals through prayer and social work according to the directives of the local bishop. Using the terminology of the Roman Legions, it comprises a presidium, which is the smallest single unit or cell; a curia, namely, a group of several presidia in a district; and a senate, which is the governing body in a country. From Dublin, Ireland, the Legion spread quickly throughout the world.[2] In 1949 it had already been organized all over Catholic Europe, Africa, and Australia. In China, Fr. McGrath had traveled through most of the country and had established hundreds of presidia. Time was of the essence because communism was advancing and Fr. McGrath spared no effort to establish the Legion wherever possible before the communists took over.

When Fr. McGrath arrived in Hong Kong, I showed him around the city, put him in touch with many of our pastors and organizations and gave him publicity in *The Sunday Examiner*. Thanks to the collaboration of our PIME priests, of the Irish Jesuits and of the Maryknoll Fathers, in a few weeks he established over fifteen presidia. The bishop himself had one of his own at the cathedral.

At the center we organized our own presidium, composed of most of the members of the staff, and it did great work. One of the characteristics of the Legion is that all the members must dedicate at least two hours a week to the spiritual work of the Legion and must give a detailed report of their activities at the weekly meetings. Our presidium, among other activities, chose to visit the Tung-wah Chinese Hospital in the central district of Hong Kong. It was a hospital for the poor and possessed all the worst characteristics that go hand in hand with poverty and sickness. I must confess that every time I had to go there to baptize someone or to hear confessions I had to overcome a real repugnance to enter the place because the sights of human misery were heartbreaking. Suffice it to say that it was terribly overcrowded and for lack of space lots of patients were lying even beneath other beds and in the space between beds. In spite of the efforts of the British-trained medical staff to run a clean hospital, the smell was unbearable. But God's love had His chosen souls even in that place of suffering.

While visiting the Tung-wah Hospital, the young ladies of our presidium met a woman who was ill with tuberculosis. Her name was A-ma. She was slightly built, forty-ish, an ex-prostitute; both of her legs had been amputated and she had no family whatsoever. At first she welcomed the weekly visits of the ladies from our presidium just to enjoy conversation; then she began to take an interest in religion, and finally she asked for baptism. Even before she was baptized, with the typical zeal of a new convert, she set about converting others and teaching religion on her own to those who wanted to be baptized. We affectionately called her our "assistant chaplain."

It was a pathetic but inspiring sight to see diminutive A-ma using her arms to crawl down from her bed to the floor, then propelling herself by her arms on the not-too-clean floor, moving around the beds from one end of the fifty-bed ward to the other. When she reached the patient she had to teach, she would again pull herself up with her arms on to the bed of the patient and sit there teaching religion, comforting and inspiring poor people more miserable than herself. For several months she was the "apostle" of that ward and helped more sick people to accept the Faith than any other person I have known. I told the bishop about her work and he was so moved that he went to the hospital to personally give her confirmation. Before we could manage to have artificial legs made for her, she died. I still remember her as one of the most beautiful souls I have ever known.

Persecution Of The Legion

In the history of the religious persecution of Catholics in China, the Legion of Mary has one of the most glorious records of endurance and heroism. The communists hated the very name of the Legion and were particularly vehement toward its members. In their pathetic ignorance of anything religious and, worse still, with their biased minds closed to any kind of religious truth they saw a threat in the very name of the Legion and accused it of the worst reactionary activities. They made it a crime just to belong to it. They hated it with a passion without ever realizing how stupid and unfounded their hatred was. If only they had taken the time to read the Legion's handbook, which had been translated into excellent Chinese, they would have understood that, in spite of its name, it was an organization comprising the most pious and charitable people in the world. Yet they attacked it as persecutors have always attacked Christians from the Roman days to our time.

Miss Rose Yeung,[4] about whom I wrote in chapter 10, was but one of the tens of thousands of victims of communist hatred of the Legion. I heard from fellow missionaries and read in mission magazines of that time about hundreds of examples of heroic deaths of members of the Legion, both young and old, who suffered imprisonment, death and torture rather than renounce it.

The Diplomacy Of Love

When I was in Rome in the summer of 1948 I saw Dr. John Wu several times at the villa of the Chinese Embassy to the Vatican. As a true diplomat, he did not speak much about his work but I heard a lot about it from my old acquaintances among the Roman clergy. He was very much in demand for lectures about his conversion to the Faith and about Chinese culture.

Ambassador Wu was a sensation in the Vatican diplomatic circles. The speech he delivered on the occasion of the presentation of his credentials to Pope Pius XII was published in the official organ of the Vatican, *Osservatore Romano*, on February 17-18, 1947, and was very well received by Vatican officials and by the public. It was an original speech, a speech such as only an Oriental could give, a speech different from the routine, matter-of-fact diplomatic verbiage of the career diplomats, a speech that beautifully merged Christian and Oriental cultures. I quote here some of its salient points:

"It is a great honor for me to come to this 'mountain of myrrh and hill of frankincense' to present to Your Holiness the credential letter, wherewith I am charged by His Excellency, the President of the Republic of China, to represent the Chinese Government at the Holy See. . . .

"China, as a nation, has lived long enough to learn by experience that in the long run it is Spirit, not Matter, that triumphs; Right, not Might, that prevails. This historical insight has taught China in many a national crisis to hope against hope; it is the secret spring that keeps China perennially young in outlook and spirit in spite of her age. And it is thanks to this same historical insight that her last victory has not inflated her with pride and self-complacency, but has, on the contrary, made her more conscious than ever of her dependence upon the Providence of God, and more eager than ever to rebuild her war-torn house upon the rock of love and justice . . .

"Before I come to a conclusion, I cannot help adding a few words on behalf of my country in appreciation of what the Holy Catholic Church has done for our people. His Excellency President Chiang, in his book on 'The Destiny of China,' has referred to the great contribution that Father Matteo Ricci, Ven. Paul Hsu, and their contemporaries made to the scientific education of China. The missionaries, during all these centuries, have been like zephyrs carrying with them the perfumes from the garden of Christ. The merits of those loyal soldiers of Christ can be told only in Heaven. . . .

"Chinese people remember what great services the native Catholics and the Missionaries rendered to the nation during the war. We are convinced that during the period of our national reconstruction, the Catholics will continue to give their best contributions for, as Your Holiness has on some occasions observed, a good Catholic must be a good citizen. It is my sincere hope that there will soon be a great spiritual renaissance in our country, and the Church in China will be a flourishing garden 'full of pleasant fruits, new and old.'"

The presence in Rome of an Oriental diplomat with a family of thirteen children was also a sensation. Msgr. Montini, then Acting Secretary of State, who later became Pope Paul VI, on his own initiative decided to introduce the entire family to the Holy Father and to have their photo taken with him. When Dr. Wu realized that this was not a normal procedure he suggested cancelling the plan in order not to establish a precedent. But Msgr. Montini replied with humor, "A diplomat must have at least thirteen children before he can cite the present case as a precedent." The photograph turned out to be quite unique because it was the first time in history that a pope was photographed while sitting with a private family.

In his 364-page biography, Dr. Wu dedicated only 8 pages to his work as a Vatican diplomat. He entitled the story of his sojourn in Rome "The Diplomacy of Love." This fully confirms my impression of him in Rome. He certainly was not a conventional diplomat, but a man in love with Christ and His Church and he never hesitated to go beyond the rules and customs of the centuries-old diplomacy of the Vatican to manifest his love for the Church, for China, for the Holy Father personally.

I cannot offer an in-depth study of the work of John Wu as the first Chinese Ambassador to the Vatican. However, just for the sake of completing this story I will mention briefly how it all ended.

The End Of A Diplomat

At the beginning of 1949 the war against the communists turned sour for the Chiang government. Chiang Kai-shek, under an avalanche of criticism, at the lowest ebb in his popularity and abandoned by the United States, withdrew temporarily from the government and went to live in semi-retirement near Ningpo. He appointed Dr. Sun Fo as Prime Minister. Dr. Sun Fo, eager to form a cabinet, wired Dr. Wu in Rome and asked him to return immediately for a consultation. When they finally met in Nanjing, Sun Fo asked Wu to join his cabinet and gave him an option between the Ministries of Education and Justice. Dr. Wu chose Justice. However, before Dr. Sun Fo could announce his cabinet, his government fell and John Wu returned to Rome, arriving there on April 20 directly from Hong Kong. After his return to Rome, Dr. Wu realized that the Nationalist government of Chiang Kai-shek was on the verge of collapse, resigned from the ambassadorship, and accepted the offer of a position as Visiting Professor of Chinese Philosophy at the University of Hawaii for 1949-1950.

Dr. Wu's Translation Of The New Testament

One day in April 1949 when he stopped in Hong Kong on his way back to Rome, Dr. Wu suddenly appeared at my office at the center carrying a huge bundle wrapped in Chinese cloth. After a warm exchange of greetings, pointing to the bundle he said, "Father Nicholas, this bundle contains all my manuscripts of the complete translation of the New Testament in modern literary Chinese. I had promised to give it to the Commercial Press in Shanghai but under the present circumstances it is not prudent to do so. I am entrusting it to you. Please have it published by the Catholic Truth Society."

Under normal circumstances I would have been almost insane with joy at being chosen by such a scholar as Dr. Wu to publish the most important religious book of his life. On the contrary, on that day in April we both almost wept with sorrow. Our old dream of publishing religious books through the largest and most influential publishing house in China to present Christianity to the Chinese masses had come to a sorrowful end. In fact, only a few weeks later, the Commercial Press became a communist publishing house and the whole of China was engulfed by communism.

A couple of days after John's visit, Fr. John Chen and I rushed to a Chinese printing press and made arrangements for the publication of Dr. Wu's work. It had taken him more than eight years to complete it. He had worked on it from the days of poverty and fear in the pigsty of Guilin to the good days of his life as ambassador in Rome. Scores of people had helped him to make it the literary masterpiece it is. The list included President Chiang Kai-shek, Madame Chiang, John's illiterate wife and numerous scholars from the East and West. As I wrote in another chapter, part of this manuscript was the only thing his family saved when they escaped from Guilin. John continued his work in the hot and cold days in Chungking, later in his beautiful home in Shanghai, and finally at the embassy in Rome. It was a translation done neither for money nor for glory. It was done for love—love of the Gospel and love of China. It represented the very best of Chinese literature placed at the service of the Gospel. However, Divine Providence had decreed that when John Wu's gift to China was ready to be presented, China, sealed and isolated behind the Bamboo Curtain, could no longer receive it..

The translation was printed by the end of 1949 just as the communists took over. Early in 1950 I proudly advertised in the *China Missionary Bulletin*:

"THE NEW TESTAMENT (In Chinese Literary Style) by Dr. JOHN C. H. WU, Chinese Minister to the Holy See, with congratulatory letters by His Holiness Pius XII and by His Eminence Cardinal Fumasoni Biondi."

For more details about the history of this translation, please read Dr. Wu's autobiography, chapter 19, entitled "A Chinese Tunic for Christ." The ways of Divine Providence are not the ways of man. This translation of the New Testament, a literary masterpiece, was John's last religious book in Chinese. During the remaining thirty-six years of his life he published many books in English but not one in Chinese. For me, as a publisher, it was also my last gift to China. For both of us—John, the Christian Chinese scholar and writer, and me, the foreign missionary and his publisher—it was a symbol of our love and dedication: the gift of the Word of God to the largest nation on earth, in the best literary style of its own language.

An Unfulfilled Dream

As I have mentioned in several chapters in this book, the evangelization of the intelligentsia was a cherished dream I shared with John Wu, Francis Yeh and many others. The Sino-Japanese war, the appointment of Dr. Wu to the Vatican, and the untimely death of Francis Yeh had all contributed to placing this ambitious plan on the back burner. However, early in 1950, when the exodus of Chinese refugees began, I realized that many Catholic intellectuals, especially from the staffs of our Catholic universities, were among them. It dawned on me then that in the midst of the catastrophe there was a ray of hope. Before the war, as I wrote in chapter 15, John, Francis, Alice and I had initiated the publication of a series of Christian classics by the Commercial Press for the Chinese general public. Now when Dr. Wu passed through Hong Kong in April 1949, we discussed the situation together and formulated a plan. We visualized a team of scholars from East and West, working together for the purpose of studying Chinese culture and its classic books and discovering in them that seed of truth the Holy Spirit has implanted in every culture and religion. In plain words, we visualized an "Institute of Chinese-Christian Studies" run by Chinese scholars and Catholic theologians. The Institute would be totally dedicated to presenting Christ's teachings to China as a logical development and fulfillment of the very best in the Confucian and Taoist traditions. It was no longer a mere matter of "baptizing" the Chinese classics but of developing a total concept of Christian life embracing both the Gospel and Chinese culture, rejecting what was obviously superstitious or spurious in it, while retaining and developing whatever was true and noble and great.

The establishment of such an institute would provide a living for Chinese Catholic scholars who had been compelled to leave China. In return they would use their talents to prepare a return of the Church to China and the beginning of a real work of evangelization of their country. We had the human resources capable of doing the work. All we needed was an influential sponsor and the funds to begin the work.

I thought that if we could secure the support of the Congregation for the Evangelization of Peoples in Rome we would have no difficulty in raising funds. When the opportunity came, in 1950, for me to go to Rome to attend the International Convention of the Catholic Press (as I will explain in the next chapter) I took that opportunity to personally submit my plan to Archbishop Celso Constantini, a former Apostolic Delegate to China and then Secretary of the Congregation for the Evangelization of Peoples.

On the day designated for the audience with the archbishop I hurried to the centuries-old papal palace of "Propaganda Fide" in the Spanish Square in Rome. As I walked up the magnificent stairs, trodden by many great saints and famous missionaries, I was excited thinking of the tremendous opportunity Divine Providence was offering the Church in China. I dreamed that good Archbishop Constantini would gladly sponsor our plan and I would return to Hong Kong a happy man to begin the new institute of Chinese Christian Studies.

A few moments later, as I sat on a red velvet chair opposite the archbishop, I spoke at length and with my usual enthusiasm about the plan. Constantini listened to me attentively but without showing any reaction. At last, when I finished, he joined his hands in front of his chest and with the tips of his fingers barely touching his lips, and without as much as looking at me, said in a tone of pitiful compassion, "Maestrini, you understand nothing about Rome. Rome never takes any initiative. You do it. If you succeed we will take over your work; if you fail we will chastise you. Goodbye." He rose as a definite sign that the audience was over and that he wanted no part of our plan.

I returned to Hong Kong a humiliated and frustrated man, and to this day I believe that the Church missed a wonderful opportunity, but I also believe that that was the Will of God at the moment and that Divine Providence had other ways and means, besides my plans, to bring China to Christ when the time is right.

The Consecration Of Bishop Lawrence Bianchi

In the morning of Sunday, October 9, 1949, a rare event took place at the cathedral in Hong Kong: a long procession of Chinese seminarians in their white surplices, followed by scores of Chinese and foreign priests in their priestly robes, a cardinal in his magnificent purple robe and several bishops in their ritual apparel, moving slowly from the mission house to the church's entrance. When the cardinal and the bishops entered the church, enthusiastic applause by the large crowd greeted them as they moved slowly along the aisle. After everyone was seated, only two lonely figures remained standing at the main altar under the dome: Bishop Henry Valtorta in his pontifical robes and by his side a humble-looking, middle-aged priest, of medium height, with a beardless face and black-rimmed spectacles: Fr. Lawrence Bianchi, soon to be consecrated Auxiliary Bishop of Hong Kong.[6]

The complex, two-hour ritual of consecration proceeded smoothly under the able direction of Cardinal Tien's secretary as Master of Ceremonies while another priest and I assisted. The new bishop spoke very briefly, limiting himself to emphasizing the program of his future work: "I came to serve, not to be served" (Mt. 20, 28). When the ceremony concluded and the new bishop emerged from the church door, he was greeted with thunderous applause by an immense crowd, which had occupied every square inch of available space in the vast compound to greet him.

A large group of poorly dressed Chinese in the midst of the crowd distinguished itself for its very enthusiastic and prolonged applause: it was the group of Catholics (and many non-Catholics, too) from the Haifeng district, where the new bishop had worked for twenty-six years, since his arrival in China in 1923. They had traveled two hundred miles, some by boat, some even on foot, for the privilege of seeing their beloved priest consecrated a bishop. Poor as they were, they brought him as a gift a brand-new, all-gold pectoral cross.

In the midst of the splendor and magnificence of the consecration rite and the rejoicing of the people, there was something poignant and saddening. First of all, Bishop Valtorta's health was failing badly and this is why he had asked, and Rome had granted his wish, to have an auxiliary bishop with the right of succession. Even though we welcomed the new bishop with all our love and enthusiasm, still we could see with our eyes that Bishop Valtorta's end was not far away. Secondly, only nine days before, on October 1, Mao Zedong had officially proclaimed from

Tiananmen Square in Beijing the new Popular Democratic (communist) Republic of China, sealing that great nation behind the Bamboo Curtain. The communist army was marching on nearby Guangdong and again the Hong Kong Diocese was on the verge of being cut off from the mainland.

Bishop Bianchi did not remain long in Hong Kong after his consecration. On October 15 the communist troops invaded the Haifeng area and two days later, as soon as he could find a junk, he left for Haifeng, together with three other missionaries from that district, defying the communist ban on traveling. They managed to evade communist surveillance but they risked losing their lives because of a violent storm. The trip, which under ordinary circumstances took from ten to twelve hours, took them eight full days to complete because of the bad storm, which broke the masts and rudder of the junk, leaving the stranded passengers without water and food.

They made land at last and, on foot, arrived at their residence at midnight. They knocked on the door but the Chinese priest refused to open it, thinking they were bandits. When he finally recognized their voices, in utter amazement he exclaimed: "How come you are here? Aren't you dead? For eight days we had no news of you, and so we all presumed you had provided a good meal for the fish!"

Bishop Bianchi's crest was especially designed: it represented a Chinese sailing junk and one star with the simple Latin motto "Respice stellam": look at the star! It was truly symbolic of the perilous life he led in his mission district. The Divine Star, which had saved him from communist execution twenty-two years before, had now guided him to safety again through that risky journey.

Bishop Bianchi had anticipated that the communists would continue their policy of tolerance toward religion and that he might take care of the area of the Hong Kong diocese on the mainland. But his hopes were soon shattered. The communists began to implement their policy of repression and he and the other missionaries were soon placed under house arrest, unable to perform their ministry.

When Bishop Valtorta died on September 3, 1951, petitions were sent to the communist authorities to release Bishop Bianchi so that he could return to Hong Kong and take over the diocese, but in vain. It was only on October 17, 1952, that he was unexpectedly brought to trial and "as a person unworthy of living in China" quickly condemned to "immediate expulsion in perpetuity from popular [Red] China." The next morning, dressed as a peasant in tattered clothes, without any money, he was placed on a train and brought to Shenzhen on the Chinese side of the Hong Kong border. He was kept there more than three hours without food or drink. At dusk, when all the other passengers had gone, he was pushed across the bridge to freedom and into the arms of a British police officer.

A few hours later he was in Hong Kong singing the "Te Deum" hymn of thanksgiving at the cathedral with an immense crowd, which had suddenly gathered there to welcome him.

Notes

1. Fr. Aidan McGrath is a missionary of the Irish St. Columban Missionary Society. He was assigned to China as a missionary and in 1946 he was officially commissioned by Archbishop A. Riberi to organize the Legion of Mary in that country.

2. The Legion of Mary is "an association of lay Catholics founded in Dublin, Ireland (1921), for the spiritual advancement and the general intensification of Catholic life. On September 7, 1921, a small group of lay people, stimulated by an awareness of the Christian vocation to be witnesses and urged on by the writings of the popes, met with their parish priest in St. Nicholas of Myra parish, Dublin, to discover some practical means of translating their discussions on the doctrine of the Mystical Body of Christ and the writings of St. Louis Marie Grignon de Montfort" into concrete action in the service of their fellow men. The Legion demands high standards of Christian life; the method employed consists of prayer and active work in the apostolate. Consequently, the two most fundamental requirements for membership are, first, attendance at the weekly meetings, where the Legion prayers, spiritual readings, and guidance by the spiritual director form the member, and, second, the performance of a substantial amount (two hours minimum) of assigned apostolic work each week. Discipline, very much a part of the ideal of membership, is measured by the individual's adherence to the system; in addition, each member has a personal responsibility to recruit new members, both active and auxiliary.

"Despite some criticism of the detailed and inflexible rules of membership and other aspects of Legion organization, the Association has received high praises from many sources, including several Popes, Archbishops and Bishops" (summarized from the *New Catholic American Encyclopedia*.)

3. The Legion's Manual and Handbook, which contains detailed information about the Legion's organization and work, was translated not only into Chinese but into 25 languages and 125 dialects all over the world.

4. The Legion in Canton was founded by Fr. A. McGrath and later developed by Fr. Bernard F. Meyer, MM, who went to work in Canton after establishing the St. Nicholas' Club in Hong Kong. When the communists took over Canton there were eleven presidia working in the city. Fr. D. Donnelly, SJ, in an article about the Legion in Canton, which appeared in the *China Missionary Bulletin*, wrote: "From the very beginning [of the foundation in Canton] the Legionaires showed themselves possessed of great zeal and enthusiasm and the growth of the Legion in Canton has "followed very closely the growth of this splendid body in other cities. The works undertaken include: visiting lukewarm Catholics in their homes; visiting the parents of the children, pagan and Catholics, in our Catholic schools; teaching Catechism in preparation for Baptism and Confirmation; visiting hospitals; visiting the Municipal Cripples' Home; selling Catholic papers and devotional objects at the Church door."

5. Bishop Lawrence Bianchi was born on April 1, 1899, near Brescia in Northern Italy. On November 4, 1920, he entered the PIME Theological Seminary in Milan, was ordained a priest in 1922 and left for Hong Kong on July 29, 1923. Assigned to the Haifeng mission, he witnessed the first rising of communism and was saved by a miracle (see chapter 12).

He assumed the government of the Diocese of Hong Kong on October 17, 1952, and after seventeen years as a bishop he resigned and retired to Italy in 1969. He died there on February 13, 1983.

6. The details of his liberation are quite interesting. He was soon taken to the police office for questioning. When he said, "I am the Bishop of Hong Kong," the policemen laughed, but realizing that he was a missionary, an officer immediately phoned our Fr. A. Poletti to come to identify him as they used to do with all expelled missionaries.

Fr. Thomas F. Ryan continued: "No more was required. The motorcycle was on the road in an instant, and Fr. Poletti's beard waved in the wind as he flew along the road to Lowu. There he found that it was indeed the bishop. The police with their usual courtesy had brought him to a nearby restaurant for some refreshment while they were waiting for the priest. The next stage of the journey was made on the back of the motorcycle, and at Taipo Fr. Poletti and the bishop caught the 8:00

evening train to Kowloon. It was October 17, three years to the day since Bishop Bianchi had left Hong Kong after his consecration."

When the bishop and Poletti arrived at Kowloon at about 9:00 P.M. a large crowd of priests and lay people had already gathered to greet him and they accompanied him as if in a triumphal march across the harbor and up to the cathedral where a solemn "Te Deum" of thanksgiving was sung.

The author (left) and a sickly Bishop Valtorta in 1950.

29

My Last Years In Hong Kong

The House Of Joy

As a result of my visits to the Grail in the USA and Holland and of our plans for work in China, more Grail members, in addition to Miss Tully, were sent to Hong Kong.

First to arrive, in April 1948, was Miss Veronica Forbes. She had different characteristics from Miss Tully. While the latter was more the "Mary" type, Miss Forbes was the "Martha" type. Tall and sturdy, physically very robust, she could tackle any kind of work. Her Grail training had taught her to willingly help in any need, whether it be moving furniture around, writing an article for a paper, or giving spiritual counseling. Endowed with a great love for China and the Chinese, she had no difficulty in adapting to the life style of the center's staff. Her coming was providential because unfortunately Miss Tully's health was deteriorating and she needed help.

The Australian Grail also decided to take an active part in the lay missionary apostolate in China and assigned Miss Elizabeth Reid to come to Hong Kong. She arrived in December 1948. Almost six feet tall, with reddish hair, freckled face, and smiling eyes, Elizabeth looked like the typical Irish lass, full of life, bubbling with energy. A trained journalist, an excellent speaker, and also a one-hundred-percent Grail-trained lady, she was a tremendous asset to the Catholic Center and did great work for the Church in Hong Kong.

With the arrival of Miss Reid, there were three Grail members in Hong Kong and it was no longer practical for them to board separately

with Chinese families. We needed a house so we decided to build one.
The bishop placed at our disposal a piece of land located about ten miles
out of town on a sparsely populated hill, with a spectacular view of the
ocean. Miss Tully prepared the basic design. It was an extremely modest
house of rectangular shape, about thirty feet long and fifteen feet wide,
divided into three sections: a bedroom at each end and a room in the
middle, which served as a dining room and living room. Toilets and
kitchen facilities were outside. Built along very economic lines, it cost
us only $2,000 US, which was all we could afford.

It was the type of house usually occupied by poor Chinese families
and not much better than the house of our Lord at Nazareth, so we called
it "The House of Joy." Total lack of any luxury did not prevent the
young women from being happy because they came there to learn
spiritual values, not to seek human comforts. The house soon became a
center of spiritual activities. For periods of time Chinese girls lived there
with Grail members to learn more about the life of the spirit. Prospective
converts were instructed, troubled girls were counseled, and Christian
doctrine was presented first by example and then by words.

The second phase of our program for lay missionary work in China
required Chinese girls trained by the Grail. Grailville College in Loveland, Ohio, offered us scholarships for Chinese girls to be trained there.
From among the several applicants we selected three girls from the St.
Joan of Arc Association and they went there for one year. One of them
was Miss Rose Yeung, who later spent over twenty years in Chinese
prisons.

In the meantime, Miss Tully's health kept deteriorating. It was a
typical case of complete burnout, due to her intense work and poor
nourishment. She became totally exhausted and on the advice of her
doctor she returned to the States in February 1950. It took her a couple of
years to recuperate. Another Grail member, Miss Nan Johns from
Australia, arrived late that year to replace her.

Mao Zedong And The Catholic Truth Society

The year 1949 brought a great change in the work of the center. The
publishing activities of the Catholic Truth Society began to decrease
while the work of assisting refugees increased beyond measure. With the
communists occupying north China and the communist army invading
the south, there was no longer much of a market for Catholic books.
Postal communications with communist-controlled areas were disrupted

again as had happened during the Japanese invasion. Orders for books became fewer and fewer.

Early in 1950 Mao "honored" the Catholic Truth Society with a special decree forbidding people in liberated China to own or to read books published by the Catholic Truth Society. I had to give up.

A Chinese refugee told me about the following episode. Unfortunately, at that time I made no record of the place or names, so I will report it here simply as it was told to me.

When the communists arrived in a certain village they searched, as usual, every house for anti-communist literature, hidden arms, etc. In the house of a Catholic family they found one of our pamphlets about Our Lady of Fatima. A communist party member glanced through it and, even though he did not understand the content, he was shocked to read about Mary's promise that Russia would one day be converted to Christ. That sounded very reactionary. He impounded the book and told the head of the family to appear at the courthouse in a nearby village the following day.

On the morning of the trial there were several people loitering in the room while waiting for the judge. The impounded book was on the judge's desk. A visitor, wanting a cigarette, casually tore off one of the pages of the book, rolled himself a cigarette and smoked it. When the trial of the Catholic man came up, the judge asked for proof of the crime. The plaintiff grabbed the book from the table, looked for the incriminating page, but the page was no longer there!

"Case dismissed!" the judge barked angrily. The defendant said a prayer of thanksgiving to Our Lady and walked happily home.

This case was a warning to me that by sending books into China, even purely doctrinal books, we were compromising the safety of our Catholics. We had to give up and stopped sending books to "liberated" areas.

Work For The Refugees

Since the beginning of the colony in 1841, Chinese people had migrated from the mainland to the British colony, and the number of immigrants increased with the passing of years. At times there had been exceptional influxes of people following local wars or political disturbances in China. However, there had never been such a gigantic flood of refugees as the one that followed the communist takeover at the end of 1949.

The causes of this exceptional new migration were totally different from those of earlier years. Refugees came in search of freedom, seeking to escape imprisonment and death at the hands of a fanatical dictator and his cronies. The waves of refugees included business people, merchants, industrialists, professors, priests, nuns, Protestant missionaries and Christians of any denomination. Those who escaped for religious motives wanted freedom to practice their religion and to secure a Christian education for their children.

The flood of refugees started as a trickle early in 1948. It grew rapidly in the summer of 1949 and reached its peak in 1951-1952. In a little over three years almost one million people escaped from Mao's "Paradise" to find a new life in Hong Kong. This is how Fr. Ryan described the situation:

"The first wave was from Shanghai and the country above it, of business people and industrialists who knew that ruin and probably death would be their lot if they remained under communist rule. They came out with their families and their wealth, to begin life anew somewhere else. They came to Hong Kong to see what opportunities it offered. If prospects were good they would remain.

"In numbers this proved the smallest group. After them came the people from the south, mostly from Guangdong, fleeing from the Red terror. In spite of early hopes and assurances that the communist advance meant only a change of rule and new hope for the less fortunate among the population, it proved instead to be accompanied everywhere by wholesale murder and confiscation, and it held out no hope of a future except one based on force and fear from which all truth and all justice had disappeared. All who had any education, or owned a farm or any property, or managed a shop, all who had opposed communism in the past, all who had been in any way connected with the previous military regime, and all who had practiced religion regularly, all were in danger of 'liquidation,' so those who could escape and were not too far from Hong Kong migrated to the Colony. The majority came with few or no possessions. Those who had relatives in Hong Kong relied on them for help; the rest had to begin life again as best they could. Within less than a year the population doubled; it was one of the largest influx of refugees that any place of the size of Hong Kong had ever known.

"All this naturally made a great demand on the charity and generosity of the entire population, and reference has already been made to the part which Catholic organizations played in helping the distressed. There was also another aspect: the sudden great growth of the Catholic population. There was, too, the profound effect on Catholic life made by the bitter persecution of religion that was part of the communist regime in China."

These events deeply affected the work of the center. Early in 1948 it became obvious that the communists were going to occupy the whole of China, and Archbishop Riberi, in the name of the Holy Father, exhorted all missionaries to remain at their places despite communist threats so as not to abandon their flocks. He set an example by remaining at his residence in Nanjing when it was occupied by the communist army. Chinese priests and foreign missionaries all over China, in the true Christian tradition, followed the directives of the Holy See and remained at their places. However, a number of priests and nuns, because of age or ill health, had to be evacuated in advance of the communist arrival. This first wave started late in 1948.

By early 1949 the flood of refugees assumed vaster proportions. It included a large number of Chinese priests and seminarians sent out of China by their respective bishops. The purpose was to send some of them to Europe for further ecclesiastical studies or merely to be reserve personnel in case religious freedom would be allowed by the new masters. In addition to these Chinese priests and seminarians, there was also an additional wave of elderly and sick foreign missionaries. There was a specific need to provide shelters and care for these clerical refugees, who obviously could not live in tenement houses.

The House of Bethany, a rest and convalescent home built by the Paris Foreign Missions Society for sick and elderly members of their many missions in the Far East, was built on a hill on the south side of the island of Hong Kong. The House of Bethany boasted a spectacular view of the ocean, and could accommodate over fifty people in private rooms with all the facilities of a rest and rehabilitation residence.

As Bethany's regular clientele had dwindled to a very few, the local superior offered it to the bishop to be used as a temporary refuge for Chinese priests, seminarians and missionaries passing through Hong Kong. Bishop Valtorta asked Fr. MacGuire and me to head this project. First we adapted the house to the new needs, placing several cots in every room, and appointing Fr. Lou, Vicar General of the Diocese of Ankwo, as rector. We built and furnished a new kitchen with facilities for preparing Chinese food. We also made arrangements to continue the education of priests and seminarians. We provided special courses in sociology, moral and pastoral theology, and practical training for nurses, tailors and shoemakers, in case some of the Chinese priests would be compelled to earn their living on their return to China. We anticipated that this house would fulfill the same role that seminaries in northern France had played for the Church in Ireland and England during the persecution of the Church in those countries in previous centuries. From 1949 on, the Catholic Center played a very important part in the work of assisting bishops, priests, nuns, and Protestant missionaries when they arrived in Hong Kong from mainland China. The center was the first place they came to get information, find hospitality, and make travel arrangements for the continuation of their trip to Europe. For this purpose I asked my friend, Aloysius Gonzaga, a very active Chinese business man, to set up a branch of his travel agency at the center in order to help and advise refugee missionaries about their traveling to the USA and Europe.

Even more important than this was the center's work with lay people, Catholic and non-Catholic, who arrived in the colony destitute, having little more than the clothes they were wearing. The government promptly organized several inter-religious committees to prepare and supervise refugee camps. Fr. Ryan played a prominent part in this work of settling refugees. Miss Reid, besides editing *The Sunday Examiner*, became the center's representative on these committees and did a great deal of field work in various camps. She looked upon her work as a person-to-person ministry of love among the poor.

The Communist Army At The Hong Kong Border

In October 1949 the Communist Liberation Army occupied the Chinese territory along the colony's border. Those were anxious days for all of us in Hong Kong as nobody knew whether the communists intended to occupy the colony or not. Military preparations to defend it were not made because everybody realized that, if the communists wanted to "liberate" Hong Kong, no military action could stop them. Only in time did it become obvious why the communists decided not to occupy Hong Kong. They needed it as a window on the Western world, as a gate for communist spies to come and go and, above all, as a good source of foreign exchange. However, although in the early days there was great uncertainty, we kept on praying and working for the refugees, hoping for the best.

The closest we came to the Liberation Army was when we saw them across the barbed wire they soon installed along the border with Hong Kong. The occupying forces were made up mostly of teenagers, fifteen to eighteen years old, boys and girls. Each was sporting two or three toothbrushes sticking out of breast pockets in the midst of leather belts containing ammunition. These "soldiers" were poorly dressed, poorly armed, but certainly afire with enthusiasm. Their bright eyes, their arrogant attitude, their contemptuous glances at us "poor capitalists," all evidenced their pride in being members of the Liberation Army. There was a professional soldier for every three or four of these youthful guards. These youths had made the communist takeover of China possible. In addition to army duties, they did the real work of spreading the communist gospel. Day and night they scattered throughout the countryside organizing peasants, indoctrinating them, arranging people's tribunals to conduct trials of landlords, business men, former civil servants, missionaries and prominent Christians.

A Quick Trip To Rome

In the midst of all this turmoil I had to leave for a couple of weeks. The International Congress of the Catholic Press was convening in Rome in February 1950 and I decided to attend it together with my good friend Mr. Jim Doyle. He was the advertising manager of the Milwaukee Diocesan paper, *The Herald*, and we both were interested in the international Catholic press as a means of presenting Christ's message to non-Christian countries. Moreover, the new political developments in China made it necessary to review our plans for the work of lay missionaries in China and so I decided to visit the Grail headquarters in Holland again.

Mr. A. Gonzaga presented me with a ticket to Amsterdam and Rome and I left Hong Kong on a Constellation plane of the Belgian Airline for Brussels via Delhi and Cairo. I was due to arrive in Brussels early in the morning two days after leaving Hong Kong, but we met with strong headwinds over Arabia and arrived in Brussels at 11:00 at night instead of 9:00 A.M. Miss Donders, the head of the Grail, welcomed me at the airport, where she had been waiting for my plane since early morning. At midnight we started driving to Amsterdam in a heavy snowstorm and arrived at the Grail early the next morning. The same evening, after a full day of meetings, I left by train for Rome, in time to meet Jim Doyle at the airport the following day.

The congress was something of a disappointment. There was very little English spoken and most of the papers dealt with European problems. However, I learned a great deal. It was the first time I was exposed to the intricacies and problems of the Catholic press worldwide and it did me good to look at it from an international point of view.

I never forgot a caustic comment of the Romans on the occasion of this convention. The congress met in the historic Palace of the Chancery,

not far from the Vatican. The entrance to the building was decorated
with a crest representing a large, open book displaying two white pages
with nothing written on them. An Italian journalist, pointing to the
emblem, told me: "Father, do you know what the Romans say about that
crest? They say it's a perfect symbol of the Catholic press: it says
nothing!" The Romans have a good sense of humor!

As soon as the week-long congress ended I flew back to my work in
Hong Kong.

The End: A New Assignment

One morning in March 1950 I received a letter from PIME headquarters
in Milan that changed the course of my life. The superior general of
PIME, Fr. Luigi Risso, informed me that in view of the certain expulsion
of missionaries from communist China (we had 150 men there), PIME
had decided to open a new field of missionary work in Japan. He asked
me to go there, to make a survey of the missionary situation, and to see if
any bishop there would accept our missionaries. I must confess that due
to the sufferings I had endured under the Japanese I hated the very
thought of going to Japan. However, an order was an order and, setting
aside my personal feelings, I made immediate arrangements to go to
Japan by boat.

My Jardine and Matheson liner docked in Osaka and I took a train to
Tokyo. Traveling through the countryside I was struck by the scenic
beauty of Japan. The lush green of the meadows, the soft contours of the
hills throughout the country, the rich, blooming rice paddies, the small,
doll-like houses of the farmers dotting the countryside impressed me
deeply.

In Tokyo I lived at the Franciscan mission house, where an experienced Franciscan, Fr. L. Bianchi, took me under his wing and introduced
me to Japan and Japanese life. To my amazement I discovered that
Japanese civilians are totally different from the military I had met in
China and Hong Kong, and I fell in love with them. Their kindness,
sensitivity and friendship won me over.

For two months I traveled through Japan from north to south, inter-
viewing bishops, foreign missionaries and Japanese priests. In those
days, many Catholic and Protestant missionaries were convinced that
this was the hour for the conversion of Japan to Christianity and many
bishops were eager to get more missionaries. With no difficulty I com-
piled a list of twelve areas where Japanese bishops would welcome

PIME, and sent a full report to Rome, returning then to my work in Hong Kong.

In September a second letter from Fr. Risso informed me that, on the basis of my report, PIME had decided to accept two mission districts (each consisting of several parishes) in Japan, respectively in the Dioceses of Yokohama in central Japan and Fukuoka in the south. Fr. Risso asked me to return to Japan to make final arrangements with the two bishops and to prepare a house for the first PIME missionaries, who would arrive there in November. I was then to proceed to the States on a temporary assignment to raise funds for the new Tokyo house.

I estimated that I could do all of that in about one year and accepted my new assignment promptly. Moreover, I was interested in a trip to the States in order to explore the possibility of establishing a center of Chinese Catholic studies at a Catholic university to employ Christian Chinese scholars who were compelled at that time to leave China.

And so, one afternoon in late October 1950, after a tearful farewell from the center staff and my numerous friends, and with the good wishes of Bishop Valtorta and my confreres, I walked down from the mission house to the harbor for the last time, with only one suitcase containing all my earthly possessions. Boarding the freighter bound for Japan, I had a feeling deep in my heart that my work in Hong Kong had come to an end and that this was my farewell to my beloved mission.

While the sun was setting behind the Kowloon hills, the ship slowly steamed out of the harbor. I could not help remembering another sunset, another ship, another painful farewell, almost twenty years earlier in Venice, when I had left my family and my country, bound for China. As I had done then, I tried to stifle my heartache and boldly turned to the future and a new life in the same old pattern of following in the steps of Christ.

When the sun rose next morning in a beautiful, blue sky, the ship was peacefully sailing over shimmering waters toward Japan and, for me, ultimately the USA. Distance-wise, Hong Kong was now many miles behind, but I was still carrying it in my heart and with it the unforgettable memory of the best twenty years of my life, twenty years with the Chinese.

Hong Kong revisited: the author with Misses Mabel and Frances Chen in 1979.

30

Hong Kong Revisited

Hong Kong Thirty Years Later

On a Sunday afternoon in September 1979, from a window of a Pan American plane approaching the Hong Kong airport, I watched the spectacular and fascinating sight of the Pearl of the Orient. It was my first return there after an absence of almost thirty years. Although I had seen photos and films of the incredible development of the city, nonetheless I was thrilled to see, for the first time, the imposing high-rises dominating the skyline, rising majestically among the chaotic confusion of houses, villas, office buildings and tenement houses stretching from the north slope of the Peak, all across Kowloon as far as the foot of the Lionhead hills.

For years I had anticipated that joyous moment of my return to the place of my youth, and now that it had finally arrived I was ecstatic. When the plane finally came to a stop at the ramp of the new, imposing airport building, I rushed toward the exit with my faithful companion Fr. James Bregola. Emerging into the cavernous lounge, I heard a warm applause but, thinking that it was for some other passenger, I kept walking straight ahead. Then I saw tall, handsome Bro. Mario Colleoni coming toward me, followed by a wildly applauding group of people, among whom I soon recognized old friends such as Mabel and Frances Chen, Mr. Poon Cheung, May Wong, Joseph Lee, Anna Chu and many others. In true American style I felt like hugging and kissing everybody, but remembering my former Chinese training, I limited myself to some vigorous handshaking and enthusiastic greetings. However, the ill-repressed emotion of the moment was all too apparent from the many tearful eyes, mine included.

A Grown-up Church

The days following my arrival I spent making the rounds of churches, institutions, schools and hospitals, and visiting old friends and acquaintances. I spoke at length with fellow missionaries of the old days and the younger missionaries of the new generation. I was greatly impressed by all I saw and heard.

Old Rosary Church and St. Teresa's parish were still there, of course. The buildings looked older but their respective congregations were very much alive, and had grown far beyond my expectations. While in my days parishioners had been counted by the thousands, now they were numbered in the tens of thousands. Weddings, which in my days had been celebrated at the rate of a few score every year, were now celebrated at the rate of twenty to twenty-five every weekend. Holy Communions, which had been counted by the thousands, were now counted by the millions.

All over the colony the number of priests, religious and sisters, both native and Chinese, had grown by the hundreds, and there were lots of new institutions, including several refugee camps for Vietnamese and dozens of new hospitals, scores of new schools, new parishes and new churches to serve a Catholic population which had grown from 30,000 in my days to over 250,000 now.

It was altogether an exciting visit, which thrilled my heart and delighted my eyes. My greatest joy was to realize how the mustard seed of the faith, which, together with my fellow missionaries, I had helped to plant and nurture in my days, had grown into such a gigantic tree. To me the Church in Hong Kong was *not* a new Church, it was a *grown-up* Church. I saw in the Hong Kong Church the features of the Church I had known as a young man thirty years before. The old familiar features were still there and I blessed the Lord for its growth and grand adulthood. I really felt like a father who leaves his children in their teens and sees them again several decades later. He recognizes in them the old features, and rejoices seeing them now fully developed and grown up.

The Old And The New

Old Rosary Church had been enlarged and given a facelift, but the old shell was still there as Fr. John Spada had built it in 1902. The congregation still included a large number of Portuguese parishioners, but the largest number now were Chinese. St. Mary's School was still run by the Canossian Sisters, but it had more than trebled its enrollment. As I visited the school and saw the eager, young faces of Chinese students, I could not help remembering the eager, young faces of my days, like those of Ruby Moy and Bella Ma.

I had the same experience at St. Teresa's. The old St. Teresa's was there, with its slender belfry, its pure architectural lines, its dome, its marble altar, but all around everything was new. In my days the church building had stood out as the tallest building in the neighborhood, overshadowing the two-story houses lined along Prince Edward Road. Now it seemed buried and overshadowed by a lot of taller buildings all along that major traffic artery. The new rectory, the buildings around the church were a far cry from the humble buildings of my days. They were in keeping with the new development.

The interior of the church still looked the same, still warm and inspiring, still pulsating with life. The Mass I celebrated there was rich with nostalgic memories, like a spiritual trip in the past. I remembered and prayed a lot for my good, old pastor and mentor, Fr. Granelli, for the late Mr. L. A. Barton, and especially for my unforgettable friend and classmate Fr. Orlando. He had been pastor there from 1949 to 1966, the years of the most phenomenal growth of the parish, which he had overseen and directed with zeal and wisdom. Unfortunately he had not waited for my return and had died of a heart attack barely a month before I arrived there.

The cathedral, the grand "Old Dame" of all the Hong Kong churches, was also still there, still looked the same both outside and inside, still gray in color, slender in its simple Gothic lines, still a real church. I was very much moved when on a Sunday morning I celebrated Mass there and saw the church filled to capacity with Chinese Catholics. I remembered the hard days of my pastoral work, the living agony of the war years and the triumphant end of the war on August 15, my "second birthday."

The landscape around the cathedral was greatly changed. The four-story mission house had been replaced by an eighteen-story high-rise. All the old, small buildings on every side of the church had been torn down and replaced by high-rises, which now dwarfed the grand, old church.

The person I missed most was dear, good Bishop Valtorta. But as much as I was saddened by his death, I rejoiced meeting his worthy successor, Bishop John B. Wu, now Cardinal Wu. His kindness, intelligence and his wise administration of the multinational diocese have made him worthy of the "red hat." He acknowledged that it was the work of Bishop Valtorta, of Bishop Bianchi, and the work of the missionaries of my time that had made possible the growth of the diocese as I was seeing it again thirty years later.

Bishop Wu, Chinese, replacing Italian Bishop Valtorta, was the best visible proof of the success of the 150 years of PIME's work in Hong Kong. True to its goal of forming a competent and zealous Chinese clergy to replace its own missionaries, PIME had gladly handed over the flourishing diocese to them. Gradually the Italian missionaries had withdrawn from all positions of responsibility, thus passing from a directive role to a subsidiary one. This was the goal for which I had worked, hoping to see it fulfilled all through China. My dream had failed in China, but at least it came through in Hong Kong.

My Successor At The Center: Msgr. Charles Vath

One September day in 1948, during my visit to Italy, I had been to the St. Beda Seminary for adult vocations in Via San Nicola da Tolentino to see my good friend Charles Vath.

"Charles, have you decided where you want to work as a priest after your ordination? Have you asked any bishop to sponsor you?" I had asked him.

"No, Father Maestrini," Charles had answered, "I haven't given it much thought yet. My desire is to work as a priest in some missionary diocese rather than in my native Germany."

"Then what about Hong Kong?" I had asked with eagerness in my voice as I saw the possibility of securing a valuable subject for our mission.

"Oh, I would love that," Charles had answered with emphasis. "Do you think you can persuade Bishop Valtorta to sponsor me?"

"Consider it done," I had said. "I guarantee you that Bishop Valtorta will be delighted to incardinate you in our diocese."

This had brought to an end our conversation that day in the dimly lit parlor of the Beda Seminary. I had not known then that through that conversation I had secured not only my successor in the work of the Catholic Center but that I had also won for the Hong Kong Diocese a "miracle man."

In order to understand the importance of this conversation and of its consequences, I must give some background information. I had already met Mr. Charles Vath in Hong Kong during the Japanese occupation when he had come to see me at the cathedral on a pastoral matter. I had learned then that he was a German, thirty-five years old, unmarried and a very devout Catholic. Also, he had been a very successful businessman engaged in import and export trading with his native Germany, and the Japanese had allowed him to travel on business between Guangzhou, Hong Kong and Shanghai. I had found him a very friendly and charming man.

After the war, on my visit to Shanghai in 1947, I had seen him again. Much to my surprise he had told me that he wanted to become a priest and had asked my advice about finding a seminary to accept him. I had suggested the Beda Seminary in Rome, conducted by a British organization for delayed vocations to the priesthood. He had gladly accepted my suggestion and I had given him a letter of introduction to the rector of the seminary, and a few weeks later he had been on his way to Rome.

The conversation I have reported above took place at the Beda a year later. On my return to Hong Kong, I had spoken about him to Bishop Valtorta, who had been very glad to sponsor him for the Hong Kong Diocese. Fr. Vath had been ordained in 1951 and on his arrival in Hong Kong had been assigned as director of the Catholic Center.

Fr. Vath At The Helm

When I left Hong Kong in 1950 Bishop Valtorta had appointed Fr. O. Liberatore as director of the center and Bro. Mario as his assistant. They had bravely weathered the initial difficulties caused by my absence and the work of the center had not suffered.

When a year later Fr. Vath had taken over as director, Fr. Liberatore had been very happy to return to his pastoral work. With his brilliant mind, business experience and organizing ability Fr. Vath had developed the center beyond even my wildest dreams. Only five years after my departure, on the occasion of the tenth anniversary of the opening of the center, Bishop Bianchi had stated: "Even outside of Hong Kong, the center has gained the reputation of being one of the best organizations in Asia."

In 1958 a visitor from the National Office of the Society for the Propagation of the Faith in the USA, after a visit to the center, had remarked: "It is in the establishment of the Centre that the Church has done something which finds its comparison only in the great work of the dispensation of the Sacraments."

I will not tire the reader with figures and statistics but will give here only a brief summary of the work accomplished by Fr. Vath.

The Catholic Center Chapel. In 1958, on the anniversary of the first one hundred years of the work of PIME in Hong Kong, Vath wrote: "The work of the Catholic Center has played its part under God's grace in the wonderful increase in the number of the faithful. Spiritually, its chapel, situated as it is in the midst of the business district, has been a principal attraction. Mass is said daily both in the morning and in the late evening and there is hardly a time during the day when there are no groups of people before the Blessed Sacrament. Confessions are heard at any hour of the day in all the common languages including several Chinese dialects."

The Work of the Catholic Truth Society. Vath wrote: "The distribution figures for Chinese publications translated and published by the Catholic Truth Society and works in foreign languages imported from Europe and America have increased from some 200,000 copies in 1952 to its present figure of nearly two million copies annually. The two Catholic weeklies, the Sunday Examiner in English and the Chinese Kung Kao Po have not only steadily increased their circulation but also doubled their size."

The English Book Shop. In 1958 it was offering six thousand Catholic books, publishing a monthly review of new Catholic books, and had opened a Catholic Magazine Subscription Office, which accepted subscriptions for magazines from all over the world.

In addition to all this work, Fr. Vath had organized a Diocesan Public Relations Office, a Central Catholic Library for the diocese, and even a library of Catholic films for Catholic schools and institutions. The Students' Press Corps organized by Miss Reid in my days was going strong and attracting the cooperation of hundreds of students.

In 1959, when the old Kings Building had been slated for demolition to make room for a modern high-rise, Fr. Vath had been able to secure German charity dollars and had purchased six floors in a nearby, newly constructed building to house the chapel, the publishing offices of the Catholic Truth Society, the Catholic Center and a host of other diocesan activities. In the 1970's, when Bishop Wu had built the new eighteen-story mission house up the hill on Caine Road, he had transferred the offices of the Catholic Truth Society there but had left the chapel and the Catholic Book Shop in the downtown center.

A few years later, Fr. Vath became the representative of the German Bishops Relief Work in the Far East and was able to obtain millions of dollars for the Hong Kong Diocese to help build hospitals, schools and churches. His magnificent work led to his appointment as President of Caritas International and he moved his headquarters to Rome, where he died in the late seventies.

After his departure, the center and the Catholic Truth Society were entrusted to able Chinese priests who to this day continue the great work. The present Director is Fr. Edward Khong, a highly intelligent, well-trained Chinese priest who continues to guide the vast network of activities with great wisdom and ability.

Farewell To Hong Kong

I spent only ten days in Hong Kong and then with Fr. James I continued my journey westward to England and Italy. It was late in the evening when the Pan American jet winged its way out of Hong Kong. As I settled down in my seat for the long eighteen-hour flight to London, I wondered whether that was the last time I would see Hong Kong. But I felt that whatever the future had in store for me, I was leaving Hong Kong with the deepest sense of gratitude to the Lord. Many years before He had called me as a young, inexperienced youth to follow in His steps and to bring the message of salvation to non-Christian nations. Trusting His word I had followed Him to China and had worked planting the seed of Faith through twenty years of work, pain and sweat. Now, I had been given the privilege of seeing that little mustard seed grown to the stature of a big tree and I felt grateful and perfectly fulfilled. My life had not been in vain: love had triumphed.

Appendix A

Communism And Christianity In China Today

Forty Years Of Persecution

In light of the Tiananmen Square events of May-June 1989, Chinese communism has finally been recognized by world opinion for what it really is, namely, the most inhumane, the most vicious, the most totalitarian regime in the world. Unfortunately, too many have failed to see that the government that ordered the Tiananmen Square massacre is the same inhumane, dictatorial government that for the last forty years has imposed its tyranny on over a billion people by sheer force. Yet we have befriended this government and have helped it to consolidate its stronghold on the people.

The unjustifiable cruelty against the young people in Tiananmen Square, the number of victims sacrificed there, and the lies told by the government to justify its barbaric behavior have justly aroused the ire of the free world. However, too many fail to realize that this senseless cruelty and unrestrained lying are virtually nothing compared to the more than thirty million victims the communists have murdered and the countless millions they have persecuted, imprisoned, tortured and relegated to forced-labor camps during their forty years in power. Included in those millions of victims are thousands of Chinese priests, sisters, expelled foreign missionaries, and hundreds of thousands of lay Catholics who have endured persecution and death in the name of the "liberation" of China.

In order to better understand what forty years of persecution have done to the Church in China, it is very important to know what the status of the Church was in 1949, when the communists came to power and unleashed a furious attack against all religions, with the ultimate goal of destroying them all.

That year, the Catholic Church in China was in better shape than it had been for the previous four centuries. According to statistics published in the *China Missionary Bulletin* of that year, there were ninety-six dioceses in China, scores of Chinese bishops, one Chinese cardinal, and the archbishop of the then capital of China, Nanjing, was Chinese too: Paul Yu-Pin. There were 2,888 well-trained and devoted Chinese priests; 2,500 foreign missionaries; about seven thousand sisters, both foreign and Chinese; several thousand parish churches and mission chapels; six hundred thousand students in Catholic schools from kindergarten through three universities; hundreds of hospitals, outpatient clinics, orphanages and homes for the aged serving a total of over three and one-half million Catholics, and millions of non-Catholics too. Both Catholic and Protestant denominations enjoyed freedom and served the people, especially the poor, with generosity and dedication. All these works were the result of four hundred years of uninterrupted missionary work, of the blood and sweat of priests and nuns, both Chinese and foreign, and of countless thousands of heroic lay Catholics.

The communists wiped it all out in a single blow! They closed all the churches and the Catholic schools, forbade religious services under the penalty of imprisonment and death, and gradually expelled all foreign missionaries after imprisoning and torturing many of them. They also disbanded entire communities of religious men and convents of nuns; they compelled Chinese priests and sisters to return to lay life, and imprisoned, tried, executed or condemned to labor camps those who refused. All church buildings were confiscated and desecrated; many were turned into stables or put to profane use. Hospitals and schools and all other church properties were forcibly expropriated without even a suggestion of compensation. Thus the nearly four million Catholics were suddenly and forcibly deprived of their priests, their churches, their religious services and their schools. The Church then went underground and became the Church of silence. But, as in the days of the Roman persecutions, and in spite of lack of external help, it remained very much alive and flourished.

Before too long, the communists realized that religion could not be uprooted from the hearts of the people, and the government decided to use it or, better, to manipulate it to its own advantage. To do so, it created a central Religious Affairs Bureau with branches all over the country. The purpose of the bureau was, and still is, to make every religion, regardless of its beliefs, completely subservient to the interests of the Communist Party. To this end, the powerful members of the bureau were not chosen on the basis of their qualifications in religious matters, but simply according to their proven record in promoting the party line.

The Religious Affairs Bureau, in order to control the Catholic Church, organized the Chinese Catholic Patriotic Assn. (CCPA), ordered Chinese priests and bishops to join it, and then compelled it to sever any tie with the pope. In the beginning the party appointed and ordained bishops and priests even thought they had no qualification whatever, appointed pastors and assistants, and required nothing of them but to be active communists and completely loyal to the party.

The establishment of the CCPA with its proclaimed independence from the pope caused a severe split within the underground Catholic community; a large number of priests and lay people defied persecution and refused to join the CCPA, remaining loyal to the Faith and to the pope. However, some of the former priests and even some bishops were compelled to or cajoled into joining it, and some did so of their own accord, believing that joining the CCPA was the only way to keep some form of Christianity alive.

Thus, through most of the last forty years the loyal Church of China, though silent, lived the life of the catacombs, continued to be steadily persecuted, and practiced the religion secretly. On the contrary, the existence of the CCPA, as an organ of the party, was officially recognized, received government subsidies, and was given some of the old church buildings, and was hailed as the Catholic Church of China by the foreign press.

What is remarkable about the underground Catholic Church in China is that neither the mighty power of the communist state with its network of spies and police force nor the violence, suffering and bloodshed of the Cultural Revolution (1966-1976) could destroy it. The faith that foreign missionaries and Chinese priests had planted in the hearts of Catholics through centuries of hard work and countless sufferings could not be stifled and uprooted from their hearts.

The Great Leap Backward

Fr. G. Politi, PIME, writing in the June 1, 1990, issue of *Asia News,* described the present situation in China as "the great leap backward," in opposition to Mao's popular slogan of the initial days of the communist revolution, "the great leap forward." On the basis of a detailed analysis of the results of the forty years of the communist regime, Politi proved that the work of the regime in bringing China into the modern world has been a complete failure from the economical, sociological and religious points of view.

With regard to the government attitude toward the Church, he demonstrated that, after the Tiananmen tragedy, the persecution of the underground Catholic Church has resumed with unabated violence and insidious practices.

Louise Branson, writing for the Palm Beach-Cox News Service, in an article that appeared in the Easter Sunday 1990 issue, gave a masterful and up-to-date picture of the situation of the Christian churches in China. She affirmed that the Church in China today is under renewed communist attack. The details are sketchy: thirty-two church leaders seized in raids across the north of China; an American expelled for conducting "illegal missionary work"; Rev. Lin Xiangao arrested in his tiny Guangzhou (formerly Canton) church while church members were interrogated and Bibles seized; many other Christians disappeared, presumed arrested.

These are only a few recorded cases, but countless more are happening. The message is clear: for the hard-working Chinese leadership, Christianity is now a potential lightning rod of discontent and Western subversion.

A witch hunt is now on. The targets are the leaders of the underground who have refused to join the CCPA because of its subservience to the communist regime, its communist-controlled religious teachings and its severance of ties to the pope. On the contrary, the CCPA is allowed to continue worshiping openly, because it has renounced all ties with the Vatican and has pledged allegiance to the communist party.

According to Chinese statistics (though they are not very reliable) the CCPA counts several million members and runs the Catholic churches in Beijing and in many other parts of the country. But underground Christians, also in the millions, want no compromise. Several of the underground priests have spent decades in prison for their refusal to join the CCPA while others are constantly under surveillance and are periodically punished. The present round of detentions provides a barometer of the repressive regime.

Church sources say that after some relaxation during the last decade the current persecution began in earnest after the Tiananmen crackdown and gathered speed after the collapse of communist regimes in eastern Europe, where the Church has been a progressive force.

These Church sources have documented the arrests of dozens of members of the "silent Church"—sometimes even as they gathered to pray on hillsides and in fields.

In its new report on human rights abuses, the US State Department said that detention of leaders of unofficial religious groups (mostly underground Catholics) is continuing, "often with no notification to followers or family members."

The new arrests indicate that a chilling internal communist party directive, known as "Document No. 3," issued in 1989 in Beijing, is now being put into effect. The document details practical ways and means to stamp out the underground church by violent persecution. It explicitly advises party members to target small groups of Catholics in every district and to publicly attack them as reactionaries.

Many church members in China fear that this could mark a return to the persecution during the 1966-1976 Cultural Revolution, when all religious practice was outlawed and when believers were tortured and killed.

The unofficial attitude of many church authorities, including bishops and cardinals, is to show cordiality to the leaders of the CCPA, ignoring its xenophobia, as they realize that many of these leaders and their followers are still true Catholics at heart, and hope that religious freedom will one day be reestablished in China.

Louise Branson concluded her article with these words: "A young woman attending Mass celebrated by a CCPA priest in the former Catholic Cathedral of Beijing recently bore out their fears. She said that in her heart she considered the Pope the head of the Church, though she was not allowed to say so.

"More important, she said the church filled a spiritual void for her and that more young people were turning to the Church for some meaning since the Tiananmen massacre and their disillusion with the Communist leadership."

I'd like to quote here a statement made as recently as April 1989 in Guangzhou by a Chinese businessman at a business dinner and reported by Fr. Politi in Asia News: "I am ashamed of our present government. It even makes me ashamed of being Chinese. To remain silent is the only dignity left to me. But, make no mistake: the violence of our present leaders is not an expression of the soul and feelings of the Chinese."

Appendix B

A Word About PIME

The Spirit And Work Of PIME

PIME is an international organization of Catholic priests and brothers (also called "lay associates") exclusively dedicated to working in the foreign missions of the Catholic Church in order to bring the message of Christ to non-Christian nations.

PIME is an acronym comprising the initials of its title, which means: Pontifical Institute for Foreign Missions.

The spirit and work of PIME are well expressed in the following mission statement:

"We, the PIME missionaries of the United States Region, are an expression of the missionary nature of the Church in the United States and of the international character of PIME. We are a family of apostles committed to the ongoing discovery, witness and proclamation of the Kingdom of God through evangelization, particularly of non-Christians in other parts of the world.

"We live in community, offering one another mutual support. We work as a team, while respecting and encouraging individual initiative and creativity. We embrace a simple and hospitable lifestyle."

The Beginning And Growth Of PIME

PIME was started by a group of bishops and diocesan priests in Milan, Italy. On July 31, 1850, after years of diligent preparation, they formally established the new Foreign Missions Society exclusively dedicated to bringing the message of Christ to non-Christian lands. Two years later the first missionaries went to work for Christ in Papua, New Guinea, Oceania. Blessed John Mazzucconi suffered martyrdom there in September 1855. A few years later, in 1858, the society sent missionaries to Hong Kong, and later to China, India and Burma.

Today there are close to seven hundred members of PIME and over a thousand sisters of the Immaculate Conception, a religious society of women founded by PIME. Today, besides in Italy and in the USA, the PIME missionaries work in the following places: Japan, Bangladesh, Hong Kong, Taiwan, Burma, Thailand, the Philippines, India, Papua New Guinea, Guinea-Bissau, the Ivory Coast, Cameroon, and in six provinces of Brazil—Amapa, Amazonas, Mato Grosso, S. Paulo, Parana, S. Caterina.

PIME In The USA

The presence of PIME in the USA began in 1948 when Cardinal John Mooney of Detroit, MI, invited his old personal friend Fr. G. Margutti, PIME, from Bangladesh, to establish a residence in Detroit to help the PIME missions devastated by World War II.

In 1951, when my work for the Chinese came practically to an end in Hong Kong, due to the communist takeover of China, I was assigned to assume Fr. Margutti's work, as he had returned to Italy for health reasons. In 1952 PIME decided to become international and to establish its first branch outside Italy in the States. Thus, the purpose of PIME's work in the States was extended to recruiting, preparing, sending and supporting PIME missionaries in the foreign missions.

The Work Of PIME In The World Today

The work of the PIME missionaries involves more than bringing the knowledge of Christianity to non-Christians and administering the sacraments. It also involves helping the poor, raising their standard of living through education, and alleviating the suffering of millions of underprivileged people, orphans, leprosy victims, the aged and ill by providing food, clothes and medicines for them.

The vast array of PIME's work includes: nine seminaries in mission countries for the training of local clergy; over a thousand schools educating three hundred thousand students; orphanages caring for eight thousand poor children; about 2,400 churches and mission stations, leper colonies, leper hospitals and anti-leprosy programs, mission hospitals and outpatient clinics that treat millions of people every year; an Institute for Asian Studies in Italy and a News Agency for Asian News.

The international headquarters are in Rome, and the Very Rev. Franco Cagnasso is the superior general. In the States, the regional headquarters are in Detroit, MI, and the Very Rev. Steven Baumbusch is the regional superior.

Places Where This Book Can Be Purchased

UNITED STATES

PIME WORLD PRESS
17330 Quincy Avenue
Detroit, MI 48221

Fr. NICHOLAS MAESTRINI
1550 Beach Road
Tequesta, FL 33469

ITALY

CENTRO PIME
Via Mose' Bianchi 94
20149 MILANO, ITALY

SEDE GENERALIZIA PIME
Via F. D. Guerrazzi 11
00152 ROMA, ITALY

HONG KONG

PIME FATHERS
315 Clear Water Bay
New Territories
HONG KONG

CATHOL. CENTER BOOKSHOP
15-18 Connaught Rd.C.
HONG KONG

INDIA
PIME FATHERS
Xaviernagar
Eluru, 534 006 AP.
W. Godiv. Dt. INDIA

JAPAN
PIME FATHERS
8841-20-1 Fuchu-Machi
Fuchu-shi
Tokyo, 183 JAPAN

Index of Names and Places